The Politics of the Stuart Court Masque

This book takes a new look at the courtly masque in early seventeenth-century England. For a generation, the masque has been a favourite topic of New Historicism, because it has been seen as part of the process by which artistic works interact with politics, both shaping and reflecting the political life of a nation. These exciting new essays move importantly beyond a monolithic view of culture and power in the production of masques, to one in which rival factions at the courts of James I and of Charles I represent their clash of viewpoints through dancing and spectacle.

All aspects of the masque are considered, from written text and political context to music, stage picture and dance. The essays, written by distinguished scholars from around the world, present an interdisciplinary approach, with experts on dance, music, visual spectacle and politics all addressing the masque from the point of view of their speciality.

David Bevington is the Phyllis Fay Horton Professor in the Humanities in the Departments of English and of Comparative Literature at the University of Chicago. His books include *From 'Mankind' to Marlowe: Growth of Structure in the Popular Drama of Tudor England* (1962), *Tudor Drama and Politics* (1968) and *Action is Eloquence: Shakespeare's Language of Gesture* (1984). He is editor of both The Bantam Shakespeare (1988) and *The Complete Works of Shakespeare* (1992, updated 1997).

Peter Holbrook is a Lecturer in the Department of English, at the University of Queensland, Australia, and is the author of *Literature and Degree in Renaissance England: Nashe, Bourgeois Tragedy, Shakespeare* (1994).

THE POLITICS OF THE
STUART COURT MASQUE

EDITED BY

DAVID BEVINGTON
AND PETER HOLBROOK

CAMBRIDGE
UNIVERSITY PRESS

PUBLISHED BY THE PRESS SYNDICATE OF THE UNIVERSITY OF CAMBRIDGE
The Pitt Building, Trumpington Street, Cambridge CB2 1RP, United Kingdom

CAMBRIDGE UNIVERSITY PRESS
The Edinburgh Building, Cambridge CB2 2RU, United Kingdom
40 West 20th Street, New York, NY 10011–4211, USA
10 Stamford Road, Oakleigh, Melbourne 3166, Australia

First published 1998

Printed in the United Kingdom at the University Press, Cambridge

Typeset in 11/12 $\frac{1}{2}$ pt Mono Baskerville [GC]

A catalogue record for this book is available from the British Library

ISBN 0 521 59436 7 hardback

To
Peggy Bevington
Annabel Hickey
and
William Noel Holbrook

Contents

Illustrations

ix

Chapter 11

List of contributors

LEEDS BARROLL is Presidential Research Professor at the University of Maryland (Baltimore County). Editor of *Shakespeare Studies*, he is also the author of numerous books and articles on Renaissance drama and literature. His *Politics, Plague and Shakespeare's Theatre* was awarded the Barnard Hewitt Prize by the American Society for Theatre Research (1992).

DAVID BEVINGTON is Phyllis Fay Horton Professor in the Humanities in the Departments of English and of Comparative Literature at the University of Chicago. His books include *From 'Mankind' to Marlowe: Growth of Structure in the Popular Drama of Tudor England* (1962), *Tudor Drama and Politics* (1968) and *Action is Eloquence: Shakespeare's Language of Gesture* (1984). He is editor of both The Bantam Shakespeare (1988) and *The Complete Works of Shakespeare* (1992, updated 1997).

TOM BISHOP is Associate Professor of English and Director of the Baker-Nord Center for the Humanities at Case Western Reserve University. He is the author of *Shakespeare and the Theater of Wonder* (1996). He has co-produced a full reconstruction of *Oberon, the Fairy Prince* for stage and videotape.

MARTIN BUTLER is Reader in Renaissance Drama at the School of English, University of Leeds. He is currently completing an edition of *Cymbeline* for the New Cambridge Shakespeare, and a book on *Courtly Negotiations: The Stuart Masque and Political Culture 1603-42*.

HUGH CRAIG teaches in the Department of English at the University of Newcastle, Australia. He edited *Ben Jonson: The Critical Heritage* (1990).

PAUL E. J. HAMMER is Senior Lecturer in History at the University of New England, Australia. He is the author of *The Polarisation of Elizabethan Politics: the Political Career of Robert Devereux, 2nd Earl of Essex, 1585-1597* (1998).

PETER HOLBROOK is Lecturer in English at the University of Queensland and the author of *Literature and Degree in Renaissance England: Nashe, Bourgeois Tragedy, Shakespeare* (1994).

BARBARA K. LEWALSKI is William R. Kenan Professor of History and Literature and of English Literature at Harvard University. Her recent books include *Writing Women in Jacobean England* (1993) and *'Paradise Lost' and the Rhetoric of Literary Forms* (1985).

DAVID LINDLEY is Reader in Renaissance Literature in the School of English, University of Leeds. He has edited a collection of essays on the court masque (1984) and an anthology of masque texts for the World's Classics series (1995). His most recent monograph is *The Trials of Frances Howard* (1993).

LEAH S. MARCUS is Edwin Mims Professor of English at Vanderbilt University. Her most recent book is *Unediting the Renaissance: Shakespeare, Marlowe, Milton* (1996).

STEPHEN ORGEL is Jackson Eli Reynolds Professor of Humanities at Stanford University. He is the author of *The Jonsonian Masque* (1965), *The Illusion of Power* (1975), and, with Roy Strong, *Inigo Jones: The Theatre of the Stuart Court* (1973). His most recent book is *Impersonations: The Performance of Gender in Shakespeare's England* (1996), and he has edited *The Winter's Tale* (1996) and *The Tempest* (1987) for the Oxford Shakespeare.

BARBARA RAVELHOFER is a Junior Research Fellow at St John's College, Cambridge. She has written and lectured on Renaissance choreography and dance. An edition of a pre-1620s dance manuscript is forthcoming.

NANCY E. WRIGHT teaches English literature at the University of Newcastle, Australia. She has published interdisciplinary studies of literature, law and theology in seventeenth-century England and America.

Acknowledgements

This book originated in a week-long seminar on 'The Court Masque' at the University of Newcastle, Australia, in 1993. In addition to the contributors to this volume, a number of whom took part in the seminar and some of whom have subsequently joined this project, we wish warmly to thank the following participants in the seminar itself: Curtis Breight, Mary Chan, Tony Cousins, Lloyd Davis, John Gillies, Richard Jordan, Philippa Kelly, Heather Kerr and Erica Veevers. For supporting the seminar, we are grateful to the Department of English at the University of Newcastle and to the University's Research Management Committee headed by Professor Ron MacDonald. For generous practical assistance we are greatly indebted to Associate Professor Wayne McKenna of the Newcastle Department of English. Secretarial and technical support from Karyn Asher and Jenny McKinnon at Newcastle, as well as from Elizabeth Mitchell, Chris Rintel, Cathy Squirell and Angela Tuohy of the Department of English at the University of Queensland, Australia, has been essential to the completion of this project: to them many, many thanks. Anna Bemrose's assistance with proofs was much appreciated. For helpful editorial advice we wish to thank Anne Barton and, for her wonderful patience, encouragement and support throughout the making of this book, Sarah Stanton of Cambridge University Press.

David Bevington and Peter Holbrook

Note on the text

Quotations from English Renaissance texts have been modernized throughout. For Shakespeare, we have relied on David Bevington (ed.), *The Complete Works of Shakespeare*, 4th edn (1992, updated 1997).

CHAPTER I

Introduction

David Bevington and Peter Holbrook

Masques were often dismissed as mere trifles of entertainment during the Jacobean years when that genre experienced its most remarkable development. Francis Bacon declared 'masques and triumphs' to be 'but toys'. For illustration, he need have looked no further than the featherbrained Sir Andrew Aguecheek in *Twelfth Night*, who 'delight[s] in masques and revels sometimes altogether' (1.3.111–12). Even Prospero in *The Tempest*, as deviser of a wedding masque for his daughter, passes the event off as 'Some vanity of mine art' (4.1.41).

Writers of masques were of course sensitive to the charge. Ben Jonson, in his *Neptune's Triumph* (1624), devised to celebrate the return from Spain of Prince Charles without a Spanish bride (much to the delight of most English observers), brings forward a Poet with his tale of woe. Wryly comparing his craft with that of the Cook, with whom he is conversing, the Poet calls himself 'The most unprofitable of [the King's] servants . . . A kind of Christmas engine, one that is used at least once a year for a trifling instrument of wit, or so' (lines 20–2). Jonson was all too aware of what his critics said of his courtly enterprises. Plutus, masquerading as Cupid in Jonson's *Love Restored* (1612), scornfully characterizes masquing as 'a false and fleeting delight', nothing more than 'The merry madness of one hour' that is sure to cost its devotees 'the repentance of an age' (lines 31–3).[1]

Writers of masques and observers of the courtly scene were none the less at pains to defend masquing. Jonson lauded the masque as 'lay[ing] hold on more removed mysteries'.[2] In Thomas Campion's *The Lords' Masque* (1613), no less an authority than Orpheus assures Entheus (Poetic Fury): 'Nor are these musics, shows, or revels vain / When thou adorn'st them with thy Phoebean brain'.[3] Bacon's demeaning reference to 'toys' occurs in an essay in which he offered shrewd advice to the aspiring masque presenter. The royal and noble sponsors of these shows took them seriously, to judge by the time, energy and money expended on them.

The Poet's acknowledgement in *Neptune's Triumph* of the triflingness of his masque is, in this context, a complex idea. While he drily acknowledges an outward resemblance between his own vocation and that of the Cook, both of whom serve up dishes, poetic and otherwise, to the court's taste, the Poet also takes a sly dig at the Cook. In that person's self-confidence, officious advice-giving and willingness to cater to every taste, Jonson skewers the presumptuous incomprehension of his art by a court that is complacently willing to equate his artistic concerns with those of the appetite and to expect that the court's tastes are to govern every aspect of the artist's production. At the same time, the likening of a Poet to a Cook has a defensive value for Jonson. Through it he can disown any riskily large political intention, and take shelter behind the innocuous role of entertainer from those malicious 'state-decipherer[s]' and 'politic picklock[s]' who plagued him in the public theatres.[4]

The contradictory significances of this exchange between Poet and Cook reflect the difficulties of Jonson's position. For, as author of a masque celebrating the return of the brideless prince, he was in a delicate spot. Was he in effect to celebrate the failure of James's long-cherished hopes of a Spanish marriage for his son, as ecstatic London crowds had done some months earlier?[5] Or was he to insinuate regret at the collapse of the King's plan for peace with Spain – a plan with which Jonson may well have sympathized? Together, Cook and Poet explore the difficult matter of their satisfying, each in his own way, the diverse tastes of their customers:

COOK: Were you ever a cook?

POET: A cook? No, surely.

COOK: Then you can be no good poet, for a good poet differs nothing at all from a master-cook. Either's art is the wisdom of the mind.

POET: As how, sir?

COOK: Expect. I am by my place to know how to please the palates of the guests; so, you are to know the palate of the times, study the several tastes, what every nation, the Spaniard, the Dutch, the French, the Walloon, the Neapolitan, the Briton, the Sicilian, can expect from you.

POET: That were a heavy and hard task, to satisfy Expectation, who is so severe an exactress of duties; ever a tyrannous mistress, and most times a pressing enemy.

COOK: She is a powerful great lady, sir, at all times, and must be satisfied. So must her sister, Madam Curiosity, who hath as dainty a palate as she, and these will expect.

POET: But what if they expect more than they understand?

COOK: That's all one, Master Poet, you are bound to satisfy them.

(lines 23–40)

Jonson's pugnacious attitude towards his auditors suggests that he finds them incapable of comprehending his artistic purpose and wilfully determined to be unsatisfied. Yet he also betrays a concern lest he be unable to pick his way among the radically contradictory preferences of this audience. The rueful and bewildered tone of the Poet reflects Jonson's awareness that the factionalized nature of courtly opinion about the Spanish Match, and about foreign policy generally, dooms *Neptune's Triumph* from the start. As David Riggs has put it, 'regardless of what [Jonson] wrote, someone would take offense'.[6] The dialogue between Cook and Poet is Jonson's bid to pre-empt such offence by making explicit the hopelessness of his task. In what amounts almost to an appeal for clemency, Jonson makes it clear that his is the impossible job of entertaining an ideologically divided court with a political entertainment.

The conversation between Cook and hapless Poet in *Neptune's Triumph* encapsulates many of the interpretive problems that bear upon a consideration of the court masque. How weighty, or trifling, were masques? What was the nature of the relation between masque and audience? As to the first point, we may need to ask what 'trifling' actually meant to the Renaissance court. The art of courtliness, Patricia Fumerton tells us, was that of the artful trifle: the sonnet, the miniature, the elaborately designed and lavishly provided-for dinner party.[7] Trifling, in that courtly context, was hardly synonymous with the unimportant; in a world of small-scale, interpersonal power relations, the slightest details of self-presentation – of gesture, deportment, manner, dress – were sure to resonate with significance. The Renaissance court, as Richard Halpern observes, provided a setting in which 'the power of sovereignty work[ed] primarily by making itself visible'.[8] In such a milieu, where the surface was, in a sense, precisely what mattered, the trivial assumed a startling importance.

The case for redefining what we mean by 'trivial' has been eloquently put by Norbert Elias in *The Court Society*. Whereas status in a money economy need not be continually asserted to maintain its effectiveness, Elias argues, status in a courtly society depends for its very existence upon display. Finely nuanced conduct becomes endowed with a special weight:

We are apt to ask today: why were these people so beholden to external appearances . . . to [the] superficial? But . . . this assessment of what was centrally important to court people as 'superficial' springs from a quite specific structure of social existence. We can to some extent allow ourselves today to leave real social differences concealed . . . because the relationships between people mediated by wealth and profession, and the resulting differentiation of people, remain unambiguously real and effective even when not expressed directly in their public manifestations.[9]

In the early modern court, prestige was either visible or non-existent.

The masque, then, considered even in its most superficial aspect – as a spectacular dance party, or what David Lindley has described as 'an elaborate frame for . . . an aristocratic knees-up'[10] – was none the less socially and politically significant. In Elias's sense, it was a display of power and standing. Renaissance court culture in all its manifestations could be singularly serious and untrifling about play – in Inns of Court revelling, for example, or in Accession Day celebrations. Festivity took on the function, as Desmond Bland has noted, of a 'training-ground' in nobility, and was acknowledged as such by the involvement of monarch, councillors and nobles.[11] Accession Day celebrations were occasions of extravagant, elaborate, and, from one perspective, superficial displays, like the masque; yet they were also attempts to garner, secure and enhance prestige at the heart of power. From a courtly viewpoint, all such entertainments were, if trifling, importantly so.[12]

As the most developed courtly pastime and formal social occasion of the English Renaissance, the masque was thus significant, even if some of its spectators may have been uncomprehending of, or indifferent to, its deeper poetic and scenic meanings.[13] Moreover, as 'the most inherently topical of all seventeenth-century art forms',[14] the masque was unavoidably and consciously political. The key to its political nature, and hence the key to critical interpretation, lies in its reception. What was the nature of the court audience, and what was its relation to such spectacle? What range of responses did the masque allow for? How far did it permit sceptical or ambivalent reactions? Do we need to think of divisions among an audience, as *Neptune's Triumph* would seem to suggest? These questions are central to our understanding of the ideological effects of a major English Renaissance symbolic form.

The essays gathered here re-open the question of the 'trivial' importance of the masque and related forms of courtly entertainment chiefly in the reigns of James I, and, to an extent, Charles I. In so doing they build upon recent advances in our understanding of the relations between society and culture in the early modern period, and upon the rehistoricized temper of Elizabethan Renaissance studies over the past decade and a half that has directed special attention to the Stuart masque. The present essays take as axiomatic the proposition, advanced by New Historicist critics among others, that Renaissance literature 'did not simply reflect history but in a sense . . . helped to make it'.[15] This proposition is arguably even more true of the masque than of other literary forms in the period, if only because many of the most powerful individuals in the land participated in its elegant rituals. A literary form so devoted to the art of self-fashioning and role-playing in the drama of power has warmly recommended itself to a new generation of critics interested in the arcane processes by which political and social authority invents and replicates itself. As Martin Butler will show, in his essay that provides a theorizing basis for this collection, the 'entanglements between culture and power' presented in the court masque have inevitably fascinated New Historicist criticism.

Stephen Orgel, working in conjunction with Roy Strong, deserves to be recognized as the initiator of modern studies in the masque. More broadly, though not a New Historicist himself by any narrow or orthodox designation, he has been an important precursor of a good deal that New Historicism has uncovered in this field.[16] Although, as Martin Butler will explain, the essays in this collection undertake to move beyond Orgel's early work in the direction of seeing factional diversity at court to which the masque necessarily responded, they do so with full appreciation of the brilliant groundwork that Orgel has provided. In his own contribution to this present collection, Orgel sees division in the court as astutely as does anyone else. To the extent that Orgel's intent in his original and pioneering work focused on James as king, showing how the masque might be seen to embody Stuart power as the 'expression of the monarch's will, the mirror of his mind',[17] Orgel's findings remain importantly true even while they need, and deserve, to be enriched by consideration of other, discordant voices in the competitions for power that sought out the masque as a medium of political self-definition. Early and late, Orgel's 'thick description' of the mentality embodied in the masque has illuminated in the courtly context 'the role of symbolic forms in human life'.[18]

Orgel and others interested in the masque, and in the broader cultural phenomena to which Stephen Greenblatt has given the useful names of 'negotiation', 'circulations of energy', 'containment' versus 'subversion' and the like, owe an important and openly acknowledged indebtedness to Clifford Geertz and Lawrence Stone. Geertz, in his anthropological analysis of what he calls 'the theater state' in nineteenth-century Bali and in other studies, offers an especially pertinent model for the Stuart masque.[19] His point, in brief, is that the ceremonies and myths of political rule became, for nineteenth-century

Bali as they do for many other cultures, a kind of self-fulfilling reality in which the leaders of a culture act out roles in ceremonies designed to mythologize those leaders' divine origins and authority. Through ceremonies of music, dance and public display, the leaders essentially become what they have created through their impersonations of power; the medium of the ceremony becomes the reality of political authority. This anthropological approach is a sceptical one in that it sees power as the end product of illusions that are being consciously manipulated. New Historicism in the 1980s, for its own cultural reasons, found this view of politics immensely applicable to the California and then the United States of the Reagan era, whilst the Cultural Materialists in Great Britain found a similar wry solace in a method of analysis so germane to the social and political practices of Thatcherism. The Renaissance court masque flourished in this environment as confirmation that some things in the world of political power never really change. Whether the manipulations of power were perceived quite as cynically in Renaissance England is another question, but examination of the process itself has brought significant new illumination of the cultural context of the court masque.

Lawrence Stone's *The Crisis of the Aristocracy, 1558–1641* (1965), and his later work, including *The Family, Sex and Marriage in England, 1500–1800* (1977), have exercised considerable influence on New Historicist critics by arguing that England's great families declined in influence under the Tudors and Stuarts.[20] One result was a scramble for ways in which England's ruling class might maintain the fiction at least of their importance to the nation. An outmoded feudal aristocracy turned to chivalric rituals such as the tournament as a means of mythologizing its function as a warrior class deserving the claim of ancestral greatness. Richard McCoy, Perry Anderson, Anthony Esler, Raymond Southall, Eric Mallen, Paul Siegel and others have further enriched our understanding of this phemonenon by their analyses of ways in which a frantic neo-chivalric cult of honour by the Earl of Essex and other aristocrats sought to idealize an imagined medieval past as an ideological bulwark against what they perceived as an unravelling of the social fabric. Paul Hammer's essay on Essex in this present volume adds still more illustration.[21] Confronted with such a decline, England's aristocracy turned to the masque especially as one vital means of asserting claims of political significance and of sorting out lines of authority. The work of Stone and others thus focuses our attention on a world of frantic courtly emulation in which the masque was destined to become a potent if multi-edged instrument in the negotiation of power.

This New Historicist approach to Jacobean court politics needs to be seen as part of a larger revolution in historiography of the period, a revolution in which the 'Whig Liberal' interpretation of English history (as seen for example in the work of G. M. Trevelyan), insisting teleologically on an inevitable progression towards civil war and the securing of political liberties under a constitutional monarchy, has given way to a revisionist view concentrating on specific moments of history and rejecting any simplified binary opposition between Tudor or Stuart governments and their critics. This revisionist history has also taken as its premise the omnipresence of rivalry and factionalism in court politics, and has generally seen King James I as a more complex, intellectual and successful ruler than the champions of Whig Liberalism would allow.[22] To dispense with the old notion that civil war was inevitable in the early seventeenth century is to make possible a new view of the Stuart masque; it need no longer be represented as the doomed and empty gesture of a court culture bent on its own destruction, and can instead be viewed as a serious representation of princely power. This present volume aligns itself with the new revisionism to the important extent of arguing that the court was not monolithic, and that the masque, as the principal genre of the court's self-representation, was much more than a simple occasion for self-congratulation. It was instead the site of negotiation over England's most pressing problems and clashes of personality.

In a similar fashion, the 'linguistic turn' in historiographical developments advocated by J. G. A. Pocock and Quentin Skinner has redirected attention to the way in which shifts in discourse can announce larger ideological locutions and changes. Pocock insists, for example, that too often, in the more traditional historical methods of analysis that preceded the current revolution in the study of history, 'the coherence of a work or body of political writing, as political philosophy or as political theory, was mistakenly identified with its character as a historical phenomenon'. A historian should not attempt to 'furnish his author with a degree of coherence he did not in fact achieve'. Skinner similarly argues that a basic inadequacy afflicts both those who have attempted to understand a work of the past in the context of religious, political and enonomic factors, and those who insist on the autonomy of the text as 'the sole necessary key to its own meaning', because both methodologies 'commit philosophical mistakes in the assumptions they make about the conditions necessary for the understanding of utterances'. The modern critic or historian must realize that 'it will never in fact be possible simply to study what any given classic writer has *said* (especially

in an alien culture) without bringing to bear some of one's own expectations about what he must have been saying'.[23] These strictures, we submit, apply with particular force to the Stuart masque, and require that
a new reading of the masque attune itself to a methodology that is as
fully aware as can be of its own premises and preconceptions. In a
similar vein, we believe that interpretations of the Stuart masque must
bring to bear a reconsideration of audience and its place in the discourse
of power at court, enriched as well by an understanding of the valences
of masque performance.

A corollary of the recent revolution in historiography is that the
court masque needs to be viewed as a diverse expression of conflicting arenas of interest within the court culture, rather than as primarily
a symbolic ceremony vital to the reproduction of monarchal power.
Whereas the scholarship of the 1960s and 1970s emphasized sovereignty and the power of a prince,[24] in an attempt 'to reconstruct the
mentality of monarch-centered power',[25] today's scholarship has begun
to move towards an increasingly complex picture. The very title of
Stephen Orgel's *The Illusion of Power* (1975) declares his fascination with
Clifford Geertz's mythologizings of authority through state-sponsored
ceremonials centred on the monarchy. Similarly, Jonathan Goldberg
assumes a centrality of monarchical power in his *James I and the Politics
of Literature*.[26] Finding ambiguity at the heart of the Jacobean court
masque, Goldberg attributes that ambiguity to the divisions of James's
own personality and policies; the masque mirrors the struggle in the
King himself between order and anarchy. These powerfully resonant
theses, we will argue, can be further enhanced if the disjunctions thus
noted are also explored in multi-faceted interpretations that stress the
role of other court factions than that represented solely by the King.

For some critics of recent years, including Goldberg himself, a potential weakness of New Historicist emphasis on sovereignty is that it may
end up reproducing early modern society's ideological misdescription
of itself.[27] Jonson's *Oberon* (1611) would appear indeed at first to celebrate
a power relationship in which all is seen to flow from an omnipotent
prince, represented in this masque by the aptly-named Pan. Yet we
would do well to consider that even if Jonson's own agenda impelled
him towards a strongly monarchical model, he was not the only deviser
of masques for the court; nor was King James the only significant
patron. As Martin Butler and Tom Bishop will argue, Prince Henry's
political role in the dynamics of *Oberon* is every bit as compelling as
that of King James.

Recent studies by Richard McCoy, Leeds Barroll, Barbara Lewalski, Malcolm Smuts and others have accordingly begun to focus on cultural forms, from neo-feudal chivalry to the researches of the Society of Antiquaries into Britain's ancient constitution, that offered an alternative political agenda to the monarchy's claim to mythological greatness.[28] The present collection of essays engages in the debate at this point, adopting what Lloyd Davis has called 'a less sovereign-centred approach to the masque'[29] in order to describe in some detail the complexities, ambiguities and uncertainties of court politics and culture in the early modern period. In our view, the masque, rather than being simply the expression of monarchal power, was available for use by other interests, and functioned at the intersection of rivalrous political discourses.[30]

The court itself in this volume thus often appears as fluid and conflicted. What we hope to have undertaken is a deepening politicization of the masque; and by 'politics' we mean not solely the idealisms of Tudor–Stuart political theology but the actual political processes through which things happened. However much the Tudor and Stuart monarchs may have fashioned images of themselves as absolute rulers, authority in those regimes was less a one-way transmission of power than a complex negotiation – not wholly unlike that of more democratic societies – involving conflict, compromise and exchange. We are interested most of all in the ways in which masques negotiated among a range of commitments.[31] Our focus is on what J. R. Mulryne has recently called the 'strains and contradictions to which masquing texts and masquing occasions testify'.[32] Our approach has been to consider the court less as the organic creation of an all-powerful monarch than as an arena in which competing interest groups jockeyed for position – a court that was dynamic, unstable and volatile, and in which a poet such as Jonson might well find himself in a delicate position.[33]

Our attempt has been to provide a cohesive argument rather than a scattered selection of essays on a topic of mutual interest. We have tried to keep the project whole and unified by selection of subjects, arrangement of those subjects in a continuous line of argument, and communication among those who have taken part. The overarching argument of the book runs as follows:

New Historicism has made a huge contribution to our understanding of the Stuart masque by showing how masques thematized and enacted the Renaissance theatricalization of power. At the same time, the focus on monarchy as a pervasive influence in the creation of the masque has sometimes had the effect of homogenizing the masque into a single-minded instrument of royal policy, and has sometimes obscured the necessary matter of addressing history as process. Even Jonathan Goldberg's analysis of the masque as simultaneously subversive and self-abasing interprets this ambivalence as a reflection of a divided royal will. To the extent that we can discern fractures in place of a monolithic image of absolutism, we can better begin to appreciate the give and take of accommodation and realignment that go to make up a communal event like the production of a masque. *Oberon* (1611) divides its focus between Oberon himself (representing Prince Henry) and Pan (King James) in a form of doubleness that reflects Henry's growing emergence as a 'significant competitor in the arena of power with his father'. These 'colliding priorities' spell trouble for Jonson as author of the text (Martin Butler).

To step back for a moment into Elizabeth's last years and to the Accession Day celebrations of 1595 is to see that the events nominally devised to praise the Queen do more to dramatize, in the debate between Love and Self-Love, the Earl of Essex's predicament as challenger to what Richard McCoy has dubbed the Elizabethan 'chivalric compromise'. That compromise allowed courtiers to flaunt their ambitions in chivalric display while subordinating ambition to royal service. The Accession Day event was so crucial to Essex's campaign of self-promotion that he essentially devised it himself, with the help of Francis Bacon and others. The event was a success if we measure it by what appears to have been Essex's design: 'upstaging Elizabeth on her own special day' of celebration (Paul E. J. Hammer).

James I's pacifist foreign policy was bound to influence his view of how court festivities should celebrate his reign. His was the strategy of a *politique*, balancing off the Catholic powers of the Continent against the Dutch and other Protestant communities. James's policy, advanced for its time, had notwithstanding to contend with a legacy of fanaticism, as well as the crypto-Catholicism of Queen Anne. Strains and equivocations are accordingly evident in Samuel Daniel's *The Vision of the Twelve Goddesses*, performed at court in 1604. Though commissioned by Queen Anne, who favoured a pro-Spanish pacifism, it none the less reveals Daniel's affiliation with the more interventionist Protestant politics once championed by Sir Philip Sidney and the Earl of Essex. Daniel's successor as purveyor of masques to the crown, on the other hand, was more aligned with James's pacifism. Jonson's *The Masque of Queens* (1609) honours the ideology of peace. Queen Anne appears to have been a force behind this entertainment, as its politics suggest (Peter Holbrook).

Jonson's *Oberon* (1611), dividing its centre of attention, as we have seen, between the images of Pan (King James) and Oberon (Prince Henry), takes on intense political meaning when examined in terms of the Prince's actively performative role in that masque. Henry's 'charisma', to use Clifford Geertz's term, manifested itself in the Prince's dancing. The King's personal disinclination to join the dancing cast him in a role of supporting things as they were, while Henry's more interventionist role lent itself to a contested dialectic that was 'mapped out on the floor in the masque performance itself'. Eyewitnesses attest to the importance of Henry's grace and facility as the central figure in a performance designed to support his growing claim to eminence at court. His dancing role had to be convincingly performed to reify his authority, and evidently was so, through newly devised choreographies that were painstakingly rehearsed (Tom Bishop).

Similarly, we must realize that the first ten years of the Stuart reign saw the forwarding of Queen Anne's programmes in ways that were not always consistent with those of her royal husband. From the start, the Queen created dominant roles for her favourites among court ladies in the dancing of new masques. Her first masque, Samuel Daniel's *The Vision of the Twelve Goddesses* (1604), departed notably from its immediate predecessor, 'The Orient Knights', sponsored by the King. *Twelve Goddesses* was danced by twelve ladies and twelve gentlemen instead of the eight mostly unmarried men who had danced 'The Orient Knights'. The political significance of the ladies' performance was bolstered by the social importance of the occasion. The women dancers, some of them married, had evidently been chosen because they enjoyed the Queen's friendship and support; youthful beauty and unmarried status seem to have counted for less. Spatial arrangements of the women signified their roles in an encoding of courtly power. *The Masque of Blackness* (1605), Jonson's first masque, seems to have appealed to James as an idea, but its success came about largely through Anne's instigation. Again, the core of noblewomen dancing with the Queen were seen as literally close to Anne and enjoying her special recognition (Leeds Barroll).

Indeed, *The Masque of Blackness* shows Jonson and Inigo Jones following the lead of Queen Anne. The undertaking was designed to enlist the magic of theatrical performance on behalf of Anne's bold presentation of herself as royal consort. The costumes, designed according to her specific stipulations, revealed her more or less literally as the King's unmanageable wife. Some men were professedly shocked by the courtesan-like appearance and black complexion of the courtly women dancers, and yet the occasion struck others as exotically sumptuous. The complex issue of blackness lent to the masque an aura of strangeness that accorded well with the Queen's political agenda. Thus did Anne establish a new transgressive mode of womanliness, one calculated to arouse masculine anxiety and yet present itself as newly fashionable. Blackface was repeated some seven months later on the royal visit of Queen Anne's brother, Christian IV of Denmark, and by 1611 (in *Love Freed*) such exotic costuming had become de rigueur. By challenging the very notion of what constitutes masculinity, as in *Hymenaei* (1606), the Queen's new masques led some observers to wonder whether James was master in his own house (Stephen Orgel).

The antimasque served in all such masques as a site of contestation and potential subversion. These subversive tendencies could, in some circumstances, be viewed as 'contained' by the surrounding masque itself and its royalist celebration. None the less, the Jonsonian antimasque developed into an extended opportunity for Jonson to talk on remarkably familiar terms with the King. Such a view of Jonson's antimasques challenges the often-heard view of him as a creature of royal sycophancy. Jonson's own political biases may well have led him to support James's pacifist foreign policy and other aspects of his rule, but the antimasque was Jonson's creation, and as such it provided a space in which Jonson could give expression to what he saw as unruliness in court politics. Even if the forces of anarchy in the antimasque can often be recuperated into the spectacular triumphs of order with which the masques customarily end, the antimasque at the very least 'creates the anxiety which makes obvious the purpose and importance of containment'. The voices of holiday misrule, giving expression to discontent on the issues of the day, are not entirely silenced. Containment is more effective in Jonson's early masques; in his later work, like *Time Vindicated* (1623), we find in the antimasque a more natural home for riot and exuberant subversion (Hugh Craig).

In long-standing rivalries of court and City, as well, we can see dissonances and conflicting points of view that betoken a changing social order, along with recognition of a need for negotiation of those differences. The public shows of the London companies and the private masques of the Jacobean court are interestingly alike in their modes of presentation. Both enact through symbolic spectacle a set of ideological claims. Ceremonial traditions like Lord Mayor's Shows and masques existed not so much to exacerbate differences between civic and courtly constituencies as to 'negotiate longstanding conflicts concerning status and finance'. King James understood the need to ingratiate himself with the London companies. The installation of Henry as Prince of Wales and Earl of Chester in 1610, for example, offered a rich opportunity for negotiating an exchange of both courtesy and money. Earlier, in 1607, Henry had attended the midsummer feast of the Merchant Tailors' Company, giving occasion for a double focus of attention anticipating that of the King and Henry during the performance of *Oberon* in 1611. The Lord Mayor's Show of 1605 had celebrated *The Triumphs of Reunited Britannia* in a way that laid claim to venerable British ancestry for all parties concerned, civic and royal. The memory of Henry was to remain warm in civic pageantry long after his death, in implicit endorsement of his Protestant and interventionist ideas on foreign policy that the crown seemed increasingly to have forgotten as it steered towards the treacherous shoals of the Spanish Match (Nancy E. Wright).

Although the greatest dramatist of the Jacobean era was never commissioned to write a masque for the court, William Shakespeare did write a masque into *The Tempest*. He saw that play performed at court in late 1611 and again during the winter of 1612–13 on the occasion of the marriage of James's daughter Elizabeth to the Elector Palatine, Frederick. The play was also publicly performed, and seems to have owed its first loyalty to its paying audience. These circumstances invite a comparison of the masque in *The Tempest* with Thomas Campion's *The Lords' Masque* (1613), written specifically for the royal wedding. Campion's masque examines the role of the creative artist in the context of an art form dependent upon a hierarchical structure of authority, and is, from first to last, a celebration of the absolutism that is to be perpetuated by the royal and politically inspired marriage. Shakespeare's masque re-presents the court masque for a paying audience and, at the last, asks for that audience's applause as the confirming sign of its endorsement. Such a re-fashioning of the court masque for a popular audience is enormously suggestive about the politics of masquing. Prospero bears some resemblance to King James. Both are imperfect rulers, self-indulgent, arrogant and impolitic, too proud in their learning, too ready to cast the administration of the state onto others. At the same time, Shakespeare's masque engages with a celebrated issue of its day, the royal marriage and its presumed mediating role in continental politics. Shakespeare's version of the masque implicitly welcomes the Jacobean royal marriage as a political and dynastic event, even if Shakespeare's play first appeared some two years before the marriage actually took place. The model of political sovereignty, so central to Stuart ideology and dramatized in Prospero's plot, is revealed as deserving of loyalty even though morally flawed, while the dramatist makes clear his allegiance to his true patrons in a capitalist enterprise (David Bevington).

A masque in performance consisted of much more than its verbal script. We need always to bear in mind that the spectacle and dancing were the main event, and occupied considerably more playing time than is evident from reading a text. At the same time, deciphering clues as to the exact nature of the dance is notoriously difficult. The texts themselves repeatedly allude to the evanescent nature of dance and spectacle. How did dancing engage in the complex negotiation of political and social dialogue with which this volume is concerned? One approach is to explore early seventeenth-century comments on masquing, which are often hostile in their puritanical dislike of indecency and affectation. George Villiers, Duke of Buckingham, was a special target of vituperation for his promoting of French customs at the Stuart court. In him especially, French-style deportment was regarded as effeminate. We can tell a good deal from Puritan diatribes about 'womanish' periwigs, styles of clothing, perfume and other cosmetics; we also learn from dancing manuals about imported styles of galliard, dancing on tiptoes, *congé*, *plié*, kissing of the hands, and much more. Similarly, we can gain insights into the instabilities between 'male' and 'female' movement codes by examining the role of young performers in the masque. Here Mary Villiers, daughter of the Duke of Buckingham, offers a highly visible model. Dance integrated young performers into the masque spectacle, socializing them as young impersonators of the values of the Stuart court (Barbara Ravelhofer).

When we consider the politics of music in the Stuart masque, in the court of Charles I as well as that of James I, we observe the intrinsic power of music to incite as well as to unite. Although no complete musical score for an extant masque survives, the problematic cues of musical setting are everywhere apparent in music's ways of differentiating the subversive energies of the antimasque, for example, from the confirming resonances of a masque's finale. Musical codes, always slippery by nature, are especially so in the early modern period; we must be careful to avoid the compartmentalizations of musical settings and look for ways in which music underscores (as it were) 'the masque's omnipresent anxiety about its own legitimacy'. Elaborate and showy performances, in singing as in dancing, are unambiguous markers of sophistication through which the politically powerful like Buckingham learned to compete for courtly favour. Above all, the masque writer's task is to exploit the 'educative and curative properties that music derives from its heavenly affinity . . . bringing them down to earth in the ceremonious masque'. The use of music in the Stuart masque increasingly subordinated itself to royal power as Charles I commissioned an idealized image of his court and its entertainment, ever more dominated by metaphors of transformation and apotheosis. Milton, alienated as were many Englishmen by the increasing authoritarianism of the Stuart court, found good cause to meditate on the 'question of the source of music's authority' in his masque, *Comus* (David Lindley).

Comus (1634) is, then, the end point of our journey. Milton found himself writing in a world presided over by a king who dismissed Parliament and reissued James I's controversial *Book of Sports* encouraging dancing and festivity. Courtly masquing idealized Charles and Henrietta Maria in Neoplatonic and pastoral terms as Heroic Love and Divine Virtue, symbolically united in their joint responsibility of bringing under monarchical control all the unruly and mutinous elements of a population symbolized in the antimasque. The Queen's Roman Catholicism exacerbated divisions in England's social and political structure, helping to formulate a poetics of court entertainment that Milton and other Protestants were bound to regard as anathema. Under these polarizing circumstances, Milton found a welcome patron in the Countess of Derby, at her estate of Harefield in Middlesex, and wrote *Arcades* for performance there perhaps in 1632. In it, Milton undertook to reclaim the pastoral for a noble Protestant countess and her household, with text and music fitted to the religious politics of the occasion. *Comus* was commissioned by the Earl of Bridgewater in 1634 in the same spirit of seeking to remedy the fundamental values of a court genre perceived as having gone fatally astray. *Comus* is thus a reformed masque reflecting Puritan religious and political sensibilities. The contrast between it and *The Temple of Love* (1635), by William Davenant and Inigo Jones, encapsulates at the close of our narrative the contested role of the Stuart masque, as the rulers and intellectuals of England sought through performative art to act out in fictive personae the claims of a divided society (Barbara Lewalski).

Perhaps the foregoing summary of the book can convey our sense of its integrated argument. We should explain what the book does not attempt to do. A volume on the masque in the early modern period could, of course, begin much earlier at the start of the Tudor reign; for this story, the reader is referred to Sydney Anglo's *Spectacle, Pageantry and Early Tudor Policy* and to Gordon Kipling's edition of *The Receyte of the Lady Katerine* (written to celebrate Katharine of Arragon's marriage to Henry VIII's son Arthur), among other studies.[34] Queen Elizabeth's reign was not especially known for its masques, but she certainly did witness other entertainments that could have been included in our deliberations. The Inns of Court were actively involved in Christmas revels.

Our book chooses instead to focus on the period under James I when the masque underwent a new definition and a vast increase in expense of production. We devote somewhat less space to the Caroline masque, though the story of increased social and political polarization does provide the setting for our concluding exploration of music in the masque and of Milton's *Comus*. Our emphasis is designedly literary, though with careful attention as well to dance and music in the essays of Tom Bishop, Barbara Ravelhofer and David Lindley. Inigo Jones does not play as large a role in this study as he does in the fine edition of Jones's work by Stephen Orgel and Roy Strong, or indeed as in the masque as it was actually performed. This book devotes rather little attention to visual aesthetics of the masque, to the machinery and stunning trompe l'oeil effects that so impressed eyewitnesses. Perhaps, despite its interest in a cross-disciplinary genre, this book is ultimately wedded to a literary and even Aristotelian preference for theme and idea over spectacle. The book has few pretensions as a work of archival historical scholarship; Paul Hammer is a professional historian, while the rest of us are literary in our affiliations. We are none the less deeply interested in historical process and its interaction with the Stuart court masque, and have sought as varied a means of exploring that interaction as our training makes possible.

NOTES

1 See *Neptune's Triumph for the Return of Albion* and *Love Restored*, in David Lindley (ed.) *Court Masques: Jacobean and Caroline Entertainments, 1605–1640* (Oxford, 1995); further quotations from *Neptune's Triumph* are from this edition.

2 *Hymenaei*, lines 16–17, in Stephen Orgel (ed.), *Ben Jonson: Selected Masques* (New Haven, 1970).

3 H. A. Evans (ed.), *English Masques* (London, nd), p. 75.

4 Induction, *Bartholomew Fair*, ed. E. A. Horsman (London, 1960), line 139.

5 See Thomas Cogswell, 'England and the Spanish match', in Richard Cust and Ann Hughes (eds.), *Conflict in Early Stuart England: Studies in Religion and Politics, 1603–1642* (London, 1989).

6 David Riggs, *Ben Jonson: A Life* (Cambridge, MA, 1989), p. 289. On Jonson's two images of himself in this masque, the 'high-brow and uncompromising artist' and the 'genial entertainer willing . . . to gratify all tastes' – Poet and Cook – see Anne Barton, *Ben Jonson, Dramatist* (Cambridge, 1984), p. 297.

7 Patricia Fumerton, *Cultural Aesthetics: Renaissance Literature and the Practice of Social Ornament* (Chicago, 1991); for contemporary attitudes to the masque, see esp. p. 237, n2. See also Jonas A. Barish, *Ben Jonson and the Language of Prose Comedy* (Cambridge, MA, 1960), p. 271 (cited by Fumerton).

8 Richard Halpern, *The Poetics of Primitive Accumulation: English Renaissance Culture and the Genealogy of Capital* (Ithaca, 1981), p. 3.

9 Norbert Elias, *The Court Society*, trans. Edmund Jephcott (Oxford, 1983), pp. 93–4.

10 Introduction, Lindley (ed.), *Court Masques*, p. x.

11 Desmond Bland (ed.), *Gesta Grayorum, or the History of the High and Mighty Prince Henry Prince of Purpoole, Anno Domini 1594* (Liverpool, 1968), pp. xxiv, xvii–xviii.

12 From an anti-courtly viewpoint masques are complicit with tyranny. Representatives in a commonwealth live soberly, but a king is 'adored like a demigod, with a dissolute and haughty court about him, of vast expense and luxury, masques and revels, to the debauching of our prime gentry male and female . . .'. See *The Ready and Easy Way to Establish a Free Commonwealth* in *The Works of John Milton*, gen. ed. Frank Patterson (New York, 1932), VI, p. 120.

13 On the importance of the pleasure provided by masques, and by the dancing particularly, see Graham Parry, 'The politics of the court masque', in J. R. Mulryne and Margaret Shewring (eds.), *Theatre and Government under the Early Stuarts* (Cambridge, 1993), pp. 113–14.

14 Leah Sinanoglou Marcus, '"Present Occasions" and the shaping of Ben Jonson's masques', *English Literary History* 45 (1978), 201.

15 Martin Butler, 'Early Stuart court culture: compliment or criticism?', *The Historical Journal* 32 (1989), 435. For a similar view, see Carolyn Porter, 'Are we being historical yet?', *South Atlantic Quarterly* 87 (1988), 782.

16 On the work of Orgel, Strong, and D. J. Gordon as New Historicism *avant la lettre*, see H. Aram Veeser (ed.), *The New Historicism* (New York, 1989), p. xiii, and Jonathan Goldberg, 'The politics of Renaissance literature: a review essay', *English Literary History* 49 (1982). Goldberg argues that their work showed the 'role that art played in the court . . . and its status as a political event' (539). Key studies include Orgel, *The Jonsonian Masque* (Cambridge, MA, 1965) and *The Illusion of Power: Political Theater in the Renaissance*

(Berkeley, 1975); Orgel and Strong (eds.) *Inigo Jones: The Theatre of the Stuart Court*, 2 vols. (London, 1973); essays by Gordon collected in *The Renaissance Imagination*, ed. Orgel (Berkeley, 1975). Critics writing earlier in the century also stressed the political function of masques. See Mary Sullivan, *Court Masques of James I: Their Influence on Shakespeare and the Public Theatres* (New York, 1913) and E. W. Talbert, 'The interpretation of Jonson's courtly spectacles', *PMLA* 61 (1946), 454–73.

17 Orgel, *Illusion of Power*, p. 45.

18 Clifford Geertz, 'Thick description: toward an interpretive theory of culture', in his *The Interpretation of Cultures: Selected Essays* (New York, 1973), p. 29.

19 Clifford Geertz, *Negara: The Theater State in Nineteenth-Century Bali* (Princeton, 1980).

20 Lawrence Stone, *The Crisis of the Aristocracy, 1558–1641* (Oxford, 1965), esp. pp. 11–13; *The Family, Sex and Marriage, 1500–1800* (London, 1977).

21 Richard McCoy, *The Rites of Knighthood: The Literature and Politics of Elizabethan Chivalry* (Berkeley, 1989); Raymond Southall, '*Troilus and Cressida* and the spirit of capitalism', *Shakespeare in a Changing World*, ed. Arnold Kettle (London, 1964), pp. 217–32; Perry Anderson, *The Lineages of the Absolutist State* (London, 1974), esp. pp. 119–27; Anthony Esler, *The Aspiring Mind of the Elizabethan Younger Generation* (Durham, NC, 1966), esp. p. 224; Eric Mallin, 'Emulous factions and the collapse of chivalry: *Troilus and Cressida*', *Representations* 29 (1990), 145–79; Paul Siegel, 'Shakespeare and the neo-chivalric cult of honor', *Centennial Review* 8 (1964), 39–70; and Paul Hammer's essay in this volume.

22 See, for example, Linda Levy Peck, *Court Patronage and Corruption in Early Stuart England* (Boston, 1990); Maurice Lee, Jr., *Great Britain's Solomon: James VI and I in His Three Kingdoms* (Urbana, IL, 1990); Jenny Wormald, 'James VI and I: two kings or one?', *History* 68 (1983), 187–209; and, as an encapsulation of the older Whig-Liberal view, George Macaulay Trevelyan, *History of England* (London, 1926).

23 J. G. A. Pocock, *Politics, Language and Time: Essays on Political Thought and History* (New York, 1971), esp. pp. 6–11, and Quentin Skinner, 'Meaning and understanding in the history of ideas', *History and Theory* 8 (1969), 3–35, esp. 3–6.

24 Alan Liu, 'The power of formalism: the New Historicism', *English Literary History* 56 (1988), 725.

25 Halpern, *Primitive Accumulation*, p. 3.

26 Jonathan Goldberg, *James I and the Politics of Literature* (Baltimore, 1983).

27 Thus in Stephen Greenblatt's *Renaissance Self-Fashioning: From More to Shakespeare* (Chicago, 1980), 'all discourse' pays 'homage to the Queen': Goldberg, 'Politics of Renaissance literature', 533.

28 'Elizabethan chivalry' was a system in which the Queen 'conceded a great deal' to her 'factious aristocrats', according to McCoy, *Rites of Knighthood*, p. 18. Butler, 'Early Stuart court culture', argues that studies of English

Renaissance culture too readily see it as in 'collusion with the mechanisms of royal power' (p. 425).

29 Lloyd Davis, 'Powerful illusions: praise and presence in Elizabethan and Jacobean court drama', *AUMLA: Journal of the Australasian Language and Literature Association* 83 (1995), 14.

30 The possibility that masques 'encode . . . the political positions of [the] noblemen and women who sponsored or took part in them' is raised by David Lindley, *The Trials of Frances Howard: Fact and Fiction at the Court of King James* (London, 1993), p. 17.

31 In *Shakespearean Negotiations: The Circulation of Social Energy in Renaissance England* (Oxford, 1988), Stephen Greenblatt replaces the hitherto master concept of 'power' (oriented towards the charisma of a monarch) with 'negotiation', which stresses the ways in which cultural works and political authority are products of exchanges of one kind or another. The essays collected here tend to view the masque as the product of such transactions rather than as the unified artwork of an author-monarch; on all of these issues, see *Shakespearean Negotiations*, pp. 2–7.

32 Mulryne and Shewring (eds.), *Theatre and Government*, p. 11.

33 On the polycentric character of the English court, see Malcolm Smuts, 'Court centered politics and Roman historians', Kevin Sharpe and Peter Lake (eds.), *Culture and Politics in Early Stuart England* (Stanford, 1994), pp. 23, 24. On the independence of Queen Anne's court, see Barbara Lewalski, 'Anne of Denmark and the subversions of masquing', *Criticism* 35 (1993), and Leeds Barroll, 'The court of the first Stuart queen', in Linda Levy Peck (ed.), *The Mental World of the Jacobean Court* (Cambridge, 1991).

34 Sydney Anglo, *Spectacle, Pageantry and Early Tudor Policy* (Oxford, 1969); Gordon Kipling, *The Receyte of the Lady Katerine* (Oxford, 1990).

CHAPTER 2

Courtly negotiations

Martin Butler

NEW HISTORICISTS AND THE MASQUE

As the Introduction to this volume has already suggested, it is scarcely surprising that the English court masques should have attracted the attention of New Historicist critics. Performed by, with, and to the court; trading in stupendous images of sovereignty; shaped as acts of festive contest in which disorder is routed and subversion contained; and functioning as ceremonial arenas in which ritual exchanges between monarch and courtier mimed the ties of obligation bonding England's political elites, the masques were overtly engaged in what in recent years have emerged as some of the most characteristic themes of New Historicist writing. If much New Historicist work has typically found its point of departure in the anecdotal and the contingent, then the ephemeral character of most masques – performed once and rarely if ever repeated – has made them a suitable case for treatment. If the expectation was that masque poets should translate present occasions into political symbolism and more removed mysteries, then the frankly ideological character of this programme is no less congenial to a criticism which has been preoccupied with the mechanisms by which power is legitimated. And if the tropes of the masque typically disclosed sovereignty as a force traversing the whole of society, absorbing contradictions and transcending contingencies, then it is not unexpected that they should have come to be seen not only as participating in the Renaissance theatricalization of power but as actually thematizing and enacting it.

Though there has yet to appear a New Historicist study focused exclusively on the masques, court theatricals have been an intrinsic part of the larger arguments advanced about Renaissance culture in the output of some of the leading names associated with New Historicism.

Both Louis Montrose and Jonathan Goldberg have written searchingly about court theatre, while Stephen Orgel's work from the 1960s onwards – the single body of scholarship that has been most influential in promoting the masque as a topic for modern study – now looks profoundly prescient, and in retrospect can be perceived as having been engaged all along with issues that have finally found a collective name. As is announced in the title of Orgel's best-known book, *The Illusion of Power* (1975), it is the court masques that most conspicuously make the intersections of illusions and power available for analysis.[1]

The great advantage for the masques that the New Historicism has over the old is that it is unembarrassed by the coalescence of the political and the aesthetic within a single form. The older historicism, working within a formalist framework which reproduced the governing assumption of New Criticism that the political and aesthetic spheres were separate and even opposed, found it hard when dealing with the masques to evade the dilemma of having to deplore their flattery of the great, while admiring the lyric beauty and intellectual sophistication which, notwithstanding, they could be shown to deploy. In earlier writers concerned with court culture, this discomfort led to an exaggerated emphasis on the masques' aesthetic achievements at the expense of their political dimensions, and even in Orgel's later, more politicized studies, the aesthetic and the political are sometimes still seen as separable agendas which pull against one another or get out of step. But by starting from the point that the worlds of action and representation are constituted by one another – that the real is as imagined as the imaginary – New Historicism has usually been able to sidestep this dilemma at the outset. Far from wanting to deplore the masques, it has made them a topic for celebration, even for a certain grim satisfaction. In the developing New Historicist revision of the Renaissance, the masques have come to figure as virtually totemic exemplars of the legitimating functions of culture in the early modern period. Chiming with that resonant Renaissance idea that the state is a work of art, they are now seen as the works of art in which spectacle most emphatically became a tool of state, and as symptomatic of the ineluctable magnetism by which kingly absolutism pulled its age's representational forms into its own orbit. As a consequence, they now typically feature as the seventeenth-century cultural form par excellence in which systems of aesthetic representation were co-opted into the service of kingship, the outstanding symbolic instances of the necessary and disenabling involvements of cultural production in the economies of power.

Yet while New Historicism's preoccupations have made it especially well qualified for investigating the spectacular politics of court culture, this shift has brought several problematic consequences with it. Particularly, although these studies have re-opened the politics of masquing as a topic of study, in practice the masques have often been written back into a scenario of power and its inescapable confluences that (I shall be arguing) increasingly looks formulaic and transhistorical. Moreover, since these readings represent the masques' politics as exactly co-terminous with their aesthetic closures, the masques' ideological significance continues to be seen as, essentially, a matter of their poetic form. I want to suggest that these manoeuvres are particularly inhibiting for readings that seek to reconsider the masques as interventions in a material history, since they marginalize precisely those elements of contingency and circumstance which each masque was engaged in negotiating.

The problems can be illustrated from two of the most influential accounts of the masques that we currently possess.[2] As the *fons et origo* of modern thinking in this area, Stephen Orgel's work has been compelling, foundational and exemplary, and not least in offering the first studies that took seriously the masques' involvement in their society's circulations of power. Orgel's work has made claims for the masques on a number of fronts, and these claims have shifted over the years, but the move which I wish to isolate here is his emphasis on the poetics of masquing space. In all of Orgel's accounts, the physical relationships between masquers, King and audience – the placement of the stage, dancing area and auditorium – have always been crucial to his presentation of the masques' politics. His readings turn centrally on the assertion that the dispositions of masquing space embody the relations of power which are enacted by the text. The King, seated directly opposite the vanishing point of the newly imported single-point perspective scenery, is the dominant figure in the entire occasion. He alone can see the action as it is meant to be seen, and it is always implicitly if not overtly centred upon him. The masquers perform their dances in homage to him, and the audience watches both the event and the King watching the event, their attentive spectatorship becoming an image of the actual political structures that relate King and court.

In Orgel's model of the masque, aesthetic and political economies reproduce one another seamlessly and inescapably.[3] The King's privileged visibility manifests his surveillance of the lives of his subjects. Observing all and observed by all, he focuses the society which the event creates, and the masque functions as a channel of social exchange by which the masquers express their devotion to him and are confirmed in their own sense of social privilege. At the same time, the fictions which the King contemplates shadow his power, showing disorder subdued by order, anarchy by authority, and sovereignty instantaneously and magically victorious. Yet, argues Orgel, these fictions are no mere reflection of the King. Rather, the court is invited not so much to interpret the masques' images as to recognize them and, in a sense, 'what the noble spectator watched he ultimately became'.[4] In representing the entire body of the realm as incorporated into the King's steady gaze, the masques revealed the court's true self, and fashioned courtly display into a statement of the impossibility of ever escaping from the King's all-embracing sovereignty.

Orgel's understanding of the masques as theatres of power has been germane to his work since the 1960s. It was a crucial insight which opened the path for much subsequent masque criticism, and in the present climate it can be seen to have much in common with the strategies of other New Historicist critics who are also concerned with the poetics of space. His theatres of power are broadly congruent with other current paradigms in which the past is encountered less as a process than as a geography: the carnival, the prison, the landscape tour, the great aristocratic household.[5] Created by the methodology of thick description, such spatial metaphors recreate history as a web of cultural interconnectedness, and reorient the historical field from the diachronic to the synchronic, from a sequence of events and motives to a structure by which identity and social relations are constituted.

As do these other spatial paradigms, the perspectivist arenas described in Orgel's early work make concretely apparent the relations of power that were involved in masque performances. A risk of this model, though, is that by presenting power relations in terms which view it as circulating rather than developing, it may become difficult to speak of their relation to history as process. To these encompassing and densely articulated structures, narratives of micro- or macro-political change will make little practical difference, so that an unintended consequence of this paradigm is to make every masque seem to do more or less the same thing – legitimate the monarch. Incidental features may differ, as each masque occupies a new occasion, but each masque tends to testify identically to the authority of the royal gaze, representing the court as serenely reaffirming its unchanging sense of identity and purpose. In such a paradigm, the theatres of power which the masques presented are compellingly evoked, but their encompassing aesthetic structures seem strangely homogenized, immune to the processes of history and endlessly reiterating the same symbolic function within the courtly economy.

Jonathan Goldberg's account of the masques in *James I and the Politics of Literature* (1983) also represents them as performing more or less the same ideological manoeuvres. Goldberg's focus is different from Orgel's, however, foregrounding as it does the problem of the textuality of the past. Taking as one point of departure the assumption that cultural forms do not merely reproduce but actively instantiate the forms of power of their society, his account of the masques situates them in relation to the discourse of sovereignty which shaped Jacobean codes of representation, the languages of power which subordinated James's subjects and in which they were always-already caught. This Jacobean discourse of power he characterizes as strategically fragmented. His account of James, brilliantly stitched together from a vast range of verbal, visual and sculptural texts, presents him as the great kingly Machiavel whose power expressed itself in terms of a deliberate doubleness, the glorious outward emperor who was simultaneously the secretive inward politician. This generated a discourse which was marked by conspicuous divisions and contradictions, a language in which Jacobean authority seemed to be at one and the same time hidden and disclosed, in which the King was both publicly on show yet endlessly invisible. This fragmentary, Machiavellian discourse Goldberg refers to as James's 'sustaining contradictions'.[6]

Goldberg presents the masques as a leading instance of Jacobean doubleness. He seizes on the masques' contrary perceptions – their vertiginous shifts between satire and ceremony, mystification and disenchantment – and reads them as at once exposing James's authority and endorsing it. Yoking the scurrilous and the reverential, the sacred and the profane, the masques mystified Jacobean power even as they unveiled it. The same masques which hymned royal authority in their choruses returned in their antimasques images of court life as prodigal and anarchic, yet both of these versions of rule James admitted and allowed. To an older historicism, the conjunction of satirical antimasque and adulatory main masque was an embarrassment: the poets heaped praise upon the King, while at the same time confusingly acknowledging the realities of power and the mechanics of courtly myth-making. But in Goldberg's analysis the contradiction is enabling, since the subversions of the antimasques were already in line with the 'duplicitous norm'[7] of the Jacobean state. James allowed the antimasques' disorders just as he presided over the main masques' harmonies, because both were strategies within the contradictory double vision of his authority. His poets dramatized a radically demystifying view of power, but in ways that were entirely cognate with a mystified kingly sovereignty. They spoke for the King even (especially) as they appeared to speak against him.

This is necessarily a compacted summary of a dense argument, but I hope that it brings out the way that Goldberg's account of the masques as conduits of the discourse which shaped Jacobean reality writes them into a particularly acute version of that vexing subversion/containment debate which has followed New Historicism everywhere, and which sometimes seems to be an unavoidable consequence of the shift from politics to power, and the dissolving of power into the field of representation. Goldberg's stunning analysis of the masques as at one and the same time outrageously subversive and outrageously self-abasing interprets them as acts of rebelliousness which are countenanced in order that they may be seen to be contained, a position closely parallel to the celebrated argument of Greenblatt's 'Invisible Bullets', in which the subversiveness of Renaissance texts is produced by the very order with which the texts were purportedly in conflict. And as so often in comparable analyses, in which power is not 'out there' to be contested but is dispersed and shapes social and cultural practices ubiquitously, the possibility of anything that might once have been taken as signals of change is fundamentally disallowed. With all transactions circulating in a liquid laissez-faire economy, and with all encounters issuing in the same repetitive and relentless closure, it is almost inevitable that we will not see anything other than 'domination dominating'. In this perspective, the masques are invariably going to function as testimonies to the prison-house of Jacobean culture, glittering occasions on which the courtly elites danced in festive celebration of their own disempowerment.

But one might legitimately want to ask whether these were in fact the only possible scenarios which the masques were capable of hosting. Was there always this perfect, inescapable equivalence between what the masques said and what they did? Or can we discern fractures in the representational field which are symptomatic of factors that were working historically to transform or at least to unsettle those modes of royal power which the masques seem so fully and irresistibly to execute? As things stand, Orgel's and Goldberg's analyses of the

masques' operations seem very totalizing, even for a form as closely
associated with the monarchy as they were. Clearly the masques did
serve the ideological needs of Stuart absolutism, and did so more
intimately than virtually any other contemporary form, but it does not
thereby follow that the only social transaction which they undertook
was one of containment, or that their performances always ratified
their royal observers, and immersed performers and spectators alike
in a scenario of dazzling disempowerment. I wish to suggest that other
kinds of negotiations[8] may also have been hosted by the masques,
scenarios which did not simply reproduce an ineluctable oscillation
between resistance and authority, but which were more in the nature
of symbolic transactions between those who were competing for position in and around the courtly arena. These negotiations can be understood as acts of accommodation or realignment, give and take between
differently empowered participants in the political process, transactions
that served to shift, manoeuvre and reshape the forms in which power
circulated.

Naturally, I do not seek to imply that the masques could have
escaped from the networks of power which played across them. To
the contrary, as communal events, in which artists and patrons, performers and participating spectators all had a hand, they were embedded in the collective practices of their society with an unusual degree of
thoroughness. Nevertheless, the notion that the masques always performed the same political work depends on a view of the operations of
power at court which runs the risk of freezing the historical moment,
substituting a snapshot for what ought to be the whole movie.[9] It does
not address the historical contingencies that may have been working to
reshape the character of Jacobean sovereignty and, arguably, it overstates the generic unity of the masques, and underestimates the hybrid
character of Jacobean absolutism.

For example, one variable which current descriptions of the masques
tend not to take much into account (as the introduction to this volume
has already pointed out) is the question of faction.[10] Was the empowerment of the King in competition with other claims on power which,
though subordinate, were still in tension with the hegemony of Jacobean absolutism? Obviously there was no such thing as an 'opposition'
in the early modern period. Revisionist historiography has thoroughly
dispelled the notion of the 'high road to civil war' and emphasized that
patronage channels kept Whitehall politically diverse and heterogeneous. Even for old historicists, these developments have permitted

an escape from discredited teleologies of constitutional conflict and removed the obligation to moralize on the court's decadence. The court was, rather, an arena in which powerful individuals contended for prestige and influence, and in which a constant adjudication took place between competing interest-groups and their claims for attention and rewards.

But if we are now better placed than once we were to acknowledge the permeability of Whitehall, there has to be a corresponding recognition that the articulation of power at the centre was constantly improvised, and that relations between courtiers and groups of courtiers were constantly open to renegotiation. The family, favourites and courtiers who surrounded James were all dependent on him, but they still exerted reciprocal pressures of their own since they were channels of influence through which his power was sustained. Although subordinate, they constrained his options since without their co-operation he would not have been able to govern: he too was dependent on them as his eyes and ears, his unsalaried bureaucrats and conduits of power. In this regard, they had holds on the King which, though limited, had a significant impact on the conduct of state. Co-operation and consent would become crucial in the 1630s, when James's successor forfeited the confidence of so extensive a section of his elites that eventually he was rendered powerless, still governing but with no effective room for manoeuvre. But even under James the functioning of the court must have necessitated day to day trade-offs between powerbrokers jostling for influence, the making and breaking of alliances, accommodations and bargaining, the courting of friends and the sidelining of rivals. Furthermore, the presence of royal powerbrokers such as Queen Anne, Prince Henry, Princess Elizabeth and Prince Charles introduced larger variables into the calculus. Their presence, and the images of sovereignty which accrued to them, meant that James's authority was never an uncontested monopoly but was constantly in balance, constantly being renegotiated with figures who had their own advisors, clients and followers, and who exerted significant sovereign pressures of their own.

For the masques, the consequences of such a recognition would be to broaden the attention which has typically been monopolized in past discussions by the principal spectator, so as to take more account of the stake in the masques' transactions held by their other participants. For example, in the poetics of space initiated by Orgel's studies of the 1960s and 70s, the fit between the court that watches and the image that the masque returns is assumed to be exact and one-way: what the

King sees he eventually becomes. But this marginalizes such strategic functions as they could be seen to have performed, functions such as negotiating or mediating between different interest groups within the court or of promoting the rival views on policy which were constantly in competition.

From the throne, the masque would indeed seem to represent the King to the court. It spoke for the monarch as a propaganda tool of a most prestigious kind, one that evoked respect for his credibility as a ruler, instilled reverence for his person and fostered confidence amongst the political elites who comprised the onlooking audience. This was most often the overt programme of the Caroline masques, particularly since Charles himself often danced as the principal performer. James, though, never danced, and his masques must have been more like acts of lobbying, in which groups of aspiring courtiers conducted a symbolic conversation with the monarch, designed to persuade him of their worth or to convince the court as a whole of their own importance in larger schemes. From the performers' side, the masques would have appeared to be acts of persuasion, in which the occasion was enlisted to give prestige to factions struggling for influence, or to advertise agendas of their own. The King presided over the fictions, but a great deal depended on who was paying, and within the fictions he might find that his situation was redefined, or that images were imposed upon him which offered different views of his obligations. Or again, on those rare occasions on which masques were presented to the court from lobbies outside Whitehall, a complex double dialogue would have ensued, as for example when lawyers from the Inns of Court used *The Triumph of Peace* in 1634 as a forum in which to define their own anxieties about Charles's conduct of his government.[11]

Inevitably these encounters were constrained by limits of tact, but they might none the less make a difference to the operations of power. Even if they did not subvert the King's authority, they still might function as mechanisms through which the balance between differently empowered groups at court could be opened to reconfiguration, and they suggest a perspective on the articulation of James's sovereign authority which is rather more conditional and contingent than that which is allowed by the indivisibly absolutist model. Given the permeability of Stuart Whitehall, the presence of significant reversionary interests, the lack of a fully-salaried bureaucracy and the crown's concomitant need to rule with the consent of its subaltern elites, the character of Stuart absolutism cannot be said to have been entirely integrated, but had a residual element of power-sharing which from time to time significantly impacted upon the conduct of British kingship. And as a consequence, in festive transactions such as the Whitehall masques, James's authority was having to be negotiated rather than simply affirmed.

Additionally, it is by no means clear that a perfect fit always obtained between the aesthetic designs of the masques and the playing-out of those iconic patterns on the Whitehall floor. The transcendent closures of the masques were designed to testify to the transcendent power of the King but, conversely, any fracture within the masques' aesthetic order must have unsettled that comfortable equivalence. Indeed, as is notorious from reports of eyewitnesses, contemporaries were all too well aware of the likelihood of the idealised images of the texts being less than persuasive (not to say comprehensible) on the night. While this was often a matter of the intervention of unforeseeable accidents, sometimes the gap between representation and performance was indeed symptomatic of forces which were working over a period of time to disturb the culture's chain of circulation and compel refiguration of royal power. At such moments, inequivalences within the imagery potentially bespoke faultlines within the structures of power which could not simply be closed back into aesthetic harmonies, but signified failures of containment, or challenges to that hermetic ordering. I now want to read Jonson's *Oberon* (1611) and *Neptune's Triumph* (1624) as masques in which the customary rituals of containment and legitimation did not, in fact, get performed as anticipated, but in which faultlines in the structures of power were unusually apparent.

COMING OF AGE IN JACOBEAN ENGLAND

Oberon was danced on New Year's Day, 1611. In its fable, Prince Henry, as Oberon, Prince of the Fairies, was presented to his father, addressed in the name of Pan. There were three scenes, arranged as progressively deeper revelations along James's line of sight. The masque began with a scene of rocks, before which satyrs led by Silvanus were playfully awaiting Oberon's arrival. The rocks parted to reveal the fairy palace, guarded by sleeping sylvans whom the satyrs taunted for their unpreparedness. Then the palace itself opened, Oberon came forth, and Silvanus and another sylvan explained that that night fairyland was doing homage to the British throne, and expounded the virtues of Pan's kingship.

For both Orgel and Goldberg, *Oberon* is a problem: specifically, the shift of focus from Oberon to Pan seems disconcerting. In Orgel it is regarded as a lapse of decorum which violates the controlling royal gaze and shows Jonson's failure to devise a fable complimentary to both James and Henry. James is decked in the familiar rhetoric of British imperial power, but Jonson first establishes a fairy iconography for Henry that has little to do with classical imperialism and involves the masque in a lurching gearshift.[12] For Goldberg, the felt loss of unity is still there but it is described as yet another of those contradictions which sovereign power pretends to ignore but which are in fact its secret strength. The decorum of the masque has to be violated since such startling disruptions empower the King, and by making Silenus, the leader of the randy satyrs, into a spokesman for James's dignity the masque figures the King in a double persona, as simultaneously King of wonder and King of sensual fulfilment.[13] But in my view, neither regret for lost unity nor celebration of a power which delights in its own doubleness adequately accounts for the transactions taking place in *Oberon*. Both interpretations overlook the extent to which Henry was already coming to function as a significant competitor in the arena of power with his father.

Henry was only sixteen in 1611, but politically he was coming of age.[14] His household had been functioning for a year, and in 1610 he had been invested as Prince of Wales and presented to Parliament. More crucially, there was already visible a difference between the pacific, internationalist and British iconography deployed around the King, and the more militaristic images which accrued to his son. In tilt, pageant and dedication Henry was constructed as a godly prince, notable for his interest in arms, scholarship and colonization, and concerned to run a strict household and promote alliances with other Protestant states. Particularly, he had become associated with a current of public nostalgia for the reign of Elizabeth which linked her to ideals of Tudor militarism and godliness of which, quite unhistorically, she was supposed to have been a promoter. Already in Daniel's *Tethys' Festival* (1610) he had been presented with the sword of the ocean and somewhat ambivalently acclaimed as Astraea's heir.

Now, patently, such images do not give us access to an impossibly authentic Prince Henry, whose identity they unproblematically express. They were, rather, counters in the ongoing struggle between the powerful for influence over the royal heir, and for a stake in the reversionary interest of which he would inevitably become the centre. But these competing iconographies also defined alternative strategies of legitimation, each marshalling sovereignty according to its own priorities and suggesting agendas which were in tension with one another. James tried to limit the circulation of his son's iconography (for example at Henry's investiture he prevented the Prince from processing through London on horseback),[15] and his own iconography cannot have been unaffected by the emergence of a powerful set of images which appropriated the memory of his predecessor in the service of a more forward idea of kingship. The legitimation of Prince Henry had consequences for the legitimation of King James, and *Oberon*, I wish to suggest, was centrally involved in this legitimation crisis.[16]

From this point of view, the tensions in *Oberon* can be seen to be neither Orgel's failed unity nor Goldberg's Machiavellian duplicity, but a point of contest between two rival but royal iconographies. On the one hand is King James: principal spectator, cynosure of eyes, clothed in language which legitimates him in terms of Union, the British monarch, Pan himself. On the other hand there is Prince Henry, the competing centre of the event, principal performer, also cynosure of eyes, accompanied by his knights and decked in language which tenses itself against that used of the King. As the Fairy Prince, Henry's iconography connects him with the Fairy Queen, the sainted Elizabeth, triggering resonances which associated him with more ideologically-motivated policies on religion and Europe than his father would countenance, and co-opting for the Prince a mythology of romantic heroism attractive to those that hoped Henry might be induced to become a more militaristic and activist monarch than his father.

Granted, Henry's action is to do homage to James and rehearse gestures which fix him in the royal gaze and attest to his deference. But there is an ambiguity to this coming of age which permits of a doubt as to which inheritance is being celebrated. If Oberon is Henry, he is James's son and heir to the British crown, but if Henry is Oberon, so to speak, he is heir to Elizabeth, whose moon illuminates the whole event (albeit taking her light, tactfully, from the greater royal sun). And the masque's edge of iconic competition is reinforced by the tropes of reborn heroism which attach to Oberon's followers. As Silenus explains, the heroes are reborn annually from the hidden 'seats of bliss' (line 151)[17] where they otherwise reside, and until their renewal all we have at this festival are frisking satyrs and sleeping sylvans. Is the masque affirming the inheritance which Henry will one day take from his father? Or has he already shattered the structures of lineage, by settling himself into a prior inheritance, and not at all the one which his father would have prepared for him?

Admittedly, in the perspective offered by Goldberg's paradigm, this opposition is an illusion. Henry cannot subvert his father without admitting his dependence on the parentage which empowers him in the first place, and in any case the masque fails to repudiate the satyrs, whose sensuality shadows what everyone knows but pretends not to know about power. But the masque has a special role for the satyrs, as antagonists to both the King and the Prince. Their anarchy and lechery project the downside of court life, and their freely-playing desire does indeed suggest the subversion/containment thesis, by its very licence provoking authority to reign it in. From this angle the satyrs' antithesis is King James, whose kingly transcendence supplies the needful opposing term. As Silvanus says, the satyrs' rudeness only testifies all the more to James's dignity: 'He is above your reach; and neither doth / Nor can he think, within a satyr's tooth' (lines 338–9; Silvanus is punning on the supposed homology between *satyr* and *satire*).

But if James transcends satyr/satire, Henry is presented as being engaged with it. The satyrs threaten his iconography, since they predict that he will license their sensuality, and they sing an insultingly lewd song about his patroness, the moon. Further, they adumbrate the educational enterprise which the masque is for the Prince. Goldberg calls them 'fierce pleasure seekers',[18] images of courtly libertinism, but this slants their role, as they are also said to be 'wantons', 'wags' and 'Elves' (lines 89, 198, 224), children, in fact, who unlike the Prince have yet to come of age. Oberon is greeted as their new leader, but his arrival reforms their hopes rather than fulfils them. Living a chaster life than they expect and attended by heroes, he can be said to enact a reformation of satire. True, the satyrs are not repudiated, but they are marginalized and silenced, so that the praise of Pan can be heard: in effect, they have been accommodated. The reform of satire does not hurt the King, whose glory is thereby proclaimed, but it does presuppose a promotion of the claims to empowerment of the Prince. There may not be subversion here, but there has been accommodation, a model for change in gradualist rather than cataclysmic terms. And while the masque's negotiations do not unseat the King, they have involved a dialogue with him and allowed his son to adopt a pose which projected an ideological competition with him even as it deferred to him.

So *Oberon* can be seen as participating in transactions which, while not subverting the King, nonetheless involved a significant challenge to him and which have, maybe, been hidden from modern view by the fact of Henry's premature demise. Who knows what his masques would have delivered had he spent the next fourteen years as monarch-in-waiting?[19] With *Neptune's Triumph for the Return of Albion*, designed to be danced by Prince Charles after his journey back from Madrid in 1623 but never actually staged, there has been an even more remarkable failure to read the intimations of contest within the tropes of praise. Again this is probably because Charles usually gets written off as a historical no-hoper, whose experiences in 1623 were an early premonition of the political incompetence which would later cost him his crown – returning from Madrid as he was, embarrassingly unencumbered by the Spanish bride whom he had gone to collect. It is the endurance of just such a Whiggish teleology that has led most current accounts to treat the masque simply as ideological misrepresentation, a blatant attempt to rewrite fiasco as victory.[20] But considered in relation to a different historical narrative, one which finds space for acknowledging the possibility of challenges to James's sovereignty and the likelihood of radical shifts in power at this historical moment, the masque might be said to display a royal discourse in crisis, in which the usual languages no longer signify because of a now open collision between ruler and heir.

Neptune's Triumph transparently reworks the events of 1623 as a myth of reunion. It opens with a dialogue between a Poet and a Cook, on the difficulty of pleasing one's customers (already discussed in another context by the Introduction to this volume). The Poet's fable will represent the joy of Neptune at his son's safe return from his hazardous voyage, but he leaves it to the Cook to devise the vulgar antimasques. The main masque consists of Albion's return and the greetings of the sea deities.[21] Neptune has sent Albion to Celtiberia to achieve a mysterious discovery, and accompanied by Hippius, his devoted master of horse, he has evaded the temptations posed by the voices of the sirens. It would have been easy (had the masque actually been performed) for spectators to have decoded this as a version of Charles and Buckingham's momentous trip to Madrid in false names and false beards, and of the outburst of rejoicing at Charles's safe and Infanta-less return. But whereas a Whiggish historiography always took this episode to be another disastrous step on the inexorable road to civil war, the political revisionists are now resituating it in relation to the struggle for political control at the end of James's reign.[22]

It is by no means clear that Charles went to Spain as the dupe of his father's pro-Spanish policy. He may have been willing to co-operate in the appeasement of Spain, but his trip (undertaken against James's wishes) effectively cut through the protracted diplomacy. When it became evident that the Infanta was not going to be offered without impossible conditions being attached, it left James's hopes looking bankrupt and Charles holding the political initiative. Returning from Spain as an advocate of reversing James's most cherished alliances, and backed by the man who six months earlier had been James's dearest dependent, Charles had hitched himself to his brother's star and was now profoundly at odds with the discredited pacificism of his father. Moreover his new militarism and anti-Spanish posture were popular with the nation at large, and involved him for the first time in cultivating parliamentary support as a way of putting pressure on the King.

Clearly *Neptune's Triumph* could neither celebrate a unified court nor put a brave face on disaster. Rather, the masque is everywhere troubled by intimations of tension which, while they cannot anywhere be fully articulated, can neither be unproblematically transcended. Ostensibly, the triumph is Neptune's. It is he, King James, who rules the seas, whose 'great commands' (line 130) Albion has executed, and who dispatches a floating island to waft his son home. But for the first time in any Jonsonian masque, the secret purposes of the King, which normally signify the impenetrability of his will, are represented as shared. Albion has not only done his task, he has participated in the hidden decision to do it. The strategy remains unexplained to the audience but it is a plan 'to *themselves* best known' (line 135, my emphasis), while even Buckingham, as Hippius, seems to be in on the plans, and Cottington, as Proteus, has contributed 'counsels wise, / In all extremes' (lines 139–40). Albion is still the subordinate partner, but no earlier masque ever suggested that a masquer might have a privileged insight into the royal will, let alone participate in policy-making as a joint enterprise.

Furthermore, it is evident that this enterprise can mean different things from different perspectives. From the King's view, the tropes of peace are still there. This is a return, a renovation, and the banquet stages the harmony of royal purposes. But from the Prince's view, this is a marine masque which coincides with the policies of naval aggression which Charles was shortly to be laying before Parliament and asking it to support by voting uncommonly generous subsidies. The masque dwells on the strengths of the navy; the sailors who accompany

Albion home shout 'a hay for our young Master' (line 523); and the concluding song anticipates that Neptune might now delegate some of his cares to his son, so that 'young Albion doth thy labours ease' (line 542). Without the canons of acceptability being broached, there are two agendas here, competing for possession of the same theatrical space.

Inevitably, these colliding priorities spelled trouble for the author, and the opening dispute between Poet and Cook may be read, in part, as eloquent of Jonson's discomfort about dancing in this particular minefield (the Introduction to this volume has already discussed the Poet and Cook as hinting at Jonson's almost impossible task of providing political entertainment for a deeply divided court). No less eloquent is the masque's studied vagueness about the 'discovery' which is being celebrated. What Albion has done can never quite come into view, since it would be tactless in the extreme to admit that all the merry-making was for the supplanting of James's peace by Charles's war. Similarly, there is a great deal of stress on the loyalty of Buckingham which, by its very emphasis, crystallizes precisely those intimations of disloyalty which it purports to dispel.

And, crucially, there is an insoluble contradiction between the courtly joys of the main masque and the popular acclamations which the antimasque incorporates in order that they might be disparaged. The main masque, praising the pure incense which flames from the masquers, says that Albion's return came about 'In answer to the public votes, / That, for it, up were sent' (lines 353–4), but the public votes which we actually see in the antimasque represent the national rejoicing as the cavorting of contemptible plebeians. The Poet explains that although Albion came home in October, the courtly love-fest was held off until January in order not to bastardize it with the popular tumult. 'It was not time, / To mix this music with the vulgars' chime', he says, contrasting his songs to 'th'abortive, and extemporal din / Of balladry' (lines 161–3). The muses waited for the national enthusiasm to boil down before they opened their mouths, 'For they love, then, to sing, when they are heard' (line 174). There could scarcely have been a more visible statement of the masque's problems in achieving an accommodation acceptable to all its participants. Charles had acquired an unprecedented popularity, but one that made him dangerous to his father and which therefore had (in show at least) to be disparaged; and popularity was a two-edged sword, since it bound him to anti-Catholic expectations which were betrayed when, a year later, he took Henrietta Maria as his bride. Seeking to envision Charles's popularity but also to constrain it, using tropes of peace but hinting at war, this masque is, to say the least, seriously overdetermined. It is caught in the incompatible negotiations caused by the diverging political agendas of its moment of production.

In the event, this crisis of discourse was demonstrated in the most absolute way imaginable: James simply refused to allow the masque to be performed. The masque itself became an object of negotiation. The Spanish ambassador complained about it, and the French ambassador seized the opportunity of humiliating the crown, refusing to co-operate in the usual charade by which he would stay away from the perform- ance so that his Spanish rival could be invited. James himself inter- vened and demanded cuts in the text to make it less anti-Spanish, but even with these the masque was still unpalatable, and he preferred to abandon the event altogether rather than undergo the embarrassment which its performance would have involved. The whole affair is a remarkable insight into the relations between masquing and practical policy-making at the Jacobean court. It uniquely exposes the canons of acceptability within which it was necessary for masques to operate.

Obviously this was an unusually critical moment within James's reign. At no other time was James's hold on policy so uncertain, nor did any other competitor ever pose quite so dramatic a challenge. Even so, it is remarkable that Jonson's masque should have been amongst the casualties of the moment, as it shows how intimately engaged the ceremony was in the competition over power between ruler and heir. In less polarized circumstances, the masque might have been the occa- sion for a symbolic act of appeasement, or for gestures towards harmony, understanding or rapprochement. But on this occasion the stakes were so high and the differences so gaping as to have made the prospects for such a public accommodation negligible. And the failure to perform the masque can, I suggest, be taken as symptomatic of larger break- downs within the culture's chain of circulation, and implies that this was indeed a moment of unusually acute historical crisis.

FROM DOMINATION TO NEGOTIATION

Undeniably the Stuart masques were 'an inherently royal form' (as Goldberg puts it in relation to Jonson in particular).[23] The agenda to which they were tied was explicitly that of the legitimation of sover- eignty, whether overtly in terms of the praise of kingly wisdom, or implicitly in terms of the gestures of obedience and social solidarity

which their performances rehearsed. And certainly the masques' ceremonial forms were in line with the political culture of Europe's emer-
ging absolutisms more generally. They closely replicated the ceremonial
vocabulary of kingly festival as it was cultivated at courts the length
and breadth of the Continent. But as is also apparent, the institutional
foundations of Stuart absolutism were not without their strains, and
had structural weaknesses the consequences of which were to be trau-
matically played out in the ensuing decades. Under James, subversion
in its larger sense was indeed effectively contained, but this should not
predispose us to ignore the more mundane conditions of consensus
within which the crown had to operate. In effect, James could not
dominate without also being prepared to negotiate.

I have been trying to suggest that the tensions within *Oberon* and
Neptune's Triumph are symptomatic of such points of strain within Jacobean absolutism. There are contradictions apparent in these masques,
but they are not 'sustaining contradictions'. They are, rather, indications of faultlines within Stuart power which James could not ignore
and which represented material challenges to his own conduct of policy.
In the case of *Neptune's Triumph*, the loss of consensus was especially
marked, and on this occasion the gaps between the participants could
not be bridged even symbolically. By attempting to make an adjust-
ment of the balance of power between father and son so extensive
as to be impermissible, *Neptune's Triumph* had the unintended effect of
demonstrating the limits of the negotiable. But even in *Oberon*, which
offered a forum in which gestures of deference and reciprocity could
be played out between King and Prince, the contradictions were far
from easily resolvable in favour of the King. The masque promoted
Henry's image as a reformer, and sanctioned dissident affiliations which
were at odds with his public filiation to his father. And although political
challenges are most conspicuously to be found in the festive exchanges
between the King and his impatient heirs, masques sponsored by the
Queen, by dissident noblemen, by critics of Jacobean pacifism and
Caroline absolutism must scarcely less have borne the character of
ceremonial confrontations. In such cases, the symbolic contests were
unsettling and did not testify unproblematically to the monarch's transcendence. On the contrary, they opened up precisely that possibility
that, just occasionally, domination might not always be dominating.

Of course these masques remained embedded within the circulations
of power which structured their courtly societies. The competitions for
position which I have been describing were contiguous with countless

other contests taking place within the Jacobean court, which would
have had an effect upon the struggles that I have isolated and would
have been in turn affected by them. But my point is that in enabling a
positioning and repositioning of King and courtier, the masques in
general were not simply reaffirming power's enduring configurations
but were participating in processes of negotiation that over a period of
time were working to transform the courtly environment. Domination
may have dominated in the masques, but they were not without space
for transactions of the kind through which the historical field would
eventually be reconfigured, and which testified to developing rifts in
the work of art that was the Jacobean state. In these respects, the
masques may have been merely ephemeral and contingent, but in
terms of their historical functions they were still very much making
a difference.[24]

NOTES

1 In a recent anthology of New Historicist writing (*The New Historicism Reader*,
   ed. H. Aram Veeser (New York, 1994)), an extract from *The Illusion of
   Power* is positioned as the lead essay, signalling one possible moment of
   inception for the new movement.
2 I would particularly like to acknowledge the influence of Lawrence Venuti's
   Our Halcyon Dayes: English Prerevolutionary Texts and Postmodern Culture (Madison, WI, 1989) on the shaping of the critique that follows. Although Venuti's
   analysis of Orgel and Goldberg (pp. 166–81) is couched in neo-Marxist
   terms, our views of the issues at stake run in close parallel.
3 In his most recent work, such as the essay 'Jonson and the Amazons' (in
   E. D. Harvey and K. E. Maus (eds.), *Soliciting Interpretation* (Chicago, 1990),
   pp. 119–39), Orgel has indeed begun to unsettle this equivalence. None
   the less, the tendency of his model has generally been to promote the idea
   that the masques' politics are to be read through their spatial matrix.
4 Stephen Orgel, *The Illusion of Power* (Berkeley, 1975), p. 39.
5 This point is made strongly by Alan Liu in 'The power of formalism: the
   New Historicism', *English Literary History* 56 (1989), 721–73.
6 Jonathan Goldberg, *James I and the Politics of Literature* (Baltimore, 1983),
   p. 116.
7 *Ibid.*, p. 126.
8 The Greenblattian term 'negotiation' is subjected to an interesting redefinition in relation to Renaissance culture by Ted Leinwand in 'Negotiation
   and the New Historicism', *PMLA* 105 (1990), 477–90.
9 I am of course thinking of Carolyn Porter, 'Are we being historical yet?',
   South Atlantic Quarterly 87 (1988), 743–86.

10 There has latterly been some interest in Queen Anne, her circle and her masques. See particularly Leeds Barroll, 'The court of the first Stuart Queen', in Linda Levy Peck (ed.), *The Mental World of the Jacobean Court* (Cambridge, 1991), pp. 191–208, and Barbara K. Lewalski, *Writing Women in Jacobean England* (Cambridge, MA, 1993). Neither of these critics really qualifies as a New Historicist, though.

11 See Martin Butler, 'Politics and the masque: *The Triumph of Peace*', *The Seventeenth Century* 2 (1987), 117–41.

12 Stephen Orgel, *The Jonsonian Masque* (Cambridge, MA, 1965), pp. 88–90.

13 Goldberg, *James I*, pp. 123–6.

14 Currently the fullest study is by Roy Strong, *Henry, Prince of Wales and England's Lost Renaissance* (London, 1986). However, this book overstates its case about Henry's artistic and political leadership and is marred by significant factual misconceptions. For some corrections, see Timothy V. Wilks, 'The Court Culture of Prince Henry and his Circle, 1603–1613' (unpub. DPhil dissertation, University of Oxford, 1987), and Pauline Croft, 'The parliamentary installation of Henry, Prince of Wales', *Historical Research* 65 (1992), 177–93.

15 *Calendar of State Papers Venetian [CSPV], 1607–10*, p. 496. One reason for this refusal was the security scare which followed the assassination of Henri IV earlier that summer, but James also disallowed Henry's desire to perform an equestrian ballet in place of *Oberon* (*CSPV, 1610–1613*, p. 79).

16 Cf. William Hunt, 'Spectral origins of the English Revolution: legitimation crisis in early Stuart England', in Geoff Eley and William Hunt (eds.), *Reviving the English Revolution* (London, 1988), pp. 305–32.

17 All quotations are taken from Stephen Orgel (ed.), *Ben Jonson: The Complete Masques* (New Haven, 1969).

18 Goldberg, *James I*, p. 123.

19 Some forward continuity is provided by the masques staged in 1613 for the Palatine wedding, the programmes for which may have been influenced by Prince Henry. See D. Norbrook, '*The Masque of Truth*: court entertainments and international Protestant politics in the early Stuart period', *The Seventeenth Century* 1 (1986), 81–110.

20 Orgel, *Illusion of Power*, pp. 70–7; Goldberg, *James I*, p. 71.

21 In classical myth, Albion was the ruler of the island before the arrival of Brute, and the son of Neptune by a mortal mother.

22 There has been an extensive historiographical debate over the interpretation of Anglo-Spanish relations in this period. The major revisionary narrative is by Tom Cogswell, *The Blessed Revolution: English Politics and the Coming of War, 1621–1624* (Cambridge, 1989), but see also Simon Adams, 'Foreign policy and the parliaments of 1621 and 1624', in Kevin Sharpe (ed.), *Faction and Parliament* (Oxford, 1978), pp. 139–72; Conrad Russell, *Parliaments and English Politics, 1621–1629* (Oxford, 1979); Kevin Sharpe, *The Personal Rule of Charles I* (New Haven, 1992); and Tom Cogswell's forthcoming study of the 1620s parliaments.

23 Goldberg, *James I*, p. 65.

24 This essay was originally given as the Dan S. Collins lecture at the University of Massachusetts at Amherst in April, 1991. It has subsequently been read, in a much revised form, at seminars at Dublin, Leeds, London, Oxford, Stratford and York. I am very grateful to all my audiences for their thoughtful responses; and, as ever, to David Lindley's friendly editorial eye.

CHAPTER 3

Upstaging the Queen: the Earl of Essex, Francis Bacon and the Accession Day celebrations of 1595

Paul E. J. Hammer

Some perspective on the faultlines in the Jacobean court masque can be gained by first examining the politics of public spectacle in the last years of James's predecessor. In recent years, scholars of English Renaissance culture have devoted considerable attention to the ceremonies associated with formal appearances by the monarch and the celebration of public anniversaries. This scholarly concern has been particularly evident for the reign of Elizabeth I, who has always proved a source of fascination by virtue of her status as both a woman and the only royal personage in her realm. With no husband, children or acknowledged heir, Elizabeth presented a unique problem for a highly personalized monarchy like that in Tudor England. Many studies have described how this fact was overcome, or manipulated, in the great variety of ceremonies which sought to define and reaffirm her rule.[1] In this context, the commemoration of Elizabeth's accession to the throne on 17 November has been a subject of special interest.[2] By the early 1580s, these Accession Day celebrations had developed as an occasion for the spectacular reaffirmation of loyalty to the Queen. Significantly, this was also precisely the period when it was finally apparent to all that Elizabeth herself would never bear any children. It was also a time when plots to both the person and authority of the Queen seemed to threaten from every direction. Only God, it seemed, stood between these conspirators and the extinction of Elizabeth's Protestant regime. As if in compensation for the lack of the usual certainties about the royal succession – a lack even more complete than that which had driven Elizabeth's own father to strain the English polity almost to breaking point half a century before – the celebration of the Accession Day became ever more elaborate during the 1580s and 1590s.

Above all, these annual celebrations focused on a great tournament held at the palace of Whitehall. In light of Elizabeth's unique status, obvious social and sexual symbolism can be seen in this event. With its emphasis upon weaponry (especially lances) and conspicuous display, jousting was a quintessentially male activity. More precisely, it was an exercise performed by male aristocrats who were of an age to fight in battle. A tournament provided an opportunity for competitive display by these virile rivals, but it was also a stylized form of homage to the whole notion of chivalry, which was embodied in the rules of the combat and the heralds who supervised it. These heralds were the very same men whose primary duty was to regulate membership of the social elite itself, by registering or disallowing coats of arms. At the same time, the individual contests which occurred during a tournament were traditionally dedicated to female 'beauty'. Competitors often wore a glove or handkerchief in token of their mistress's affection. This chivalric convention sometimes even extended outside the Tiltyard. In 1591, for example, the Earl of Essex challenged an enemy knight to a duel on the grounds that his cause was superior, that he himself was a better man than the enemy knight and 'que ma maistresse est plus belle que la vostre'.[3] Honouring the elevation of the Virgin Queen with a tournament therefore had a certain symbolic appropriateness.

The anniversary of Elizabeth's accession marked the beginning of a new regnal year, which regulated the dating of all official government documents. In a very real sense, the Accession Day tournament at Whitehall also represented the start of a new cycle of life at court. For courtiers, these celebrations heralded the beginning of a busy social season, leading up to the festivities of the royal Christmastide. Physically, the public displays of 17 November marked the return of the court to London and its immediate vicinity, after its absence during the summer months on progress and at the 'country' palaces of Nonsuch, Richmond, Greenwich and Oatlands. Thus, the City worthies eagerly assembled in all their finery to attend a formal sermon at Paul's Cross, after which 'the trumpets sounded, the cornets winded, and quiristers sung an anthem' from high up on the church. Elsewhere in London, cannon were fired, bells rung and bonfires set ablaze.[4] In this perspective, the Accession Day tournament can be seen as the most conspicuous element in a whole series of celebrations which proclaimed the continuation of the Queen's reign, and the renewed royal bond with London itself. The presence of large numbers of spectators from the City at the Tiltyard can be seen as the controlled, and strictly limited, interpenetration of court and City.

The sheer size and splendour of the Accession Day tournament was a public event perhaps matched only by coronations and royal weddings.[5] The Tiltyard at Whitehall was a permanent structure and apparently had room for 10–12,000 spectators, accommodated in conditions which ranged from the spartan to the opulent. Entry for the day was set at 12d.,[6] so the Accession Day events were performed not only before the assembled court, in all their finery, but also before thousands of Londoners eager for a good day's entertainment. For the ambitious young aristocrats who participated in the show, the whole chivalric nature of the tournament, with its mock combat and heroic connotations, was peculiarly appealing. Those who watched them clearly also found their own meaning and pleasure in the spectacle. Riding in the lists, courtiers could make a bold bid for renown in a way which contrasted sharply with the long hours of dreary waiting around the court. For weeks before the event, prospective jousters practised to ensure that they would make a good impression on the big day. Even before this, the leading devotees of the tournament, such as the Earl of Essex, spent much time and money preparing all the things necessary to make certain that their appearance in the Tiltyard would have the maximum possible impact. Elaborate costumes were designed and made for themselves and their servants. A grand chariot might be built for their triumphal entry and an *impresa*, or illustrated motto for the occasion,[7] would be created and displayed. Those great courtiers who controlled the tournament, such as Sir Henry Lee and later the Earls of Essex and Cumberland, might also take advantage of their status to accompany their own participation in the jousts with some kind of special entertainment.

Of all the Elizabethan Accession Day celebrations, perhaps the best-known is that of 1595. This occasion is probably better documented than any other during Elizabeth's reign.[8] The evidence about this event is also particularly interesting. As well as various lists of those who tilted, we have speeches from an entertainment which was performed before and after the competition, descriptions of the events, and a painted miniature which also may commemorate the occasion.[9] Finally, the 1595 Accession Day is significant because it sheds light on the central figure of political culture during Elizabeth's last decade, Robert Devereux, second Earl of Essex.

As Sir Roy Strong pointed out some years ago, Essex's actions on Accession Day 1595 and the entertainment which he staged to mark that occasion must be seen as part of the Earl's own bid for 'domestical greatness'.[10] More recently, Richard McCoy has developed this notion by characterizing Essex's performance in 1595 as an example par excellence of the 'dangerous image' which he presented to Elizabeth and her regime. In this perspective, Essex was the great challenger to what McCoy terms the Elizabethan 'chivalric compromise' – the view that aristocrats were allowed to exhibit their vaunting ambitions by means of chivalric display but, if they were to win reward from the sovereign and political weight commensurate with their birth, they must ultimately subordinate their personal honour and pride to the dictates of royal service.[11] According to McCoy, the tensions inherent in this 'chivalric compromise' are symbolically played out in the set-piece entertainment which Essex puts on for this occasion: the struggle between the forces of Love and Self-Love are a public dramatisation of Essex's own predicament.[12]

One feature is immediately striking about McCoy's account of the 1595 Accession Day celebrations – the person whom he casts as the *primum mobile* of this display, Francis Bacon. Again and again, McCoy emphasizes that Francis Bacon was the creator of Essex's entertainment and that it represented Bacon's vision for a rapprochement between Essex and the Queen, which might advance his own career.[13] For McCoy, the entertainment staged by Essex was very much Bacon's show and reflected Bacon's own agenda. Yet this assumption begs a number of basic questions. Who, as it were, 'owned' such occasions as this? Whose agenda was being pursued – the author's or that of the aristocrat who employed the author, or both? Indeed, what does authorship actually mean in this context? Such questions are also intimately related to judgements about the success of an occasion, since whether an entertainment achieved its intended goals obviously depends upon whose goals it should be measured by.

McCoy is certainly justified in claiming that Francis Bacon had a crucial role in scripting the Accession Day performance. Bacon had apparently performed similar work for Essex in the past.[14] Moreover, several draft fragments of this piece survive in Bacon's own hand.[15] A long line of commentators have also confidently asserted Bacon's authorship of the remainder of the show.[16] However, the situation is more complex than such assertions suggest. Although Bacon himself penned a fair copy of five speeches from the entertainment,[17] another quite separate fragment is written in the hand of Edward Reynoldes, the personal secretary to the Earl of Essex.[18] Whether Reynoldes might have acted as a copyist for Bacon on this occasion – rather than for the Earl – is difficult to judge.[19] Matters are further complicated by the attribution of another manuscript copy of the entertainment to another of Essex's secretaries, Henry Cuffe.[20] In addition, there is an incomplete translation of part of the Hermit's speech into French by Anthony Bacon, the elder brother of Francis and an intimate of Essex.[21] Unfortunately, it is impossible to know whether Anthony Bacon's translation was part of the actual preparations for the Accession Day show (the speech in Reynoldes's hand is also in French) or whether it was made afterwards for the benefit of Essex's French friends, or even merely represents a form of private recreation.

The question of authorship is compounded by two further pieces of evidence. In addition to those fragments in identifiable hands, there are also a number of contemporary copies of what seems to have been the main part of the entertainment: an exchange between Essex's squire and a Hermit, a Soldier and a Statesman.[22] About half of these copies include a short introductory speech by the Hermit which is not part of Bacon's text.[23] In the light of arguments raised below, this variation and the multiplicity of copies are both highly significant. Secondly, there is a statement written some forty years after the event by Sir Henry Wotton, another member of Essex's secretariat. In praising the Earl's 'serious habits', Wotton specifically refers to his 'impresses and inventions of entertainment, and above all his darling piece of love, and self-love'.[24] This clearly suggests that Essex himself was responsible for the entertainment in 1595, and for its theme of Love and Self-Love. Given the involvement of Reynoldes and the alleged involvement of Cuffe, this claim must be taken seriously. It also striking that Anthony Bacon has endorsed his translation: 'The speeches of the Hermit turned into French. November, 1595. Essex'.

Clearly, this exploration of the archival base for evidence about the entertainment has taken us some distance from McCoy's emphasis on Francis Bacon and Bacon's personal agenda. It seems indisputable that Bacon wrote the great bulk of the text for this entertainment. Nevertheless, it would probably be wrong to place too much emphasis on its allegedly Baconian character. Indeed, the whole thrust of the spectacle seems contrary to Bacon's plea for Essex to woo the Queen with 'obsequious kindness'.[25] Almost certainly, the true provenance of the 1595 Accession Day piece must be seen in a corporate effort within Essex's circle, and probably also under his personal direction. Wotton was serving Essex in a secretarial capacity by late 1595 and his singling out this occasion forty years later suggests that this entertainment involved some unusual effort by the Earl and his associates, including Bacon. Essex had certainly been served by cooperative efforts before.

When the Queen demanded that he produce a set of instructions for a notional secret agent being sent to France in 1593, Essex made use of both Francis Bacon and Thomas Phelippes to produce a draft for him.[26] In 1596, he had no compunction in delegating the writing of an important document to Henry Cuffe, before editing the resultant text according to his own requirements.[27] I have argued elsewhere that Essex's friends and secretaries also pooled their talents for the Earl on other partisan literary projects during the 1590s, including a letter of travel advice purportedly from Essex to the young Earl of Rutland.[28] As will be seen below, this is a document which has distinct thematic and chronological parallels with the Accession Day piece.

Our knowledge about the entertainment which Essex staged on 17 November 1595 is tantalizingly incomplete. The best source of information is a letter written by Rowland Whyte to his master, Sir Robert Sidney, governor of the Dutch port of Flushing, on 22 November.[29] There is also a verse description of the tournament by George Peele, *Anglorum Feriae*, although this is highly stylized and much less informative.[30] Other poetic commemorations of the occasion have not survived.[31] By contrast, when it comes to texts for the show, there is something of an embarrassment of riches. Indeed, it seems clear that some of the fragments which survive must be sections of the entertainment which were edited out before the piece's final form was settled. Bacon's draft of a speech for the Hermit, for example, was subsequently rewritten for the statesman.[32] There are two separate speeches which perform the same function of requesting permission for the characters to speak in the royal presence.[33] There is also a tradition that Essex himself deleted a separate interlude which would have reflected favourably upon Sir Walter Ralegh's recent voyage to Guiana – a claim which, if true, would confirm his editorial control over the performance.[34] A more fundamental problem concerns the number of fair copies of the entertainment. Until these various manuscripts are properly collated, no authoritative text for the show can be established. This means that any attempt at a really close 'reading' of the entertainment would be highly problematical.

Despite these difficulties, comparing the extant documents with the descriptions of the occasion suggests a fairly solid outline for Essex's performance. Before the tournament itself began, each competitor made his ceremonial entry. First came the Earl of Cumberland, the Queen's champion, whose gilded appearance reflected a dragon theme.[35] Next came Essex, his friend and regular jousting partner, dressed in the colours of love: 'innocent white and fair carnation'.[36] Before making his entry, Essex sent a page ahead to address the Queen. In response to the page's speech, Elizabeth bestowed her glove upon Essex, who was thus able to arrive in the arena already bearing a royal token. When the Earl himself finally entered the Tiltyard, he was met by a Hermit, a Soldier and a Statesman (or secretary of state), the representatives of Philautia (Self-Love),[37] and also by his own Squire, who acted as an intermediary between the three men and his master. These characters had apparently been exchanging opinions before Essex's arrival but fell silent upon his approach. The three men then presented Essex, through his Squire, with books representative of their callings, all in total silence. This touch was characteristic of Essex's flair for the dramatic, and vaguely reminiscent of his appearance at an earlier Accession Day tournament dressed, not in festive garb, but 'all in sable sad'.[38] However, the Earl's inventive streak was not yet exhausted – even though Cumberland (and presumably also the other competitors waiting to make their entry) stood 'impatient of delay'.[39] No sooner had the elaborate charade been conducted than a packet of letters was delivered to Essex, via the secretary, with the sudden arrival of 'the ordinary Postboy of London, a ragged villain all bemired, upon a poor lean jade, galloping and blowing for life'.[40] Where the silence of the book presentation had contrasted with the previous hubbub of the arena, the arrival of the Postboy contrasted with the elaborate costumes and splendid horses which would now have been milling around the Tiltyard. Perhaps more importantly, the Postboy's delivery of genuine letters to Essex deliberately punctured the artificial world of Philautia with an unexpected intrusion from the real world. Many observers would recognize that letters were emblematic of the Earl's recent recovery of royal favour.[41]

After the day's jousting was completed and the Queen and her subjects had enjoyed their supper, Essex's entertainment began again in a seemingly more intimate manner. The show commenced with the Earl's Squire calling upon the Queen to observe how his master was 'tormented with the importunity' of the three representatives of Philautia.[42] After this brief introduction, the focus shifted decisively away from Elizabeth. Philautia's envoys addressed the Squire, each in turn urging that his master, whom they called Erophilus (Love), should abandon his love for his mistress and instead seek contentment in their own particular profession. This is a familiar scenario of threefold temptation. Instead of maintaining his devotion to the Queen, with all the

tribulations inherent in such Love, Erophilus/Essex was being urged
to look to his own desires and seek personal satisfaction in either contemplation and study (the Hermit), martial glory (the Soldier), or political power (the Statesman). However, the trusty squire dismisses these
'enchantments' of Philautia and reaffirms his master's undying devotion
to the Queen. Thus, only at the very end of this show does the figure
of Elizabeth herself return to the foreground. In keeping with the conventions of a *discordia concors*, the Squire claims that Elizabeth herself
embodies the unique conjunction of all the qualities previously ranged
in opposition to one another: 'all these are in the hands of his mistress
more fully to bestow than they can be attained by your addresses'.[43] The
final message of the entertainment is therefore a reaffirmation of the
Love of Erophilus/Essex for his royal paragon and a pledge to harness
all the qualities with which he had been tempted to her service alone.

In its outline, Essex's entertainment seems an appropriate vehicle
for honouring the Queen's day. However, the details of this show, and
the resonance which they were intended to have among the audience,
suggest a rather different interpretation. This becomes apparent when
the contexts for the entertainment are explored.[44] During the mid-
1590s, Essex recognized that old Lord Burghley was slowly dying and
made a determined effort to convince Elizabeth that he should assume
Burghley's mantle as her chief advisor. Essex therefore worked hard as
a privy councillor and invested heavily in the pursuit of foreign intelligence. In late 1595, these earnest efforts seem to have been supplemented by a deliberate campaign to advertise Essex's intellect and
judgement, both to Elizabeth herself and also to those who frequented
the court and its margins. The timing of this propaganda campaign
was determined by a revival of tensions in May 1595 with Burghley
and his son, Sir Robert Cecil, after about twelve months of relative
calm. These stirrings at court centred not only on the long-vacant post
of secretary of state but also on whether England's war effort should be
directed at the Continent or in Ireland, a matter of urgent concern
from mid-1595. Essex's push for self-advancement therefore came with
a definite series of strings attached – he was the arch-Europeanist at
Elizabeth's court and wanted to entangle England more fully in continental affairs. Accordingly, he sought a secretary of state like Thomas
Bodley, who would support this policy against the Queen's own mis-
givings, not Sir Robert Cecil.

Although Essex's campaign of self-advertisement was aborted in
early 1596 as a result of his involvement with the Cadiz expedition,[45]

elements of this effort can be seen in the Earl's conspicuous patronage of university scholars during this period, the funeral of Sir Roger Williams in December 1595 and the large-scale circulation in manuscript of Essex's letter of travel advice to the Earl of Rutland. Essex's Accession Day entertainment – on the biggest public occasion of the year – must surely also be added to this list. Apart from close chronological affinities, there are obvious thematic continuities between these endeavours. The Rutland letter, for example, emphasizes Essex's qualities as a sober counsellor, often in terms rather similar to those used in the speeches of Philautia's three envoys. The political effectiveness of the Rutland letter can be gauged by the wide dispersion of manuscript copies of this document and its ultimate migration into print in 1633.[46]

In this light, the number of surviving manuscript copies of the post-supper section of the Accession Day entertainment is highly instructive, for they indicate that this text was also deliberately circulated among Essex's friends. If the Rutland letter is any guide,[47] this probably means that the surviving texts of Accession Day entertainment represent a cleaned-up version of what was performed in the Tiltyard, rather than an accurate 'script' of the performance. Circulating the manuscript should therefore be seen as a deliberately literary reinforcement of the spectacle itself. The inclusion of a brief additional speech by the Hermit, for example, may represent an attempt to give the circulated text greater coherence.[48] Together with the Hilliard miniature (if this is indeed the occasion which it commemorates[49]) and any of the printed works which may have been encouraged by Essex or his friends, the circulation of this document would constitute a second stage of capitalising on the public platform provided by Accession Day, carrying the Earl's propaganda well beyond the confines of the show and its immediate audience. By circulating a version of the text in manuscript, the audience could be carefully targeted and the problems associated with censorship of the printed works could be avoided.[50] Moreover, the after-life of a document circulated in this manner could be substantial. As noted above, several of the surviving copies of the 1595 entertainment date from the 1630s or later. Ironically, Essex's efforts at self-advertisement proved more enduring than his political career.

A more immediate context for the Accession Day performance can be seen in developments at court in the weeks immediately before the big day. In late September, rumours were circulating of a 'vile book' dedicated to Essex by an enemy of the Queen.[51] This was *A Conference*

About the Next Succession of the Crown of England, published abroad by the pseudonymous R. Doleman, which singled out the second son of the Earl of Hertford as a legitimate contender for the English throne.[52] Hertford and his sons were arrested at the end of October.[53] At the start of November, when many of his preparations for the Accession Day were presumably already drawing close to completion, Essex was shown Doleman's book by an angry Elizabeth. He left the audience looking 'wan and pale' and immediately took to his sickbed. Despite a visit from the Queen herself on 4 November, it was not until the 12th that the Earl's health and political fortunes were recognized as being fully recovered. By then, it was old Burghley who was on his sickbed.[54]

These general and specific contexts had a direct impact upon the Accession Day entertainment, and upon how the audience perceived it. The occasion itself provided Essex with the most public opportunity possible to trumpet his return to royal favour. His triumphant entry into the arena already wearing the Queen's glove proclaimed this fact to all and sundry.[55] The arrival of the Postboy also demonstrated the Earl's renewed importance in the Queen's affairs, and all the more strongly because it represented such an unexpected intrusion of everyday life into the Tiltyard drama. The shock of his recent hiccup may also explain Essex's apparent decision to remove a scene which would have allowed Sir Walter Ralegh a share of the limelight.[56] The longer-term context of Essex's campaign to demonstrate his intellect and judgement, both to the Queen and the political class at large, is also evident in the whole emphasis of the entertainment upon Essex's personal qualities. More particularly, this helps to explain why so many of the spoken words in this entertainment are devoted to discussing the written word.

When Essex first entered the Tiltyard, he was greeted with a silence which gave a dramatic quality to his arrival. This silence, and the dumb show which followed, also focused special attention on the fact that the emissaries of Philautia presented him with books. Since Essex already enjoyed the public reputation of being a pre-eminent patron of writers,[57] this ceremonial delivery of books probably seemed appropriate to many of the audience. However, the significance of this act was developed in more explicit manner after supper. Each of the speeches by Philautia's envoys begins by harking back to the kind of book which he had given to Erophilus/Essex earlier in the day, emphasising the direct practical value of their gift. For the Soldier, for example, 'the Muses are to serve martial men, to sing their famous actions', thereby

displaying the cardinal virtues in active operation.[58] Even the Statesman, who cautions that reading books should 'possess not too much of
his time', enjoins Erophilus/Essex to immerse himself in the paper-
work of government.[59] This constant emphasis upon the practical util-
ity of books for those who are entrusted with the direction of human
affairs was something of a commonplace in educated discourse. The
manner in which this idea is elaborated would certainly have given
some amusement to the cognoscenti among the audience. The Statesman's speech, for instance, is a deliberate parody of Machiavellian precepts of government. The Squire of Erophilus/Essex also mocks these
speakers by introducing them as 'a melancholy dreaming Hermit, a
mutinous brain-sick Soldier, and a busy tedious Secretary'.[60] However,
despite such humour, the cumulative effect of Essex's entertainment is
ultimately to reinforce the association between books and government,
and the Earl's association with both.

The somewhat academic cast to this show was further reinforced by
the actors who played the leading roles. As he had done in the previous
year, Essex staged his Accession Day celebrations with scholars whose
thespian credentials lay in the sphere of university drama. According
to Rowland Whyte, Toby Mathew played the Squire to Erophilus/
Essex, while the three envoys of Philautia were played by Morley, 'he
that in Cambridge played Giraldy' and 'he that played Pedantique'.[61]
Mathew was an Oxford man[62] and the latter two both fellows of
Queens' College, Cambridge.[63] Morley was probably Thomas Morley,
the musician and member of the Chapel Royal.[64] Other observers
may not have been as well informed as Rowland Whyte, but Essex's
reliance upon university men would have been obvious to all. Considering that Essex could only have appeared before the Queen in
the company of gentlemen, and not with members of the socially
inferior world of professional theatre, this connection was perhaps hardly
surprising. Nevertheless, the association with university scholars did
have a certain political resonance. Over the course of 1595, Essex had
begun to act as a conspicuous benefactor for academics. With his
help, Thomas Smith became a clerk of the Privy Council, while Henry
Wotton, William Temple and Henry Cuffe entered the Earl's own
secretariat. During the closing months of the year, Essex also made
a very public effort to make Henry Savile the provost of Eton, even
though he was already warden of Merton College, Oxford, and lacked
the traditional ecclesiastical qualifications.[65] For at least some of those
watching in the audience, the Accession Day show would have seemed

another example of Essex's willingness to help university men find preferment in the wider world. It would also perhaps have been a general reminder that the Earl's personal qualities were admired by many of the best and brightest in the realm.

Essex's Accession Day entertainment also included a number of more fleeting references which would have elicited flickers of recognition among the audience. Midway through his speech, for example, the Hermit touches upon the court of the Muses: 'there shall he find secrets not dangerous to know, sides and parties not factious to hold, precepts and commandments not penal to disobey'.[66] Many of his auditors would no doubt have smiled at this description in light of the well-known bitterness between Essex and the Cecils over the previous few months. The Earl's own more recent ups and downs also gave an ironic, but perhaps unintended, topicality to the Hermit's advice for Erophilus/Essex: 'the gardens of love wherein he now playeth himself are fresh today and fading tomorrow, as the sun comforts them or is turned from them'.[67] Reality also intrudes into the entertainment in what appear to be more calculated allusions to the world outside the drama. The Soldier's reference to champions wearing the glove of their mistress seems to reflect directly upon Essex himself, who had been granted the Queen's glove even before he entered the Tiltyard. Similar references to the world of the audience seem to crowd more thickly in the latter part of the Squire's speech, as if deliberately dissolving the barriers between artifice and reality even as he brings the *discordia concors* to its expected conclusion. In criticising the dissimulation of the 'untrue Politique', the Squire complains that 'your life is nothing but a continual acting upon a stage'. Soon after, he for the first time shifts the focus of the drama to Elizabeth herself ('that mistress whom you undertake to govern'), which invites speculation of a direct gesture towards the Queen seated in the audience.[68] The Squire's declaration to the envoys of Philautia that all of their professions 'are in the hands of his mistress more fully to bestow' also takes its force from the reality of life at Elizabeth's court. All major decisions, and certainly the fate of Essex's own lofty political ambitions, lay in the hands of the Queen herself. For both Erophilus and the real-life Earl of Essex, therefore, it was hardly surprising that 'the hearing of her, the observing of her, the receiving of instructions from her, may be . . . a lecture exceeding all dead monuments of the Muses'.[69]

Elizabeth herself was far from pleased by the entertainment staged by Essex. According to Whyte, she tartly stated 'that if she had thought there had been so much said of her, she would not have been there that night, and so went to bed'.[70] In light of this royal scorn for the Earl's self-aggrandizement, Strong, McCoy and Young have all concluded that the Accession Day entertainment was 'an extravagant flop'.[71] However, Whyte begins his letter by informing his master that 'My Lord of Essex's device is much comended in these late triumphs'.[72] There is also no suggestion of failure in Peele's verse account of the occasion.[73] Elizabeth's reaction was also far from unique to this entertainment. Time and again, when faced by dramas or sermons which she did not like, Elizabeth walked out. Essex himself had experienced this royal disdain at least once before. In September 1588, he and the Earl of Cumberland – his opponent again in the Accession Day tilts of 1595 – led off a display of jousting as part of the celebrations to mark the defeat of the Spanish Armada: 'when they had finished with the lance they drew their swords, but when Her Majesty saw this she made a sign with her hand that they were to cease, but they set to and she shut the window, in order not to see them'.[74] The observer of this incident clearly thought it worthy of note but, again, there is no mention of any disquiet among the audience or any sense that Essex and Cumberland had done wrong. Indeed, the young earls continued 'at it for some time', even after the Queen had withdrawn her presence. Clearly, these public performances had a certain life of their own. Although performed in the presence of the Queen, and even in her honour, such entertainments did not depend for their success merely upon a favourable royal response, but also upon that of the audience at large.

This naturally raises the question of whether Essex himself would have regarded the Accession Day show as a success. If the Earl's principal aim was to win the Queen's favour and to demonstrate his special devotion to her, the result of the entertainment would indeed merit the verdict of failure. However, the whole thrust of the performance suggests that this was not the primary aim. Although staged upon the occasion of Elizabeth's own Accession Day, Essex's entertainment was far from being the customary display of obsequious loyalty or glorification of the Queen. Instead, as Elizabeth complained, it was first and foremost a drama about Essex himself. Recalling the larger political context for this entertainment sketched out above, there can be little doubt why the Earl sought to appropriate the biggest public occasion of the year in this way. As with his circulation of partisan documents in manuscript, his patronage of scholars or the funeral which he gave for Sir Roger Williams, Essex's intention was less to sway the Queen herself – always a difficult task, as he knew from personal experience – than to build up political momentum and put pressure on her to surrender to his views on policy. If anything, Essex's aim on the Accession Day seems so transparent that it must be regarded as a measure of his frustration with the Queen. During the preceding months, Essex and Antonio Perez had been describing Elizabeth in their private correspondence as a Juno to the Earl's Aeneas.[75] In the weeks that followed the Accession Day, this frustration provoked Essex into even more dangerous action. Faced with Elizabeth's persistent refusal to succour Henri IV, he secretly ordered Sir Henry Unton, the new ambassador to France, deliberately to exaggerate his reports in order to force a change in royal policy.[76] During 1596, Essex went still further and tried to entangle the Queen in continental affairs by seeking to hijack the Cadiz expedition, and almost succeeded.[77]

Only a tiny handful of the audience for the Accession Day entertainment would have been aware of Essex's growing willingness to exert pressure on his sovereign. Nevertheless, those watching the performance had no doubt that it was a thoroughly partisan display. As Rowland Whyte despaired, 'the world makes many untrue constructions of these speeches, comparing the Hermit and the Secretary to two of the lords [of the council], and the Soldier to Sir Roger Williams'.[78] Despite the explicit claims in the entertainment that the envoys of Philautia were meant to represent distinct personal qualities, the audience and those who only heard about the show at second-hand chose to interpret it in terms of their understanding about courtly politics. For them, the show was a satirical attack on the Cecils, with old Burghley cast as the Hermit and Sir Robert as the dissimulating Statesman. There was, indeed, some justification for this view. The tensions between Essex and the Cecils at court were widely known, and perhaps even somewhat exaggerated by gossip. There was also a direct connection between the Cecils and the characters featured in the entertainment. In 1591, when he had first tried to persuade the Queen to appoint his son to the vacant office of secretary of state, Burghley had staged a show during her visit to Theobalds which made much play upon the office of secretary and upon the idea of Burghley himself as an old hermit.[79] The identification of the Soldier with Sir Roger Williams is rather less clear-cut, since he was a well-known intimate of the Earl.[80] Those watching the performance may have thought that Essex was having some fun at his friend's expense, possibly as an unsuccessful way of making his attack on the Cecils less obvious. Alternatively, some of the audience may have felt that the Soldier appeared in a more positive light than the other envoys of Philautia. Either way, Rowland Whyte's complaint is a reminder that what an author intends and what an audience perceives may be quite different things.

The entertainment which Essex staged for the Accession Day must clearly be seen as a reflection of the Earl's own predicament in 1595, not that of Francis Bacon. Bacon took the leading hand in scripting this show, but it was ultimately Essex's production. Bacon may well have harboured personal hopes for this occasion, as McCoy suggests, but they were submerged, and perhaps even drowned, in the pursuit of Essex's larger political objectives. For Essex, the Accession Day tournament provided the opportunity to parade his credentials for leadership at the biggest public event of the year, and he took it with both hands. In doing so, Essex played a complex and risky game with the Queen. By presenting his case, as it were, on an occasion intended to honour Elizabeth, and before her person, Essex was in a sense trying to co-opt royal approval in a matter upon which the Queen had pointedly refused to make any firm judgement in the preceding months. Faced with pressure from both Essex and the Cecils over the war and the post of secretary, Elizabeth had consistently prevaricated and tried to avoid making any hard decisions. Now the entertainment which Essex staged for the Accession Day invited her to endorse the Earl's qualities and her special trust in him in the most public circumstances possible. Even if for political reasons alone, Elizabeth had no choice but to undermine the performance by making her distaste for its contents apparent. To do otherwise would have been interpreted as supporting Essex over the Cecils, as the comments reported by Rowland Whyte make clear. However, Elizabeth was also clearly upset at the whole manner of the performance. In seizing upon the occasion of the Accession Day for his own political purposes, Essex was overbearing enough to upstage the Queen on her own special day of celebration.

In a sense, this action was typical of Essex when baulked. When a polite request or logical argument failed, he often resorted to more direct means of persuasion. This was true not only of his dealings with lesser men but also with the Queen herself. Time and again during the mid-1590s, Essex tried to force his sovereign's hand on matters in which she had refused him. As noted above, the Accession Day entertainment was only part of a pattern of events which included the circulation of propaganda in manuscript form, conspicuous acts of patronage and ultimately even an attempt to subvert the purpose of the Cadiz expedition. It is in this context of rival policies and a struggle over political power, rather than merely in a chivalric sense, as McCoy argues, that Essex came to embody a 'dangerous image' to Elizabeth. This can be seen in the way in which Bacon explained his warning to Essex less than a year later:

> But how is it now? A man of a nature not to be ruled; that hath the advantage of my affection, and knoweth it; of an estate not grounded to his greatness; of a popular reputation; of a military dependence: I demand whether there can be a more dangerous image than this represented to any monarch living, much more to a lady, and of Her Majesty's apprehension?[81]

As Bacon complained, Essex's excessive commitment to policies associated with continental war and his unwillingness to accept the Queen's rejection of them led him into an ever more dangerous position. Again and again, Essex was able to commit what amounted to gross acts of insubordination – even in public, as at the Accession Day tournament – and escape without obvious penalty. However, as Bacon realized, no monarch could tolerate such flagrant abuse of their authority for long. When it came, Essex's punishment could only be sharp, and perhaps even fatal.

Why did Elizabeth allow Essex to try and bully her in this way? More accurately, why did she fail to stop Essex? Unavailing though it proved, she certainly tried to make him fall into line, as her rejection of Francis Bacon's suits for high legal office showed.[82] However, Elizabeth was unable to force her will upon Essex, in part because she needed his enormous talents and energy, as showcased in the Accession Day performance. With her realm involved in a dangerous war, she could not afford either to lose Essex's soldierly skills or to risk an open rupture within her regime. Taking severe action against Essex would also not only weaken his ability to serve her but even perhaps undermine her own authority, by recognising resistance to her will. Moreover, removing Essex would have left her wholly dependent upon the Cecils. Although she instinctively shared many of the concerns of her old lord treasurer, Elizabeth clearly recognised the need for Essex's dynamism as a counterbalance to Burghley's profound conservatism, which had become greatly accentuated by his long years of holding key offices of state. The loss of Essex would also have destroyed her fundamental strategy for what was, literally, man-management: building up rivals and forcing them to compete for her favour. This is precisely what occurred in the last years of the reign. After the fall of Essex in

1601, Sir Robert Cecil finally achieved the kind of *regnum Cecilianum* which critics alleged his father had tried, and failed, to create.[83] Having avoided the Essexian Scylla, Elizabeth succumbed at last to the Cecilian Charybdis.

Elizabeth's long unwillingness to dispense with Essex therefore shared part of its motivation with her similar reluctance to accede to Essex's push to displace the Cecils in the mid-1590s, and thus also with her dissatisfaction with the nature of his Accession Day show of 1595. At heart, Elizabeth's problem came down to the elemental difficulty of her reign – the fact that she was a female prince among men who thought that they knew better than any woman. As Essex complained to a visiting French envoy in 1597, 'they laboured under two things at this court, delay and inconstancy, which proceeded chiefly from the sex of the Queen'.[84] Similar comments had been passed by councillors to Elizabeth since the beginning of her reign. Her military leaders were equally consistent in ignoring her instructions as soon as they were safely out of the realm.[85] Elizabeth's only defence against this kind of male chauvinism, apart from impassioned rage, was a version of the old strategy of divide and rule. When Essex and Burghley combined to back Francis Bacon for the post of solicitor-general in early 1594, for example, she consistently sought to destroy their united front.[86] Elizabeth simply could not afford to seem to be dictated to in this way by her leading, male subjects.

At the broadest level, then, the entertainment which Essex staged on Accession Day 1595, like so many other occasions in her reign, was yet another episode in the constant struggle of Elizabeth I to resist the pressures of male courtiers. More significantly, though, this occasion demonstrated the lengths to which one particular courtier, the Earl of Essex, would go in his efforts to change the policies of Elizabeth. This was evident not only in the elaborateness and obvious expense of the performance but also in the brazenness of its primary message. Although gift-wrapped as a celebration of love and devotion to the Queen on her Accession Day, Essex's show was overwhelmingly about the Earl himself and the talents which he could deploy in royal service. In political terms, it was another blow in his campaign to take Burghley's place as chief minister and to push England into the very centre of European affairs. Far from being a public display of submission and duty to the Queen, Essex's entertainment was self-aggrandizing, and probably pitched at the audience as much as at Elizabeth herself. Frustrated by his inability to win the struggle over place and policy by more conventional means, Essex seized upon the Accession Day tournament as a vehicle to put pressure upon the Queen, even at the cost of upstaging Elizabeth on her own special day.

That Essex could do such a thing is yet another reminder of the extraordinary malleability of Elizabethan public occasions. Because they had to pay for so much out of their own pockets, and because the chivalric mode placed so much stress upon the individual, Elizabethan aristocrats could, and did, manipulate public entertainments for the sovereign to suit their own ambitions. No other courtier had the ability or the self-confidence remotely to match the breathtaking arrogance of Essex's behaviour in 1595. Yet, even much lesser instances of this malleability – such as Sir Robert Carey's illicit appearance as the forsaken knight at the 1593 Accession Day tournament[87] – make Elizabethan public occasions seem quite different from the spectacles of the early Stuart period. Under James I and Charles I, chivalric endeavour increasingly lost place in royal celebrations to the carefully scripted medium of the masque.[88] Significantly, this greater emphasis on stage-managed, state-funded royal propaganda saw a physical retreat from the open arena into the secure, closed environment of the court itself. The potential for ceremonial dissent was resurrected, in conscious reaction to this general trend, by the revival of chivalric display around Prince Henry.[89] However, both the prince and his festivals proved to be short-lived. Under the Stuarts, unlike in Elizabeth's reign, political point-scoring among courtiers had increasingly little opportunity for expression outside the confines of the palace. As many commentators have noted, this raised the prospect of political dissent assuming other, more dangerous forms than ceremonial display.

However, in November 1595 such developments lay in the future, unforeseen. Far more immediate matters would have absorbed the thoughts of the masses who observed the Accession Day entertainment in the Tiltyard – the glories of the spectacle, enjoyment of a break from work, admiration for the competitors, pride in their monarch and praise for Essex. Yet, some of the audience, and certainly the courtiers among them, also clearly viewed events with a more sophisticated, political eye. For them, the immediate significance of the occasion was what it expressed about Essex himself and the pressures to which the elderly Elizabeth was now exposed in her latter years. More subtle and premeditated than mere bullying, Essex's tactics – as they would have seen – sought to force Elizabeth's hand by building up political momentum behind himself and the policies which he espoused.

This was playing to the gallery on a grand scale. It is little wonder, then, that Francis Bacon came to fear that Essex represented an increasingly 'dangerous image' in the eyes of Elizabeth.

NOTES

1 Recent studies include: P. Berry, *Of Chastity and Power: Elizabethan Literature and the Unmarried Queen* (London, 1989), ch. 4; C. Breight, 'Caressing the great: Viscount Montague's entertainment of Elizabeth at Cowdray, 1591', *Sussex Archaeological Collections* 127 (1989), 147–66, and 'Realpolitik and Elizabethan ceremony: the Earl of Hertford's entertainment of Elizabeth at Elvetham, 1591', *Renaissance Quarterly* 45 (1992), 20–48; M. Colthorpe, 'Pageants before Queen Elizabeth I at Coventry', *Notes and Queries* ns 32 (1985), 458–60, and 'Anti-Catholic masques performed before Queen Elizabeth I', *ibid.* ns 33 (1986), 316–18; S. Doran, 'Juno versus Diana: the treatment of Elizabeth I's marriage in plays and entertainments, 1561–1581', *Historical Journal* 38 (1995), 257–74; S. Frye, *Elizabeth I: the Competition for Representation* (Oxford, 1993); R. McCoy, '"This wonderful spectacle": the civic progress of Elizabeth I and the troublesome coronation', in J. Bak (ed.), *Coronations: Medieval and Early Modern Monarchic Ritual* (Berkeley, 1990), pp. 217–27; R. Strong, *The Tudor and Stuart Monarchy: Pageantry, Painting, Iconography*, 3 vols. (Woodbridge, 1994–7), II, *passim*; J. Wilson, *Entertainments for Elizabeth I* (Woodbridge, 1980).

2 See, for example, M. Colthorpe, 'Lord Compton's Accession Day speech to Queen Elizabeth I in 1600', *Notes and Queries* ns 33 (1986), 370–1; R. Strong, *The Cult of Elizabeth: Elizabethan Portraiture and Pageantry* (London, 1977), ch. 5, and *Tudor and Stuart Monarchy*, II, pp. 101–9, 121–43; F. A. Yates, *Astraea: The Imperial Theme in the Sixteenth Century* (London, 1975), pp. 88–111. For celebrations of this public holiday at the popular level, see D. Cressy, *Bonfires and Bells: National Memory and the Protestant Calendar in Elizabethan and Stuart England* (London, 1989), ch. 4, and R. Hutton, *The Rise and Fall of Merry England: The Ritual Year, 1400–1700* (Oxford, 1994), pp. 146–52.

3 [Pierre Cayet], *Chronologie Novenaire, contenant l'Histoire de la Guerre, sous le Regne du Tres Chrestien Roy de France et de Navarre Henry IIII*, 3 vols. (Paris, 1608), II, fol. 502v.

4 John Stow, *The Annals of England, faithfully collected out of the most authentical authors, records and other monuments of antiquity, from the first inhabitation until this present year 1601* (London, 1601, *STC* no. 23336), p. 1281. Note that Paul's Cross had been newly refurbished for the Accession Day sermon of 1595, which was delivered by Richard Fletcher, bishop of London and the Queen's chief almoner.

5 The following paragraph is indebted to A. Young, *Tudor and Jacobean Tournaments* (London, 1987). For historical background and more general discussion of chivalry, see M. Keen, *Chivalry* (New Haven, 1984), esp.

chs. 5 and 11, and M. Vale, *War and Chivalry: Warfare and Aristocratic Culture in England, France and Burgundy at the end of the Middle Ages* (Athens, GA, 1981), esp. ch. 3. The techniques of jousting are discussed in S. Anglo, 'How to win at tournaments: the technique of chivalric combat', *Antiquaries' Journal* 68 (1988), 248–64, and H. Watanabe-O'Kelly, 'Tournaments and their relevance for warfare in the early modern period', *European History Quarterly* 20 (1990), 451–63. For the Earl of Leicester's use of tournaments in Mary's reign and the early years of Elizabeth, see R. McCoy, 'From the Tower to the Tiltyard: Robert Dudley's return to glory', *Historical Journal* 27 (1984), 425–35.

6 This is the minimum cost of entry in 1584, as reported by the visiting German Lupold von Wedel. By 1620, the cost had risen to a full shilling (Young, *Tudor and Jacobean Tournaments*, p. 86). The price of entry in the 1590s is unknown.

7 In recent years, a significant body of literature has developed around the subject of *imprese*. See especially A. R. Young, *The English Tournament Imprese* (New York, 1988).

8 For convenient summaries of the manuscript evidence relating to this tournament, see Strong, *Cult of Elizabeth*, p. 209, and Young, *Tudor and Jacobean Tournaments*, p. 204. Note that there is a typographical error in the latter list: Queen's College, Oxford, MS 121, pp. 405–7 should read pp. 450–7.

9 The miniature in question is Nicholas Hilliard's well-known image of Essex wearing tournament garb. It is printed, for example, as plate 42 of Strong's *Cult of Elizabeth* and plate 80 of Young's *Tudor and Jacobean Tournaments*. For discussion of this miniature, see R. Strong and V. J. Murrell, *Artists of the Tudor Court: The Portrait Miniature Rediscovered 1520–1620* (London, 1983), pp. 136–7, and E. Auerbach, *Nicholas Hilliard* (London, 1961), pp. 125–8, plate 98.

10 *Cult of Elizabeth*, p. 141. Note that the original version of Strong's essay was first published in 1959.

11 R. McCoy, *The Rites of Knighthood: the Literature and Politics of Elizabethan Chivalry* (Berkeley, 1989), ch. 1.

12 *Ibid.*, pp. 84–6. An earlier version of this argument was rehearsed in McCoy's '"A dangerous image": the Earl of Essex and Elizabethan chivalry', *Journal of Medieval and Renaissance Studies* 13 (1983), 313–29.

13 For example: 'this deft achievement . . . reflected *Bacon's* broader aims in this performance. *He* saw the Accession Day Tilt as a means of gratifying both the Queen and Essex, and thus reconciling their conflicting interests'; '*Bacon's* device . . .'; 'in 1595 *Francis Bacon* certainly felt *he* needed more room to manoeuvre . . .' (McCoy, 'Dangerous image', pp. 314, 314–15, 321, emphasis added). Virtually identical phrases recur in *Rites of Knighthood*. By contrast, Alan Young is much more circumspect: 'the authorship of the text has never been completely determined' (*Tudor and Jacobean Tournaments*, p. 172).

14 J. Martin, *Francis Bacon, the State and the Reform of Natural Philosophy* (Cambridge, 1992), pp. 64ff. For a text of this entertainment, see J. Spedding (ed.), *A Conference of Pleasure, Composed for some Festive Occasion about the year 1592 by Francis Bacon* (London, 1870).

15 L[ambeth] P[alace] L[ibrary], MS 936, no. 274. These are printed in J. Spedding (ed.), *The Letters and Life of Francis Bacon, including all his Occasional Works*, 7 vols. (London, 1861–1874), I, pp. 376–8.

16 Spedding himself is adamant that the other fragments of this entertainment are also the work of Bacon. Spedding's conviction is based upon stylistic comparison, a notoriously treacherous form of evidence. F. J. Burgoyne in his *Collotype Facsimile and Type Transcript of an Elizabethan Manuscript preserved at Alnwick Castle, Northumberland* (London, 1904) unquestioningly accepts the view of Spedding and prints this edition of the entertainment as 'by Francis Bacon' (pp. 55–63).

17 LPL, MS 933, no. 118. This is printed in Spedding, *Letters*, I, pp. 378–86. It is also printed in J. Nichols, *The Progresses and Public Processions of Queen Elizabeth*, 3 vols. (London, 1823 edn), III, pp. 372–9.

18 P[ublic] R[ecord] O[ffice], S[tate] P[apers] 12/254, fols. 141r–v. For Reynoldes and Essex's other secretaries, see P. E. J. Hammer, 'The uses of scholarship: the secretariat of Robert Devereux, *c.* 1585–1601', *English Historical Review* 109 (1994), 26–51.

19 In touching upon this point in my article on Essex's secretariat, I suggested that Reynoldes was involved in the 'composition' of the text for the entertainment ('Uses of scholarship', 47). This is probably an exaggeration. I now believe that the word 'composition' should be replaced by 'production'.

20 Pierpont Morgan Library, MA 1201, fols. 12–21v, cited in P. Beal, *Index of English Literary Manuscripts*, 4 vols. (London, 1980–93), I, 1450–1625, part i: Andrewes-Donne, p. 51, item BcF 314. This attribution may well be erroneous (the volume of papers which includes this document was only brought together about 1630), but it does suggest an enduring perception that the 1595 entertainment was the work of Essex and his secretariat.

21 LPL, MS 652, fol. 141r. For Anthony Bacon, see D. du Maurier, *The Golden Lads: Sir Francis Bacon, Anthony Bacon and their Friends* (New York, 1975). J. T. Freedman, 'Anthony Bacon and his World, 1558–1601' (unpub. PhD thesis, Temple University, 1978), adds little. Note that Bacon moved into Essex House, where he lived as the Earl's guest, at the end of August 1595 (LPL, MS 651, fol. 326r). LPL, MSS 647–62 comprise the bulk of Anthony Bacon's surviving papers. A selection of them was printed in T. Birch, *Memoirs of the Reign of Queen Elizabeth, from the year 1581 till her death*, 2 vols. (London, 1754).

22 Beal lists four contemporary copies (excluding those by Bacon or Reynoldes) and three copies made in the seventeenth century (*Index*, pp. 51–2). There was also another seventeenth-century copy among the family papers of Sir Thomas Winnington, Bart., at Stanford Court, Worcestershire (*Historical*

Manuscripts Commission. First report, appendix (London, 1870), p. 54). This document may have been destroyed in the 1880s. I am indebted to Dr Beal for this reference and gratefully acknowledge my debt to his work, which provides the foundation for any discussion of this manuscript evidence.

23 Beal, *Index*, pp. 51–2 (entries BcF 312, 313, 314, 315).

24 Sir Henry Wotton, *A Parallel between Robert, late Earl of Essex and George, late Duke of Buckingham* (London, 1641, Wing No. W 3647), sig. B1v.

25 Bacon is emphatic on this point: 'win the Queen: if this be not the beginning, of any other courses I see no end' (Spedding, *Letters*, II, p. 40).

26 LPL, MS 653, fol. 189r.

27 You shall receive a discourse ... penned very truly according to his lordship's large instructions, by which besides my own knowledge he informed me of sundry particulars of moment in the process thereof. And after I had penned it as plainly as I might, altering little or nothing of his own draught, I caused his lordship to peruse it once again and to add *extremam manum*, which he hath done, as you may perceive by the interlining (LPL, MS 658, fol. 88r, Cuffe to Reynoldes, July 1596).

28 Hammer, 'Uses of scholarship', 46ff. Cf. also my 'The Earl of Essex, Fulke Greville and the employment of scholars', *Studies in Philology* 91 (1994), 167–80. The letter to Rutland (actually only the first of three such letters) is printed in Spedding, *Letters*, II, pp. 21–6. Note that, like the Accession Day entertainment, this letter has also been ascribed wholly to the authorship of Francis Bacon. Once again, I find this attribution simplistic: P. E. J. Hammer, 'Letters of travel advice from the Earl of Essex to the Earl of Rutland: some comments', *Philological Quarterly* 74 (1995), 317–325.

29 C[entre for] K[entish] S[tudies], Maidstone, U 1475, C 12/26. (Quotations from this document in the De L'Isle Manuscripts, a private collection, by kind permission of Viscount De L'Isle.) This letter is printed (with modernized spelling) in Spedding, *Letters*, I, pp. 374–5.

30 D. H. Horne, *The Life and Minor Works of George Peele* (New Haven, 1952), pp. 265–75. Presumably Peele wrote this poem to cash in on the excitement generated by the Accession Day spectacles. However, it is not clear whether Peele's poem was actually published during Elizabeth's reign (*ibid.*, p. 178). It might be noted here that Peele had published works in praise of the martial qualities of Essex and Cumberland in the past (*ibid.*, pp. 224–43), as well as Essex's brother-in-law, the Earl of Northumberland (A. R. Braunmuller, *George Peele* (Boston, 1983), pp. 26–7). At the risk of stretching a rather long bow, it may also be significant that Peele had a prolonged association with Christ Church, Oxford, a college with which Essex, in particular, had close links. His long-serving secretary, Thomas Smith, had been a senior fellow in the college when Peele was also a fellow there (*Dictionary of Literary Biography* (Detroit, 1978–), vol. 62 (Elizabethan Dramatists), pp. 243–4).

31 Two ballads about the occasion were entered in the Stationers' Register by John Danter and another by William Blackwall (E. Arber (ed.), *A Transcript of the Registers of the Stationers' Company of London, 1554–1640 AD*, 5 vols. (London, 1875–94), III, p. 53). It is uncertain whether any of these entries is connected to Peele's work.

32 Spedding, *Letters*, I, pp. 377–8, 381–3.

33 These speeches seem to be mutually exclusive and embody two apparent alternatives to the problem of opening the exchange. One is put in the mouth of the Squire (*ibid.*, p. 378), while the other is given to the Hermit (Burgoyne, *Facsimile*, p. 57).

34 Spedding, *Letters*, I, p. 387. Young suggests that this interlude was actually used by another, unknown participant in the tournament (*Tudor and Jacobean Tournaments*, p. 175). This speculation is unconvincing.

35 *Anglorum Feriae*, lines 172–80 (Horne (ed.), *Minor Works of Peele*, p. 270). For Cumberland's tournament pageantry, see A. R. Young, 'Tudor Arthurianism and the Earl of Cumberland's tournament pageants', *Dalhousie Review* 67 (1987), 176–89.

36 *Anglorum Feriae*, line 191 (Horne (ed.), *Minor Works of Peele*, p. 270).

37 From the surviving evidence, it is not clear how the audience was informed that these men were representatives of Philautia, nor of her precise nature. One of the fragments surviving in Bacon's hand is a kind of letter of credence from Philautia for her envoys but it is unclear if this was part of the entertainment in its final form (Spedding, *Letters*, I, pp. 376–7). Presumably, the scenario was laid out to the audience in the exchanges which took place before Essex's entry into the arena.

38 This occasion was the Accession Day of 1590, described in Peele's 'Polyhymnia' (Horne (ed.), *Minor Works of Peele*, p. 235).

39 *Anglorum Feriae*, line 181, *ibid.*, p. 270.

40 CKS, U 1475, C 12/26.

41 On 12 November, Elizabeth had demonstrated her renewed faith in Essex by giving him sole responsibility for answering recent letters to her (A. Collins, *Letters and Memorials of State . . . from Penshurst Place*, 2 vols. (London, 1746), I, p. 360). The circumstances of Essex's loss of favour and rehabilitation are discussed below.

42 Spedding, *Letters*, I, p. 378.

43 *Ibid.*, p. 385.

44 For much of what follows, see P. E. J. Hammer, 'Patronage at court, faction and the Earl of Essex', in J. Guy (ed.), *The Reign of Elizabeth I: Court and Culture in the Last Decade* (Cambridge, 1995), pp. 65–86, and 'Essex and Europe: evidence from confidential instructions by the Earl of Essex, 1595–6', *English Historical Review* III (1996), 357–81.

45 Note that this expedition also became a vehicle for Essex's self-advertisement: P. E. J. Hammer, 'Myth-making: politics, propaganda and the capture of Cadiz in 1596', *Historical Journal* 40 (1997), 621–42.

46 Hammer, 'Letters of travel advice', p. 317.

47 *Ibid.*, pp. 320–2.

48 Based on the present range of evidence, it is impossible to tell whether this extra speech by the Hermit was added to the circulated text or actually used in the performance. In the latter case, Bacon's text would be a cut-down version of the show. The text of this 'Hermit's first speech' is: 'Your Majesty, which loveth to be just, and your Justice, which loveth to be indifferent, will not suffer you to condemn any unheard. We beseech your Majesty to assign us a time when we may before you plead for ourselves and then it shall quickly appear whether this compliment be just, or our importunities injurious' (Inner Temple Library, Petyt MS 538, vol. xxxvi, fol. 111r).

49 A connection between this image and the 1595 Accession Day tournament cannot be proven. However, the likelihood of this is strengthened by the political relevance in 1595 of the military scene in the background (war being the chief bone of contention between Essex, Elizabeth and the Cecils during this period) and by Essex's clear tendency to commission new images to commemorate significant events (Strong, *Cult of Elizabeth*, ch. 2). The self-aggrandizing *impresa* recorded on the picture also seems highly appropriate: *Dum formas minuis* (In shaping me, you destroy me).

50 On this phenomenon in general, see H. R. Woudhuysen, *Sir Philip Sidney and the Circulation of Manuscripts, 1558–1640* (Oxford, 1996), chs. 1–6, and H. Love, *Scribal Publication in Seventeenth-Century England* (Oxford, 1993), chs. 1–2.

51 *Historical Manuscripts Commission. Report on the manuscripts of Lord De L'Isle and Dudley preserved at Penshurst Place*, 6 vols. (London, 1925–1966), ii, p. 165 (hereafter cited as *HMCD*, ii).

52 Published Antwerp(?), 1594 (*STC* no. 19398). The authorship of this book is often ascribed to the Jesuit Robert Parsons (or Persons), although it is the subject of some debate: P. Holmes, 'The authorship and early reception of *A Conference about the Next Succession to the Crown of England*', *Historical Journal* 23 (1980), 415–29. For the impact of this work on the Earl of Hertford and his family, see Breight, 'Realpolitik and Elizabethan ceremony', 38ff.

53 *HMCD*, ii, pp. 177, 183. Hertford was not released from the Tower into the custody of the Archbishop of Canterbury until the beginning of January 1596 (BL, Harleian MS 6997, fols. 156, 158; PRO, SO3/1, fol. 567).

54 *HMCD*, ii, pp. 182, 183, 184.

55 Although no text survives of the page's address to the Queen, it is possible that he explicitly requested this kind of chivalric token for his master. In the Soldier's speech, there is what seems like a deliberately topical allusion: women 'will quickly discern a champion fit to wear their glove, from a page not worthy to carry their pantofle' (Spedding, *Letters*, i, p. 381).

56 Upon Ralegh's return from the Orinoco in late September, his friends immediately began urging the Queen to restore him to her favour (*HMCD*, ii, pp. 163, 166, 169). By 19 October, Ralegh was hopeful of being able to

secure the offices held by Sir Thomas Heneage, who then lay dying (*ibid.*, p. 175). Ralegh finally abandoned the vicinity of the court in early November, but 'his friends are many, and I hear he shall be sent for again' (*ibid.*, p. 182).

57 G. L. Bird, 'The Earl of Essex, Patron of Letters' (unpub. PhD thesis, University of Utah, 1969).

58 Spedding, *Letters*, I, p. 380.

59 *Ibid.*, pp. 381–2.

60 *Ibid.*, p. 383.

61 CKS, U 1475, C 12/26. Whyte is apparently referring to a performance of *Laelia* staged at Cambridge on 28 February 1595, which was attended by Essex and some of his friends. The actors to whom Whyte refers were George Meriton and George Montaigne (or Mountaine). See F. S. Boas, *University Drama in the Tudor Age* (Oxford, 1914), pp. 289–90; A. H. Nelson, *Records of Early English Drama: Cambridge*, 2 vols. (Toronto, 1989), II, pp. 905–6.

62 For Mathew, see *Dictionary of National Biography*. Like Peele, his college was Christ Church. Mathew's father, a former dean (i.e. master) of Christ Church and now bishop of Durham, had also performed in university drama during his time at Oxford (J. R. Elliott, 'Queen Elizabeth at Oxford: new light on the royal plays of 1566', *English Literary Renaissance* 18 (1988), 227).

63 The two fellows of Queens' College were George Meriton and George Montaigne. Meriton was made a fellow of Queens' College in 1589 and Montaigne in 1592. The former subsequently became dean of York and the latter archbishop of York (see *Dictionary of National Biography*). Both men were experienced players and (possibly) playwrights: Nelson, *Records*, I, p. 337; II, pp. 856, 906, 973, 1228.

64 *Dictionary of National Biography*. Various connections between Morley and Essex are explored in L. M. Ruff and D. A. Wilson, 'The madrigal, the lute song and Elizabethan politics', *Past and Present* 44 (1969), 3–51.

65 Hammer, 'Uses of scholarship', pp. 28–9, 45–6.

66 Spedding, *Letters*, I, p. 379.

67 *Ibid.*

68 Spedding, *Letters*, I, p. 385.

69 *Ibid.*

70 CKS, U 1475, C 12/26.

71 Strong, *Cult of Elizabeth*, p. 141. Cf. McCoy, 'Dangerous image', p. 323; and *Rites of Knighthood*, pp. 85, 86; Young, *Tudor and Jacobean Tournaments*, p. 176. A contrary view is advanced by E. S. Mallin, 'Emulous factions and the collapse of chivalry: *Troilus and Cressida*', *Representations* 29 (1990), 166. I am grateful to David Bevington for the latter reference.

72 CKS, U 1475, C 12/26.

73 Horne (ed.), *Minor Works of Peele*, pp. 270–1.

74 *Calendar of Letters and State Papers Relating to English Affairs, Preserved in, or Originally Belonging to, the Archives of Simancas, Elizabeth,* ed. M. A. S. Hume, 4 vols. (London, 1896–1899), IV, p. 419.

75 G. Ungerer (ed.), *A Spaniard in Elizabethan England: The Correspondence of Antonio Perez's Exile,* 2 vols. (London, 1974–6), I, pp. 329, 354.

76 LPL, MS 652, fol. 264.

77 W. T. MacCaffrey, *Elizabeth I: War and Politics 1588–1603* (Princeton, 1992), pp. 117–20; J. S. Corbett, *The Successors of Drake* (London, 1900), pp. 109–11.

78 CKS, U 1475, C 12/26.

79 BL, Egerton MS 2623, fols. 15–16, 17–18. Elizabeth herself responded to this self-characterization by addressing an elaborate mock charter to Burghley as 'the disconsolate and retired sprite, the hermit of Tybott' (a copy of this manuscript, dated 10 May 1591, is BL, Reserved Photocopy 2895). Robert Cecil was knighted ten days later, at the conclusion of the court's residence at Theobalds (W. Murdin, *A Collection of State Papers relating to Affairs in the Reign of Queen Elizabeth, from the year 1571 to 1596 . . .* (London, 1759), p. 796).

80 *Dictionary of National Biography*; J. X. Evans (ed.), *The Works of Sir Roger Williams* (Oxford, 1972).

81 Spedding, *Letters,* II, p. 41.

82 See, for example, Martin, *Bacon, the State and Reform,* chs. 3–4; J. Marwil, *The Trials of Counsel: Francis Bacon in 1621* (Detroit, 1976), pp. 71–83; MacCaffrey, *War and Politics,* pp. 482–4.

83 For Burghley's wounded reaction to accusations about a *regnum Cecilianum,* see C. Read, *Lord Burghley and Queen Elizabeth* (London, 1960), pp. 319–21.

84 [André Hurault, sieur] de Maisse, *A Journal of all that was accomplished by Monsieur de Maisse ambassador to England from Henri IV to Queen Elizabeth anno domini 1597,* ed. G. B. Harrison and R. A. Jones (London, 1931), p. 115.

85 C. Haigh, *Elizabeth I* (London, 1988), ch. 7.

86 LPL, MS 650, fols. 33r, 45r, 148r, 197r; *ibid.,* MS 653, fol. 75v.

87 F. H. Mares (ed.), *The Memoirs of Robert Carey* (Oxford, 1972), p. 29.

88 See, for example, G. Parry, *The Golden Age Restor'd: the Culture of the Stuart Court 1603–1642* (Manchester, 1981); R. M. Smuts, *Court Culture and the Origins of a Royalist Tradition in Early Stuart England* (Philadelphia, 1987); Young, *Tudor and Jacobean Tournaments,* pp. 37–42; J. S. A. Adamson, 'Chivalry and political culture in Caroline England', in K. Sharpe and P. Lake (eds.), *Culture and Politics in Early Stuart England* (Stanford, 1993), pp. 161–97, esp. p. 165. Note also N. Council, 'Ben Jonson, Inigo Jones and the transformation of Tudor chivalry', *English Literary History* 47 (1980), 259–75.

89 See, for example, Parry, *Golden Age Restor'd,* ch. 3; Smuts, *Court Culture,* pp. 29–31; R. Strong, *Henry, Prince of Wales and England's Lost Renaissance* (London, 1986), pp. 138–83; Young, *Tudor and Jacobean Tournaments,* pp. 38–40, 177–83; Adamson, 'Chivalry and political culture', pp. 161–3.

CHAPTER 4

Jacobean masques and the Jacobean peace

Peter Holbrook

> SECOND SERVINGMAN Why, then we shall have a stirring world again. This peace is nothing but to rust iron, increase tailors, and breed ballad makers.
>
> FIRST SERVINGMAN Let me have war, say I. It exceeds peace as far as day does night. It's spritely walking, audible, and full of vent. Peace is a very apoplexy, lethargy; mulled, deaf, sleepy, insensible; a getter of more bastard children than war's a destroyer of men.
>
> SECOND SERVINGMAN 'Tis so. And as wars in some sort may be said to be a ravisher, so it cannot be denied but peace is a great maker of cuckolds.
>
> FIRST SERVINGMAN Ay, and it makes men hate one another.
>
> THIRD SERVINGMAN Reason: because they then less need one another. The wars for my money!
>
> *Coriolanus*, 4.5.227–41

England's momentous change of rule in 1603 brought with it a number of transitions that were crucial to the role of court festivities and entertainments. The ruler was now male, Scottish and partial to his favourites from the North. At the same time, his royal consort, Anne of Denmark, brought with her a fascination for a new and expensive style of court dramatic entertainment that was to change the cultural landscape. The new king preened himself on his considerable learning, and longed to be an architect of rapprochement in European state affairs. His commitment to peace, eventually symbolized on the one hand by the marriage of his daughter Elizabeth to Frederick the Elector Palatine in 1613 and on the other by negotiations aimed at a Spanish wife for his son Charles, were sure to become topics of intrigue in the new style of masquing. The contested rivalries of Queen Elizabeth's Accession Day celebrations, studied by Paul Hammer in the previous essay, now found expression in the Jacobean court masque.

King James's pacifism was probably not just a political reaction to the continental wars of his day; it was deeply ingrained in his personality and early experiences. James had come to England from a violent and anarchic kingdom dominated by unruly Presbyterian extremists and turbulent aristocrats. His love of peace seems to have been a reaction against the violent conditions in which he had grown up.[1] Peace was, in his view, the greatest blessing a monarch could bestow upon his subjects. His proud boast, on the occasion of his first speech to the English Parliament, was that he had brought peace to his new kingdom.[2] In his commitment to peace and horror of sectarian violence he was ahead of most of his contemporaries. Today we can view James as an early exponent of a liberal tradition of western political thought (beginning with the *politiques* in France) that advocated tolerance and deplored religious factionalism.[3] His foreign policy was bent on keeping England out of the bitter struggles between Protestants and Catholics in western Europe.[4] As a result, the cultural life of his court – in marked contrast to that of Elizabeth – was saturated with pacifist ideology.[5] Whereas Elizabeth, the reluctant warrior queen, had been content to be celebrated as a Protestant champion, a Judith of the Reformation, James's preferred self-image was that of the law-giver, Solomon, *Rex Pacificus*. Blessed are the Peacemakers was his motto.

When James came to the English throne in March, 1603, England was still formally at war with Catholic Spain, though that war was perceived as drawing to an end.[6] Philip III of Spain saw the futility of his father's long attempt to crush the rebellious Dutch Protestants. The English, for their part, understood that the Hollanders were now able to stand alone against Spain.[7] Spanish power had begun to decline, even if many Englishmen still looked upon Spain as an expansionist and aggressive superpower unalterably hostile towards English nationhood, freedom and religion. Accordingly, the way was open to the first major act of James's reign: a peace treaty between the two countries, signed in London in August, 1604.[8] Robert Cecil, Elizabeth's chief minister and adviser on the side of caution against the aggressively interventionist policies associated with Leicester, Sidney and Essex, stayed on as secretary of state with the king he had helped to bring to the English throne. The Spanish–Dutch war lingered on until the stalemate was formally acknowledged by both sides in the Treaty of Antwerp of 1609, initiating the Twelve Years' Truce between the Dutch Republic and Spain.

Measured by his objective of keeping England free of religious strife on the Continent, James's foreign policy was a success throughout most of his reign – until 1619, at any rate, when his son-in-law Frederick accepted the Bohemian throne, thus involving James in German politics and in events that would lead to the Thirty Years' War. In 1604 England was at peace for the first time since 1585, when she had gone to the aid of the Dutch states. James wanted friendship with Spain, but understood how vital it was to English interests that Spain and France, traditional enemies, should remain at enmity.[9] He was wary of the growing commercial power of the Dutch, who, as a maritime and trading people, were potential rivals to England.[10] Though a committed Protestant, James had no wish to see England at the head of a Protestant international coalition confronting the Habsburg powers. He dreamed instead of mediating European religious conflict by building alliances with both sides.

He was of course well placed in regard to Protestant Europe. Relations with the Catholic powers were more difficult. The idea of a marriage between Prince Charles and the Spanish Infanta, first proposed during the peace negotiations with Spain by James's crypto-Catholic queen, Anne of Denmark, became an obsession of his reign.[11] This so-called Spanish Match was immensely unpopular at home. It cost James a serious loss of public support in the early 1620s when the marriage negotiations were in process.[12] Predictably, he had better political success in 1613, when he married his daughter Elizabeth to the most militantly Calvinist of the German princes, the Elector Frederick of the Palatinate in Germany. Yet this marriage too eventually brought him trouble by embroiling him in German political strife. Marriage was for James a necessary instrument of state policy, as he sought to insinuate himself into the centre of European affairs where he could play the role of mediator, but the hazards of his attempt were everywhere apparent.

James's pacifist and dynastic foreign policy, the strategy of a *politique* rather than a religious fanatic, had no shortage of enemies. His was an essentially political approach to foreign affairs, whereas his critics thought of foreign relations in religious terms.[13] Because the differences were ideological, no issue divided the court more bitterly.[14] International affairs were inseparably linked to the survival of Protestantism and the English church. To militant Protestants, friendship with Spain meant an attack on true religion and was thus tantamount to appeasement of the enemy.[15] Protestants idealized the Elizabethan years, when England had led the fight against Antichrist. Images of heroism in this 'Elizabethan Legend' linked two seemingly different traditions, that of aristocratic honour and that of the Protestant apocalypse: Sidney at Zutphen, Drake and his sea-dogs, the Earls of Leceister and Essex in the Low Countries and in Ireland on the one hand, and John Foxe triumphantly reinventing Reformation history as an epic confrontation between Protestantism and the Whore of Babylon on the other.[16]

From this romantic-chivalric-Protestant perspective, James's political approach to foreign policy was cowardly and treacherous.[17] The protest was not confined to the countryside and the City of London; those who yearned for a more partisan and ideological management of foreign affairs could be found at the centres of power. Factionalism in James's court was probably even more acute than in the reigns of his predecessor or successor. Elizabeth's ministers differed as to the means of containing the Spanish menace,[18] some (like Burghley and his son Robert Cecil) being more cautious than others, but the threat of invasion discouraged open opposition to the Queen's official policy. Charles I avoided the appearance of division in his court by surrounding himself with like-minded ministers who stood more or less united against Parliamentary opposition.[19] James deserves credit for having brought a state of peace to England that provided the luxury of occasion for men to hate one another (as the quotation from *Coriolanus* above suggests), and for not insulating himself from criticism by a phalanx of yes-men, but a price had to be paid for peace and freedom.

The result was a factionalism both bitter and organized. A pro-Spanish party, grouped around the Howard family under the leadership of the Earls of Northampton and Suffolk, joined forces with the Catholic queen.[20] The Howards, long-time opponents of the Tudor regime, had suffered at the hands of royal power. Young Prince Henry, on the other hand, attracted the devotees of the Sidney–Essex tradition. His name was, until his untimely death in 1612, the rallying-cry of the Elizabethan war-party.[21] After his death, Protestant hopes transferred to the sister whom he so cherished, Elizabeth.[22] When Elizabeth and her husband Frederick lost the Palatinate to the Habsburgs in 1620, their cause was endorsed by militant Protestants. Many hoped that one of their offspring would succeed to the English throne, rather than Charles, whom they deplored for running off to Madrid in 1623 with the idea that he had fallen in love with the Infanta. The Palatine couple, living in exile in The Hague and dependent for charity on Protestant princes, became a standing reminder of the apparent pusillanimity of James and, later, Charles.

James's pacifism was in the best tradition of Christian humanists such as Erasmus, Thomas More and (later) Milton, who were sceptical of the neo-chivalric militaristic culture dominant in the centres of European power. Unfortunately, it was also too enlightened and tolerant to win general assent in a time of international crisis. The cause of peace was not helped by the widespread perception that his court was decadent, slothful, effeminate and unpatriotic. To James's critics, eager to find fault, shockingly low standards of conduct in high places seemed of a piece with a lack of commitment to the Protestant cause.[23]

The rhetoric of attack on James as a peacemonger was at times remarkably frank. The King, wrote Sir Anthony Weldon,

naturally loved not the sight of a soldier, nor of any valiant man . . . His sending ambassadors were no less chargeable then dishonourable and unprofitable to him and his whole kingdom; for he was ever abused in all negotiations, yet he had rather spend 100,000 li. on embassies, to keep or procure peace with dishonour, then 10,000 li. on an army that would have forced peace with honour . . . He was infinitely inclined to peace, but more out of fear than conscience . . .[24]

Foreign observers noted the restiveness among many of the King's subjects. The Venetian ambassador observed in 1607 that James 'loves quiet and repose, has no inclination to war, nay is opposed to it, a fact that little pleases many of his subjects'.[25]

The controversial character of James's foreign policy has consequences for the interpretation of the masques performed during his reign. Divided and factionalized debate over foreign policy led in turn to a contested negotiation among those for whom the masque provided a highly visible and politically significant forum for ideological statement. The Jacobean masque was politicized by foreign policy differences.

Many masques of the Jacobean and Caroline eras choose pacifism as a major theme.[26] Insofar as they customarily depict chiefly the avoidance and transcending of conflict by means of supernatural guidance and aid, these masques invite interpretation – outwardly at least – as formal expressions of the pacifist theology that was so dear to the heart of James and his Queen (though less so to their son Henry). Such masques appear to valorize passivity. The mere presence of royalty magically imposes order and harmony on Bacchanalian satyrs, ranting witches and other figures of disorder.[27] Samuel Daniel expresses this view when he refers to masques, in a letter to Lucy, Countess of Bedford, as 'these ornaments and delights of peace'.

Indeed, *The Vision of the Twelve Goddesses*, Daniel's masque for the first Christmas of James's reign, performed on 8 January, 1604 at Hampton Court, is ostensibly a celebration of the 'blessings' that James's accession has brought – most of all 'this glory of peace'.[28] Though the 'peace' here may refer to the end of the Irish rebellion, occurring around the time of James's ascension of the English throne, it almost certainly also alludes to the rapidly developing amity between England and Spain that would be formalized in the London treaty of August of that year. One of James's first acts as King of England, in June 1603, had been to repress English forays against Spanish merchant shipping. Diplomatic activity between England and Spain had increased in the autumn of that year, confirming what was in reality a cessation of hostilities; as King of Scotland, after all, James had maintained friendly relations with Spain. Relations with England's former great enemy improved so substantially that in August, 1603 the King found it necessary to dispatch Sir Ralph Winwood to the Dutch States with assurances that England would not abandon their struggle.[29] Daniel wrote *The Vision of the Twelve Goddesses* during this auspicious but disconcerting outbreak of peace. For all its stiffly formal action in which the twelve goddesses approach the Temple of Peace and dedicate their various attributes to that ideal, Daniel's masque registers, in its preface and elsewhere, the conflicting discourses that attended James's controversial policy. The masque itself was, for a writer like Daniel, a double-edged sword. Regarded widely as at best a frivolous 'trifle' or 'vanity', as we saw in the Introduction to this book, the Jacobean masque was further compromised by its role in symbolizing the disgraceful frivolity and lack of militancy of the Stuart court to which Protestant activists so vehemently objected. In Scotland, James's ministers had taken offence at Queen Anne's 'night-walking and balling';[30] now the chorus of disapproval grew louder. At the same time, masque writers were keenly aware of the extraordinary potency of a form of entertainment so aptly fitted to fictionalized enactments of royal authority.

The problem for a writer like Daniel, then, was to transform a 'vanity' into something kingly and powerful. James's pacifism faced a similar problem: how to make a policy of inactivity appear honourable and chivalrous rather than devious and cowardly. The trick, evidently, was to look wise and temperate, as Prospero wishes to present himself in *The Tempest*, rejecting vengeance not out of weakness but as 'the rarer action' in which the 'nobler reason' overcomes baser, more primitive drives (5.1.26–7). For Daniel, accordingly, the dual problem of bestowing genuine dignity on masques and on pacifist state policy was in essence a single problem, since masquing entertainments and royal policy were so intertwined. Jacobean masques were, outwardly at least, designed to be the aesthetic embodiment of a pacifist culture.[31] Justifying 'these ornaments and delights of peace' is to justify that culture, and vice versa. Paradoxically, then, the masque writer needed to laud pacific aims in the conventional language of glory, power and honour. The masques of Daniel, Jonson and others often register a contest between the cultural discourses and stereotypes of peace and war.

To be sure, the deliberate blurring of the discourses of peace and valour that we so often find in the Jacobean masque could respond to varying motives and pressures, in the writer, in his noble or royal patrons, in the social matrix. *The Vision of the Twelve Goddesses*, commissioned by Queen Anne, suggests a tripartite loyalty: to the Queen as sponsor, to James as the central spectator and to the memory of Spenser and Sidney as noble exemplars of the Elizabethan tradition of honour.[32] In other words, the masque negotiates Anne's pro-Spanish pacifism with the Protestant pacifism of James and also with an Elizabethan, nostalgic commitment to military honour that seems to have formed a central part of Daniel's political consciousness. Daniel's loyalty to the Sidney–Essex faction is easily documented: he enjoyed the patronage of Sidney's sister, the Countess of Pembroke, and was to incur the displeasure of the Privy Council in 1605 for a play (*Philotas*) that appeared to sympathize with Essex's rebellion of 1601.[33]

For Daniel's own perspective on honour and, by implication, on masquing, we need to look briefly at 'Ulysses and the Siren', a poem published by him in the year following the masque. Even if its debate between pleasure and virtuous honour rings changes on a Renaissance commonplace, the timely choice of topic, in a poem not officially commissioned as a court entertainment, may indicate some of the author's concerns more acutely than does *The Twelve Goddesses*. In this dialogue, Ulysses successfully resists the invitation of the Siren to 'joy the day in mirth the while / And spend the night in sleep'.[34] He chooses to remain true to 'fame [and] honour', which are not, he points out sternly, 'To be attained with ease': 'To spend the time luxuriously / Becomes not men of worth'. The entire poem is a debate between pleasure and virtue, but without the fantasy of reconciliation that is so much a part of Jonson's masque on that topic. Here, Ulysses must spurn the Siren's enchantments:

Siren: Ulysses, O! be not deceived
　　With that unreal name;
This honour is a thing conceived
　　And rests on others' fame;
Begotten only to molest
　　Our peace, and to beguile
The best thing of our life, our rest,
　　And give us up to toil.

Siren: Delicious nymph, suppose there were
　　Nor honour nor report,
Yet manliness would scorn to wear
　　The time in idle sport;
．　．　．　．　．
But natures of the noblest frame
　　These toils and dangers please;
And they take comfort in the same
　　As much as you in ease;
And with the thought of actions past
　　Are recreated still;
When pleasure leaves a touch at last,
　　To shew that it was ill.

To the Siren's blandishing suggestion that 'Our sports are without blood' and that 'The world we see by warlike wights / Receives more hurt than good', the honourable soldier has the firm reply:

Ulysses: But yet the state of things require
　　These motions of unrest;
And these great spirits of high desire
　　Seem born to turn them best;
To purge the mischiefs that increase
　　And all good order mar,
For oft we see a wicked peace
　　To be well changed for war.

Ulysses carries the day, the poem finely articulating the perspective of those Essexian 'spirits of high desire' who still hoped that England might exchange the 'sports' of the Siren of pacifism for the 'action' of a campaign. Ulysses comprehensively spurns the irenic outlook: 'For oft we see a wicked peace / To be well changed for war'. How then is Daniel, fired with such a chivalric idea of honour, to write an officially court-sponsored masque in which pleasure and virtue, pacifism and warlike honour, are to be reconciled? It is a problem with which Jonson too would have to grapple.

The Vision of the Twelve Goddesses plentifully suggests the kinds of strain and equivocation that we would expect of a work produced in response to such varied ideological positions as the Queen's, the King's and Daniel's own. Daniel's dedicatory letter to the published text seems deliberately to call upon traditional ideals of honour and heroism, as though in response to the doctrine of disengagement from Europe. He aligns himself with the Queen, whom he characterizes as 'magnificent' and 'heroical' (lines 10–11). He explains his willingness to see the masque printed in language that is at once cool towards the masque as a form and openly admiring of military preparedness. He has consented to publication, he says

seeing . . . that these ornaments and delights of peace are in their season as fit to entertain the world and deserve to be made memorable as well as graver actions, both of them concurring to the decking and furnishing of glory and majesty as the necessary complements requisite for state and greatness. (lines 12–16)

While praising both masques ('these ornaments and delights of peace') and military glory (the 'graver actions' that deck our kings and nobles) as necessary for 'state and greatness', Daniel makes clear his sense of priority. Masques are fine 'in their season', but, as the products of an unwarlike culture, they are secondary to 'graver actions'. Although both deserve to be 'made memorable', the antithetical structure here and in the dedicatory letter as a whole invokes a scale of values in which war, glory and honour are more truly to be celebrated than mere 'ornaments and delights'. Emphasis falls audibly on military values rather than irenic ones as the sentence quoted above leads up to its resonant conclusion of 'state and greatness'. A few lines later, in Daniel's tribute to 'this glory of peace, with the accession of so great state and power', we hear a similar cadence. Peace is redescribed as war, by a strategic blurring of the discourses of peace and glory and especially by the oxymoronic 'glory of peace'.

When we turn to the masque itself, we find a similar blurring in Daniel's presentation of the twelve goddesses, some of whom at least have an ambiguous relation to the official irenic ideology: 'Juno, the Goddess of empire and *regnorum praesidi* [protectress of kingdoms]', is associated with the 'blessing of power', Pallas with 'wisdom and defence', and Tethys with 'power by sea' (lines 25–27, 30). Astraea, or Justice (line 29), is especially significant in this context, since she is certain to remind her courtly spectators of the cult of Astraea that

Queen Elizabeth's poets and courtiers so assiduously cultivated on her behalf. Daniel's dedicatory letter lays out his interpretation of the twelve goddesses in such a way as to confirm his belief in military preparedness. *The Vision of the Twelve Goddesses*, he explains,

> first presented the hieroglyphic of empire and dominion, as the ground and matter whereon this glory of state is built. Then those blessings and beauties that preserve and adorn it: as armed policy, love, religion, chastity, wealth, happiness, concord, justice, flourishing seasons, plenty: and lastly power by sea, as to imbound and circle this greatness of dominion by land. (lines 49–54)

All of these attributes of English greatness are consonant with Daniel's loyalty to the 'Elizabethan legend' of Sidney and Essex. Juno and Tethys, in first and last place, signify empire and sea-power, supremely needful to England in her quest for that victory over Catholic Europe that the patriots longed for in their dismay at the peace treaty of 1604. 'Armed policy', represented by Pallas, is given second place. Even 'chastity' may recall Elizabeth, while other seemingly irenic attributes are seen here as arms of England's might. Diana desires peace but will fight when necessary:

> chaste Diana, in her robes of green,
> With weapons of the wood her self addrests
> To bless the forests where her power is seen,
> In peace with all the world but savage beasts.
>
> (lines 309–12)

Many a Jacobean spectator would have matched this observation about a lasting peace not being possible with 'savage beasts' with their feelings about the Spanish Habsburg emperor, Philip III.

The weight of Daniel's description of his masque thus falls on a discourse of glory and, by implication, war. Sea power, embodied in Tethys, is given an especially dominant role, as though to remind a Jacobean audience of the crucial importance of maritime strength in England's military preparedness and of the Sidney–Essex faction that supported the cause of naval might.[35] An island nation like England must cultivate a singularly close relation with the sea. Hence Tethys is 'Albion's fairest love',

> Whom she in faithful arms doth deign t'embrace
> And brings the trident of her power t'approve
> The kind respect she hath to do him grace. (lines 344–7)

Such a tribute to Albion and sea-power is common enough in the literature of the time, as for example in John of Gaunt's praise for

England as 'This precious stone set in the silver sea' (*Richard II*, 2.1.46), but here, in the context of the political alignments at court in 1604, it also reflects a polemical view of English naval power that the anti-Spanish faction would have heartily endorsed. Significantly, King James and his son differed on the issue of seapower. Henry befriended Ralegh, one of England's hawks and a hero of the expedition against Cadiz in 1596, even though that gentleman had been arrested for conspiring against James in 1603 and was still confined to the Tower of London in 1604. James's mind had been set against him and much else that was naval. Henry, to the contrary, took a keen interest in naval construction and design, supporting those who wished to rebuild the fleet that James had let run down. (Tom Bishop provides further details in his essay on *Oberon* in this volume.) Not surprisingly, then, when Daniel was called upon to write another masque at Queen Anne's behest, celebrating the Prince's creation as Prince of Wales, he called it *Tethys' Festival*.[36]

The part played by the Queen in *The Vision of the Twelve Goddesses*, 'war-like Pallas', offers an intriguing prospect when we consider Anne's role as sponsor of Daniel's masque and at the same time an influential proponent of rapprochement with Spain. The description of Pallas seems designed, albeit tactfully, to enlist the Queen on the side of those who favour military preparedness:

> Next war-like Pallas in her helmet dressed
> With lance of winning, target of defence:
> In whom both wit and courage are expressed,
> To get with glory, hold with providence.   (lines 294–7)

This image seems sufficiently bellicose, in its conflation of 'glory' and 'providence', to have invited comparison with the Protestant chivalry that Sidney had come to epitomize. Yet Daniel is careful not to antagonize his patroness with a suggestion of undue militancy. Pallas Athene, after all, can be associated with wisdom and handicrafts; Daniel presents her (and Anne) as a goddess 'In whom both wit and courage are expressed'. Such a portrait is conventional enough to flatter the King's royal consort and at the same time pursue indirectly the programme of military boldness that Daniel evidently wished to support.

In a similar vein, the religion denoted by Vesta would appear to be of a distinctly reformed and even zealous kind. Vesta appears in 'a white mantle . . . with a dressing like a nun', and holds 'a burning lamp in one hand, and a book in the other' (lines 71–2):

> Next holy Vesta with her flames of zeal
> Presents herself clad in white purity:
> Whose book the soul's sweet comfort doth reveal
> By the ever-burning lamp of piety.   (lines 304–7)

Once again, the point is made without introducing an avowedly strident tone of Calvinism. Daniel could scarcely have attempted such a thing in a masque written for the King and Queen. Still, the passage certainly does not disallow an actively Protestant conception of England's role in Europe. Throughout the masque, peace is to be obtained through 'armed policy', 'true zeal', 'might / And power by sea' (lines 378, 379, 381–2). The rhetorical emphasis is more on these securities of peace than on peace itself. History affords countless examples of political leaders whose desire for 'peace' manifests in a show of force or preemptive strike. If Sir Walter Ralegh had been permitted to see the *The Twelve Goddesses*, he might not have been affronted by its vision.

Although Daniel provided the first Whitehall masque for the new regime, he was 'only mildly successful' as a court entertainer, and Ben Jonson soon took over the role.[37] One reason for Jonson's ascendancy may have been his greater sympathy with the prevailing Jacobean ideology. He seems to have developed a good working relationship with the Queen, whose influence on masquing was now considerable and whose pro-Spanish and pro-Catholic opinions were not always in accord with her husband's views, even though both desired peace. As a humanist, Jonson supported a renewal of Western culture along neo-classical lines, and accordingly was drawn (like Erasmus and More) to a pan-European and pacifist view of history. Whereas Daniel's masque of 1604 redescribed peace as war by blurring the discourses of peace and glory, Jonson's *The Masque of Queens*, performed on 2 February, 1609, skilfully uses the discourse of war to make honourable the cause of peace.

When Jonson wrote *The Masque of Queens* he had already written two masques at the behest of Queen Anne. James's order to the Exchequer makes clear the extent of the Queen's involvement in 1609: 'the Queen our dearest wife hath resolved for our greater honour and contentment to make us a mask this Christmas attended by most of the greatest ladies of the kingdom'.[38] As Barbara Lewalski has pointed out, and as other essayists in this volume concur, Anne's views, especially 'her Roman Catholic proclivities' and 'blatant pro-Spanish politics', sometimes diverged from those of the King.[39] Moreover, Anne was a Danish princess, intent upon preserving her separate dignity as the daughter of a king. Her masques, especially those of the first decade of the century, 'contest[ed] the gender ideology dominant in the King's Court . . . as they insisted upon the Queen's (and womankind's) worth and power'.[40] Jonson, as author of the masque, plainly found it necessary to bear in mind Anne's views about gender and politics while at the same time producing a public entertainment that would not openly offend the King and his policy.

Queen Anne's views on the worth and dignity of women are especially evident in the way Jonson opens *The Masque of Queens*.[41] Witches appear in an antimasque, bent on disrupting the night's celebrations. Instead of succeeding, they are vanquished by Heroic Virtue, the father of Fame, and are replaced onstage by the warrior queens who occupy the House of Fame. This action should be read, Lewalski argues, as a demonstration of Anne's self-assertion: the queens are independent rulers, 'subversive' of James's authority because they are seen as 'historical women who fought battles and ruled kingdoms in their own right'.[42] As such, they may have been an uncomfortable reminder to the King of the independent-minded women – Queen Elizabeth, Mary Stuart, Arabella Stuart – who for years had had such influence on James's destiny. 'These militant Queens, whose force is directed against Kings and husbands, need, and find, a female referent – Queen Anne, not King James.'[43] However much the masque may appear to honour the Jacobean court and its monarch, *The Masque of Queens* is a bid for transfer of power from King to Queen.

Such a jarring hint at struggles for control in the royal family could scarcely have been staged without the softening effects of apparent harmony elsewhere in the masque. Fortunately for Jonson, the central issue of peace in foreign affairs offered a topic of mutual accommodation between King and Queen, even if the Queen had a foreign policy programme that was discernibly her own. In these terms, *The Masque of Queens* attempts a non-militaristic redefinition of fame and virtue, by transforming the language and trappings of war into the language of peace, while at the same time providing a role for Queen Anne as one who can subtly shape James's image as peacemaker to her own advantage. By making peace honourable and fame-worthy, *The Masque of Queens* implicitly encourages a tilt in English foreign policy in the direction of Spain. It still supports the official royal position on international affairs in outline, but leaves open the possibility of a more pro-Spanish stance than James's middle way would have countenanced.

The masque thus manages to reconcile two aims that must have weighed heavily with Jonson: asserting the 'dignity of [the] persons' of the queen and her ladies (line 5), while also attempting to revive and make admirable, by redefining the language of war, the tradition of humanist and Christian-humanist pacifism. The irenic tradition of Erasmus, More and Castiglione took an entirely different view of war and honour from that of the Renaissance militarists like Machiavelli, Sidney and Ralegh, who, as Steven Marx observes, regarded 'war as an end in itself' and as the fount of fame.[44] *The Masque of Queens* transforms the language of one tradition into that of the other, redeploying the terms of a militaristic code in the service of what Marx calls 'the dominant Stuart mode of expression . . . [the] culture of pacifism'.[45] The redeployment thus serves the aims of Jonson's humanism even while it also implicitly promotes Anne's cause of the Pope and Spain.

Jonson's dislike of militarism is discernible in *The Masque of Queens*'s distinction between mere Fame and Good Fame. The passions that make for war – 'wild Suspicion', 'stupid Ignorance', 'quick Credulity', 'Murmur, with the cheeks deep-hung', 'Malice, whetting of her forked tongue', 'Slander', 'black-mouthed Execration', 'flame eyed Rage' (lines 105–19) – are 'the opposites to good Fame' (line 16). Deplorable qualities of malice and rage contribute to the fanaticism of war and Fame, whereas good Fame possesses all the manly attributes of honour and glory but is peaceful as well.

Jonson's antimasque figures illustrate all that is opposite to the positive image of Good Fame. The witches announce that they have come 'To overthrow the glory of this night' (line 101). They speak in an inflated, blood-and-thunder rhetoric that is unmatched by deeds: 'we have set the elements at wars, / Made midnight see the sun, and day the stars' (lines 213–4). Although their Dame speaks like a great commander at a solemn council – 'Holds our great purpose?' (line 102) – the witches are grotesquely and comically ineffectual.[46] Their invocations to the 'fogs' to 'strike a blindness through these blazing tapers' (lines 227–8) become more and more desperate and petulant:

> *Dame* Stay! All our charms do nothing win
> Upon the night; our labor dies!
> Our magic feature will not rise,
> Nor yet the storm! We must repeat
> More direful voices far, and beat
> The ground with vipers till it sweat.

Charm 6

Bark dogs, wolves howl,
Sea roar, woods roll,
Clouds rack, all be black
But the light our charms do make.

Dame   Not yet? My rage begins to swell;
Darkness, devils, night and hell,
Do not thus delay my spell!
. . . . . .
        . . . Still are you deaf?
. . . . . .
        . . . I'll speak a charm
Shall cleave the ground as low as lies
Old shrunk-up Chaos, and let rise
Once more his dark and reeking head
To strike the world and nature dead.

(lines 268–97)

By way of contrast with all that the witches ineffectually defy, the main body of Jonson's masque glorifies Heroic Virtue, Good Fame and the peaceful arts of poetry. When Heroic Virtue – 'heroic and masculine' (line 342) – appears in 'a sound of loud music' (line 334), the witches vanish. In their place appears Fame, the daughter of Heroic Virtue, whose neoclassical house features columns that are

Men-making poets, and those well made men
Whose strife it was to have the happiest pen
Renown them to an after-life, and not
With pride to scorn the muse and die forgot.

(lines 362–5)

Fame's house is thus supported by those poets and great men of the past who eternize true virtue. The virtuous queens, too, 'are of times long gone' (line 374) – except for 'Bel Anna' (line 391), who possesses 'all virtues, for which one by one / they were so famed' (line 393). Queen Anne assumes a central role as the embodiment of the irenic yet manly qualities that the masque lauds.

Implicit is a narrative of cultural modernization: the virtues of the ancient warrior queens are embodied in the modern champion of peace. This synthesis of warlike vigour and peaceful civilization is expressed by various emblems and motifs. *Fama bona* bears '*in her right hand . . . a trumpet, in her left an olive branch*' (lines 423, 426–7). The trumpet of Fame paradoxically blazes not war but James's 'peace' (line 411).[47]

The fusion of bellicose form with peaceful content is evident throughout, as the machinery of war and the spirit of peace come together in
triumphal invocations of epic poetry and dancing (lines 471–79, 489–
94, 505–13).[48] 'Triumphing' (line 513) and the mounting of chariots
lead unexpectedly to the repudiation of martial glory at the end of
the masque. The 'power' (line 516) of Virtue, now clearly distinguish-
able from a purely militaristic ethic, has transformed itself into Good
Fame:

> Th'Assyrian pomp, the Persian pride,
> Greeks' glory, and the Romans', died;
>   And who yet imitate
> Their noises, tarry the same fate.
>   Force greatness all the glorious ways
>   You can, it soon decays,
>   But so Good Fame shall never:
> Her triumphs, as their causes, are forever. (lines 519–26)

In *The Masque of Queens* we thus see an attempt to render honourable,
by shrewd use of the language of war, the ideology of peace (or appeasement, as the Protestant war-party would have it). Peace is bold and
honourable; war atavistic, stupid and benighted. The ancient warlike
queens have contentedly taken up residence in the house of Fame,
while the witches – those figures of dark violence, superstition, raving
and impotence who stand vainly in the way of history – are consigned
to obscurity. True fame belongs to modernity; the ancient virtues of
war are now domiciled, apparently without any sense of strain, in the
orderly house of peace. The masque serves Anne's cause, as Lewalski
suggests, not only in that it is female-centred in such a way as to
enhance her dignity and that of her household, but also, perhaps,
in that it embraces James in an ideology of pacifism that takes him
further in the direction of Spain and abandonment of the Protestant
cause than he might otherwise wish to go. Jonson's dedication to Prince
Henry in the quarto version is similarly significant, addressing Henry
principally as a patron of the arts and lover of poetry rather than as a
soldier.[49] The masque is an attempt to make the war-party – the party
of 'noise' – look ridiculous, and to suggest that the tide of history runs
against it.[50]

In a fundamental sense, masques found their justification and authority in the king. They were obliged to please him, and one way to do
so was to articulate his ideology. Still, the Jacobean court was not

monolithic, and the royal interest was not the only one that had to be considered. Even where the writer of the masque supported the royal outlook, this ideological position had to be negotiated. Daniel, in *The Vision of the Twelve Goddesses*, held true to the tradition of Sidney and Essex, even as he made his obligatory offering at the Temple of Peace. Jonson, on the other hand, discovered that he had to co-opt and transform the honour- and glory-centred rhetoric of the war-party if his masque was to succeed as a pacifist statement. In so doing he found he needed to take account of varying points of view, even of significant opposition to the King's policy. Anne's Catholic and pro-Spanish interests were not synonomous with James's pacifist views; though the two positions converged on the central issue of peace, 'peace' in this context came to mean many things.

NOTES

1 On James's 'abhorrence of violence', see S. R. Gardiner, *The History of England from the Accession of James I to the Outbreak of the Civil War, 1603–1642*, 10 vols. (London, 1904–9), II, p. 221. See also L. J. Reeve, *Charles I and the Road to Personal Rule* (Cambridge, 1989), p. 9, and G. P. V. Akrigg (ed.), *Letters of King James VI and I* (Berkeley, 1984), p. 3.

2 Gardiner, *History of England*, I, pp. 165–6.

3 See Roger Lockyer, *The Early Stuarts: A Political History of England, 1603–1642* (London, 1989), p. 16, and Roy Strong, *Henry, Prince of Wales and England's Lost Renaissance* (London, 1986), p. 84.

4 For James's foreign policy I have drawn on Gardiner, *History of England*; Lockyer, *The Early Stuarts*; Simon Adams, 'Spain or the Netherlands? The dilemmas of early Stuart foreign policy', in Howard Tomlinson (ed.), *Before the Civil War: Essays on Early Stuart Politics and Government* (London, 1983); G. M. D. Howat, *Stuart and Cromwellian Foreign Policy* (London, 1974); J. R. Jones, *Britain and Europe in the Seventeenth Century* (London, 1966); Maurice Lee, Jr., *James I and Henri IV: An Essay in English Foreign Policy, 1603–1610* (Urbana, IL, 1970) and *Great Britain's Solomon: James VI and I in His Three Kingdoms* (Urbana, IL, 1990).

5 Steven Marx, 'Shakespeare's pacifism', *Renaissance Quarterly* 45 (1992), 58, and Graham Parry, *The Golden Age Restor'd: The Culture of the Stuart Court, 1603–42* (Manchester, 1981), pp. 17–18, 21–2.

6 Simon Adams, 'Britain and the world under the Tudors: 1485–1603', in J. S. Morrill (ed.), *The Oxford Illustrated History of Tudor and Stuart Britain* (Oxford, 1996), p. 414.

7 Adams, 'Spain or the Netherlands?', p. 93.

8 Lee, *James I and Henri IV*, p. 12.

9 *Ibid.*, p. 14.

10 Adams, 'Spain or the Netherlands?', p. 84. James and Charles disliked the Dutch as rebels against established authority: see Jones, *Britain and Europe*, p. 17; Kevin Sharpe, *The Personal Rule of Charles I* (New Haven, 1992), p. 76; Simon Adams, 'Foreign policy and the parliaments of 1621 and 1624', in Kevin Sharpe (ed.), *Faction and Parliament: Essays on Early Stuart History* (Oxford, 1978). For James and Charles, writes Adams, 'the House of Habsburg represented social order and monarchical legitimacy and stability in a world threatened by Dutch and presbyterian republicanism' (p. 141). See also Reeve, *Charles I*, p. 183.

11 On Anne's conversion to Catholicism, see D. H. Willson, *King James VI and I* (London, 1956), p. 95. On her role in the marriage scheme, see Lockyer, *The Early Stuarts*, p. 13, and Adams, 'Spain or the Netherlands?', p. 88.

12 On the 'fury' of the Protestant clergy regarding the match, see Louis B. Wright, 'Propaganda against James I's "appeasement" of Spain', *Huntington Library Quarterly* 6 (1942–3), 149.

13 Many of the subjects of James and Charles preferred a 'godly' rather than pragmatic foreign policy: Adams, 'Spain or the Netherlands?', p. 101. In 'Foreign policy and the parliaments of 1621 and 1624', Adams argues that Jacobean and Caroline debates over international affairs were 'conducted between men who saw contemporary events as part of a pattern of Protestant apocalyptical history and men who, fearing the revolutionary implications of such an ideology, sought a policy more conducive to the stability of the political and social *status quo*' (p. 140). Cf. Reeve, *Charles I*: the early Stuart foreign policy struggle was between 'confessional politics' and 'reason of state' (pp. 292, 293).

14 See R. Malcolm Smuts, *Court Culture and the Origins of a Royalist Tradition in Early Stuart England* (Philadelphia, 1987), pp. 6–7. On 'court factions and the foreign policy debate' in the Stuart era, see Adams, 'Spain or the Netherlands?', p. 90.

15 On the public controversy over the 1604 treaty, see H. R. Trevor-Roper, 'Spain and Europe: 1598–1621' in volume IV of *The New Cambridge Modern History* (Cambridge, 1970), p. 265, and Linda Levy Peck, *Northampton: Patronage and Policy at the Court of James I* (London, 1982), p. 105.

16 On 'The Stuarts and the Elizabethan legend', see Smuts, *Court Culture*, pp. 15–50: over time 'Elizabeth's name was associated with austerity, military preparedness, and Protestant alliances, in contrast to the perceived extravagance and pro-Spanish policies of James I' (p. 29). See also chapter 1 of Frances Yates's *Shakespeare's Last Plays: A New Approach* (London, 1975). Richard McCoy stresses the 'zeal for martial glory' of the male Elizabethan aristocracy in '"A dangerous image": the Earl of Essex and Elizabethan chivalry', *Journal of Medieval and Renaissance Studies* 13 (1983), 313.

17 A good account of this perspective is in Vernon F. Snow's description of the leading role in the Protestant war-party of the third Earl of Essex, a

champion, along with Oxford and Southampton, of what the seventeenth-century dramatist and historian Arthur Wilson called 'old English honour': see 'Essex and the aristocratic opposition to the early Stuarts', *Journal of Modern History* 32 (1960), 226. According to Snow, the Essexians 'bemoaned the decline of honor and other military ideals' in James's court, believing that 'new titles and dignities should be won on the battlefield and not sold in the anteroom of the presence chamber' (227, 226). The third earl thus continued in the tradition of his father – himself, in Mervyn James's words, 'a legatee of Sidneian chivalric romanticism' – which wanted 'a European Protestant league, a larger investment of resources in the war with Spain, wider military commitments abroad, westward oceanic expansion, and an extended naval assault on the Spanish empire'; see his *English Politics and the Concept of Honour: 1485–1642* (Oxford, 1977), p. 72.

18 Adams, 'Spain or the Netherlands?', p. 90.

19 Charles excluded from his circle 'that basically orthodox approach to politics which espoused the Dutch alliance, war with Spain, the Protestant cause, the sitting of Parliament and the established Calvinism of the English Church' (Reeve, *Charles I*, p. 181). On the 'ideological flexibility' (p. 180) and pluralism of James's court by comparison with his son's, see pp. 179–81.

20 Charles H. Carter, 'Gondomar: ambassador to James I', *The Historical Journal* 7 (1964), 193–4.

21 Strong, *Henry, Prince of Wales*, p. 70.

22 Reeve, *Charles I*, pp. 221–3.

23 On the lack of 'morality and decorum' at James's court, see Parry, *Golden Age Restor'd*, p. 58. Lee, more sympathetic to James than earlier historians, concedes in *Great Britain's Solomon* that James's court was 'corrupt and disorderly' (p. 132). See also Smuts, *Court Culture*, p. 28.

24 Quoted in Robert Ashton (ed.), *James I By His Contemporaries* (London, 1969), pp. 13, 14–15, 16.

25 *Ibid.*, p. 10.

26 On the Caroline peace cult, see Smuts, *Court Culture*, pp. 247–53.

27 On this point, in the context of Jonson's *Masque of Queens*, see Martin Butler, 'Private and occasional drama', in *The Cambridge Companion to English Renaissance Drama*, ed. A. R. Braunmuller and Michael Hattaway (Cambridge, 1990), p. 140.

28 The quotations from the letter to Lady Bedford (which was included in the octavo 1604 printing of the masque) are found at lines 12, 18 and 20–21 of Joan Rees's edition in *A Book of Masques in Honour of Allardyce Nicoll*, ed. T. J. B. Spencer and Stanley Wells (Cambridge, 1967). Further quotations are from this edition; references (by line number) are included in the text.

29 For these events, see G. B. Harrison (ed.), *A Jacobean Journal: 1603–1606* (London, 1941).

30 Their remonstration is quoted in Willson, *King James*, p. 94.

31 On the ancient association of peace with revels, see James Hutton, *Themes of Peace in Renaissance Poetry*, ed. Rita Guerlac (Ithaca, 1984), pp. 274–5.

32 For Daniel's loyalty to Elizabeth, see Joan Rees, *Samuel Daniel: A Critical and Biographical Study* (Liverpool, 1964), p. 138. Snow, in his article on Essex, regards Daniel as a member of the Jacobean Protestant opposition (p. 224). See David Norbrook, *Poetry and Politics in the English Renaissance* (London, 1984), p. 196. For Norbrook, Daniel was a member of a Spenserian poetic circle out of step – unlike Jonson – with the new political culture, which had 'rejected the Elizabethan ideals of Protestant chivalry' (p. 199); see chapters 7 and 8 ('Jonson and the Jacobean peace: 1603–16' and 'The Spenserians and King James: 1603–1616'). Norbrook discusses Daniel's critical view of masquing in 'The reformation of the masque', in David Lindley (ed.), *The Court Masque* (Manchester, 1984), p. 96.

33 Rees, *Samuel Daniel*, pp. 11–12, 97–8.

34 The text is edited by E. K. Chambers in *The Oxford Book of Sixteenth Century Verse* (Oxford, 1932; repr. 1976).

35 It was recognized that a forward Protestant policy for England would be a maritime one: Reeve, *Charles I*, p. 207.

36 Rees, *Samuel Daniel*, pp. 147–8.

37 *Ibid.*, p. 144.

38 Quoted in Barbara Lewalski, 'Anne of Denmark and the subversions of masquing', *Criticism* 35 (1993), 346.

39 *Ibid.*, 431. For Anne's pro-Spanish tendencies, see Gardiner, *History of England*, ii, p. 224, and Adams, 'Spain or the Netherlands?', p. 91.

40 Lewalski, 'Anne of Denmark', p. 350.

41 Quotations from Jonson's masques are from Stephen Orgel (ed.), *Ben Jonson: The Complete Masques* (New Haven, 1969); references (by line number) included in the text.

42 Lewalski, 'Anne of Denmark', p. 347.

43 *Ibid.*, p. 348.

44 Marx, 'Shakespeare's pacifism', p. 51; on humanist anti-militarists, see p. 49. For the hostility of humanists such as Ascham towards chivalry, see Norman Council, 'Ben Jonson, Inigo Jones, and the transformation of Tudor chivalry', *English Literary History* 47 (1980), 261–2.

45 Marx, 'Shakespeare's pacifism', p. 58.

46 David Lindley comes independently to a similar view of the witches, as dramatizing 'the ridiculous self-delusions of witchcraft', in *Court Masques: Jacobean and Caroline Entertainments, 1605–1640* (Oxford, 1995), p. 225.

47 Stephen Orgel makes this point about *Queens* in *The Illusion of Power: Political Theater in the English Renaissance* (Berkeley, 1975): 'the highest virtue is that of the pacific king, not a warrior, but a classical scholar and poet' (p. 65).

48 Even the triumphalism of the masque operates within an irenic ideology. According to Hutton, the Romans regularly associated Pax and Victoria. Pax is sometimes represented 'with spear and shield or trophies of war' or

'setting foot on the necks of the conquered' (cf. the binding of the hags in
Queens): 'The Roman mission is bluntly stated in the legend *Mars pacifer*'
(*Themes of Peace*, pp. 30–1). I am grateful to Dr Anthony Miller of the
University of Sydney for showing me his discussion of this topic in his
forthcoming book on the Renaissance triumph.

49 See *Complete Masques*, ed. Orgel, pp. 478–9.

50 Jonson's representation of war in *The Golden Age Restored* (1616) parallels
that in *The Masque of Queens*. Pallas banishes Iron Age, thus introducing the
(Jacobean) Golden Age. Iron Age's war-lust beings forth 'a tumult and
clashing of arms' (line 23), 'pyrrhic' dances (line 49), 'drums, trumpets,
and a confusion of martial music' (lines 69–70). The showing of Pallas's
shield re-establishes the Golden Age (line 70). As in *The Masque of Queens*,
martial properties – Pallas's 'chariot' (line 1) and shield – are reactivated
as engines of peace, pre-empting the traditional attack that peace is dishonourable and soft. Jonson's armed Athena, enemy of strife and harbin-
ger of peace, is an example of Jonson rededicating martial types to the
cause of pacifism. Moreover, Jonson subverts the 'war is honour' ideology
by providing a psychopathology of the war-drive, reducing it to 'malice',
'spite', 'hate', 'fear', 'Rapine', 'Treachery' and 'Folly' (lines 68, 86, 139,
46, 47, 48). As in *Queens*, the appeal is to modernity: true 'virtue' (equated
with peace) has been 'pressed' and must 'grow'; 'buried arts' must 'flourish'
(line 119). Both masques appropriate the iconography of war for the sake
of its cultural prestige, pressing it into the King's service; both redescribe
unflatteringly the traditional martial ideology.

On the dating of *The Golden Age Restored* see Martin Butler and David
Lindley, 'Restoring Astraea: Jonson's masque for the fall of Somerset',
English Literary History 61 (1994), 807–27, especially 808–9, and John Orrell,
'The London Stage in the Florentine Correspondence, 1604–1618', *Theatre
Research International* 3 (1977–8), especially 173–4. Following Orrell, Butler
and Lindley challenge the theory, as set forth in C. H. Herford and Percy
Simpson (eds.), *Ben Jonson*, 11 vols. (Oxford, 1925–52), x, pp. 545–6, and
followed ever since by most editors and scholars, that the last two masques
in the 1616 Folio (*Golden Age* and *Mercury Vindicated*) were printed in reverse
order, and that the date there given for *Golden Age* of 1615 is the 'right' one,
with *Mercury Vindicated* being the masque for the following year. Butler
and Lindley argue that *The Golden Age Restored* is in fact in its 'right' place,
having been performed 1616 in the midst of the Overbury murder trials.
Mercury Vindicated was thus the masque for the previous year. This present
volume accepts this argument.

CHAPTER 5

The gingerbread host: tradition and novelty in the Jacobean masque

Tom Bishop

> On Tuesday the Prince gave his masque, which was very beauti-
> ful throughout, very decorative, but most remarkable for the grace
> of the Prince's every movement.[1]

> In a society mad for novelty, I knew I could become something of
> a fad by clinging to bits of the past, but I also recognized that the
> strange is acceptable only if it fits people's familiar notions of it.
> An oddity that suits everyone's preconceptions must be nothing
> more than a slight variation on the ordinary. If a dancer turns left
> instead of right, or shrugs after the fourth beat instead of the
> third, then her daring will be endlessly discussed; but if she insists
> that dancing itself is absurd, forget it.[2]

Enlarging on Martin Butler's and Peter Holbrook's analyses of the
representation of political 'negotiation' in the Jacobean court masque,
I wish to reconsider the relations between aesthetics and politics in the
masque over the first fifteen years or so of James's reign. I will argue
that in the masques of these years a politics of charisma was waged
through the selection and performance of personal images, and that
this politics and the masques that represented and enacted it were
generated out of a dialectic of tradition and novelty that characterized
the earlier Jacobean court in both its individual and its group workings. My particular example will be Prince Henry's *Oberon, the Fairy
Prince* of New Year's Day 1611.

My interest in re-examining the political character of the court
masque stems from a sense that recent masque criticism has to some
extent taken its eye off the central concern of the genre with performance, preferring a discursive model of masque politics that focuses on
texts rather than action.[3] Valuable and important as this commentary
has been in drawing attention to the connections between the masque
and its political contexts, and in linking the masque to Jacobean political

theory, it has tended to concern itself especially with the masque's rumination of policy rather than its presentation of politics.[4] Certainly the masque spoke of and to policy issues. Yet our analysis of the positions announced in texts or in iconic images conceived as texts can be usefully complemented by consideration of the masque as a formal and kinetic event whose politics are not simply uttered, but enacted. For a political culture exists not only in ways of writing or talking, but also in ways of moving, grouping and seeing. In the performance of the masque we have an unusually clear opportunity to see Jacobean court politics actually unfolding, in process rather than in abstraction, and to see it, in a sense, theorizing itself as it does so. The masque's poetic understanding of court politics as a present activity is registered in its orchestration of charisma, and it is this aspect that I wish to highlight here.[5]

COURTIERSHIP AND CHARISMA

Politics at court stems from the culture of courtiership, which has important similarities through all levels, lowest to highest. Courtiership in Elizabethan and Jacobean England is perhaps most conveniently imagined as a continuous dialectic between individual distinction and group co-optation or solidarity, with the relative effectiveness of strategic choices between these changing constantly. As Frank Whigham has shown in detail, Renaissance courtiership evolved a vocabulary of rhetorical performances which located the courtier and his or her deserts in terms of status, abilities and allegiances.[6] These performances worked within a dialectic that had two basic polarities, which we might call novelty and tradition. By rhetorical manipulation of this dialectic, the courtier worked to get himself and his or her party 'in' and keep others 'out'. *Topoi* of stasis and change variously served those both in and out to advance or solidify their positions. The court often functioned like a series of locked rooms, with those outside always trying keys and those inside constantly changing the locks.

The fundamental political activity to be observed at court is the movement of individual courtiers into and out of groups, often several overlapping ones at once. Some of these groups were clearly and even officially defined (the Privy Council, the Gentlemen of the Bedchamber), some much less so (the 'Sidney Circle'). Some offices came with groups of persons entailed on them in turn (the Master of the Horse, the Lord Chancellor), others created their own. There was even an office whose prerogative it was to challenge the very idea of office: the Royal Fool. 'Getting a place' at court was largely a matter of getting oneself attached to these more or less constituted groups. And one did so by making oneself distinctive in some manner to those in whose gift an office lay. At each level, there was a complex and delicate system, conscious at all times of its complexity and its delicacy. And, as with all highly-refined courtierly cultures, the mechanisms for negotiating with and for authority were often very subtle. Above all, the maintenance and management of a repertoire of representations, of oneself and others, was a daily necessity.[7] Distinction was the outcome of careful or lucky calculation as to the relative amounts of new and old, change and stasis, which would have maximum effect at a specific moment. Too much of either at the wrong time could prejudice potential advancement. The careers of many contemporary poets (Edmund Spenser, John Donne, Ben Jonson, Emilia Lanyer) can be charted through their success or failure in just these calculations.

Usually, progress through these nested hierarchies was gradual and subject to long delays. Yet it was always possible to imagine a performance or distinction so unparalleled and overwhelming that it would compel the wholesale reconfiguration of these delicate networks in a single stroke. No doubt this was the stuff courtierly dreams were made on, but not without cause: Robert Dudley seems always to have looked to some such coup d'oeil, as did his sorrier epigone, Robert Devereux. George Villiers, on the other hand, succeeded wildly. New and novel configurations were constantly forming, and a great skill of courtiership consisted in the successful arrangement of such new filiations and coalitions in one's own interest. Nothing galvanized a court like the emergence of a powerful novelty, whether it was a royal favourite or a fad in dress.

Representation of both the individual and the group was thus a paramount activity at court. By careful control of a whole panoply of representations, from handwriting to skill in arms, from facility at debate or jest to taste in clothes or doctrine, a courtier made his case as a candidate. The court swelled with performances, or eloquent disavowals of performance. The press of competing modes and instances of representation could grow hectic, if not chaotic. Semiosis might become at different times, or the same time, a tournament, a carnival, a marketplace, a Field of the Cloth of Gold. The labile and layered character of this *mundus symbolicus* has been well caught by D. G. Gordon, who speaks of

> that late Renaissance world where the relationship between image and what was imaged, sign and what was signified, was still patient of ambiguous readings, and in part powerful by very reason of that ambiguity. Here a king might move delicately but potently between fiction, representation, enaction, identification or participation. This was a world where the 'real', the 'historical', could cohabit with the feigned, where the hard political programme could, without distortion, undergo translation into symbol.[8]

Such fluidities were open not only to kings, though perhaps kings were more likely to lose themselves in them. The main point is the recurrent openness in semantic relations, the malleability of semiosis that a canny or a bold politician could use to advantage. How a particular image or symbolic gesture would resonate was always in question, but an image or resonance firmly enough embedded in the vocabulary of the court might prove a formidable asset, in part because it might then become an established mode of courtierly comportment in turn, attracting to itself the attentions of imitators, adherents and even patrons.

The glue to make such an image stick was often, in the masque and elsewhere, a combination of resolve in the execution and coherence in the design – a coherence for which the criteria might be aesthetic as much as political, if the distinction holds. And in a world where politics was conducted most of all through personal contact and physical access, images of political personality were often displayed on or enacted through the person itself. In a world where no important public event went unmarked by the display and exercise of an institutional authority, the ability to marshal and manage a convincing personal imagery, though not everything, was very useful. This ability may be thought of as a courtier's 'charisma', defining his or her skill at creating personal distinction and attracting to that distinction the desired attention within the fluid universe of values and symbols at court, that 'kaleidoscopic pattern that was perpetually changing its shape'.[9] Interventions in the circulation of symbols at court, and especially when they were sudden and dramatic, were thus like wagers attempting to exercise charisma to capture attention and endorsement. They could be wild successes, like Buckingham's debut, or terrible disasters, like the Essex revolt. Charisma, like Machiavellian *virtù*, was the dream of perfect control of an everchanging moment. And at the earlier Jacobean court, whose systemic character was newly complicated, it assumed an especial importance.

THE MULTIVARIATE COURT

As Martin Butler and Peter Holbrook have already suggested, recent literary accounts of the Jacobean court and its politics have sometimes left the impression that it sprang fully formed from the head of James, as though the courtiers all started from the King's line as they found it in, say, *Basilicon Doron*.[10] On this view, the 'masque-in-performance' becomes a kind of book, one ultimately both written and read by the King, so that the performance 'is only a pretext to present the recurrent motif of the king's wisdom'.[11] This 'discursive' politics was certainly an important element at the court of a king who prided himself on his intellectual accomplishments, and it would be a foolish courtier who did not know the King's published views. Yet reading a book and watching a masque are not, after all, the same. For one thing, masque emblems are constantly in motion. In a courtly arena where social 'mobility' is the central issue for almost everyone, the invitation to scrutinize an image of mobility is charged with something more than the merely readerly.[12]

In Elizabeth's day, the figure at the centre of the court labyrinth was, of course, the Queen, and though she might variously diffuse herself into powerful subordinates such as Leicester or the Cecils, her court remained basically unifocal. Under James, however, a different state of affairs emerged, greatly complicating the court's political architecture. As several commentators have pointed out, for the first time in forty-three years, the English court had a royal family, hence, and increasingly between 1603 and 1612, several foci of authority.[13] With the King often absent hunting, no single site of court activity, and the Queen and, later, Prince Henry looking to advance their own agendas, court culture fragmented into groups of intersecting images and constituencies, to which, as Malcolm Smuts notes, 'young innovators like Prince Henry and Arundel, older and more traditional English noblemen and Scots like James himself . . . each brought their own cultural preferences . . . and became models of different patterns of courtliness'.[14] Rather than a strict hierarchy and smooth transmission of power and representation downwards, the court was a loose, amorphous and multiple configuration of trends and possibilities. Three stones thrown into a pool make a more complex pattern than one.

In this novel environment, lacking a consistent lead and increasingly pressured into fractions, if not factions, novelty itself assumed a more prominent role in the dynamic of stasis and change, doubling and redoubling in complexity the hermeneutic patterns of court life. A policy option or appeal, a stylistic choice, which failed in one quarter might find welcome in another. Within a broad, continuing commitment to institutional traditions inherited from Elizabeth, there developed a more insistent pressure for distinction, affecting alike the tempo of fashion, the taste for innovation and the scale of display. Tensions between the three major court powers over matters of personality and policy created corresponding distinctions in the cultural and social arenas, radiating opportunity for the recruitment of novelty to highlight this or that posture. This pattern was repeated in turn at and between other levels of the court. Competitive display, connoisseurship, importation of continental novelty, enrolment of artist clients and reactions to all these, became the order of the day.

The masque was a kind of crisis in this hectic of signification. As an intense focus for the collective court eye, staged in a hall frequently full to bursting with confirmed and aspirant courtiers, the masque was saturated with significance. Its ambition to synthesize all the arts may be a direct outgrowth of this semiotic intensity. It was power and influence inflected as complex and novel motion, where a tussle of displays and potential meanings sought to reshape networks of policy through the creation and ordering of images, ideas and pleasures, extolling the delights of literal and figural mobility. Above all, and singularly unlike the public stages in this, the masque displayed the formation and movement of *groups*. Court politics is here imagined and presented as the complex motions of constituencies comprised of individuals articulating themselves through a common symbolic regime: knights, fairies, queens and so forth, each grouping newly minted and usually led by a 'head' figure. There is, in other words, not solely an absolutist politics on display here; there is also a representative one, an enacted image of 'parties'.[15]

Contrasting pressures thus appear in the Jacobean masque, as in other aspects of court life: one towards the production of novelty, and one towards the confirmation of 'things as they are'. With the King's consistent disinclination to join the dancing, the antinomies of mobility and stasis at court were even mapped out on the floor in the masque performance itself.[16] The dialectic between these two impulses leads to a constant need to restate again just how things as they are really are, with different groups competing for the right to define the terms of that restatement to their advantage. Hence, perhaps, the regularity with which masques, as central self-presentations of the court, came to be performed in James's England.

THE RITUAL OF THE FUTURE PERFECT

The political and social community of the court, like most early modern communities, expressed its sense of cohesion and collective endeavour through the authority of ceremony and ritual. One has to page only briefly through the voluminous compilations of John Nichols to note how much ceremonial activity there was 'at court'.[17] Seeking the stability of a traditional set of gestures, the masque often counterfeited a ritual aura for itself, affecting a high degree of solemnity. This impulse, however, did not draw directly on the Church, the ritual centre of English society, for the masque's accoutrements or rhetoric, since that would have been blasphemy. Often masque inventors, and especially Jonson and Jones, borrowed instead from the great reservoir of Renaissance 'second culture', using the fragmentary record of pagan religious practices – mysteries, orgies, and so forth – to set their nonce imaginings implicitly alongside church ritual as a secular counterpart with yet a quasi-religious ambience, and the dignity and prestige of antiquity. Thus to ratify as a political contract what the Church had performed as a spiritual one, Jonson and Jones mounted a second wedding *à l'antique* for Essex and Frances Howard, producing *Hymenaei* (1606) as an elaborate and detailed reconstitution of a Roman marriage rite. To lend *Oberon* (1611) a similarly solemn air, Jonson's Silenus describes the action as though it were a ritual of long standing, declaring:

> These are nights
> Solemn to the shining rites
> Of the fairy prince and knights,
> While the moon their orgies lights.   (lines 37–40)

Heralded by Dionysiac revels and Silenic mysteries, the Prince's inaugural masque becomes a traditional chivalric ceremony in which the Prince and his fairy knights 'come of right to pay / Their annual vows' (lines 245–6), as if Princes of Wales had always done so.

The usefulness of the doctrinally 'empty' character of pagan antiquity can be clearly seen here. As an acknowledged site of fictions, it was as fundamentally malleable as church ritual was inflexible, and could lend itself to constant reconstruction that served a political imperative for novelty even while balancing this with the suasive illusion of solemnity and tradition. The impulse towards ceremony spills over also into the antimasque, which presents the parallel, lesser orgies of a subgroup or even a malefic faction, as with *Oberon*'s satyrs or the witches of *The Masque of Queens* (1609). These in turn are later transfigured by the true ritual that supervenes. The masque thus offered a useful forum for exploring the current complexion of relations between the various court powers, performed within the aura of a kind of miraculous stasis lent by its evocation of a ceremonial potency of word and gesture. Finding an apt conjugation of symbols was the central task of the 'invention' of the masque. But the right invention, framed by large investments in money, in time, in symbolic resources, in prestige, could promote this conjugation as a symbolic assertion with which other assertions would have to negotiate in their turn, in future.

This latter point – the implicit inclination of the masque towards the future – is what most distinguishes it from the ecclesiastical ceremonies to which it so longingly looks. Despite the quasi-ritual ambience with which it cloaks its penchant for novelty, the content of the masque is not exhausted, is not even fully realized, in the present. As a political statement, the masque necessarily tends to look forward, if only towards the morrow on which the masquers will have acquired a sort of symbolical aura or 'afterglow' from their night's exertions. Yet even this small increment might be significant for the dancer who had chosen rightly or performed well. The masque aims above all, in the annunciations articulated by all its theatrical prophecies, acclamations and 'discoveries', to reveal the very moment when the future begins, even (perhaps most of all) when that future takes the form of a revived past.[18] The masque wishes to summon into being, according to the designs of its sponsors, the form and pressure of a future body. Hence the necessity for the antimasque to be always an ante-masque, not an interruption or a postlude. And hence also the masque's insistently hortatory tone and preference for fictions of the magical in invention, language and action, since magic also brings into being through invocatory power.

The secret anxiety of the masque, which its ritual character attempts solemnly, fervently to deny, is that its magical gestures will turn out in reality every bit as ephemeral as the endings of many masques admit they themselves are. Or, to put it another way, had Prince Henry not died when he did, we might now see *Oberon, the Fairy Prince* as a performance figuring and announcing a radical change in the direction of English history. *Oberon* comes forth on the New Year's Day of Henry's first full year of majority; as it turned out, his only one. It is insistently present before us. Yet its fullest political meaning remains unrevealed, is couched in a sort of future perfect – it 'will have been' the sign announcing the glory to come, the promise of primacy.[19] In this, the

masque's basic difference from the rituals it often apes is clearly manifest. No ritual is, qua ritual, its own precedent. Yet this is what *Oberon*
wishes to be. By the force of its imagining, it seeks to make itself an
inevitable coordinate for future representation, an act of novelty which
instantly renovates courtly tradition in its own name. Masques being
much less semiotically self-contained than plays, one result of Prince
Henry's early death is that a whole array of symbolic precedents that
Oberon may have sought to assert never came into being.

THE BODY OF THE TIME

To be effective, however, this ritual arraying of the body of the time
with new symbolic meanings had to be performed publicly, and above
all by the figure whom it most concerned to be transformed, the representative 'head' of the symbolic push. King James was, throughout his
reign, content to repose in his immense reserve of institutionally guar-
anteed, divinely ratified charisma. Not so his Queen and Prince, who
took opportunity year by year to restate or rephrase their claims to
eminence. Yet this undertaking was not without risk. Above all, the
masque had to be well and convincingly performed. As a 'sacrament
of novelty', the masque could not rely on institutional authority alone
to make up deficiencies.[20] A new masque had to argue its case each
time through the rhetoric of the performance, and, in particular, through
its dancing.[21]

Dancing a lead role in a masque was thus a deliberate gamble.
Having become a hypothesized emblem of himself, the masqued courtier had to 'argue out' the hypothesis by enacting the coherence and
decorum of the emblem as a functioning body. If you tripped while
tripping, you could lose your symbolic all. It is not therefore surprising that the eyewitnesses we have, much to the disappointment of
literary historians, tend to speak little of the poetry, a little more of the
music, but much of the design, costumes and dancing, and of the
performances of particular figures. Dancing was where the real action
was. Orazio Busino's account of *Pleasure Reconciled to Virtue* (1618), for
instance, noted of Prince Charles that he was not 'once seen to do a
step out of time when dancing, whereas one cannot perhaps say so
much for the others', and Ambassador Correr's politic delight at Prince
Henry's performance in *Oberon* is evident in the epigraph quoted above.[22]
Conversely, the French ambassador at *Queens* in 1609 had arranged in

advance through 'a Lady friend of mine' that Queen Anne should *not* invite him to dance, since it was not his forte and 'I did not wish to make the assembly laugh, as the Spanish ambassador did last year'.[23] Such emphases confirm a point made years ago by Stephen Orgel: the key moment of the masque is not the 'discovery' of the device, but the moment when the hypothetical body that proposes that device proffers its hand and asks the court to accept its reality by joining it in the dance.[24] In dancing, the moving figure was making a case, inscribing with fluidity of gesture and perfection of poise a certain convocation of politic terms.

Charisma, ritual and magic, the currency of the masque's political trading, are all intent on bodies. In a bureaucratic and technological age, or an academic milieu, we may forget how much authority as a living bodily presence was important to earlier polities. Important statements of policy were made through its exercises, its tastes, its touches, and its posture. Its image was used to betoken its authority through coins and seals, signatures and portraits.[25] And among the rhetorics of the gentle body developed over the sixteenth century, dancing was one of the most powerful, perhaps because, like its rivals fencing and horsemanship, it was complex and hard to master.[26] Dancing was singled out for attention in treatises on courtly behaviour from Elyot on, and specific manuals of dancing were available from Robert Copland's *Manner of Dancing* of 1521 to John Playford's chauvinist *English Dancing Master* of 1651.[27] Above all, these treatises emphasize the dance as a rhetorical arena for the efflorescence of noble character through demeanour and gesture, through virtuosity and vigour of bodily control. Dancing was social signing.

It thus becomes clear why the performance of the masque invested so much energy and preparation not only in dancing, but particularly in *new* dancing. It was not enough merely to prove that one was a good dancer, though there was plenty of opportunity for caprioles, high-stepping galliards and the like in the revels. It was also necessary to be seen offering newly devised, preferably challenging, choreographies, painstakingly rehearsed over weeks and now performed without a false step, as though the easiest thing in the world. There is some evidence that the dances for *Oberon* may have been particularly complex, as composer Ferrabosco and choreographers Confesse and Herne had their 'rewards' increased by order to compensate them for their 'pains bestowed almost six weeks continually', presumably in devising and rehearsing the dances.[28] Prince Henry's early return from Royston,

according to Correr 'to arrange a masque for Christmas', may have
been for these extended rehearsals.[29] Such pains bespeak a special care
to ensure both the invention and the execution of the dances was of
a superior standard. By the time the dancer came forward, he needed
to be footing-perfect. For *Oberon*, Correr's report of 'the grace of the
Prince's every movement' suggests a distinct success. But for all the
pleasure taken in his ease, the dancer walked a political tight-rope.

In fact, the pleasure in his ease was the foundation of the dancer's
success. The caprioles of George Villiers, the future Duke of Buckingham, in various court masques of James's middle years make this
connection especially clear. *Mercury Vindicated* of 6 January 1615 was
young George's first masque and, according to John Chamberlain,
principally intended as his vehicle. Donne notes in a letter of 18 December that the rising favourite, recently made the King's cupbearer,
was already 'practising' for it three weeks in advance, and even sardonic Chamberlain, though he did not like the masque, conceded it
'excellent dancing'.[30] The King ordered it repeated two days later.
In April of that year, Villiers was knighted and made a Gentleman of
the Bedchamber, and the following year, perhaps between appearances
in *The Golden Age Restored* (performed at court on 1 and 6 January 1616),
he was appointed Master of the Horse (4 January). Another year, and
the recently-created Viscount Villiers was promoted Earl of Buckingham on the same day as *The Vision of Delight* (6 January 1617), at which
'the newmade Earl . . . danced with the Queen' before the King and
court, including 'the Virginian woman Pocahontas'.[31] And at *Pleasure
Reconciled to Virtue*, when King James grew impatient and shouted out
'Why is there no dancing? What did you make me come here for? The
devil take all of you, dance!', Buckingham 'at once sprang forward . . .
cutting a set of high and very minute capers, with so much grace and
agility that he made everyone admire and love his person and ap-
peased the ire of his angry Lord'. Five days earlier, he had been made
a marquis. James patted his face tenderly.[32]

Any account of the masque in performance that rests content with
the static elaborations of emblem and motto without fixing its eye on
the kinetic suasiveness of the dancing figure will miss much of this
central action. The hieroglyphics of invention, the elaborated learning,
the machinery of the *impresa* are condensed and absorbed into the
body and make their address through it. Gordon's epitome of the
mode catches this almost accidentally when he insists that in such
symbolic ambiences 'a King might *move*'.[33] Motion is of the essence.

The masques themselves regularly speak of this motion. In *Oberon*, a song calls on the masquers to show 'the virtue of their feet' since 'with you it still should fare / As with the air of which you are' (lines 318, 321–2). In *Pleasure Reconciled To Virtue*, several songs educe the complex rhetoric of dance, as when Daedalus exhorts the masquers:

> Come on, come on; and where you go,
>   So interweave the curious knot,
> As ev'n th' observer scarce may know
>   Which lines are Pleasure's and which not.
> . . . . . .
> Then, as all actions of mankind
>   Are but a labyrinth or maze,
> So let your dances be entwined,
>   Yet not perplex men unto gaze;
> But measured, and so numerous too,
>   As men may read each act you do,
> And when they see the graces meet,
>   Admire the wisdom of your feet.
> For dancing is an exercise
>   Not only shows the mover's wit,
> But maketh the beholder wise,
>   As he hath power to rise to it.   (lines 224–7, 232–43)

Daedalus calls the onlookers specifically to an awareness that dancing is charged with more freight of meaning than at first appears, that it demands an act of deliberate intelligence. The exhortation that the dance be not overly labyrinthine or amazing necessarily promotes the suspicion that some further subtle thread might be encrypted in it and its occasion, just above the reach of ordinary wit. And in the later *Masque of Augurs* (1622), which inaugurated Jones's rebuilt Banqueting House, dancing Roman priests, the Salii of Mars, combined choreographic prophecy with the use of antique ritual already discussed.

An unusually large amount of music survives from *Oberon*, allowing us to make more specific observations on the particular effects sought from the dancing in this masque, despite the absence of any choreography.[34] The music for the antimasque dance of satyrs, described by Jonson as 'full of gesture and swift motion' and by a Spanish eyewitness as danced 'with a thousand strange gestures affording great pleasure', shows many shifts of rhythm and metre in short strains and bursts, encompassing five changes of time-signature, together with other devices of contrast, such as fermatas followed by rapid scale passages. Andrew Sabol comments, 'one senses very clearly that this is antic music composed in close collaboration with a choreographer'.[35] The point here is the attention thrown by the piece on the movements of the dancers' bodies as disorganized, piecemeal and chaotic. Typically, it is less the melodic or harmonic than the rhythmic register which expresses disorder here, anchoring its perception as much in the body as the ear. By contrast, the three dances written for the Prince and masquers are much smoother and more regular, with a single time-change to mark the final exit.[36] The relative simplicity of these dances no doubt aids their accurate performance by non-professionals, but it also showcases the smoothness and control of the courtly performers, their homogeneity of style achieved within the decorum of the device, and hence frames the political rhetoric of moving bodies for the piece as a whole.

PLEASURE RECONCILED TO POLITICS

Along with the dancing, eyewitnesses in their private accounts emphasize the masque's careful creation of a concerted decorum of pleasures. Ambassador Guistiniani's comments on *The Masque of Beauty* (1608) are typical:

I must just touch on the splendour of the spectacle, which was worthy of her Majesty's greatness. The apparatus and the cunning of the stage machinery were a miracle, the abundance and beauty of the lights immense, and the music and dance most sumptuous. But what beggared all else and possibly exceeded the public expectation was the wealth of pearls and jewels that adorned the Queen and her ladies, so abundant and splendid that in everyone's opinion no other court could have displayed such pomp and riches.[37]

Even Francis Bacon, though he condescends to the masque as trivial and superfluous, concedes that its proper function is to offer a regime of pleasure for the eye of the court, as when he remarks that 'the alterations of scenes, so it be quietly, and without noise, are things of great beauty, and pleasure: for they feed and relieve the eye, before it be full of the same object'. Likewise, he reflects the anticipatory aura of the action when he calls for masque dances before the revels: 'for it draws the eye strangely, and makes it with great pleasure, to desire to see that, it cannot perfectly discern'.[38] The role of Dame Pleasure in promoting the acceptance of the emblem embodied through the magic of charismatic performance is quite clearly suggested here, and if Bacon in the end rejects such pleasures as 'but toys' and no true ground of courtiership, we should recall his own recurrent failure to temper his ambition with charisma.

Oberon is characteristic of the masque in its invocation of pleasure's appeal. The satyrs in particular confidently expect that the arrival of the Fairy Prince which will set the cap on their reveling will be accompanied by an increase in both quantity and quality of pleasure. A kind of ultimate Master of the Revels, he will provide 'larger caves', 'ivory staves' and 'better wine', improved costumes and ornaments such as 'powders sweet', 'silver loops', 'bracelets', 'garlands' and special 'bells' for dancing.[39] These satyrine sensualities are also to be complemented, we later learn, by the moral and intellectual 'bliss' associated with 'fairyland' and with the beneficent rule of King James.

It is important to note how many kinds of bodily and intellectual pleasure are invoked together in the masque, as though to maximize the appeal being made by making it through as many channels as possible. The masque's regular association with banqueting is relevant here, and even its usual consignment to the status of 'afterpiece', which connects it with the sweetness of a dessert or confectionery.[40] Jonson himself seems to acknowledge the analogy even in denying it when he speaks of the nourishing meat offered the intellect by the masque, and consigns sauces, jellies and booze to the fringes of the antimasque. It is as if the evening's entertainments are a dish to be consumed.[41] What Bacon refers to as 'pleasure', 'grace', 'elegancy' – all the appeals that the emblem-in-motion can manufacture through its brightness, quickness, clarity, even its fragility – are sweet suasions, to help the symbolic meringue go down the courtly gullet and into the political bloodstream. And though this lightness might seem to conflict with the masque's reach after ritual solemnity, the two are sides of the same coin, inflecting again between them a flickering dynamic of change and stasis, and offering a strategic line of retreat in the sad case of a failed representation. Though a gingerbread host is an odd idea, it nicely captures the composite flavour of the Jacobean court antinomies.

THE PROPER HEIR

The several elements of the Jacobean masque are now assembled. The masque proposes a novel complexion for court politics through a rhetoric of performance that reshapes the symbolic order and reassigns charisma at pleasure's lead. I want now to examine in detail Prince Henry's 'coming-of-age' masque, *Oberon, the Fairy Prince* of 1611. But in order to evaluate the work done by the performance of this masque and the poetic means invented to do it, it is necessary first to be acquainted with the Prince as competitor.

The year preceding *Oberon* had already been a remarkable one for the sixteen-year-old Prince, as Martin Butler has suggested in his essay for this volume.[42] At its outset, he had had himself presented as man-at-arms and Brittanic hero in his Twelfth Night *Barriers*, in which he and six companions challenged opponents to joust at a standing bar in the masquing hall. Ben Jonson, commissioned to write speeches for the occasion, produced a pageant in which Merlin and a stellified Arthur prophesy (at length) glory and empire for Henry.[43] The image of the virile young Prince clearly diverged from his father's pacific policy and offered to revive the 'war party' symbology of the now-dead Essex, and, before him, of Leicester. The European political context suggests that Henry was grooming himself to join an upcoming Franco-Protestant crusade against Habsburg power in Western Europe.[44]

In May of that year, however, Henri IV of France was assassinated, throwing the English court into panic and sinking hopes of any Grand Alliance, as Marie de Medicis became regent of the child Louis XIII. Though negotiations went on for form's sake, and resulted in a watered-down treaty, it soon became clear that France was much less interested.[45] At home, the court went into mourning, and measures were taken to strengthen security. These included the expulsion of all Catholic clergy and Jesuits, the banishment of all recusants from within ten miles of the court, and the administration of the Oath of Allegiance to all court officers, lawyers, university students and clergy. The Commons and Lords also took it voluntarily, and the Lords administered it in turn to all their servants and sacked any who refused.[46]

Henry's next substantial public appearances were the celebrations around his investiture as Prince of Wales in June. Though not as extensive as he wished, these included a water-borne pageant entry to London (31 May), the creation of twenty-four Knights of the Bath (3 June), his investiture as Prince of Wales in the Court of Requests before the nobility, Parliament and Lord Mayoral party, followed by a great ceremonial banquet (4 June), the Queen's masque *Tethys' Festival* (1610) stressing martial and maritime traditions and including the presentation of a jewelled sword to Henry (5 June), and finally a great tournament followed by a mock seafight against the Turks, with magnificent fireworks (6 June).[47]

Nor was Henry's commitment to the military merely symbolic. With keen interest, the Prince was following the construction at Woolwich of the great ship which was to head the refurbished Royal Navy.[48] He visited it often in this year – on 31 January, 25 April, 18 and 19

June (the latter with the King on his birthday), 24 September, and 6 December – and was in regular contact with Phineas Pette, the master-shipwright and his servant, who rode to Nonsuch to consult with Henry on 31 August and received from him a buck 'killed with his [Henry's] own hand' on 20 September.

On 24 September, the Royal Family and the court converged on Woolwich for the great launching, the King having first ascertained that no 'persons disaffected might have bored some holes privily in the ship to sink her'. However, the event was disappointing: the tide was low, the adverse wind strong and the ship so crowded that it stuck fast on the bottom and could not be launched until the next tide. The King, diarrhetic from overeating grapes, took the court away, but Prince Henry, who was to have named the ship, returned with his train about two in the morning, crossing Blackheath through a violent thunderstorm, 'his invincible spirit daunted with nothing'. The Prince then performed the naming ceremony 'standing upon the poop . . . with a great deal of expression of princely joy . . . solemnly calling her by the name of the Prince Royal, the trumpets sounding all the while'.[49] The name is nicely suggestive of his aspirations.

Continental affairs reappear in November with the visit of Christian, Prince of Anhalt and chief general of the United Provinces armies that had fought that summer, with English assistance, for the Protestant claimant to the Duchy of Cleves. Henry is not mentioned in connection with this visit,[50] but Correr reported on 25 November (15 old style) that the Prince was returning to London early to arrange his masque, which 'he would have liked to present on horseback could he have obtained the King's consent'.[51] Martial images were still uppermost.

A further context for reading Henry's political development and persona at this time is his move to reform his household finances, followed by his undertaking a general review of his revenues and estates as Prince of Wales and Duke of Cornwall. Sir Charles Cornwallis, his Treasurer, speaks of him in this respect as 'more like a grave, wise, and ancient counsellor . . . than so young and great a prince'. Such testimony recorded of Henry by his followers suggests a comparison with his father's ongoing fiscal difficulties, which had come to a head in this year with the failure of the Great Contract, Salisbury's latest attempt to put the crown's fiscal house on a reliable foundation.[52]

Henry's shaping of himself as a figure with specific symbolic resonances was far advanced by the time he appeared on the stage in *Oberon*. Yet the opportunity to cement these connotations the more firmly to his person through public performance at the head of a masquer group was eagerly and resolutely grasped. Correr informs us that the masque had originally been intended to form part of the special celebrations to welcome the French emissary, Marshal de Laverdin, when he brought over the new treaty for the King's signature. Marie de Medicis, averse to such publicity for a treaty she no longer supported, delayed the Marshal's departure for England, which seriously displeased the English court, as Correr overheard the Queen remarking to Salisbury at *Oberon*.[53] Had de Laverdin been present, Henry's danced evocation of a chivalric reawakening would no doubt have had an added point.

'WHO RISETH HERE?'

The preceding set of contexts helps us see how the political stakes at the Jacobean court on New Year's Day, 1611 brought the basic, recurrent polarities of tradition and novelty into unusually clear definition. The Prince himself, it seems, was beginning to appropriate novelty as a banner, and his move to do so forced the usual antinomies of court culture into sharper relief. His recent majority, his reform of his household, his sponsorship of a revived navy, his new push on behalf of a more militant Protestantism, his very youth formed a sort of magnetic field beginning to affect other aspects of the court, like so many iron filings. Novelty, prophecy, change and the future tend to become the domain of the Prince, while tradition, stasis and the received remain with the King. Between these two sets of terms, and perhaps the object of their struggle, lies the present, the moment of *Oberon, the Fairy Prince*. Each novelty and each traditional gesture discovered in *Oberon* is drawn into this delicate hermeneutic spiderweb. The fantastical and elaborate satyr dances, the stage design with its first use of the *scena ductilis*, the mix of Italian, French and English architecture in the fairy castle with its novel 'perspective' interior, the avant-garde musical texture – all these point to the newness of the Prince.[54] Yet this newness is balanced by an equal emphasis on the past, on the tradition of 'homage' being enacted. Newness is in the service of imagined ancient rites for which Jonson printed scholarly glosses. And yet again, in these rites, the past is being reborn, 'quickened by a second birth' for the future, that future which *Oberon* inaugurates as its claim about 'how things are'. Though the present is the moment the masque addresses, it is the future it most imagines. And though the King's presence (and treasury) is what calls this charismatic ambience into being, the potency of that ambience arises as much from the figure of motion as from the one at rest, even at rest on the throne. The present, like the dancer, lives a delicate and shifting balance.

For though symbol was the currency of the court, the masque gives the King no monopoly on coining, let alone circulation. It has often been noted that Jones's stage-designs for masques took the King as their focal point.[55] Less remarked is the necessary consequence: if the King saw the show as 'naturally' oriented on him, other courtiers – the further off, the more – saw it as artificially so, as in fact distorted in order to be so. The implications of this built-in ambivalence of view-point can be extended, and in *Oberon*, under the pressure of Henry's 'personal' charisma, such multiplicity of resonance becomes itself a poetic method. Singleness of focus is doubled and deepened in the textures the masque offers for interpretation: what relation is there between the rowdy carnality of the satyrs and the increasingly seedy reputation of James's court?[56] Is there some especial point to the fact that 'the Prince took the Queen' to dance three times in the revels, as the Spanish observer remarked? Was it really tiredness that caused the King to end the performance? Such questions are inscrutable now, and perhaps any latencies were never fully realized. But though we cannot recover *Oberon*'s full wardrobe of nuances – the turn of a foot, the crook of a leg, the offer of a hand – we can see in some detail how Jonson's script registered and figured its own occasion as an ambival-ent weaving of tradition with novelty, the established with the emer-gent. This detail casts important light on the political significances borne by *Oberon*'s performance of novelty.

An allusive ambivalence governed from the very outset. The sight that greeted the audience upon arrival is recorded in our eyewitness account:

The new hall of the palace was furnished as usual with its galleries round about, a green carpet on the floor, a dais at the top for the king and queen. At the bottom a very large curtain painted with the kingdoms of England, Scot-land and Ireland, with the legend above *Separata locis concordi pace figantur* [May what is separated in place be joined by harmonious peace].[57]

This opening image is not simple. The motto appears to refer to the map of Britain it surmounts, united in peace under James. Yet this is no more than a pretext or first viewing, and there is more behind. Jones's design for the unfolding masque, with its series of discoveries and its careful placement of Henry and James at opposite foci of its perspective, allows a second, rather more charged reading of 'what is separated' to a courtier with a quick eye and a pregnant mind. What is on the one hand an unobjectionable rubric of the Jacobean *imperium* becomes a sidelong comment on the divided complexion of affairs at court.

A third resonance brings us specifically to Jonson's contribution to the occasion, and suggests that he may have been responsible for the motto. The line is in fact adapted from Ovid's *Metamorphoses* (I.25) where it appears as *'dissociata locis concordi pace ligavit'* and refers to God's (or Nature's) activity in settling and ordering the warfare of elemental atoms at the time of Creation.[58] In addition to its variously specific political applications, then, there is here a 'metapolitical' or philosophic implication. The shaping activity of creation is the exercise of an ordering power over the threat of chaos, hence the presence of an apprehending intelligence ordering the masque itself as an act of balance or concilation between disparate impulses, political atomies in constant mobility. Politics and poetics order one another's flux into the purposive activity of performance. It is a reasonable assumption that these implications would not have been lost on at least some in the classically literate assembly.

We can go further still in this series of allusive veils or 'discoveries', and when we do so we come to the heart of Jonson's responsiveness to the ambivalent weightings of novelty and tradition in the politics of *Oberon*, here metamorphosed into or fused with a more strictly poetic ambivalence that picks up the same charged polarities and orients itself along the same lines of force. The Ovidian passage in turn alludes to Virgil's Sixth Eclogue, as Jonson surely knew, since he had made the latter the foundation of his invention in *Oberon*. And the Sixth Eclogue provides Jonson not only characters and poetic language for the action of his masque, but also deeply frames and glosses his and his work's central ambivalences, both poetic and political, through its own exploration of tradition, novelty, ripeness and poetic prophecy.

Virgil's poem is itself strangely diffuse and ambivalent. Like many of the *Eclogues*, it is heavily conscious of its own poetic inheritance, as Virgil works to locate and assert himself as a new poetic presence in a crowded tradition.[59] The poem, whose first word is 'prima', opens with a prologue in which Virgil ties his own poetic production allusively to Theocritus's *Idylls* and Callimachus's mythographic *Aitia*. But Virgil explicitly balks at taking up the greater onus of epic, despite the apparent request of his friend and patron, Varus. Instead the body of the poem tells how two boys, Chromis and Mnasyllos, caught Silenus asleep in a cave, bound him with his own garlands, and extorted a song from him.[60] For his release, the mantic Silenus sings of the Creation, epitomizes various myths of forlorn love (following, as we are later told, a lament of Apollo for Hyacinthus), and addresses the question of poetic vocation, only ceasing at the reluctant approach of night. The poem moves through a variety of stances – prophetic, mythographic, elegaic, encomiastic – to conclude nowhere in particular, and scholars both ancient and modern have reached little consensus over its patterning. For all its eloquence and virtuosity, anxiety about its own poetic maturity – its relation to the figure of poetic capability it imagines in Silenus – seems a dominating concern.[61]

Jonson mines Virgil's poem pervasively in *Oberon*, not only for his satyrs with their own prophetic Silenus as leader or shepherd, but for small details of diction and image everywhere. Silenus's tankard in Virgil ('gravis . . . cantharus') reappears in the masque as 'Hath his tankard touched your brain?' (line 15).[62] The sylvans that are 'caves / of sleep' (lines 116–117) recall Silenus lying asleep in a cave ('in antro / Silenum . . . somno . . . iacentum'), and display Jonson's witty reading of Virgil's studied *homoioptoton*. Jonson's praise of James who 'keeps the age up in a head of gold' (line 268) picks up Virgil's reference to Saturn's reign ('Saturnia regna'), and the King's sunlike power that 'quickens everything / Like a new nature' (lines 272–273) is Virgil's new sun that amazes the earth ('novum terrae stupeant lucescere solem'). Most prominent of all, Silenus's powerful Creation hymn in Virgil revives again in Jonson's cosmic and elemental song for Oberon's meeting with James:

> Melt earth to sea, sea flow to air,
> And air fly into fire,
> Whilst we in tunes to Arthur's chair
> Bear Oberon's desire.   (lines 220–3)[63]

Moreover, Jonson's entire conception of satyrs and fairies dancing together seems to be a response to the poetic power of Silenus's song, which makes Fauns and wild beasts dance in metre ('in numerum Faunos ferasque . . . ludere').[64] This confirms an implicit identification between Jonson and Silenus as poets, and invites special attention to the latter's role as prophet and exponent of Oberon in the masque. Virgil's insistence that 'I do not sing uncommanded' ('non iniussa cano' line 9) becomes Jonson's licence as the Prince's midnight laureate.[65]

What in particular seems to galvanize Jonson's response to Virgil's poem in *Oberon* is its ambivalence towards its own claim to mature poetic status, encoded in the figuring and practice of echo. Echo inhabits Virgil's verse as phonic effect ('si quis tamen haec quoque, si quis / captus amore leget'), as narrated event ('ut litus Hyla, Hyla omne sonaret'), and as allusion to earlier works of Theocritus, Callimachus and Hesiod. And as the eclogue develops and accumulates its own sonorities, so its ability to harness the threat of echo also increases, so that its last instance evokes Virgil's own strong aspirations to prolonged poetic resonance: 'He sings: the smitten valleys carry it up to the stars' ('ille canit: pulsae referunt ad sidera valles' (line 84)). Having made this ringing assertion, as though it had reached its goal, the eclogue immediately closes.

In *Oberon*, Jonson takes over Virgil's concern with the figure of echo and adapts it to place his work at once poetically and politically. Echo is where the performance begins. An echo of 'his cornet' at first deceives the first satyr into believing the time is ripe for sport, and only when this echo is diagnosed and mythographized as an unwanted haunting can licit reveling get underway:

> Or I doubt it was the vain
> Echo did me entertain.
> Prove again –   *He wound the*
>   I thought 'twas she!   *second time and*
> Idle nymph, I pray thee, be   *found it.*
> Modest, and not follow me;
> I nor love myself nor thee.
> *Here he wound the third time and was answered by another satyr . . .*
>
>   (lines 17–23)

Yet though both Echo and Narcissus are conjured away, she remains everywhere in the masque – and perhaps he too, despite denials, has his place in the general self-eyeing of both Prince and poet in the masque occasion. 'Vain echo' may not be allowed to 'entertain' this night, but other kinds of echo are harnessed to good purpose, and Virgil's echoing of Theocritus and Callimachus is itself echoed in Jonson's use of Virgil, whom he in turn calls, in deference and self-interest, 'the most learned of poets'.[66]

In *Oberon, the Fairy Prince*, the issues of prematurity, priority and succession that swirl around poetic echo are redoubled in the politics of the occasion, so that relations between Prince Henry and his father are interpreted through precisely the same *topoi*. The masque's treatment of Henry figures him complexly as a successor to his father, and attaches this generational transition to Jonson's assertion of his own emergent poetic prowess. Thus while the first satyr's opening question 'See you not who riseth here?' ostensibly refers to the moon, it also takes in Henry's rising star at court and with it Jonson's ambitions as his poet, singing 'not without orders'. In *Oberon*, we have an unusually clear example of political and literary negotiation self-consciously sharing a set of central tropes wherein each interprets the other. It is not simply a matter of either providing a ground for the other, for it is as true to say that Prince Henry interprets Jonson's dilemma as the reverse.

Silenus's description of Oberon before he is 'discovered' makes these complex tensions especially apparent, even as it hides them in the codes of mythography. The key comparison is of Henry/Oberon with 'Phoebus, when he crownèd sung' (line 51). Jonson's note tells us, citing Tibullus, that on this occasion 'Apollo is said, after Jupiter had put Saturn to flight, to have sung his father's victory to the harp'.[67] A song sung in praise of a son who has just deposed his father is a risky analogue for *Oberon*, and Jonson does not dwell on the point. But the very fact that he includes it suggests the inevitability with which scenarios of supplanting are drawn into the masque. Oberon is at once like Apollo, the chanter of paeans in praise of his father, and, more remotely but not less urgently, like the hymned deposer himself. The contraries of encomium and rebellion fold together as Jonson has Apollo sing what Jonson/Henry would do: dazzle the world with novelty, even at the risk of seeing Jacobean/Virgilian 'Saturnia regna' overthrown.[68]

At the same time, of course, such aggression is hardly admissible as a motive either for masquing or for poetry, and gestures of solemn and ceremonial deference hedge it all around. Tension between these impulses is focussed throughout the masque in the figure with which it both begins and ends: the moon. The masque returns with a certain obsessiveness to the moon which floods the dancing floor with its reflected light. The provocative opening query, 'Who riseth here?', points to it, the satyrs tease it in song, a 'full song . . . by all the voices' hymns it, the day-star chants its fading at the close. It is clearly the central emblem of the evening's revels. As an image of 'reflected glory' the moon serves Jonson's purpose well, and insofar as it 'now borrows from a greater light' (line 306) it provides a visual counterpart to acoustic echo, pointing decorously at James's sunlike majesty and Virgil's 'novum . . . solem'. Yet other aspects of this moon's secondariness are less easily subservient. The satyrs in their song, for instance, harbour a suspicion that she may be both more and less than she appears:

> Now, my cunning lady, moon,
> Can you leave the side so soon
>   Of the boy you keep so hid?
> Midwife Juno sure will say
> This is not the proper way
>   Of your paleness to be rid.
> But perhaps it is your grace
> To wear sickness i' your face,
>   That there might be wagers laid
>   Still, by fools, you are a maid.   (lines 186–95)

This mockery is very much germane to the issues of maturity and self-advertisement that subtend the poetics and politics of echoing in the masque. The moon, say the satyrs, is pretending to an innocence she does not have. Her pale and secondary character is a mere mask for a more calculated knowingness. She is more advanced than she appears in the wiles of the world, and her fake innocence disarms the audience she would deceive. If the moon figures the rising young Prince whose 'orgies' she chiefly lights, the implications are bold. The satyrs' question to the sylvan guards is one to the audience also: 'Be your eyes yet moon-proof?' (line 168). Are we certain we are looking on these revels in the right light?[69]

If this is still equivocal, the later treatment of the moon's light in *Oberon* is less so. Despite, or perhaps because of, its echoing luminosity, moonlight becomes the preferred ambience of the masque's annunciations. The song that follows the opening dances of the masque proper, for instance, declares that

> The solemn rites are well begun,
>   And though but lighted by the moon,
> They show as rich as if the sun
>   Had made this night his noon.
> But may none wonder that they are so bright;
> The moon now borrows from a greater light.
>
> (lines 301–6)

Here moonlight outshines the sun by borrowing from the splendour of James. Yet the invocation of the pair sun/moon against the pair son/father here suggests by the pun that this night is in fact the son's noon, a time in which sonship shows itself in its fuller glory, even in the face of the father. The couplet appended to the quatrain seeks belatedly to allay or finesse an intimation of Henry's emergent authority already echoing in the ear.

Though the rhetoric of the masque formally defers to James and day (and Virgil) as the reigning powers, its secret self-investment in night is disclosed not only through a plangent longing for the latter's 'rich' prolongation, but, more conclusively, by Jonson's tactic of reversing the final sequence of Virgil's poem, where Silenus sings all day 'until Vesper came forth in an unwilling Heaven and ordered flocks to the folds and their number told' ('cogere donec ovis stabulis numerumque referre / iussit et invito processit Vesper Olympo' (lines 85–6). In *Oberon*, this reluctance is transferred to the return of that day, at the King's command, that puts an end to the reign of the moon:

> Oh yet how early, and before her time,
> The envious morning up doth climb,
>   Though she not love her bed!
> What haste the jealous sun doth make,
> His fiery horses up to take,
>   And once more show his head!
> Lest, taken with the brightness of this night,
> The world should wish it last, and never miss his light.
>
> (lines 361–8)

In Jonson's vision, Vesper and Phosphorus exchange places, and it is the latter, 'the herald of the day', who is the messenger of what is allusively an 'unwilling Heaven'.[70] Jonson's troping reversal enlists Virgil in strengthening the case for night as the time for 'solemn rites' that announce the new, against the 'jealous sun'. The question of that sun's connection to James who, 'as it was about midnight and the King somewhat tired . . . sent word that they should make an end' remains patient, like the opening curtain motto, of reading from several perspectives, and could only have disclosed its fuller resonances in the future, that is to say, as prophecy.[71]

FIGURES OF OCCASION

This analysis of *Oberon* may seem to have returned exploration of the Jacobean masque to the very point that I began by wishing to depart from: a focus on discursive at the expense of performative concerns. Yet the insistently deictic character of the text ties its allusiveness directly to Henry's performance and suggests that it is there that the common tropology of Jonson's aspirations as poet and Henry's as Prince will be justified. The participation of each in the project of the masque interprets the other's delicate situation as potential supplanter,

but only the immediate physical presence of Prince Henry as a brilliant performer before a delighted spectatorship can realize the full
subtlety of Jonson's poetic response to him. Only Prince Henry's personal and charismatic 'participation' makes this night a noon, so that
the figure of the Prince, the figure Jonson makes for him, and the
figure Jonson makes from him for himself come down before their
audiences inextricably intertwined. The literary and political histories
that participate in the present essay likewise discover themselves mutually precipitated.

Oberon is a striking example of what might be called the figurative
character of occasion in the masque, peculiar most of all because of
Prince Henry's early death. By a mortal irony, this night was indeed
his noon. But almost every masque given under James can be discussed in some analogous way. We miss much of the masque's significance as a symbolic performance if we insist on assimilating it to a
general pattern or policy, whether aesthetic or political. Its development is related rather to the way local politics offers the opportunity
for a figure of occasion of this kind, so that the chief examples of the
genre necessarily resist convenient typology. The figuring of occasion
requires for its coming into being the mobile and sensual energies of
performance, not conceived, as Jonson tended to do, as mere material
outwork, but as, to adapt a phrase aptly used of it, 'the *action* of the
mind'.[72] The masque as a genre thus has a dialectical momentum
greater than its counterparts in the public theatre. Its local pointednesses
are sharper, but hence also more quickly blunted. When the complex
currents of Jacobean politics change, so does the masque. What Gordon
called the relations 'between fiction, representation, enaction, identification or participation' are reconfigured, new and old forming and
reforming figures like partners in a set of branles, as the dancers turn
left instead of right.

NOTES

1 Ambassador Correr's report to the Venetian Council for 14 January
  (4 Jan. old style) 1611. Quoted from *Calendar of State Papers – Venetian* by
  C. H. Herford and Percy Simpson (eds.), *Ben Jonson*, 11 vols. (Oxford,
  1925–52), x, p. 519.
2 Edmund White, *Forgetting Elena* (New York, 1973), p. 72.
3 The distinction between 'text' and 'action' might be challenged along
  several lines, yet the differences in the general orientation of discussion it
  refers to remain, I think, clear enough.

4 Thus Graham Parry's excellent essay, after using the texts of the masques to trace the changing winds of court policy, concludes that much of a masque's 'political message' may have been inaudible to or ignored by its audience. I think this is to think of such messages too narrowly for these occasions. See Parry, 'The politics of the Jacobean masque', in J. R. Mulryne and Margaret Shewring (eds.), *Theatre and Government Under the Early Stuarts* (Cambridge, 1993), pp. 87–117.

5 In this I follow recent work in Renaissance studies (by Stephen Greenblatt, Stephen Orgel, Jonathan Goldberg, Leah Marcus *et al.*) that has emphasized how performance contributes to the social and political process, rather than merely reflects it. But I would also stress how such contribution can itself analyse the process by abstracting and symbolizing its procedures for concerted attention.

6 See Frank Whigham, *Ambition and Privilege: The Social Tropes of Elizabethan Courtesy Theory* (Berkeley, 1984). On personal comportment as political rhetoric, see Anna Bryson, 'The rhetoric of status: gesture, demeanour and the image of the gentleman in sixteenth- and seventeenth-century England', in Lucy Gent and Nigel Llewellyn (eds.), *Renaissance Bodies: the Human Figure in English Culture. c. 1540–1660* (London, 1990), pp. 136–53. On women at the Jacobean court, see also Karen Middaugh, 'The Golden Tree: the Court Masques of Queen Anna of Denmark' (unpub. PhD dissertation, Case Western Reserve University, 1994).

7 Literary criticism has tended, for obvious reasons, to focus on these representations, and charisma tends also to operate through them. It should be said, however, that political power and representational power do not necessarily go together. One index of this, and of our current weakness in confronting it, is the general absence, from the masque record and our discussion of it, of the Earl of Salisbury, a comprehensive treatment of whom we still lack. See Pauline Croft's essay in Linda Levy Peck (ed.), *The Mental World of the Jacobean Court* (Cambridge, 1991), pp. 134–47.

8 D. G. Gordon, *The Renaissance Imagination*, ed. Stephen Orgel (Berkeley, 1975), p. 32.

9 Roger Lockyer, *Buckingham: The Life and Political Career of George Villiers, First Duke of Buckingham, 1592–1628* (London, 1981), p. 13. One should perhaps distinguish here between an 'institutional' charisma, entailed by installation in the dignity of public office (and in the monarch literalized by the 'chrism'), and a 'personal' charisma, more vulnerable and perhaps for that reason more dangerous, entwined with 'personality' as we might now use the term. We could exemplify the distinction by noting that King James had the former, Philip Sidney the latter, and Queen Elizabeth, by all accounts, both. Even personal charisma, however, is largely defined and created by a relation to institutions. Following Clifford Geertz, we can see it as the personal embodiment of an institution's potential for dialectical transformation, its latent readiness for innovation through the interest and pressure of an emergent or insurgent group. This nicely

suggests the intimate connection of charisma with change, and hence with both mobility and performance. See Clifford Geertz, 'Centers, kings, and charisma: reflections on the symbolics of power', in *Local Knowledge* (New York, 1983), pp. 121–46.

10 Important discussions of the masque that have focused mainly on the King's politics in it include: Stephen Orgel, *The Illusion of Power* (Berkeley, 1975); Jonathan Goldberg, *James I and the Politics of Literature* (Baltimore, 1983); and Leah Marcus, *The Politics of Mirth* (Chicago, 1986).

11 Jerzy Limon, 'The masque of Stuart culture', in Peck (ed.), *Mental World*, pp. 209–29, here p. 228.

12 The regular reduction of our perception of meaning to a textual or semiotic model is worth reconsideration also in this context. It is an open question, I think, whether the perception of such qualities as 'grace' in a dancer or an athlete is, strictly speaking, a semiotic perception, as it is difficult to distinguish within such a perception the standard components of 'the sign'. The motion of an arm or foot *as bodily kinesis* has no further referent and our sense of its impact may be rather proprioceptive than semantic. The Saussurean model which underpins much contemporary discussion is thus ill-suited to deal with such perceptions, yet they may be central to events such as ballet or the masque.

13 See e.g. Malcolm Smuts, 'Cultural diversity and cultural change at the court of James I', in Peck (ed.), *Mental World*, pp. 99–112, Leeds Barroll, 'The court of the first Stuart queen', in the same volume, pp. 191–208, and David M. Bergeron, *Royal Family, Royal Lovers: King James of England and Scotland* (Columbia, MO, 1991).

14 Smuts, 'Cultural diversity', p. 111.

15 On this question of 'representation', see the somewhat neglected remarks of Angus Fletcher, who makes a fascinating comparison with Hobbes, in *The Transcendental Masque* (Ithaca, 1971), pp. 11–18.

16 Even here, the masque sometimes displays a dialectical turn. The outbreak of the 'tableau' effect in some masques momentarily arrests the fluidity of the proceedings into a static emblem. One such moment in *The Golden Age Restored* uses the only occurrence I know of in English Renaissance drama of the very modern-sounding stage direction, 'A pause'. See *Ben Jonson: The Complete Masques*, ed. Stephen Orgel (New Haven, 1969), p. 229. All quotations from Jonson's masques will be from this edition.

17 See John Nichols (ed.), *The Progresses, Processions and Magnificent Festivities of King James the First*, 4 vols. (London, 1828).

18 Patricia Fumerton discusses this 'annunciatory' aspect of the masque in *Cultural Aesthetics: Renaissance Literature and the Practice of Social Ornament* (Chicago, 1991), pp. 143–59. It is worth remembering here the formal descent of the masque from the earlier practice of the 'disguised entry' (cf. the relevant scenes in Shakespeare's *Love's Labour's Lost* and *Henry VIII*). In this respect, the Jacobean masque is a kind of 'royal entry' inside out, with the monarch now in the receiving position. The elaboration of the masque

entry under James gives rise to a fiction of 'influx' that accompanies the physical arrival of the masquers, who bid to have their symbolic assertions also received into the court milieu.

19 Roy Strong anticipates the pattern in commenting that 'If [Henry] had lived, the art of festival in Stuart England would have taken a very different course'. See Roy Strong, *Henry, Prince of Wales and England's Lost Renaissance* (London, 1986), p. 139.

20 At least early in his reign, King James seem to have taken the view that masques were technically private entertainments *en famille*, and not public events of state. In practice, this useful dodge helped deal with the perpetual protocol wars among ambassadors that plagued masques. For an occasion on which this was argued, see Herford and Simpson (eds.), *Ben Jonson*, x, p. 447 of *The Masque of Blackness* (1605). The notion of the masque as an event for which 'the state' was not accountable contributes to the picture of the performance as assertive but provisional.

21 It is instructive to compare the role of dance in Jacobean politics with its place at the court of Elizabeth. The Queen was fond of and proficient at dancing, though she is not known to have danced herself in any masque. A dancer who took her eye might win favour, as it appears the young Christopher Hatton did, possibly in the masque that followed *Gorboduc* at court on 18 January 1562. Yet at her court dancing was not elaborated into and embedded in the specific symbology of an occasion: dances were not devised anew according to an 'invention', and hence their political deployment was different. Hatton's success, for instance, was a personal one, where that of Villiers was orchestrated by a court faction. On Hatton, see Eric St John Brooks, *Sir Christopher Hatton* (London, 1946), pp. 31–9.

22 Busino was chaplain to the Venetian ambassador. His account is reprinted in Herford and Simpson (eds.), *Ben Jonson*, x, pp. 580–4. Other eyewitness accounts to be found in that volume include Dudley Carleton on *Blackness* (pp. 448–9), Ambassador Guistiniani on *Beauty* (p. 457), John Pory on *Hymenaei* (pp. 465–6), an unknown Spanish observer on *Oberon* (pp. 522–3), and John Chamberlain and others on *Pleasure Reconciled* and its reprise (pp. 576–7). The eyes of these witnesses were predominantly on who stood out, who took whom to dance, and who 'bare away the bell' (p. 576). Occasionally we also hear of an unfortunate who did not perform so well, as Sir Thomas Germain in Daniel's *Vision of the Twelve Goddesses* who 'had lead in his heels and sometimes forgot what he was doing' (Dudley Carleton, quoted in Andrew Sabol (ed.), *Four Hundred Songs and Dances from the Stuart Masque* (Providence, RI, 1978), p. 12).

23 Herford and Simpson (eds.), *Ben Jonson*, x, p. 498, my translation.

24 Stephen Orgel, *The Jonsonian Masque* (Cambridge, MA, 1965), p. 117.

25 The Renaissance elaboration of the portrait pose as an icon of character and policy is an important aspect of this bodily rhetoric. Jones represented this tradition and deployed it in his masques. Images of Prince Henry as a warrior had begun to circulate in books and paintings by the time

of *Oberon*, the culmination being Isaac Oliver's miniature of around 1612. See Strong, *Henry, Prince of Wales*.

26 Norbert Elias, *The History of Manners*, trans. Edmund Jephcott (Oxford, 1978), and Bryson, 'The rhetoric of status'.

27 Space prevents a systematic look at the dance treatises here, but the most important representatives (all continental) are Caroso's *Il Ballarino* of 1581, Arbeau's *Orchésographie* of 1588, and Negri's *Nuove Inventioni* of 1604. Though only Caroso's text is specifically recorded in England at this time, these were the sources drawn on by the dancing-masters of the Jacobean court, such as Thomas Giles, Jeremy Herne and Monsieur Confesse, who all worked on *Oberon*. Sir John Davies's poem *Orchestra* (1594) is also important in elaborating the courtly view of dance. For relevant discussion of the importance of grouping in the experience of dance in the period, see Michael Baxandall, *Painting and Experience in Fifteenth Century Italy* (Oxford, 1972), pp. 75–80.

28 Quoted in Herford and Simpson (eds.), *Ben Jonson*, x, p. 519, from BM Add. MS 24023. The wording of the warrant suggests an unusually protracted rehearsal period in this case. A similar phrase appears in the order for payment in the Pell Book which lists the same parties receiving twenty pounds for 'having been employed in the Prince's late Mask by the space almost of six weeks' (Herford and Simpson (eds.), *Ben Jonson*, x, p. 520). The Pell Book also records a further payment of forty pounds to the choreographer 'M. Giles for three dances' (Herford and Simpson (eds.), *Ben Jonson*, x, p. 521). This last is the same fee Ben Jonson and Inigo Jones each received from the King (with Jones receiving a further sixteen pounds from Henry). In other words, the total fees paid out for choreography from the King's Exchequer were equal to those for the script and stage design combined. Likewise, in the Queen's masque of a month later, *Love Freed from Ignorance and Folly* (1611), M. Confesse was paid more 'for teaching all the dances' than anyone else associated with the event (Herford and Simpson (eds.), *Ben Jonson*, x, p. 529). If we measure importance by compensation, it is clear where the scale was tipped.

29 Herford and Simpson (eds.), *Ben Jonson*, x, p. 518. There are also reports that Queen Anne was holding 'daily rehearsals and trials of the machinery' two weeks before *The Masque of Queens* in 1609, and that the Countess of Rutland, who was to appear in *Hymenaei* on 5 January 1606, moved into Whitehall with her attendants on December 16th (Herford and Simpson (eds.), *Ben Jonson*, x, pp. 494, 467).

30 Donne and Chamberlain both quoted in Herford and Simpson (eds.), *Ben Jonson*, x, p. 553.

31 Chamberlain to Carleton in Herford and Simpson (eds.), *Ben Jonson*, x, p. 568. On Buckingham's early advancement, see Nichols (ed.), *Progresses*, III, pp. 79, 131, and Lockyer, *Buckingham*, pp. 12–35.

32 Quoted from Busino's report, Herford and Simpson (eds.), *Ben Jonson*, x, pp. 583–4, my translation. John Aubrey later reported that at 'the Duke of

Buckingham's great masque' Buckingham tried so hard he 'did sprain a vein on the inside of his leg, of which he was lame ever after' (quoted in Herford and Simpson (eds.), *Ben Jonson*, x, p. 612). This may reflect less a real incident than a sense of Buckingham's extraordinary efforts to shine on such occasions.

33 Gordon, *Renaissance Imagination*, p. 32, my emphasis.

34 The music is reprinted and discussed in Sabol (ed.), *Songs and Dances*. See the table on p. 4.

35 Sabol (ed.), *Songs and Dances*, p. 13. The dance is given in two versions by Sabol, as his 107 and 249. Like other antimasques, it would have been performed by professionals. It may be the same as the 'dance of twelve Satyrs' (or 'Saltiers') included in Shakespeare's *The Winter's Tale*, where we are told that three of the dancers 'hath danced before the King, and not the worst of the three but jumps twelve foot and a half by the square'. See *The Winter's Tale* 4.4.338–9.

36 See Sabol's dances 188, 189, 190 (and alternative versions 251–4). The eyewitness reported that the entry dances were 'intermingled with varied figures and many leaps, extremely well done by most of them' (Sabol (ed.), *Songs and Dances*, p. 543).

37 Herford and Simpson (eds.), *Ben Jonson*, x, p. 457.

38 Francis Bacon, *Essays*, ed. Michael Kiernan (Cambridge, MA, 1985), pp. 117–18. 'Of masques and triumphs' (Essay 37) comes suggestively after 'Of prophecies' and 'Of Ambition'.

39 *Complete Masques*, ed. Orgel, pp. 162–3.

40 Fumerton, *Cultural Aesthetics*, investigates this connection in detail.

41 See the Preface to *Hymenaei* and the opening of *Pleasure Reconciled to Virtue* with its dancing bottles, and compare the tippling satyrs in *Oberon*. Coupled with the ceremonial element of the masque, the idea of an 'edible symbol' might suggest the holy communion, though this analogy needs to be carefully handled. Jonson himself referred to masque sets after performance as 'carcases' (*Complete Masques*, ed. Orgel, p. 47).

42 On Henry, see Strong, *Henry, Prince of Wales*, esp. pp. 138–83, Bergeron, *Royal Family, Royal Lovers*, pp. 92–106, and J. W. Williamson, *The Myth of the Conqueror: Prince Henry Stuart* (New York, 1978). On other political events of 1609–1611 in relation to the masque, see Mary Sullivan, *Court Masques of James I* (New York, 1913), ch. 2.

43 For the text of the entertainment, see *Complete Masques*, ed. Orgel, pp. 142–58.

44 See Strong, *Henry, Prince of Wales*, p. 141. The *Barriers* were announced by strangers challenging with trumpet and drum in the Presence Chamber. According to Drummond of Hawthornden, Henry's pseudonym on such occasions was 'Moeliades', an anagram of 'Miles a deo' (which Jonson gives as 'Meliadus'). Anagrammatization itself suggests both a certain hesitancy and the possibility of a 'new arrangement'. James forbade Henry to hold his tournament in the public tiltyard. On Henry's relation to the

Sidney circle, see Strong, *Henry, Prince of Wales*, pp. 145, 159, and on the anti-Habsburg alliance, pp. 150–1.

45 The delivery of this treaty through the French envoy, de Laverdin, forms the background of the Christmas masquing season that includes *Oberon*. The whole process was exasperating to the English court and not without its comic side, as the English tried to showcase what the French wished to play down. In April of 1611, France signed a defensive alliance with Spain. See Sullivan, *Masques*, pp. 60–7.

46 These formal steps were proclaimed on 4 June, the day Henry was created Prince of Wales. The timing was probably deliberate. Exactly a year later, the requirement of taking the oath was further extended. See Nichols (ed.), *Progresses*, II, pp. 310–13.

47 The above is summarized from Strong, *Henry, Prince of Wales*, pp. 151–60, and from Nichols (ed.), *Progresses*, II, pp. 315–62. It appears that James carefully controlled Henry's public appearances throughout, denying his request for a processional entry into London, delaying advertisement to the City Fathers and hobbling their celebration, and refusing to dine with his son at the investiture banquet, where there was nevertheless 'such state as greater could not have been done unto the King' (Nichols (ed.), *Progresses*, II, p. 360).

48 The following details are drawn from Nichols (ed.), *Progresses*, II, pp. 365–9.

49 Nichols (ed.), *Progresses*, II, p. 369. The Prince also visited the ship on 31 January and 25 April, and again when it was rigged on 6 December. It is clear that he regarded this naval buildup as important, and wished those around him to know he did. Pette had been captain of Henry's own ship in 1603 (see *Dictionary of National Biography*, xv, pp. 990–2, and Bergeron, *Royal Family*, p. 101).

50 Prince Henry had earlier in the year been the principal host and companion of his cousin, Prince Frederic Ulric, heir to the Duchy of Brunswick, taking him to a private lion fight at the Tower and himself writing to inform him at Bath of Henri IV's assassination. See Nichols (ed.), *Progresses*, II, pp. 290, 307–12.

51 Herford and Simpson (eds.), *Ben Jonson*, x, p. 518.

52 See Nichols (ed.), *Progresses*, II, pp. 370–5.

53 Herford and Simpson (eds.), *Ben Jonson*, x, p. 519.

54 See Strong, *Henry, Prince of Wales*, pp. 160–73, and John P. Cutts, 'Le rôle de la musique dans les masques de Ben Jonson et notamment dans *Oberon*', in *Les fêtes de la Renaissance*, ed. Jean Jacquot, 2 vols. (Paris, 1956), I, pp. 285–303. On the *scena ductilis* and the design of Oberon's palace, see Stephen Orgel and Roy Strong, *Inigo Jones: the Theatre of the Stuart Court*, 2 vols. (London, 1973), I, pp. 18, 22, 210–20, and John Peacock, *The Stage Designs of Inigo Jones: The European Context* (Cambridge, 1996), pp. 74–81.

55 Orgel and Strong, *Inigo Jones*, I, pp. 6–8, 17, and Peacock, *Stage Designs*, pp. 163–70.

56 This point is pursued in Goldberg, *James I and the Politics of Literature*, pp. 123–6.

57 Herford and Simpson (eds.), *Ben Jonson*, x, p. 522.

58 Jonson's change in voice of the final verb deflects attention from the question of who is to bestow peace. Perhaps Ovid's 'dissociata' was a little too suggestive for such a 'sociable' occasion. The whole passage is as follows:

> nulli sua forma manebat,
> obstabatque aliis aliud, quia corpore in uno
> frigida pugnabant calidis, umentia siccis,
> mollia cum duris, sine pondere, habentia pondus.
> Hanc deus et melior litem natura diremit.
> nam caelo terras et terris abscidit undas
> et liquidum spisso secrevit ab aere caelum.
> quae postquam evolvit caecoque exemit acervo,
> dissociata locis concordi pace ligavit.   (I.17–25)

Ovid, *Metamorphoses*, ed. Frank Justus Miller, 2 vols. (Cambridge, MA, 1971). I wish to thank Professor Martin Heltzle for locating this allusion.

59 Virgil's *Eclogues* were, throughout the period, crucial texts against and through which aspiring poets measured poetic anxieties about maturity, earliness and prophetic vocation. In English Spenser and Milton furnish other examples, the latter no doubt with Jonson in mind. *Eclogue VI* is especially important in this context in *Lycidas*, lines 76–7.

60 Chromis and Mnasyllos are said to be shepherd-boys (*pueri*) in Virgil, but Jonson followed the commentary of Servius in identifying them as satyrs.

61 For extended discussion of Virgil's poem, see: Michael C. J. Putnam, *Virgil's Pastoral Art* (Princeton, 1970), pp. 195–221; Eleanor Winsor Leach, *Virgil's 'Eclogues': Landscapes of Experience* (Ithaca, 1974), pp. 216–44; and E. Coleiro, *An Introduction to Vergil's Bucolics* (Amsterdam, 1979), pp. 198–218.

62 Quotations of Virgil are from *Eclogues*, text ed. Roger Mynors with notes by Guy Lee (London, 1984), pp. 70–5.

63 Cf. Virgil, lines 31–2: 'Namque canebat uti magnum per inane coacta / semina terrarumque animaeque marisque fuissent / et liquidi simul ignis' (For he was singing how through the great void the seeds of earth and breath and sea and liquid fire were forced together).

64 Jonson's learned note attempting to establish the derivation of 'fairies' from 'feras' seems to be a response to Virgil's line, but does not cite it directly. See *Complete Masques*, ed. Orgel, p. 549.

65 Consideration of Jonson's response to the dual role of Virgil's Silenus as drunkard and prophet also helps resolve the structural 'fissure' identified by Jonathan Goldberg in *Oberon* between the roles of libertine satyr and the eulogist of James. See Goldberg, *James I and the Politics of Literature*, p. 125.

66 *Complete Masques*, ed. Orgel, p. 549. For fuller discussion of echo and Echo in the Renaissance and elsewhere, see John Hollander, *The Figure of Echo:*

A Mode of Allusion in Milton and After (Berkeley, 1981), and Joseph Loewenstein, *Responsive Readings: Versions of Echo in Pastoral, Epic and the Jonsonian Masque* (New Haven, 1984).

67 *Complete Masques*, ed. Orgel, p. 549.

68 Stephen Orgel comments justly on these lines that 'it is surprising that the embodiment of universal order should be defined in verse of so much indirection, so little clarity and ease' (Orgel, *Jonsonian Masque*, p. 87). The indirection is clarified by considering the allusion.

69 It is here, if anywhere, that the glimmering, plastic space of imaginative invention that is Oberon's moonlight in Shakespeare's *A Midsummer Night's Dream* comes into the masque. In Jonson that insubstantiality becomes a threat to true perception, but within it some anxious and canny desires might well screen themselves.

70 The Latin can bear an even stronger reading as 'against the will of Olympus', implying that the gods themselves would prefer Silenus to keep singing.

71 Herford and Simpson (eds.), *Ben Jonson*, x, p. 523.

72 Orgel and Strong, *Inigo Jones*, I, p. 16, emphasis altered. The original sentence reads 'In the spectacular genre as Jonson and Jones developed it, marvels were *about* philosophy and theory, *action* was the action of the mind'.

CHAPTER 6

Inventing the Stuart masque

Leeds Barroll

Despite the prominence of such poets as Ben Jonson and Samuel Daniel, the court masque was always a presentation planned not by writers but by masquers – for the spectacular exhibition of themselves to an exclusive audience at their own homes or at court. Primarily associated with weddings during the last decades of Elizabeth's reign, the English masque as court entertainment enacted by nobles in the Christmas season, commonly found on the Continent, was an innovation of Anna of Denmark when she came to England as the Queen Consort of James I in 1603.[1] What critical attention these masques have attracted has centred either on their designers – Ben Jonson and Inigo Jones – or on the role of their iconology in reflecting the monarchic interests and plans of King James. Thus masques of the first ten years of the Stuart reign emerge not as *Anna's* programmes but as patriarchal product – richly tapestried expressions of King James's agendas as understood by other *men* who were his own artisans.[2]

This essay waives this traditional approach to view the first Stuart masques as a forwarding of the *Queen's* programmes. As a cultural activity primarily involving noblewomen, these royal spectacles deflected attention from the King and his own circle to focus on the new court of the Queen. Indeed, Anna of Denmark was so effective in showcasing herself and her own interests by means of her masques that by 1613, when she had lost appetite for these shows, they were appropriated for similar purposes by her husband. Lying outside the scope of this essay, these *King's* masques, maintained in the years after 1612 – beyond Anna's death in 1619 and up to the end of James's own reign in 1625 – differed in form from those sponsored by the Queen, but certainly not in political means and ends. For Anna used the masque to generate not only entertainment or art, but the idea of herself and her new court.

When at the beginning of the Stuart reign, Anna claimed the masque at the first opportunity for her own purposes, she was not, of course, inventing the form, for there had been masques at the English court. But, importantly, in Queen Elizabeth's time, the masque seems to have been the possession of men, a prerogative reflected in the drama of the period.[3] The masquing in *Romeo and Juliet*, for example, is a pastime for rich young *men* of good family who could playfully invade the homes of similar families such as the Capulets to present their show. In fact this carnivalesque convention of masqued invasion from outside the household (nostalgically recalled by Capulet from his own younger days) was obviously behaviour available only to men. It was they, not the young women of their social class, who could wander through the streets of Verona *en masque* and unchaperoned in advance of their appearance at the ball; or, to take another example, through Venice, where Gratiano, Lorenzo, Salerio and Solanio, on the way to visit Antonio, could parade past Shylock's house to abduct Jessica disguised as her lover's page-*boy* (2.7; 2.8).

The actual masques found at the court of Elizabeth during the latter part of her reign seem to have been similarly gendered. In 1589 Arthur Throgmorton wrote to Robert Cecil about a masque he and other gentlemen wanted to present at court, and, in 1595 and 1599, two of the all-male Inns of Court – Gray's and the Middle Temple – presented the masques from their own annual revels before Elizabeth during the holiday seasons.[4] In Scotland too, James VI had embellished the inner-circle marriage he arranged between the Earl of Huntly and the Duke of Lennox's sister in 1588 with a dialogue of men which refers to the coming of 'strangers in a masque'.[5] Thus, at James's English accession in 1603, if masques were to be presented at all, English custom and Scottish precedent argued that men would enact them. And since their own revels were an annual affair, young gentlemen from the Inns of Court might again have been obvious and available candidates to mount these aristocratic shows during the Christmas revels. We know, for example, that in 1613 Inns of Court men presented masques at the palace for the wedding of Princess Elizabeth to Frederick.

But notwithstanding this male monopoly, women in England had not themselves been strangers to this pastime prior to 1603. Among themselves, and within doors, they seem to have organized masques as private, patriarchally supervised entertainment. For example, in the summer of 1600 Anne Russell, one of Queen Elizabeth's maids of honour, had married the heir of the Earl of Worcester with festivities at Lord Cobham's house in Blackfriars where Queen Elizabeth's seven other maids of honour danced a masque to celebrate their fellow's marriage, even persuading Queen Elizabeth to join them.[6] Indeed, thirteen years later, a few months after the accession, Queen Anna showed herself familiar with such female, in-house festivity. When, during the autumn of 1603, the royal family had removed to Winchester because of the plague, they were joined there by the nine-year-old Prince Henry, and between 11 October, when Henry arrived, and 17 October, the Queen and her ladies privately presented for him the first known masque of the reign.[7] The composer John Dowland may have been a contributor to this activity, for when, a number of months later, he published his famous *Lachrimae* (*Stationers' Register*, 2 April 1604), he inscribed them to Queen Anna, mentioning his 'access' to her in Winchester.[8]

At the same time as the masque to entertain the boy Prince Henry, it seems Anna was making plans for the first Stuart Christmas, for Beaumont, the French ambassador, noting the October occasion in a letter to Villeroi in Paris, remarked that the Queen proposed '*d'en faire d'autres plus beaux cet hiver*'. Indeed, he continued, it seemed that the King and his principal ministers, constantly concerned about Anna's '*esprit*', were quite content to see her so absorbed, as these activities would presumably divert her from those political self-assertions so characteristic of her Scottish reign. Ironically, however, these masques were not to be diversions from, but expressions of, this 'spirit' about which the King and his closest advisers had learned to be wary.[9] Thus, two months later, the royal couple having returned to celebrate at Hampton Court the first Christmas of the reign, Anna in effect launched the Jacobean court masque in the season of revels.

Because plague throughout the year had often postponed royal ambassadorial audiences and requisite farewell feastings, the honourings of ambassadors-extraordinary sent by different continental rulers to congratulate the new King of England were in great arrears.[10] The crown had therefore decided to dissolve this backlog during the Christmas revels so that the special emissaries from Spain, France, Poland, Tuscany and Savoy could be given their Audiences of Farewell along with their customary, individual feastings during the celebratory days of December and January.[11] By appropriating this elaborate celebratory context for her kind of masquing, Queen Anna began to use the annual regularity of the Christmas season of revelry and its recurrent diplomatic obligations to win for the masque – that sometime court event in England most often accompanying weddings – a place it never held in the days of Elizabeth.

The prestige of a new Queen Consort must have been a significant factor in her early success because even Anna's first masque was anticipated as a major occasion. The concerns of the foreign emissaries who vied to be present amply demonstrate this enhanced status. Although the French ambassador-extraordinary had been invited to an earlier male masque on New Year's evening, it was the Spanish ambassador, bidden to the masque of the Queen, who thought he had gained the greater prestige. 'The Spaniard thinks he hath carried it away by being first feasted (as he was the first holiday and the Polack the next) and invited to the greatest masque.'[12] Thus Anna's forthcoming spectacle had, merely by being exclusive, attained political weight. In fact, the sheer elaborateness of her plans had raised these stakes. As Carleton (a courtier himself) pointed out, the scenery required for the performance made the great hall at Hampton Court 'much lessened by the works that were in it, so as none could be admitted but men of appearance'.[13]

'The Orient Knights' – nothing of this masque survives but some contemporary description – emphasizes by contrast Anna's departure from those few traditions that seem to have governed masquing at the English court prior to her intervention. Presented 1 January 1604, two weeks before Anna's, it was danced by eight male, mostly unmarried nobles. They were prestigious persons – almost all Gentlemen of the Bed Chamber – but they were not the most politically significant men at court. Young and specially favoured, they lent lustre and excitement to the event, but they could hardly compete as court cynosures with the likes of Robert Cecil (the future Earl of Salisbury), Henry Lord Howard (the future Earl of Northampton), or the Earls of Suffolk, Worcester and Mar, all powerful members of James's closely-held ruling circle. Rather, the young favourites danced because masquing had always been a young man's game and the dancers in this case were the most promising and marriageable courtiers.

Queen Anna's first masque was a decided departure, if only because her own participants were noble*women* dancing not at home, but before the general court.[14] Further, most of those dancing this first masque of the reign, Samuel Daniel's *The Vision of the Twelve Goddesses*, were married. They were thus appearing not because of their youth, availability and promise, but by virtue of their positions, as members of the close circle around the Queen Consort of England. It was as if (improbably) King James had elected to dance a masque with Cecil, Worcester, Northampton and Mar. True, some women were spouses of powerful or prestigious noblemen, but this fact, except in one case, seems to have been coincidental. What determined the selection of the eight foremost dancers was that two were ladies of Anna's Bed Chamber (Bedford, Hertford) and six from her next most exclusive group, the Drawing Chamber (Derby, Suffolk, Nottingham, Rich, Walsingham and Susan de Vere).[15] Indeed, five of these eight women would form, with Anna, the core of those who danced in every one of her subsequent masques, and for this reason, they must, I think, be taken as the ladies closest to the Queen.[16]

Anna's masques differed from the (male) norm not only in gender but in number. Featuring not eight but twelve noblewomen, the mode in the French *balet de cor*, this arrangement was used by Anna not necessarily for choreographic reasons but for social and political purposes. With herself and her official ladies comprising a constant nucleus, the remaining places seem to have been reserved for visitors – for example, young noblewomen whom Anna favoured either for themselves or for their parents. This factor also accounts for the occasional presence of ladies whose husbands were of undistinguished rank.[17]

The arrangements of Anna's masques – such as that of the eleven ladies chosen for her first effort – can be fully comprehended only if we move beyond the allure of the textual remnants of these productions, the poetic language that identifies them today as 'works' of a Jonson or a Daniel. Critical tradition has situated Queen Anna and her ladies, along with the elaborate costumes and sets of her masques, as ornaments to the text; moreover, it has 'interpreted' her masques not in terms of those noblewomen who spoke no lines, but in terms of the ideas expressed in the verses uttered by the professional male talkers – I call them interlocutors. Elaborately costumed, these figures commented on the masque, explained the device, sang the songs and signalled beginnings, transitions and ends. But such figures, along with their costumes and even the spectacular sets, did not elicit half the interest accorded the noble dancers. Illustrative are the words of Dudley Carleton writing to a friend about the earlier, men's, 'Orient Knights':

On New Year's Night we had . . . a masque brought in by a magician of China. There was a heaven built at the lower end of the hall out of which our magician came down, and *after he had made a long sleepy speech to the king* [italics added] of the nature of the country from whence he came, comparing it with ours for strength and plenty, he said he had brought in clouds certain Indian and China knights to see the magnificency of this court; and thereupon a traverse was drawn and the masquers seen sitting in a vaulty place with their torchbearers and other lights, which was no unpleasing spectacle.[18]

That it was not the device or poetry but the participants themselves that were the focus of attention in these spectacles is further suggested by the correspondence of two earls. As late as 2 February Worcester wrote Shrewsbury, who had obviously been asking him about Daniel's masque: 'I have been at sixpence charge with you to send you the book which will inform you better than I can, having noted the names of the ladies applied to each goddess'.[19]

I would argue that emphasis on 'the names of the ladies' – on the women who danced – was Anna's whole point, and that this emphasis in fact dictated the very structure of these masques. Although most surviving texts (such as those of Daniel or Jonson) do not provide full descriptions of the phases or parts of the masque, some – such as a text of Campion – do. Because these parts have specific social functions crucial to our sense of the masque's significance, particularly as con-figured by Anna, they warrant brief attention here.

Part 1 (the continued use of 'part' is my own) was, from the view-point of the dancers, perhaps the most important. It was a three-stage exhibition of the masquing women (and, after 1612, the men) them-selves, displaying the noblewomen all together statically, then in pro-cession and then singly. The masquers were arranged so as to confirm or establish their relationship with respect to one another in actual life, either by means of their fictive roles, or their physical positioning. Part 1 of *Twelve Goddesses*, for instance, seems not so much concerned to enact Roman deities as to enhance and interpret the noblewomen who personated them.

The cases of several masquers seem especially illustrative here. Anna chose not to be Juno 'goddess of empire and *regnorum*'; rather, 'the person her Majesty chose to represent' was 'Pallas [Athene]', god-dess of 'wisdom and defence', an identification Anna seems to have cherished, for she would be associated with Athene in several later instances.[20] A contemporary list indicates the identities of the other goddesses and is useful in establishing principles of precedence.[21] The list is somewhat misleading in that it represents succeeding *trios* of ladies, the centre lady (as in the case of Queen Anna) presumably holding the highest position among the three (see below).

Juno	The Countess of Suffolk
Pallas Athene	Queen Anna
Venus	Penelope Rich
Vesta	The Countess of Hertford
Diana	The Countess of Bedford
Proserpina	The Countess of Derby
Macaria	Lady Hatton
Concordia	The Countess of Nottingham
Astraea	Lady Walsingham
Flora	Susan de Vere
Ceres	Dorothy Hastings
Tethys	Elizabeth Howard

In the beginning of the masque, the 'discovery' of these figures in a dim group at the top of a mountain did not yet disclose the identities of these ladies because part 1, as previously observed, was more complex than in the previous, men's, masque. 'The Orient Knights' had begun with a fully visible discovery of the knights 'sitting in a vaulty place with their torchbearers and other lights', after which they were 'brought in' by two boys and two musicians. Next they had 'presented themselves to the King' and 'in their order delivered their escutcheons with letters' with 'no great stay at any of them'. There even seems to have been a touch of humour, since James joked with one of these knights (Philip Herbert) as he presented his shield. For *The Vision of the Twelve Goddesses*, humour – and the King – were not part of the proceedings and part 1 seems to have been a much more studied exhibition.

Trumpets and cornets, played by the King's musicians disguised as satyrs lurking in the dark among rocks around broad steps, played a stately march during which a torch-lit procession slowly materialized; it descended the stairs in ranks of threes, led by the Three Graces in their silver robes holding aloft burning white torches. Behind the Graces, three more torch-bearers, hair and robes decked with stars, preceded the first rank of three goddesses that included the Queen. This first rank was followed by three more torch-bearers preceding the next row of three goddesses, these alternating groups of threes continuing until the full number of the twelve goddesses was made: 'which being all seen on the stairs at once', wrote Dudley Carleton, 'was the best presentation I have at any time seen'.[22]

This spatial context deliberately foregrounded social and political hierarchies. Anna, of course, defined the place of honour, sharing it here with two ladies whom the *Crown*, not necessarily Anna, had an interest in favouring. The Countess of Suffolk, dressed as Juno queen of the gods, was the wife of Thomas Lord Howard whom James had created Earl of Suffolk, presumably to honour Henry Lord Howard who had helped James to the throne. Penelope Rich, also in this first trio, might seem to have been a favourite of Anna – and probably was, as one of the seven ladies of the privileged Drawing Chamber – but King James himself had shown a strong political interest in honouring the kin and memory of the dead Earl of Essex.[23] Thus Penelope Rich, as Essex's sister (and indicted co-conspirator), had been restored to her position above the daughters of all other earls except those who superseded Essex in precedence. Significantly, Anna placed two daughters of the Earl of Oxford, among the few earls who did supersede Essex, *behind* Penelope, presumably to emphasize the current honouring.[24]

The political arrangement of this procession is also attested to by the status of the countesses relegated to the second of the four trios of goddesses: the Countess of Hertford, the Countess of Bedford, the Countess of Derby (as Vesta, Diana and Proserpina). All three in their mid-twenties, the Countesses of Hertford and Bedford held the highest posts in Anna's court as the only two English Ladies of the Bed Chamber. Bedford, in the middle, took precedence here as the first noblewoman appointed to any office by the new Queen. The Countess of Derby (Elizabeth née de Vere, a daughter of the Earl of Oxford) was a niece of Robert Cecil and must have stood well with Anna. Several years later she would be the countess honoured as holder of Anna's newborn daughter, Princess Mary, during her elaborate christening.[25]

As previously suggested, part 1 of a Stuart masque did not end with the procession down the steps; rather, the last phase of its triple structure allowed each lady to individualize herself. Here each was given an allegorical task requiring her to cross the 'stage' in front of the courtier-audience, displaying her status, grace, looks and costume. Thus in *Twelve Goddesses*, each masquer, to the accompaniment of music and the singing of the Three Graces, individually approached the Temple of Peace to offer her gift at the altar. As Daniel reports it,

> one after another with solemn pace ascended up into the temple and delivering their presents to the Sibylla (as it were but in passing by) returned down into the midst of the hall, preparing themselves to their dance, which, as soon as the Graces had ended their song, they [the goddesses] began to the music of the viols and lutes placed on one side of the hall.[26]

Part 1 then yielded to what I am calling part 2, in which the Queen with her ladies organized themselves to dance. Most often referred to simply as 'the measure', this designation for the ensuing action had specific implications since the English 'measure' was a slow and stately dance.[27] Requiring execution by *couples*, even when all masquers were of the same sex, the measure always began with one of the dancers holding the partner's left hand as both made obeisance first to the King, then to the onlookers and then to each other in that mutual reverence that began every dance.[28] Conventional steps were the Sideways Single, the Double, the Backward Single, the Succeeding Double and the Reprise, one whole piece – one particular 'measure' in this part 2 – presumably being a rehearsed sequence of such steps by the six couples.[29] Part 2 *in toto* included several such individual pieces or 'measures' that allowed the participants, often well-rehearsed by the dancing-master, to show their command of grace and movement, while complexity was achieved as these six couples, dancing the measure, became simultaneously part of some larger dance-structure.[30] The Queen and her ladies in *Twelve Goddesses*, appearing to have been much more accomplished than 'The Orient Knights', danced to music that moved in 'divers strains framed unto motions circular, square, triangular, with other proportions exceeding rare and full of variety'.[31]

After 'the measure', which effectively exhibited the dancing masquers before the court, part 3 initiated an active form of social interchange. Often referred to as 'the ordinary measures' – and sometimes including the pavanne, another slow measure-like dance with connotations of stateliness – part 3 increased the number of participants in the masque to include (twelve) appropriate courtly onlookers, now of the opposite sex. In the process known as 'taking out', each masquer invited an individual to dance, and here men's masques had always, of course, invited ladies (as had the 'The Orient Knights').[32] But now, in Anna's new masquing, it was ladies who conferred favour upon, or withheld it from, *male* courtiers. And although, in such a court event, some powerful noblemen had to be so honoured as a matter of necessity by the Queen of England, men who were not politically close to the King's circles might, by being taken out here, attain some prestige. Thus the ladies of Anna's masques would hardly have taken out any particular noble without the prior direction of the Queen.

A new phase – part 4 – continued the mode of part 3 but offered an opportunity for expanding the numbers of those dancing still further. As the tempo of the music changed, those already taken out seem to have been empowered to take out others, the twelve masquers issuing new invitations.[33] Younger (and hence often less exalted) courtiers were selected to accommodate the faster tempi of the galliards and corantoes that always characterized part 4.[34] But no matter how long it lasted, this more lively dancing was always ended formally, by one of the masque interlocutors recalling, by speech or song, the twelve masquers to a final phase. Part 5, the finale, referred to as the '*sorti*' in the *balet de cor*, was the 'going out' by the masquers, reaffirming themselves alone as a group in a last exhibition dance and now making their formal exit.[35]

The identity of those taken out in *Twelve Goddesses* provides further evidence of Anna's political designs for her masquing. In part 3, she directed that noblemen in James's political administration be taken out, but also added several individuals friendly to her own circle. Thus the Duke of Lennox was the only Scottish lord selected because, as the only Duke in England or Scotland, King James's second cousin and lifelong confidant and the one closest to the throne during the minority of the princes, Lennox was surely the most appropriate partner for Queen Anna in this her first inviting. But, additionally and significantly, during Anna's stand-off with her husband eight months earlier in Scotland over the physical custody of Prince Henry, Lennox had been the only noble in James's circle whom Anna had allowed access to her. Anna also lent public support to James's policies by honouring four English noblemen in his political inner circle: Henry Lord Howard (the future Northampton); the Earl of Suffolk, his nephew; the Earl of Northumberland who had been a party to the secret correspondence with James VI conducted by Cecil before Elizabeth's death, and the Earl of Worcester, Master of the Horse (whose acting company during this same Christmas season would become known as the Queen's Servants). And Anna reinforced James's previous overtures to the Essex-group by instructing her ladies to take out two ex-conspirators – the Earl of Southampton (newly restored in blood by James in the previous summer) and Lord Monteagle, fined £8,000 by Elizabeth for participating in the Essex plot, put in the Tower, but released with Southampton at James's accession.[36] But the remaining nobles who were taken out had perhaps closer relations with the Queen's own circle: Sir Robert Sidney who was her Lord Chamberlain, the Earl of Pembroke who was his nephew, and the Earl of Devonshire who had an obvious connection through his relationship with Anna's Lady of the Drawing-Chamber, Penelope Rich.[37] Finally, the ambassadors who were being feasted at this time were included in these honours, but only in part 4 (they being the only invitees at this stage for whom there is a record): 'for galliards and corantoes they [the ladies] went by discretion . . . The Lady Bedford and Lady Susan [Vere] took out the two ambassadors [Spain and Poland], and they bestirred themselves very lively.'[38]

I have been suggesting that if we are to understand Anna's court masques as cultural product of their milieu, we ought to view these spectacles not as 'works' of their particular scriptwriters but as social constructs utilized by the Queen for her own social and political purposes. Thus they are not wholly comprehensible unless we can grasp not the King's, but Anna's, aims. That these aims were more social and political than 'recreational' – and that James absorbed these lessons willy-nilly from her about masquing – seems clear from correspondence no doubt provoked by Anna's intentions for the Christmas season of 1604–05. This interchange is important because it preceded Ben Jonson's first Jacobean court offering, *The Masque of Blackness*, and thus helps to situate this well-known script in the context of the Queen's sphere of influence, a context which I would argue is critical for all narratives purporting to describe masques at the early Stuart court.

Recommendations for a second masque seem not to have come from Anna but from King James (although possibly at Anna's instigation). At some point after 7 December 1604, James, ensconced at his hunting palace at Royston, wrote to the Privy Council about a possible masque this Christmas season, observing that after the elaborate display of the year before, the absence of a masque in this second Christmas of his reign might have some 'ominous presage'. Accordingly he proposed another entertainment by the Queen, featuring 'fine ballets or dancing'. The Privy Council, responding to what they took as a financial inquiry, told James that a masque would cost £4,000. At this news, James apparently demurred, suggesting that the Queen use funds from her own court and save money by also requiring her ladies to pay for their own lavish costumes. He seems to have added that, if this was not possible, then other Christmas plans could certainly be made – 'some commandment should be given to noblemen and gentlemen to make some jousts or barriers'.

The Council's letter (corrected by Cecil) importantly defines the expectations that Anna had already managed to establish for these spectacles. It first alludes to the Christmas tradition Anna has apparently violated: 'Many Christmases pass without any such note though such things [masques] be omitted; dancing, comedies, plays, and other sports having been thought sufficient marks of mirth, except some

great strange Prince or extraordinary marriage fell in that time.'
Addressing the present, however, the Council advised that if there was
to be another Queen's masque, then James, rather than trying to think
of ways to avoid paying for it, should 'resolve beforehand that the
expense must be your own'. For, the Council opined, the Queen would
'think it a scorn to draw such as are fit to attend her Majesty in those
things and suffer them to be at charges'. They then raised what they
considered to be a much more important point – one that may absolve
Anna from the imputation of thoughtless spendthriftness that has been
her historical legacy and at the same time indicate how, with only one
performance, she had already politicized these new spectacles.

Although we must confess unto your Majesty that some expenses even in the
government of richest princes receive not at all times one and the same interpretation, yet the change of this matter now for the saving of £4,000 would
be more pernicious than the expense of ten times the value, for when ambassadors of foreign princes shall understand that either King or Queen would
have a masque *if* they had £4,000, that judgment that will follow will be neither
safe nor honourable. [Italics added][39]

James obviously must have concurred with the Council's recommenda-
tion. Clearly the Queen's masquing – or even the mere prospect of its
performance – had become an important index of the court's viability.[40]

The masque that James agreed to pay for in the Christmas season of
1604 turned out to be Jonson's first commission, *The Masque of Blackness*.[41] The sensational spectacle of Anna and her ladies representing
the black daughters of Niger has recently been included in a larger
– and important – effort to define early modern concepts of 'race'.[42]
Here, however, I want to emphasize how the masque attests to Anna's
continuing and persistent efforts to promote her circle, to establish her
presence at court and to establish a context for the exercise of her own
politics.[43]

Six of the seven core noblewomen found in *Twelve Goddesses* were
featured again in *Blackness*. What is significant about these six, furthermore, is that, for the most part, Anna had chosen them not because
their husbands held powerful office, but because she seems to have
preferred them. With the exception being the Countess of Suffolk –
her husband, the Earl of Suffolk was the Lord Chamberlain, nephew
to Northampton, and in the King's inner political circle – the five
other ladies were not married to politically active men. The Countess
of Bedford and the Countess of Derby, two ladies who seem to have
remained closest to Anna, had earls for husbands who seem to have

preferred life away from London. Penelope Lady Rich was married to a baron, Lord Rich, whom she despised and who was not a political factor at court. Instead, Lady Rich was living with the prestigious Earl of Devonshire by whom she had borne several children. Susan de Vere (the future Countess of Montgomery), younger sister of the Countess of Derby, was sixteen and still unmarried, while the fifth, Audry Walsingham, was married to a knight, Sir Thomas Walsingham, who worked for and reported to Cecil. By foregrounding this group – the women closest to Anna on and off the stage – in what had become an important public spectacle, Anna was in effect elevating their status by means of their connections with her. Additionally, she chose a number of her 'extra' dancers, or visitors, from the circle with whom her highest-ranking courtier, her only Lady of the Bed Chamber, the Countess of Bedford, was most closely associated – that of the Sidney and Essex families. And again Anna did favours for their families by inviting these extra ladies to dance. One such was Lady Bevill, wife of Francis Manners, the future sixth Earl of Rutland (26 June 1612), brother of one of the four earls comprising the group of co-conspirators in the uprising of 1602, that is, Essex, Rutland, Bedford and Southampton.[44] Another was Lady Mary (Sidney) Wroth (married the previous September), daughter of Anna's Lord Chamberlain, Sir Robert Sidney, brother of Sir Philip and of the Countess of Pembroke and uncle of the young noble, Philip Herbert, whom Anna's lady, Susan de Vere, had just married. These new brides were thus related to the last visitor, Anne Herbert, the young unmarried daughter of the Countess of Pembroke.[45] Finally she re-invited Elizabeth Howard, daughter of the Countess of Suffolk and dancing last year at seventeen in *Twelve Goddesses*. In the interim Elizabeth had married William Baron Knollys, uncle of the late Earl of Essex, created baron at James's accession. Thus, presumably, Lord Knollys, the Earl and the Countess of Suffolk were all complimented by Elizabeth's inclusion here.

Although in the selections from the Essex circle one can begin to see the contours of what would become Anna's sphere of influence in the Jacobean court, Anna's even-handed political instincts prompted her once again, in this second masque, to include some ladies whose presence might be particularly important to James. Ann Lady Effingham, for example, was not a member of Anna's Drawing Chamber and danced only in this one masque. However, her father-in-law, the Earl of Nottingham, was to leave for Spain in several months at the head of the extremely prestigious embassage to sign the Spanish Peace as a follow-up of the Spanish visit to England of the previous summer. An additional reason for Effingham's inclusion may have been that Nottingham's own new young wife, who had danced as a member of the Drawing Chamber in the previous year, was prevented from masquing this year because of a facial disfigurement. In what looks like a similar substitution, to make up for the missing Countess of Hertford who was sick with the measles, Anna invited a dancer from the previous year, Elizabeth Howard.

The importance of the *masquers* in Anna's masques is underlined by the fact that part 1 of *The Masque of Blackness* was, like its counterpart in *Twelve Goddesses* (and despite the difference in the scriptwriters), again configured to emphasize identity and status among these women. Because *The Masque of Blackness* initially presented the twelve daughters of Niger in a great concave, four-tiered shell, for example, one might expect that each tier would be occupied by three of the twelve ladies. But, significantly, despite their uniform blackness, the noblewomen were grouped asymmetrically. The first tier contained only two: Queen Anna and the Countess of Bedford. Had Hertford, Anna's only other lady of the Bed Chamber, not been sick, she would presumably have taken her place with Anna and Bedford. But despite the fact that Anna had appointed a substitute to maintain the number of dancers at twelve, no one was added to the first tier containing herself and Bedford – even though two of the remaining *Blackness* participants (including Lady Suffolk, wife of James's Lord Chamberlain) were countesses. None of the other African queens, it seems, could substitute for an absent Lady of the chief African queen's most exclusive Bed Chamber.[46]

This initial statement of the tiers was refined by the two-by-two (rather than the former three-by-three) order of the subsequent procession.[47] Couple 1 was: the Queen and the Countess of Bedford; couple 2: Lady Herbert and the Countess of Derby; couple 3: Lady Rich and the Countess of Suffolk; couple 4: Lady Bevill and Lady Effingham; couple 5: Lady Elizabeth Howard and Lady Susan Vere; couple 6: Lady Mary Wroth and Lady Walsingham. Thus, though the Countess of Derby and Susan (de Vere) Herbert were sisters and both members of Anna's Drawing Chamber, Derby, as a countess, walked with young Anne Herbert. Anne Herbert had been living away from court with her mother the Countess of Pembroke at Wilton, where Queen Anna and James had spent almost all of November and December 1603 while plague raged in London. This placement might have been a way of displaying Anne Herbert, to recognize not only the former Pembroke hospitality, but also the closeness between the Queen and this family, whose members, including the young Earl of Pembroke, Anne's brother, were all connected to the Queen's inner circles.[48]

The Stuart court masque as presented by Queen Anna was calculated to fit into, to articulate, and even to appropriate the one court season of extended revels consecrated by custom. Although noblemen continued throughout the period of her masquing (1603–1612) to dance in wedding-masques scripted by Jonson and Campion, and paid for by the participants in order to honour the weddings of kinsmen, their clannish presentations hardly held centre stage in those seasons when the Queen herself claimed and metamorphosed the form. Pre-empting Twelfth Night, excluding male nobles from all but the takings-out and arranging spectacle whose extraordinary luxury was enabled by the resources of a royal treasury, Anna showcased herself and her ladies as the centre of the Christmas revels.

In doing so, she was also defining a sphere of influence distinctly her own, one which would, in subsequent years, move beyond the politics of public ritual represented by the masque to affairs of state, the province of her husband. But in the early years of the Jacobean accession, Anna was not yet a political player in the traditional sense, as she had been in Scotland, and the masque provided her with a special kind of political voice. In this context it is significant that Anna's masques were not inevitably recurring annual events: she planned masques only when she saw fit, and she ceased masquing when masques no longer served her ends.[49]

Figures make the point. *The Masque of Blackness*, performed on Twelfth Night 1605, actually marks the end of a first phase, for the Queen did not follow up this Twelfth Night masque with another until 1608. Indeed, although she reigned in England throughout sixteen holiday seasons before dying at age forty-five, Anna planned only seven masques. The last – proposed for Christmas 1611–12 – was cancelled in rehearsal in deference to the recent death of the Queen of Spain.[50] Thus Anna's sixth and last masque occurred only halfway through her reign: in the holiday season of 1610–11, when she had just turned thirty-six.

The Vision of the Twelve Goddesses and *The Masque of Blackness* might, then, be viewed as the opening salvos of a masquing career that was deliberate and purposeful. That Anna was able to seize the opportunity represented by the masque – to redesign the form so as to produce a major annual event that was distinctively her own – suggests that the traditional view of the Queen as frivolous and empty-headed is very far off the mark. This was a woman who thoroughly understood the political power of ceremonial display, and who self-consciously exploited it for her own ends as long as it proved useful.

NOTES

1 The Queen's first name, for obvious reasons, seldom appears in the correspondence of others to whom she was simply 'the Queen', but at least three instances indicate that she considered the Danish 'Anna' her name. She so signs it in a holograph letter (1603) to James ('so kissing your hands / I rest / yours / Anna R[egina]'). Similarly, her oath of office, when she was invested as Queen of Scotland, began in a Scottish account of 1590: 'The Queen's Majesty's Oath: "I Anna, by the grace of God, Queen of Scotland."' See *Papers Relative to the Marriage of King James the Sixth of Scotland* (Edinburgh, 1828), pp. v, xviii. A doggerel poem by John Burel of the same year, describing the 'form and manner' of the Queen's Scottish coronation, has one stanza beginning: 'Anna, our well-beloved Queen': see *Papers*. John Dowland's *Lachrimae* (London, 1604) is dedicated to 'the most sacred and gracious princess Anna Queen of England', while John Florio, a gentlemen of the Queen's Privy Chamber and her Italian teacher, offered his second rendering of his well-known Italian dictionary, *Queen Anna's New World of Words* (London, 1611), to 'the Imperial Majesty of the highest-born Princess, Anna of Denmark'.

2 Since Stephen Orgel's seminal works, *The Jonsonian Masque* (Cambridge, MA, 1965), and, with Roy Strong, *The Theatre of the Stuart Court*, 2 vols. (London, 1973), discussion of the Stuart masque has been extensive, but primarily focused on the symbolism of costume, setting and allegorical sequence. Political contexts have been suggested recently, but these focus on James, the nobles in his circle and the authors of the masques themselves, rather than on Anna. But see John Pitcher, '"In those Figures Which they Seeme": Samuel Daniel's *Tethys' Festival*', in David Lindley (ed.), *The Court Masque* (Manchester, 1984), pp. 33–46 and the works cited in its full bibliography.

3 For a useful survey of Elizabethan masquing, see Enid Welsford, *The Court Masque* (Cambridge, 1927), ch. 6.

4 See E. K. Chambers, *The Elizabethan Stage*, 4 vols. (Oxford, 1923), I, p. 168.

5 James also helped William Fowler, Queen Anna's secretary, to devise some sort of male show for the banquet honouring the baptism of Prince Henry on 23 August 1593. See Chambers, *Elizabethan Stage*, III, p. 351 and James I, *New Poems*, ed. Allan F. Westcott (New York, 1911), p. lviii.

6 See Chambers, *Elizabethan Stage*, I, pp. 169–70. Again, the occasion is *intime*, the ladies, in effect, maintaining a kind of seclusion in the context of a 'private' wedding.

7 See the journal of Cecil's assistant, Levinus Munck (p. 246) in Howard Vallance Jones, 'The journal of Levinus Munck', *English Historical Review* 68 (1953), 234–58.

8 See Diana Poulton, *John Dowland* (Berkeley, 1982), pp. 60–1.

9 See Leeds Barroll, 'The court of the first Stuart queen', in Linda Levy Peck (ed.), *The Mental World of the Jacobean Court* (Cambridge, 1991), pp. 191–208.

10 'The King will feast all the ambassadors this Christmas', wrote Arabella Stuart to her uncle the Earl of Shrewsbury on 18 December. See *The Letters of Arabella Stuart*, ed. Sara Jayne Steen (Oxford, 1994), p. 197.

11 Juan de Taxis, Count of Villa Mediana, the Ambassador Extraordinary of the King of Spain, would be feasted on 26 December (St Stephen's Day) in the Great Chamber at Hampton Court and then hear a play. On 27 December (Innocents Day) Stanislaus Cikowski de Voislanice, Vice-Chamberlain of Cracow, Ambassador Extraordinary of the King of Poland, would be feasted again with a professional stage performance following; and on Twelfth Night Christophe de Harlay, Comte de Beaumont, Ambassador Extraordinary from Henry IV of France, would have his turn, the entertainment this time including not only a play but also an untitled 'masquerade of certain Scotchmen' (I have called it 'The Orient Knights'). See *Dudley Carleton to John Chamberlain: 1603–1624*, ed. Maurice Lee, Jr. (New Brunswick, 1972), p. 54. Finally, on 12 January and 2 February (Candlemas) the ambassador from Savoy, and Alfonso Count Montecuccoli, ambassador of the Grand Duke of Tuscany, were scheduled for similar revels.

12 The French ambassador, anxious to attend the Queen's masque, made 'unmannerly expostulations with the king and for a few days troubled all the court', but the problem, very significantly, was settled by Queen Anna herself. She 'was fain to take the matter upon her, who as a masker had invited the Spaniard as the Duke [of Lennox] before had done the French'. The French emissary was 'flatly refused to be admitted'. It was the Polish and the Spanish ambassadors who attended the Queen's masque 'with their whole trains' (*Carleton*, p. 55).

13 *Ibid.*

14 The vehicle for Queen Anna's masquing debut, Samuel Daniel's *The Vision of the Twelve Goddesses*, dismissed by Enid Welsford as derivative – see Welsford, *Court Masque*, p. 171 – differs in significant ways from the tradition exemplified in the presentation of 'The Orient Knights'. It could even be argued (though this is not my present concern) that Jonson's masque for Christmas 1604–05 (Anna's second) followed innovations first appearing in the masque Samuel Daniel arranged for the particular purposes of Queen Anna.

15 Many of these 'regulars' were in their twenties, but their youth was not an imitation of the mode of male masquing, owing to the fact that the Queen, herself just turned thirty a month before, found this age-group most congenial.

16 The Earl of Worcester at this time described Anna's ladies belonging to the 'Bed Chamber', the 'Drawing Chamber' and the 'Private Chamber' as if in descending degrees of status, and named individuals. Of the 'Bed-Chamber': the Countess of Bedford and the Countess of Hertford; of the 'Drawing Chamber': the Countess of Derby, the Countess of Suffolk, Penelope Lady Rich, the Countess of Nottingham, Susan de Vere, [Audrey] Lady Walsingham and [Elizabeth] Lady Southwell; of the 'Private Chamber': 'All the rest'. See Edmund Lodge, *Illustrations of British History*, 3 vols. (London, 1838), III, p. 88. A list of Anna's 'servants', compiled before 18 March 1606, is calendared in *Calendar of the MSS of the Marquess of Salisbury Preserved at Hatfield House*, ed. M. S. Giuseppi (London, 1883–1976), XXIV, pp. 65–7 – hereafter cited as *Hatfield*. That Anna did not necessarily accentuate youth is suggested by the selection of Penelope Rich, fortyish at this point, to personate the goddess of beauty. None the less, Rich was thought of by the very young Anne Clifford in 1603 as one of the younger ladies of the Queen's new court. See *The Diaries of Lady Anne Clifford*, ed. D. J. H. Clifford (Wolfeboro Falls, NH, 1991), p. 24n.

17 In *Twelve Goddesses*, Dorothy Hastings and Elizabeth Howard are good examples of unmarried 'visitors'. Dorothy Hastings, daughter of the Earl of Huntingdon, would in several years marry the Scot Sir James Stuart, the eldest son of Lord Blantyre. Elizabeth Howard was seventeen and a daughter of the Countess of Suffolk, one of Anna's ladies of the Drawing Chamber who was dancing in the same masque. Making the kind of court appearance in the Christmas revels that would not have been possible before Anna's accession, Howard would be invited back in the following year for *The Masque of Blackness*, perhaps again through her mother's influence or because Anna liked her and wanted to congratulate her on her marriage in 1605 to William Knollys, uncle of the late Earl of Essex and created baron at James's accession.

18 *Carleton*, p. 53.

19 See Lodge, *Illustrations*, III, p. 87. As Chambers has noted, the first edition of Daniel's script must have been quickly printed if Worcester could already have bought it between 8 January and 2 February. See Chambers, *Elizabethan Stage*, III, p. 281.

20 Elsewhere in *Twelve Goddesses*, Iris reinforces this identification when she refers to the other goddesses of the masque (including Juno) as 'these deities by the motion of the all-directing Pallas, the glorious patroness of this mighty monarchy, descending in the majesty of their invisible essence'. John Florio, dedicating his Italian Dictionary, *Queen Anna's New World of Words*, in 1611 addressed her as 'most absolute supreme Minerva', and still later in *Cupid's Banishment* (4 May 1617) given before Queen Anna at Greenwich, the figure Occasion, speaking an epilogue to the Queen, addressed her as 'Bright Pallas and royal mistress of our muse'. See Robert White, *Cupid's Banishment*, ed. C. E. McGee in *Renaissance Drama* ns 19 (1988), 226–64.

21 Samuel Daniel was careful to write a full description of *Twelve Goddesses* in the published quarto, but a contemporary list yields the identities of those ladies chosen by the Queen for the first masque of her reign. See W. W. Greg (ed.), *A Bibliography of English Printed Drama to the Restoration*, 4 vols. (London, 1962), I, number 207.

22 See *Carleton*, p. 55. A matter of some curiosity is the gender and identity of the three Graces and the torch-bearers. Were these figures personated by professional players? If so, they would have been men; otherwise ladies of lower rank would have assumed these places.

23 See Barroll, 'Court of the first Stuart queen', pp. 205–6.

24 In many instances, as in funeral processions, those who came before had lesser precedential status than those who followed, but Anna, occupying the *first* row in the masque procession, was obviously defining the direction of status within it.

25 See John Stow, *Annals [as continued by Edmond Howes]* (London, 1615), sigs. 4C5–4C5ᵛ [pp. 862–3]. Bedford, Hertford and Derby all had higher precedence than Suffolk which was an earldom created at James's accession. See William Harrison, *The Description of England*, ed. Georges Edelen (Washington, 1968), pp. 121–2. The last two triads (triads three and four) were obviously a miscellaneous repository that included two Drawing Chamber ladies of lesser rank: Lady Walsingham (the wife of a knight, Sir Thomas Walsingham, Chief Keeper, along with his wife, of the Queen's Wardrobe) and Susan de Vere, included in the last group. The two remaining goddesses, Lady Hatton and the newly married Countess of Nottingham, may have been least in favour although Nottingham was listed as of the Drawing Chamber. Hatton had tried unsuccessfully to use her powerful uncle, Robert Cecil, to become one of Anna's ladies (*Hatfield*, xv, p. 388) while the twenty-three-year-old Lady Nottingham (Margaret Stewart), her parents both dead and a ward of Queen Anna, may have offended by marrying the new widower, the seventy-year-old Earl of Nottingham, without Anna's permission, thus becoming an instant countess in her household: a letter from Anna to James laughs at the marriage. For Stewart's background, see *Complete Peerage*, ed. H. A. Doubleday *et al.* (London, 1910–59), IX, pp. 185–86; 786–87. Lady Nottingham, absent from *Blackness* a year later (see below), was in none of the Queen's later masques, having been banished from the court in the fall of 1606 for sending an intemperate letter of defiance to Anna's well-loved brother, the King of Denmark, for a fancied slight after his English visit in 1606 (*Carleton*, p. 90).

26 See Samuel Daniel, *The Vision of the Twelve Goddesses*, ed. Joan Rees in *A Book of Masques*, ed. T. J. B. Spencer and Stanley Wells (Cambridge, 1967), p. 29.

27 Beatrice, in *Much Ado About Nothing*, distinguishes between courtship, wedding and repentance as being like various kinds of dances. 'The first suit is hot and hasty, like a Scotch jig, and full as fantastical; the wedding,

mannerly-modest, as a measure, full of state and ancientry' (2.1.69–72). Cf. the use of 'measure' by Benvolio as he and Romeo plan the gentlemen's masque brought to the Capulet house. Deciding to forego any boring prologue or explanation of their costumes, Romeo proposes: 'But let them measure us by what they will, / We'll measure them a measure, and be gone' (1.4.9–10). For the description of an English 'measure' surviving from the period, see the Bodleian Library MS, 'My Lord of Essex Measure', whose detailed directions are discussed in Mabel Dolmetsch, *Dances of England and France from 1450 to 1600* (London, 1949), ch. 3. See also the important study by Otto Gombosi, 'Some musical aspects of the English court masque', *Journal of the American Musicological Society* 1.3 (1948), 3–19, and, most lately, Andrew J. Sabol (ed.), *A Score for 'The Lords' Masque' by Thomas Campion* (Providence, RI, 1993), pp. 22–23.

28 This reverence was performed before the music of the dance started: musicians often played an opening chord or four bars of introduction to accompany it. Exemplary are comments in 1618 when Prince Charles, dancing in the measures of *Pleasure Reconciled to Virtue*, 'excelled them all in bowing, being very formal in making his obeisance both to the King and to the lady with whom he danced'. See *Calendar of State Papers and Manuscripts Relating to . . . Venice*, 35 vols., ed. H. F. Brown *et al.* (London: HMC, 1864–), xv, p. 114. (The editor erroneously – p. 111 – refers to this masque as *The Vision of Delight*.)

29 According to the attentive Dudley Carleton, 'The Orient Knights' was perhaps under-rehearsed for this part. 'The first measure was full of changes and seemed confused, but was well gone through withal' – see *Carleton*, p. 54. Paul Reyher, *Les Masques Anglais* (Paris, 1909), pp. 435–64 has a useful discussion of masque dances.

30 Some idea of the complexity possible in these initial measures of part 2 may be derived from the annotations of Thomas Campion for *Lord Hay's Masque*. 'The nine masquers in their green habits solemnly descended to the dancing place in such order as they were to begin their dance . . . As soon as the chorus ended, the violins or consort of twelve began to play the second new dance . . .' Then a speech, a visit to a grove with music and then 'the motet being ended, the violins began the third new dance which was lively performed by the masquers, *after which* [italics added] they took forth the ladies and danced the measures with them': see Thomas Campion, *Works*, ed. Walter R. Davis (New York, 1967), pp. 222–5. Campion's part 2 thus offered three dances of increasing tempo.

31 Indeed, Carleton, who had criticized sloppy dancing in 'The Orient Knights', saw the Queen's measures here as 'nothing inferior to' the grand entrance that had so entranced him. See *Carleton*, p. 55, and *Twelve Goddesses*, p. 30. Reyher, *Les Masques Anglais*, pp. 447–8, seems to conflate part 2 with part 3.

32 *Carleton*, p. 54.

33 On the former point, the Venetian ambassador, Antoine de la Boderie, writing about a court masque in 1609, observed that Prince Charles, having been taken out by one of the ladies in the Queen's masque, returned to take out his granddaughter: 'le Duc d'Yorck ayant été pris a danser par une des Dames du ballet, il vint aussitôt chercher madite fille où elle étoit, & l'y mena'. See Mary Sullivan, *Court Masques of James I* (New York, 1913), p. 218.

34 Cf. Campion: 'Now the masquers began their lighter dances as corrantoes, levaltos, and galliards wherein when they had spent as much time as they thought fit, Night spake thus . . .' (*Works*, p. 226). In 'The Orient Knights' the clothing had not been well thought out for this lively part 4 since 'their attire was rich but somewhat too heavy and cumbersome for dancers, which put them besides their galliards' (*Carleton*, p. 54).

35 See *Carleton*, p. 54, and Campion's description of his own masque, *Works*, p. 227: 'At the end of these words the violins began the fourth new dance which was excellently discharged by the masquers . . . After the dance followed this dialogue of two voices . . . performed with several echoes of music . . . at the end whereof the masquers, putting off their vizards and helmets, made a low honour to the King.' In the French court, the dancing of all the masquers in exhibition served as the finale (Welsford, *Court Masque*, p. 166).

36 For details of Monteagle's background, see David Mathew, *James I* (London, 1967), pp. 144–6, and for the Essex connection specifically, see *Marquess of Bath MSS*, ed. G. Dyfnallt Owen, 6 vols. (London, 1980), v, p. 278.

37 Dudley Carleton listed the twelve invitees of part 3, and in this order: the Earl of Pembroke, the Duke of Lennox, the Earl of Suffolk, Henry Lord Howard (future Earl of Northampton), the Earl of Southampton, the Earl of Devonshire, Sir Robert Sidney (the Queen's Lord Chamberlain), the Earl of Nottingham, Lord Monteagle, the Earl of Northumberland, William Lord Knollys (now Lord Treasurer and future husband, we recall, of Elizabeth Howard dancing in the masque) and the Earl of Worcester.

38 *Carleton*, p. 56.

39 There remains only one letter, in draft form, from this interchange, in which the Privy Council reviews James's statements – and their own – from previous corespondences. All quotations here have been taken from this draft to be found in the Manuscripts of the Marquess of Salisbury at Hatfield House (vol. CIX, fols. 89–90) and calendered in close paraphrase in *Hatfield*, XVI, pp. 388–9.

40 This £4,000 figure interestingly reverberates throughout the remarks of those hostile to *The Masque of Blackness* at that time. See Leeds Barroll, 'Theatre as text: the case of Queen Anna and the Jacobean court masque', in A. L. Magnusson and C. E. McGee (eds.), *The Elizabethan Theatre XIV* (Toronto, 1996), pp. 175–93.

41 It is hard to imagine *The Masque of Blackness* as Jonson's idea. Jonson was merely a common playwright-artisan in the eyes of those of the Queen's

household with whom he would have to deal (he was not even on the regular court payroll). Thus it does not seem likely that he would have suggested such a startling innovation as his first piece of work for the Queen and her countesses.

42 See, for example, Kim F. Hall, 'Sexual politics and cultural identity in *The Masque of Blackness*', in Sue-Ellen Case and Janelle Reinelt (eds.), *The Performance of Power* (Iowa City, 1991), pp. 3–18; Margo Hendricks and Patricia Parker (eds.), *Women, Race and Writing in the Early Modern Period* (London, 1994); Barroll, 'Theatre as text'.

43 A glance at the text of *The Masque of Blackness* may suggest how Ben Jonson's own 'literary' interests may obscure for us the overriding importance of the presence of the Queen and her ladies to these occasions. The entire text is composed of 365 lines. Speeches by Aethiopia, Oceanus and Niger, with descriptions of scenery, consume 274 lines of the text before the eleven-line listing of the Queen and her ladies appears. The remaining seventy-nine lines present more speeches together with the songs sung by professional performers, despite the fact that there were four more parts to follow. These are summed up in five lines of text as follows. 'Their own single dance ended [part 2], as they were about to make choice of their men' [here there is a song that consumes eight lines of text]. Then: 'Here they danced with their men, several measures and corantoes [parts 3 and 4]. All which ended, they were again accited to sea with a song of etc. [part 5]'.

44 Lady Bevill's husband was the noble for whom Richard Burbage and William Shakespeare would execute the *impresa* for the tilting of 24 March 1613. She, however, died of smallpox in the October following the presentation of *Blackness*.

45 It is the occasional nature of these 'visitor' appearances that misleads. Thus both Lady Mary Wroth and Lady Anne Clifford, though significant as authors of well-known bodies of writing, are often described by commentators as 'having danced in Anne's masques'. This is literally true in that each woman made one or two appearances as a member of that year's quartet of occasional *visitors*, but these infrequent invitations should not serve as indices of these ladies' closeness to Anna or prestige at court. Despite Anne Clifford's 'in my youth I was much in court with her and in masques attended her, though I never served her' (see *Lives of Lady Anne Clifford . . . and of her Parents Summarized by Herself*, ed. J. P. Gilson (London, 1916), p. 38), the Queen invited Clifford only for two consecutive years (1608, 1609) to be a visitor: in *The Masque of Beauty* and *The Masque of Queens*. Lady Mary Wroth danced as a visitor in *The Masque of Blackness* only.

46 See Sir Ralph Winwood, *Memorials of Affairs of State*, ed. Edmund Sawyer, 3 vols. (London, 1725), II, p. 44, and *Ben Jonson*, ed. C. H. Herford and Percy and Evelyn Simpson, 11 vols. (Oxford, 1925–52), x, pp. 448–50. For what it is worth, Dudley Carleton, who described this seating arrangement, lists 'the rest' in this order: 'Ladies Suffolk, Derby, Rich, Effingham,

Anne Herbert, Susan [de Vere] Herbert, Elizabeth Howard, Walsingham and Bevill' (Winwood, *Memorials*, II, p. 44).

47 Jonson noted 'every couple (as they advanced) severally presenting their fans in one of which were inscribed their mixed names, in the other a mute hieroglyphic expressing their mixed qualities' (Herford and Simpson (eds.), *Ben Jonson*, VII, p. 177). It is possible that these emblematic dimensions reinforced in some way the political significance of Anna's pairings.

48 Physical stature may have had something to do with this arrangement, but I doubt it, unless all countesses and baronesses were taller (or shorter) than the other ladies. Penelope Rich continued to be honoured as Essex's sister and, as the only baroness in the group, preceded one of Anna's favorites, Susan de Vere, who had been given away by King James at her elaborate wedding at court on 27 December.

49 In a forthcoming book-length study of Queen Anna's political activities, I argue that in the later years of her Jacobean reign she returned to the practice of active political intervention that characterized her years in Scotland (briefly described in Barroll, 'The court of the first Stuart queen').

50 The six masques presented by the Queen are, in chronological order and with the inclusive dates for the relevant Christmas holiday season: *The Vision of the Twelve Goddesses* (1603–04); *The Masque of Blackness* (1604–05); *The Masque of Beauty* (1607–08); *The Masque of Queens* (1608–09); *Tethys' Festival* (June 1610); and *Love Freed from Ignorance and Folly* (1610–11). Lists of the dancers' names exist for the first five, but not for *Love Freed* or for the cancelled masque of 1611–12.

CHAPTER 7

Marginal Jonson

Stephen Orgel

The fictions of playwrights, Stephen Gosson told his readers, were the cups of Circe.[1] The magical power of Renaissance theatre, its ability not merely to compel wonder in its audiences but to change them, whether for good or evil, by persuasion or seduction, is assumed by both attackers and defenders of the art, and Gosson's warning fully acknowledges both the danger of the stage and its irresistible attractiveness. When Prospero, near the end of *The Tempest*, renounces his magic with a speech adapted almost verbatim from Ovid's Medea, the evocation of witchcraft through the classic exemplar of a dangerously beautiful woman encapsulates the full range of Renaissance attitudes to the theatrical magician's powers. But the literary allusion goes beyond the anti-theatrical trope; for at this moment the hero ceases to be a character and becomes a text. The script the actor recites is a book, a classic, a passage that every schoolchild in Shakespeare's England could also recite. This is a Jonsonian moment in Shakespeare, the invocation of a classic text to establish the authority of the fiction, to strike the audience with a shock of recognition, to place the drama in the context not of an ephemeral performance, but of the history of poetry.

Jonson debunks the magic of theatre in *The Alchemist*, but alchemy in the play is more than the art of charlatans making a quick fortune. It is the stuff of ingenious dramatic plotting and theatrical illusions; it also evokes the magnificent poetry of Sir Epicure Mammon and, indeed, the moral philosophy of Jonson the comic classicist. The play is, in the deepest sense, about Jonson turning the basest materials – charlatanry, greed, whoredom (and perhaps we should include theatre) – into gold; and not only the gold of poetry, but his own success as poet and playwright, establishing him as the patriarch to a family of poetic disciples who duly constituted themselves 'the sons of Ben', a father whose 'best piece of poetry' was his first son Benjamin, the 'child of my right hand', the hand he wrote with.

Theatrical magic, then, is both a quality of language and a way of establishing oneself, of rising in society; a way for servants (or employees of theatrical companies) to become masters. Like that classic exemplar of theatrical sorcery *Doctor Faustus*, *The Alchemist* is about getting rich and powerful in the world of Renaissance capitalism. The magic of *The Tempest* is less openly concerned with this, but the theme is there: in Stephano's plan to turn his islander-servant into a money-making sideshow in London; in Caliban's dream of riches dropping upon him (this is clearly not about life on the island, where riches would have no value: whose dream is this?). It is the servants who have these fantasies; when they become masters, the dreams are dreams of power – but power of a specific kind, the reverse of the servants' dreams: what Prospero's magic enables him to do is precisely to be the head of his household, to control his children and his servants. It is Ariel who, on Prospero's orders, raises the tempest and stages the disappearing banquet; both he and the bad child Caliban serve Prospero, but only under strong compulsion. Magic confers an absolute authority within very narrow bounds: the power to be obeyed by the rest of the family.

It confers, that is, a patriarchal authority, and thereby the authority to arrange marriages. The betrothal of Miranda to Ferdinand is a principal part of Prospero's scheme; in the same way, Face's miraculous larcenies are ultimately validated when he produces a rich widow for his master Lovewit to marry. Magic produces a wife – for Renaissance men the crucially enabling form of property, the key not merely to genetic posterity, but to an income, land, alliances with other powerful men. Faustus, indeed, is all but unique in wanting a wife for sex: 'for I am wanton and lascivious and cannot live without a wife'.[2] But the magic in this case is suddenly ineffective – as always, Faustus asks for too little: Mephistopheles balks at arranging a marriage (presumably because it is a sacrament), offering instead all the courtesans Faustus can handle. The magician, however, turns to books instead; and when he finally gets the woman he wants, she is neither a wife nor a courtesan, but Helen of Troy, a literary allusion, like Medea or Circe, another text.

The wife as book, compliant, silent, obedient, open only when her husband opens her, the perfect embodiment of male desire, is very much a Jonsonian topos, the topos so decisively and delusively invoked by Morose in *Epicoene*. But the problem with the topos, as Jonsonian wives like the Collegiate Ladies and Lady Politic Would-be demonstrate, is the refusal of women to enact it. The unmanageable wife embodies what Jonson's own theatrical magic could never control, the 'shrew but honest' – chaste enough, but a virago, giving him no satisfaction ('five years he had not bedded with her', he told Drummond),[3] and by the same token, impossible to satisfy.

What happened, then, when Jonson worked for women, when his success depended on his ability to satisfy them? The persona he and Inigo Jones provided for the Queen in their first Twelfth Night masque for the Jacobean court was devised according to her specific stipulations (figure 7.1); Jonson followed orders, and when Sir Dudley Carleton found fault with the result, it was not the poet and designer who were blamed, it was the King's unmanageable wife. If Queen Anne's costume in *The Masque of Blackness* was, as Carleton complained, 'too light and courtesan-like for such great ones',[4] the Queen was clearly wearing what she wanted to wear. The criticism has been taken as the truth about the masque, but it has certainly been generalized too far. If we rely for our understanding of Renaissance events solely on the evidence of the few eyewitness accounts that survive, or take these simply at face value, we become the prisoners of the tastes and prejudices of those witnesses. In this case, it is probably sufficient to observe that fashion descends from above, and it is in the nature of new fashions to displace older ones; part of the function of new styles is to surprise and defeat expectations. Carleton found the costumes transgressive, but the Queen and her ladies doubtless saw them as innovative, stylish and attractive, and they obviously set the style for the next few years. In the masquers' costume for *Love Freed* (figure 7.2) in 1611, the sheer, filmy fabric that had so offended Carleton has become the stuff of standard masquing dress. Queen Anne's clothes, like those of many women in the upper reaches of society before and since, were characteristically in the forefront of fashion; and were, indeed, what set the fashion.

As for the more basic problem of the Queen's blackness, though Carleton could not 'imagine a more ugly sight than a troop of lean-cheeked Moors' and cited the 'danger' that her makeup would soil the lips of a dancing partner who kissed her hand (as the Spanish ambassador, in what Carleton evidently considers an excess of gallantry, did), it is unlikely here again that the Queen was undertaking to present herself and her ladies as ugly or even transgressive. The black makeup no doubt did represent a problem for a partner, but hardly a new one: ladies regularly used white makeup on the exposed parts of their bodies

Figure 7.1 Inigo Jones, costume design for a nymph in *The Masque of Blackness*, 1605.

Figure 7.2 Inigo Jones, masquer's costume for *Love Freed from Ignorance and Folly*, 1611.

– not only faces and bosoms, but hands and forearms as well – and this was just as likely to adulterate the male courtly lip. Kissing a whitened hand is never claimed to be dangerous in any way except morally, though the mercury- and lead-based whiteners were actually quite poisonous. The real key to Carleton's reaction here may lie not simply in the symbolic difference between black and white, but more deeply in the fact that white cosmetics were naturalized because men employed them too.

It is, in any case, unlikely that Carleton's distaste for the performance was widely shared: the Venetian ambassador found it 'very beautiful and sumptuous',[5] and another correspondent, who did not see the performance, reported what he had heard, that it was 'a sumptuous show represented by the Queen and some dozen ladies all painted like blackamoors, face and neck bare, and for the rest strangely attired in Barbaresque mantles'.[6] What is cited in these accounts is not ugliness, but richness, innovation and exoticism. The conceit of the Queen in blackface in fact must have been been not offensive but quite pleasing, since it was repeated seven months later when Queen Anne's brother Christian IV came to visit, and the royal party were entertained by Cecil at Theobalds with a masque in which the Queen of Sheba brought gifts to the Solomonic monarchs. Sir John Harington's famous account of the resulting fiasco makes much of the drunkenness of the participants, including the two kings, but includes no complaints about the complexion of the Abyssinian Queen, a role performed by an unnamed and unfortunately clumsy court lady; nor did King Christian hesitate to dance with her for fear of being soiled by her blackness – he was in any case already quite soiled by the cream cakes and other sweetmeats she had just spilled on him.

Women's fashion and women's cosmetics, of course, were a continuing source of masculine anxiety. So, if it comes to that, was men's fashion, as all the complaints about the effeminacy of male aristocratic dress in the period make clear. Carleton's dismay at the masquers' dress is part of a larger cultural debate over the decorum and boundaries of gender itself, of what properly constituted the feminine and the manly. The real innovation in the costumes for *Blackness*, indeed, was probably the fact that cosmetics were being allowed to do the work of clothing, the fact that the ladies were not masked and had bare forearms and sheer overmantles that revealed their upper arms. It would most likely have been this, not the dresses, that Carleton registered as 'too light and courtesan-like,' too blatantly feminine, but also, in its

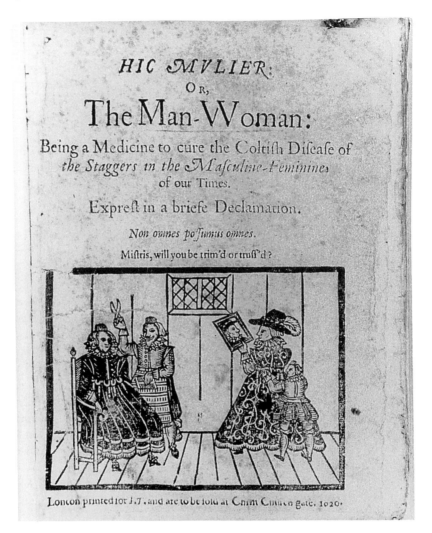

Figure 7.3 *Hic Mulier*, 1620, titlepage.

aggressive display of sexuality – Queen Anne was visibly pregnant – paradoxically masculine as well.

The King of England, the French ambassador observed, 'was not master in his own house'.[7] The fear that women were adopting the prerogatives of men is so ubiquitous as to constitute a topos in the period, encapsulated in figure 7.3, the emblematic title page to *Hic*

Mulier. It is articulated in John Chamberlain's report to Dudley Carleton of the King's fervent admonition to the London clergy 'to inveigh vehemently and bitterly in their sermons against the insolency of our women, and their wearing of broad-brimmed hats, pointed doublets, their hair cut short or shorn, and some of them stillettos or poniards . . . adding withall that if pulpit admonitions will not reform them he would proceed by another course'.[8] This admonition was directed against what the King saw as a masculine style of dress; but the ministers did not invariably understand the point of the royal injunction. 'The Dean of Westminster', Chamberlain reported a few weeks later, 'hath been very strict in his church against ladies and gentlewomen about yellow ruffs, and would not suffer them to be admitted into any pew'. Since yellow ruffs were particularly stylish at the moment, the fashionable parishioners appealed at once to the King, who was obliged to explain that 'his meaning was not for yellow ruffs, but for other man-like and unseemly apparel'.[9]

What constitutes masculinity, however, in apparel as in everything else, is a matter of opinion. Paul van Somer's portrait of the Queen (figure 7.4) shows her with broad-brimmed hat, short hair, pointed doublet – and yellow ruffs.[10] The picture, roughly contemporary with the King's expostulation, was painted for her, and shows her own palace of Oatlands in the background; it presents her as she wanted to see herself, as queen and huntress. The implications of the costume are revealed in the contemporaneous French term for a riding habit, *amazone*. Whether this is seen as transgressive or as attractive depends on where one stands; but clearly aristocratic women who dressed in this way were not imitating men, they were imitating the Queen. The royal style, moreover, whether 'light and courtesan-like' or 'man-like', was surely intended to render the Queen and her ladies *attractive*: women do not dress to be repellent.

Queen Anne's taste in clothes was individual and innovative. Her taste in poets, designers and entertainments was too. Fifteen years ago I suggested that court masques should properly be viewed as genuine collaborations between the artists and the patrons.[11] I cited an example that has to do precisely with fashion: when I was working on the Inigo Jones drawings, I was initially puzzled by the fact that Jones regularly did his costume designs in monochrome, in a brown or grey wash, and indicated the colours with annotations. Wouldn't it have made more sense to do the drawings in colour, so that the masquers and their dressmakers could see what the costume was actually going to look

Figure 7.4 Paul van Somer, *Anne of Denmark*, *c.* 1616.

like? Out of several hundred surviving drawings, only seven show
the costumes in colour. The solution became clear when I got a look
at the notes and letters accompanying the drawings: Jones would do
his designs, and submit them, with his suggestions, to the Queen. She
then chose the colours, and made whatever changes in the design that

she wished. The inscriptions on the sketch of Queen Henrietta Maria's costume for *Chloridia* (figure 7.5) read, in the margin, 'green, white, white green,' and below: 'This design I conceive to be fit for the invention, and if it please Her Majesty to add or alter anything I desire to receive Her Majesty's command and the design again by this bearer. The colours also are in Her Majesty's choice, but my opinion is that several fresh greens mixed with gold and silver will be most proper'.

Hymenaei, performed in 1606, provides an especially striking instance of the independence of the aristocratic performers at these spectacles. The costume as Inigo Jones designed it is described by Jonson: 'the upper part of white cloth of silver wrought with Juno's birds and fruits; a loose undergarment, full gathered, of carnation, striped with silver and parted with a golden zone; beneath that another flowing garment of watchet [light blue] cloth of silver . . .'. In the portrait of one of the masquers, in figure 7.6, the double skirt of Jones's design is clearly visible, though the top skirt does not appear to be 'parted', unless this means simply separated from the upper garment. But the portrait in figure 7.7 shows Lucy Harington, Countess of Bedford dressed for the same masque. Her costume has a single skirt. That is the way this aristocratic dancer preferred to appear; she paid for the costume, and her own dressmaker made it. The other dancers would have felt entitled to make their own alterations in their costumes as well.

When Jonson says that he 'apted' his invention to the commands of Queen Anne in writing *The Masque of Blackness*, he is acknowledging that his poetic invention follows, depends upon, and is subject to the authority of the Queen; the conceit of blackness is the Queen's. If we took the patronage system seriously, the Queen's invention would be as interesting to us as Jonson's. Why did the Queen want to appear black? Inigo Jones's costume emphasizes the richness and exoticism of the conceit; its sources are two figures from Vecellio's book of national costumes (figure 7.8), a Thessalonian bride for the headdress and an Ethiopian virgin for the striped and embroidered gown. But though Thessalonica was Turkish at this period, the headdress has a broader geographical history: it is called a Persian mitre – the daughters of Niger emanate from the Renaissance imagination of the Orient and of biblical antiquity. Analogously, Harington opens his account of the festivities provided for the reception of Christian IV by likening them to Mahomet's paradise – figure 7.9, for comparison, shows the costumes for a stylish mascarade designed by Boissard in 1597. Harington's analogy is certainly intended ironically, but the choice of the simile is

Figure 7.5 Inigo Jones, sketch for the Queen's costume in *Chloridia*, 1631.

Figure 7.6 A masquer in *Hymenaei*, 1606.

Figure 7.7 Lucy, Countess of Bedford in costume for *Hymenaei*, 1606.

Figure 7.8 Cesare Vecellio, Thessalonian bride, Ethiopian virgin,
from *Habiti antichi et moderni di tutto il Mondo*, 1598

Figure 7.9 Robert Boissard, Turkish masquerade, from
Mascarades recueillies, Valenciennes, 1597.

Figure 7.10 Henry Peacham (?), scene from *Titus Andronicus, c.* 1595.

not accidental, and it reveals a genuine ambivalence, both admiring
and disapproving. We inevitably see Blackamoors through the history
of black slavery and of modern racism, but in 1605 the English view
of blacks was more complex, and the language of racism was being
principally applied to the Irish, where it obviously had nothing to do
with skin colour. Interesting recent work on the English response to
Africans sometimes oversimplifies this complexity, but it reveals a much
larger black presence in Elizabethan England than has previously been
acknowledged. Eldred Jones's well-known book *Othello's Countrymen* has
now been supplemented by the work of Ania Loomba, Lynda Boose,
Margo Hendricks, Ruth Cowhig, Gretchen Gerzina and, most fully
and lucidly, Peter Fryer and Kim Hall.[12] In what follows, I am in part
indebted to their research.

To begin with, as Carleton's reference to 'lean-cheeked Moors' indicates, Negroes and Moors were often conflated, as the jet-black Aaron
the Moor in figure 7.10, the *Titus Andronicus* drawing of 1595, shows.
The conflation is almost caricatured in figure 7.11, the plate of a 'Well-
to-do Moor' in Vecellio's 1598 Venetian costume book.[13] Moors were
more likely to be slave owners and traders than slaves. Othello's 'thick
lips' similarly betoken the conflation; and Shakespeare makes him both
heroic warrior and former slave. Opinion was divided over whether
blackness was an inherent (or as we would say genetic) characteristic,
or an acquired one, the result of continual exposure to the equatorial
sun. The latter was the line taken about American Indians; it was

Figure 7.11 Vecellio, Well-to-do Moor, 1598.

claimed that if an Indian baby were kept out of the sun, it would grow up white. In contrast, George Best's observations, in 1578, are cited by several critics to indicate the absoluteness of the English attitude toward the skin colour of Africans:

I myself have seen an Ethiopian as black as coal brought into England, who taking a fair English woman to wife, begat a son in all respects as black as the father was, although England were his native country, and an Englishwoman his mother; whereby it seemeth that blackness proceedeth rather of some natural infection of that man, that neither the nature of the clime, neither the good complexion of the mother concurring, could anything alter . . .[14]

Against this notion of the black father's 'natural infection', which inevitably overwhelms 'the good complexion' of the white mother, however, we might set the evidence of Aaron the Moor, in *Titus Andronicus*, who, when Tamora gives birth to his black child, determines to substitute another:

> Not far, one Muliteus my countryman
> His wife but yesternight was brought to bed;
> His child is like to her, fair as you are.   (4.2.154–6)

This in its way is an even more frightening fantasy, a testimony to the impossibility of determining not only whether one's child is one's own, but even whether it is 'really' white or black: blackness in this case is not at all a function of skin colour. Lynda Boose, in an essay anatomizing the complexity of English Renaissance attitudes, argues that by Shakespeare's time the genetic theory – that blacks were racially 'infected' with their skin colour, not merely (like the American Indians) sunburnt – was the predominant and scientifically correct one,[15] but while this is doubtless true, it overstates the case: both theories remained current and available; the correctness of either depended on what one wished to demonstrate.

When the Prince of Morocco in *The Merchant of Venice* describes his complexion as 'The shadowed livery of the burnished sun, / To whom I am a neighbor and near bred' (2.1.2–3), he represents his blackness as acquired, and the claim serves as a mode of idealization. He comes off a great deal better than any of Portia's white European suitors, including the English one; and arguably, indeed, better too than the profligate and mercenary Bassanio. The fact that Morocco's skin colour is the only thing Portia finds to dislike about him probably says more about xenophobia, something the English understood well, than about racism (a local Italian, after all, is the only suitor Portia likes).

Cleopatra, endlessly seductive and desirable, is similarly 'with Phoebus' amorous pinches black' (1.5.29), radically, even erotically, sunburnt. This is an aspect of what Philo in the first lines of *Antony and Cleopatra* calls her 'gypsy's lust', but there is no suggestion anywhere in the play that it renders her ugly. It makes her, on the contrary, dangerously attractive. The danger here derives specifically from her designation not as black but as a gypsy, which obviously has to do with more than its etymological derivation from 'Egyptian'. Buckingham's decision in 1621 to have Jonson represent him and his family as a band of gypsies evoked from the poet an equally keen sense of both the attractiveness and the danger.

The ambiguous and imponderable issue of blackness was growing increasingly visible because English involvement in the African slave trade, which was to be considerable by the end of the seventeenth century, was already well under way. Hakluyt records John Lok's return from a voyage to Guinea in 1555 with five African slaves; by the mid-1560s, the English captain George Fenner was trading blacks for sugar.[16] Sir John Hawkins maintained a lucrative trade in Africans in the 1560s and 70s, heavily subsidized by the Earls of Leicester and Pembroke, and by the Queen herself, who not only invested in his voyages but also supplied him with two ships. As his portrait in figure 7.12 shows, Hawkins was proud enough of his continuing success in this venture to take as his crest 'a demi-Moor, proper, in chains'. ('Demi' means a half-length figure, 'proper' means in natural colouring, not heraldic colours – the blacks are real, not allegorical.) The slaves were for the most part traded to the Spanish in the West Indies, but blacks were, nevertheless, an exotic presence in London at this period, generally but not invariably as servants – a sufficiently disturbing presence, indeed, for expulsion orders to be issued twice in the decade preceding the performance of *Blackness*. The terms of the expulsion order are instructive:

Whereas the Queen's majesty, tendering the good and welfare of her own natural subjects greatly distressed in these hard times of dearth, is highly discontented to understand the great number of Negroes and blackamoors which . . . are crept into this realm since the troubles between her highness and the King of Spain; who are fostered and relieved here, to the great annoyance of her own liege people who want the relief which these people consume, as also for that the most of them are infidels having no understanding of Christ or his Gospel: hath given especial commandment that the said kind of people shall be with all speed avoided and discharged out of this Her

Figure 7.12 Robert Boissard, engraved portrait of Sir John Hawkins, *c.* 1590.

Majesty's dominions; and to that end and purpose hath appointed Casper van Senden, merchant of Lubeck, for their speedy transportation, a man that hath very well deserved of this realm in respect that by his own labour and charge he hath relieved and brought from Spain divers of our English nation, who otherwise would have perished there. These shall therefore be to will and require you and every of you to aid and assist the said Casper van Senden . . . to take up such Negroes and blackamoors to be transported as aforesaid, as he shall find within the realm of England; and if there shall be any person or persons which are possessed of any such blackamoors that refuse to deliver them in sort as aforesaid, then we require you to call them before you and advise and persuade them . . .'[17]

Van Senden is here apparently being repaid for his assistance in repatriating English nationals marooned in Spain, presumably after unsuccessful maurauding ventures, by being granted the right to expropriate and sell blacks resident in England. The order initially describes the blacks as refugees, but subsequently makes it clear that they are, or at least are to be considered, property: 'any person or persons possessed of such blackamoors' are commanded to give them up. The language is once again xenophobic but not racist; the blacks are foreign and heathen, and in a time of spiraling inflation and unemployment are crowding the Elizabethan welfare rolls and threatening English access to work. The fact that the foreigners are infidels relieves the commonwealth of any claim on its Christian charity; the fact that they are property renders them valuable, and a marketable commodity. Blackness is not presented as the primary issue; and in fact the Irish were similarly expelled at this period, though with no suggestion that they were to be sold. Perhaps they were not felt to be marketable; however the first slaves sent to the English plantations in the West Indies in 1623 were Irish. I should add that I can find no evidence that van Senden succeeded in possessing himself of any blacks.

It is doubtful that any of this has any direct connection with the conceit of the Queen's masque; but the idea of aristocratic women as blacks, that is, as marketable commodities and rich possessions, is surely not irrelevant to the age's construction of women generally, and specifically of their negotiation in marriage, their status as the property first of their fathers and then of their husbands. Queen Anne in blackface is, in this sense, merely representing herself in the terms set by the culture. Of course, the point of *The Masque of Blackness* is ultimately to render the ladies white and English; but this is something that is only projected to take place a year later (in the event, the sequel was delayed for three years, until 1608) and outside the confines of the fiction:

Blackness is, properly speaking, only half the conceit, the antimasque to the transformation scene, which is its sequel *The Masque of Beauty*. What is probably most notable about the resolution, however, is the means by which the ladies are ultimately transformed: they become white by becoming English, by subjecting themselves to the English King, whose 'beams shine night and day, and are of force / To blanch an Ethiope, or revive a corse', both proverbial examples of the monarch's ability to do the impossible. The option of a royal miracle was not offered to the blacks at whom Elizabeth aimed her expulsion order, but even the rhetoric of that document suggests that their essential defect is not the colour of their skin or any racial infection, but simply – like the daughters of Niger before their enlightenment – a failure of comprehension and conversion: 'the most of them are infidels having no understanding of Christ or his Gospel'.

The beneficent magic of whiteness here is the magic of masculine and patriarchal authority, and the final gesture of subjection to it was one that was built into the Jacobean masque as a form, which always acknowledged the King as its centre. Three years later when the Queen commanded Jonson to present her and her ladies as military heroines, the problem of subjecting her to a pacifist King who, moreover, disapproved of masculine behaviour in women, must have seemed an especially stringent test of the poet's powers of invention. How he fulfilled it I have discussed in an essay called 'Jonson and the Amazons': the women are disarmed even as they are empowered; their militant presence banishes the malevolent witches of the antimasque, but Jonson's embodiment of Heroic Virtue is not Athena or Bellona, warlike goddesses and prototypes of the armed Queen and her ladies, but Perseus, slayer of Medusa, the gorgon, who embodies all the dangerous potential of the feminine.[18] If Jonson's mythography subverts the Queen's interests, it fully supports the King's. For James, the defeat and decapitation of the primary sensual and beautiful woman in his life was the crucial act of empowerment.

The attitudes towards women expressed in *The Masque of Queens* are, however, not altogether accounted for by the politics of Jacobean royal patronage. The militant heroines were the Queen's idea, but the witches, after all, were the poet's, and they represent an obvious declaration of the community of Jonson's interests with those of the King. The royal treatise on *Demonology*, the fruit of both scholarly research and of continual attendance at witch trials, testified to James's credentials as Britain's principal expert on the subject; but Jonson's elaborate glosses, elucidations, citations of authorities, declare his own expertise to be fully the equal of the King's. The witches are as much a gesture of self-assertion as of compliment, and the fact that they are presented as the alternatives to female heroism says more about Jonson's psychology than about the terms of his employment.

As 'a foil or false masque' to heroic virtue, infernal evil is not an inevitable choice. A year later, devising the antimasque antitheses to the heroic persona of Prince Henry's Oberon, Jonson created a group of rowdy and good-natured satyrs, whose vices were all the lusty and indecorous pleasures that Jonson obviously shared: drinking, sex, practical jokes. Anatomizing his poetic options in *The Forest*, Jonson rejects the classical pantheon en masse, but his strictures specifically against the two female goddesses, Athena and Venus, reveal anxieties that have nothing to do with the composition of poetry, and resonate significantly with the styles of both his royal patrons:

> Pallas, nor thee I call on, mankind maid,
> That at thy birth made the poor smith afraid,
> Who with his axe thy father's midwife played.
>
> Go, cramp dull Mars, light Venus, when he snorts,
> Or with thy tribade trine invent new sports;
> Thou nor thy looseness with my making sorts.
>
> (*Forest* 10, lines 13–18)

Athena here is both masculine and responsible for the feminization of Jove and Vulcan; Venus is not only a wanton who exhausts even Mars, but one who engages in lesbian sex with the Graces – 'tribade', the earliest term in English for a homosexual woman, is first used in print by Jonson. The masculinity of the martial Athena, 'mankind maid', leads to the much more hostile response to genuinely self-sufficient women, who are both sexually active and erotically independent of men – as in figure 7.13, the frontispiece to Saxton's *Atlas* (1579), Justice and Peace, realized as Pallas and Venus, seem about to be. The decisive and contemptuous rejection of Venus as Jonson's muse is especially striking since his 'making', which he declares to be so incompatible with her wantonness, must be not only his poetic craft but his own kind of sex as well, that 'doing' which, he says, following Petronius, 'a filthy pleasure is, and short; / And done, we straight repent us of the sport' (*Underwood* 88). Is the problem with lesbian sex precisely its ability to 'invent new sports', its revelation of a world of erotic alternatives (and of alternatives to men: the martial goddess on Saxton's frontispiece is replacing Mars) – and its revelation thereby of the insufficiency of his

Figure 7.13 Justice and Peace, detail from the frontispiece of Christopher Saxton's
Atlas of England and Wales, 1579.

own sexuality, determined as it is by all its good classical masculine precedents?

Clearly women are profoundly destabilizing. Even in explaining 'Why I Write Not of Love', the love that eludes Jonson's verse is male, not female, Cupid, not Venus. In contrast, for Donne and his libertine correspondents a decade earlier, women were the only subject – the subject, indeed, that binds men together – and tribadry was the very essence of poetry. The word is deployed, in the earliest example I have found (not recorded in the *OED*), in a way that is neither uncomprehending nor hostile. Donne's correspondent T. W. writes in a verse letter,

> Have mercy on me and my sinful muse,
> Which, rubbed and tickled with thine, could not choose
> But spend some of her pith, and yield to be
> One in that chaste and mystic tribadry.[19]

Nevertheless, and paradoxically, to praise women for their masculine qualities is often the bottom line of Jonsonian idealization:

> Only a learned and a manly soul
>   I purposed her, that should, with even powers,
> The rock, the spindle, and the shears control
>   Of destiny, and spin her own free hours.
>
> (Epigram 76, lines 13–16)

What is extraordinary here is not that Lucy, Countess of Bedford, is being offered control over her fate, and that that is conceived as the work of a 'manly soul'; it is that the control is depicted as involving the most traditional of feminine accomplishments: what the fates do is the domestic work of spinning, and this is the work of the manly soul. What prevents Jonson from imagining a soul so conceived as quintessentially womanly? Women's virtues, as we derive them from the poems in praise of those women whose patronage he courted, are to maintain a well-run and hospitable household, keep a bountiful table, but most of all to stay clear of the world of action and temptation, 'Not to know vice at all, and keep true state', as he puts it in the 'Epode' – to be, in short, fruitful, chaste and (the unspoken corollary) silent. How difficult Jonson found it to believe in the reality of such an ideal, however, is evident enough simply from the topography of his epigrams, in which a poem in praise of his patron the Countess of Bedford appears immediately after a poem asserting that the words 'woman' and 'whore' are synonyms, or from the chronology of his theatre, in which the play composed immediately after *The Masque of Queens* is *Epicoene*.

The three poems written To Elizabeth, Countess of Rutland may serve as an epitome of Jonson's difficulty in negotiating his feelings about the idea of female patronage. Daughter of Sir Philip Sidney, she is praised in the *Epigrams* specifically as a successor to her father. Sidney had no sons 'Save', as Jonson puts it, 'that most masculine issue of his brain', his writing, and Nature therefore created, in the Countess, a poet – but a poet who outdoes her father. The praise is evidently heartfelt, since Jonson asserted to Drummond that her poetry was 'nothing inferior' to Sidney's; but embodied in the epigrammatic text, the genial equivalence ('nothing inferior') becomes a hostile confrontation: poetry is male, the woman's excellence is realized only through an invidious comparison with her father, and her success, indeed, does not merely outdo his, but incinerates it: 'if he were living now',

> He should those rare and absolute numbers view
>   As he would burn, or better far, his book.
>   (Epigram 79, lines 11–12)

Implicit in the articulate woman is the obliteration of the masculine text. In contrast, the much more modest praise of the Countess's talent expressed in the epistle to her included in *The Forest* leaves Sidney's reputation intact:

> . . . what a sin 'gainst your great father's spirit
>   Were it to think that you should not inherit
> His love unto the muses, when his skill
>   Almost you have, or may have, when you will?
>   (*Forest* 12, lines 31–4)

Almost; may have. The final epigram in *The Underwood*, addressed to the Countess in her widowhood, praises her hospitality, virtue and passion not for writing but reading:

> . . . you make your books your friends,
>   And study them unto the noblest ends,
> Searching for knowledge . . .   (*Underwood* 50, lines 27–9)

Her poetry is not mentioned; neither is her father. Both Sidney and Jonson are safe from her at last.

The Jacobean years were good ones for Jonson as a court poet. He maintained both his place and his self-esteem through a finely poised rhetoric of hyperbolic compliment, including as much self-aggrandizement as praise of his patrons. Royal idealization was framed and legitimated by classical authority and historical example. Court

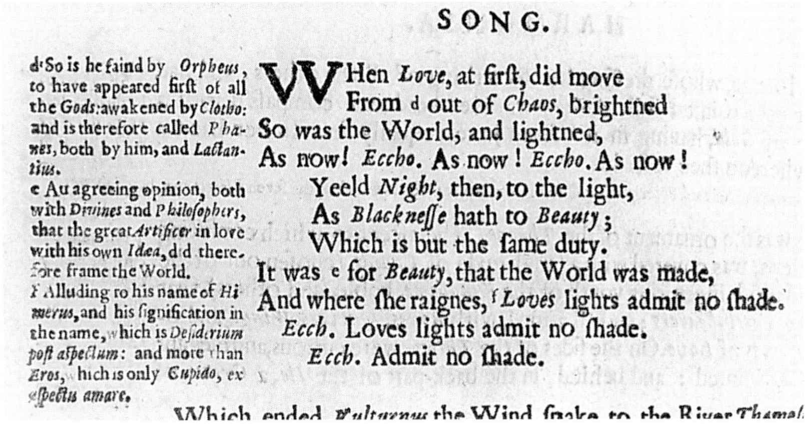

S O N G.

d·So is he faind by *Orpheus*,
to have appeared firſt of all
the *Gods*:awakened by*Clotho*:
and is therefore called *P ha-*
nes, both by him, and *Laɡan-*
tius.
e Au agreeing opinion, both
with *Diuines* and *Philoſophers*,
that the great*Artificer* in love
with his own *Idea*, d·d there.
ſore frame the World.
f Alluding to his name of *Hi*
merus,and his ſignification in
the name, which is *Deſiderium*
poſt aſpeɡum: and more than
Eros, hich is only *Cupido*, ex
aſpeɡtu amare.

WHen *Love*, at firſt, did move
From d out of *Chaos*, brightned
So was the World, and lightned,
As now! *Eccho.* As now ! *Eccho.* As now !
Yeeld *Night*, then, to the light,
As *Blackneſſe* hath to *Beauty* ;
Which is but the ſame duty.
It was e for *Beauty*, that the World was made,
And where ſhe raignes, f *Loves* lights admit no ſhade.
Ecch. Loves lights admit no ſhade.
Ecch. Admit no ſhade.

Which ended *Vulturnus* the Wind ſpoke to the River *Thamel.*

Figure 7.14 *The Masque of Blackness*, song with marginalium, from the 1616 folio.

masques were not the 'toys' they were for Bacon, the 'punctiloes of dreams' they were for Daniel, the 'vanity of my art' they were for . . . well, at least for Prospero; they were 'the donatives of great princes', 'high and hearty inventions . . . grounded upon antiquity and solid learnings', whose 'sense . . . should always lay hold on more removed mysteries'. They were, that is, on the one hand, royal utterances, and on the other, scholarship, philosophy and poetry. As such, they validated both Jonson's social place, his authority to speak for the monarch, and his literary credentials, his authority to speak for the ages. They were, in short, not only texts, but even more powerfully, subtexts.

But perhaps most important in terms of Jonson's ability to assert his continuing control over his masques, and thereby over the world to which they granted him access, they were marginalia (figure 7.14). In a sense the masques of these years pose a far more complex and interesting question than the question of why Queen Anne wanted to appear in blackface: why did she want marginalia? The easy answer would be that she did not want them. Jonson in fact invites this answer in the dedication to the presentation manuscript of the copiously annotated *Masque of Queens*, where Prince Henry is credited with issuing the 'command to have me add this second labour of annotation to my first of invention'.[20] The logical corollary is, then, that the annotations to the prince's masque *Oberon* were similarly done at his command, and that the annotations to the Queen's masques of *Blackness and Beauty* and to the two wedding masques *Hymenaei* and *The Haddington Masque* were Jonson's own idea.

This is certainly a possible scenario. It is suspect only because it allies Jonson a little too easily and completely with the scholar King on the one hand and his filial disciple on the other, Jonson the royal deputy acting as both servant and master to the young prince, Aristotle to Henry's Alexander. Where is the Queen in all this? Was the learning simply thrust upon her? It was she, after all, not the King, who was Jonson's patron for much of the first decade of the reign, though he courted James's favour tirelessly. Why was the Queen attracted to this poet? Why did she change her masque writer from the Daniel of 'punctiloes of dreams' to the Jonson of 'antiquity and solid learnings'? Peter Holbrook has suggested, earlier in this volume, that Jonson was more sympathetic with James's ideology as a whole than was Daniel. No doubt this is correct, but it was largely the Queen who established Jonson as court poet. She has traditionally been represented as both flighty and morose, with a particular and somewhat reprehensible interest in masquing; but since Jonson's only court entertainment before *Blackness* was the brief pastoral at Althorp, it can hardly have been his previous successes in the genre that recommended him to her. Perhaps in fact Queen Anne was a patron of taste and discernment – the resistance of modern critics to this idea has been quite striking (though Leeds Barroll has recently mounted a strong defence of her acumen, and pursues the point in his essay in this volume). Frances Yates, for example, discussing the career of one of the Queen's most impressive and original protégés, John Florio, describes Anne as 'a rather stupid, rather frivolous person', who, however, 'spoke the Italian language most perfectly'.[21] This is offered as a testimony to Florio's talents as Queen Anne's Italian reader; but surely it may be allowed to redound to the Queen's credit as well. In fact, she already knew Italian when Florio came to her attention, having studied it with Giacomo Castelvetro in Edinburgh for five years. Graham Parry is more appreciative, but the condescension is still palpable, with Jonson's genius 'transforming the flimsy, gay devices of the Queen into fables of monarchical divinity'.[22]

In fact, Florio provides a good index to the genuine value of the Queen's artistic patronage. The first edition of his Montaigne, published in 1603, had six dedicatees, all socially prominent women, four of them notably literary: the Countesses of Bedford and Rutland, Lady Anne Harington, Penelope Lady Rich, Lady Elizabeth Grey and Lady Mary Neville. For the second edition ten years later, the six ladies were replaced by the Queen, who clearly constituted, for a scholar, a much better investment. Florio provided two dedications, the second an Italian poem, a tribute to his patron's linguistic proficiency. The Queen subsequently underwrote the revision of Florio's great Italian dictionary, duly re-entitled *Queen Anna's New World of Words*. This surely says as much about the Queen's influence on Florio as about his influence on her.

Perhaps, then, the Queen was attracted to Jonson precisely for the artistic authority he could bring to her Twelfth Night entertainments – for just what she is claimed to have had no interest in, his seriousness and learning. In that case the marginalia would be as much a validation of her taste as of Jonson's scholarship, her way of justifying and maintaining her control over these extravagant ephemera, just as they were his way of asserting the power and authority of his learning. Patron and poet shared a need for a space in which they could operate independently of the constraints of their situations. Is it irrelevant that both were converts to Roman Catholicism? All Jonson's masques for the Queen imagine her transformed, freed, militantly victorious: are these only Queen Anne's fantasies?

But the fantasies are contained, enveloped, by the obsessive marginalia; if they serve the Queen's purposes, they serve Jonson's even more. It can hardly be accidental that the witches are far more elaborately authenticated than the Queens. Appearing only in the text of the masque, and only after it is no longer a performing text, the glosses are finally all Jonson's; and indeed, the marginalia to *Queens* record a moment of scholarly invention that approaches *lèse majesté* (figure 7.15). Beside an assertion that witches' conventicles commonly begin with dances, Jonson cites an authority:

> See the King's majesty's book (our sovereign) of *Demonology*.

To acknowledge the King's expertise on the subject of witchcraft is doubtless no more than the price of royal patronage; but in fact the note does not acknowledge the King. It is pure ventriloquism: King James does not discuss witches' dances anywhere in *Demonology*. That Jonson should presume to speak as the King is perhaps not surprising in the playwright who brought Queen Elizabeth onstage to conclude *Every Man Out of His Humour*, treating the monarch as a prop for his drama; but the note records, as I have remarked elsewhere, a subtle antagonism along with the obvious, if meretricious, compliment. Jonson's true source for information about dancing at covens appears to be Reginald Scot's sceptical treatise *The Discovery of Witchcraft*, a tract

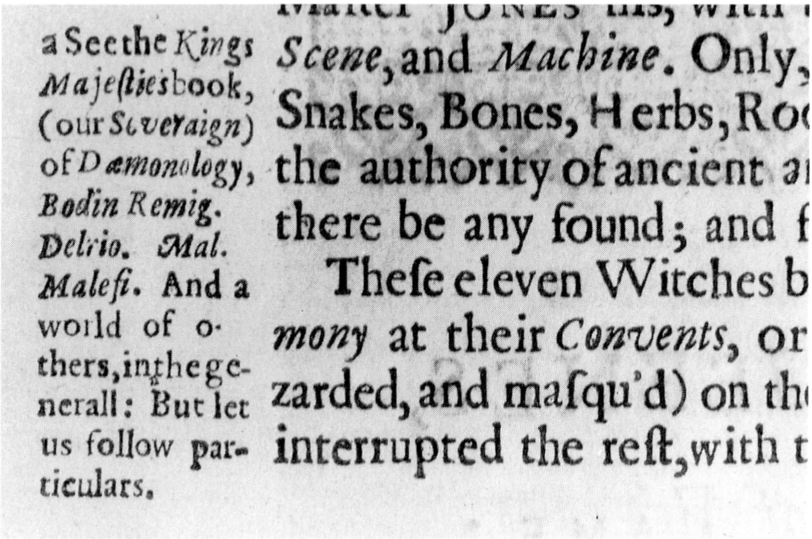

a See the *Kings Majesties* book, (our *Soveraign*) of *Dæmonology*, *Bodin Remig. Delrio. Mal. Malefi.* And a world of others, in the generall: But let us follow particulars.

Scene, and *Machine*. Only,
Snakes, Bones, Herbs, Ro
the authority of ancient a
there be any found; and
These eleven Witches b
mony at their *Convents*, or
zarded, and masqu'd) on th
interrupted the rest, with t

Figure 7.15 *The Masque of Queens*, marginalium from the 1616 folio.

d. See the Kings Ma.ties Booke (of Soveraigne) of Dæmonologie. Bodin. Remig. Delrio. Mall: Malefi. and a world of others, in the generall: but, let vs follow particulars.

These eleven Witches beginning to daunce (wch is an vsuall d Ceremony at theyr Convents, or meetings Where, sometimes, also they are vizarded, and masqu'd) on the sodayne, one of them miss'd theyr Cheife, and interrupted the rest, wth this Speach.

Sisters, stay; we want or Dame.
Call vpon her, by her name,

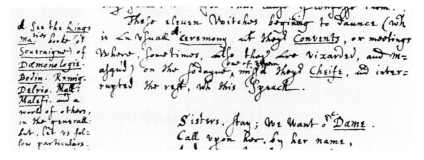

Figure 7.16 *The Masque of Queens*, marginalium in the holograph, 1609.

that James attacks in *Demonology*. Jonson thus marginalizes the King's scholarship even as he praises it, usurping the royal authority with a subversive rival expertise.

What particularly interests me here is that parenthetical 'our sovereign'. This seems designed to preclude any ambiguity about what royal work on demonology is intended (not, e.g., that of the King of Naples); but in that case, to whom is the marginal note being addressed? Jonson says the notes were prepared at the command of Prince Henry; they first appear in the beautiful holograph dedicated to the Prince and presented by Jonson to the Queen (figure 7.16). This is the most personal

Figure 7.17 King James on Bodley tower, 1616.

of copies of the work. Surely the King's wife and son were in no danger of confusion on the question of which King is intended. But equally clearly the note is not really addressed to Jonson's royal patrons, but to all his projected readers; and the parenthesis thereby transforms prince and Queen into subjects, not only of the King, which of course they are, but even more significantly of the sovereign poet. The masque, indeed, concludes with a realization of the power and permanence, the ultimate authority, of poetry: the House of Fame, an architectural emblem adopted from Chaucer. It is adorned with statues of Homer, Virgil and Lucan on the lower tier, and of Achilles, Aeneas and Caesar on the upper. The heroes' fame is supported and preserved by the immortal poets; heroism (and the heroism now is all male) depends on the ordering and eternizing power of poetry.

Jonson's claims for himself are royal claims too: poet and King in this text assert the same authority. Outside the fiction but at the centre of the spectacle, James occupies his seat of state, declaring by his presence that in this masque of Queens, heroism may be allowed to be the royal consort, but the highest virtue is that of the Rex Pacificus, scholar and poet: it is finally not the triumphant Queens but the King's peace that Fame's trumpet sounds. James had himself represented on the tower of the Bodleian Library precisely as a scholar, to commemorate his gift to Oxford of the folio of his works, published, like Jonson's, in 1616 (figure 7.17). It is for this that Fame, at his right hand, blows her trumpet. The masque, for all its Amazonian heroines, celebrates the sovereign and masculine word. Empowering women was not a Jonsonian ideal, and the Queen was not the patron he sought.

NOTES

1 Stephen Gosson, *The School of Abuse* (London, 1579), sig. A2ᵛ.
2 *Doctor Faustus* (B text, 2.1.141) in Christopher Marlowe, *Doctor Faustus and Other Plays*, ed. David Bevington and Eric Rasmussen (Oxford, 1995).
3 *Conversations with Drummond* in C. H. Herford and P. and E. Simpson (eds.), *Ben Jonson*, 11 vols. (Oxford, 1925–52), I, p. 139.
4 Cited in Herford and Simpson (eds.), *Ben Jonson*, x, p. 448.
5 *Ibid.*, p. 447.
6 *Ibid.*, p. 449; the writer is identified only as 'Vincent', and may not be the herald Augustine Vincent.
7 The remark concerned the diplomatic squabbles over invitations to *The Masque of Beauty*, in which the Queen countermanded the King's orders; see Herford and Simpson (eds.), *Ben Jonson*, x, p. 456.
8 *Letters of John Chamberlain*, ed. Norman E. McClure, 2 vols. (Philadelphia, 1939), II, pp. 286–7.
9 *Ibid.*, p. 294.
10 See Graham Reynolds's discussion of the painting in James Laver (ed.), *Costume of the Western World: Fashions of the Renaissance* (New York, 1951),

p. 146: 'The lace of the ruff and cuffs and round the yoke of her bodice is dyed with saffron.'

11 Stephen Orgel, 'What is a text?', repr. in David Scott Kastan and Peter Stallybrass (eds.), *Staging the Renaissance* (New York, 1991), p. 85. See also my 'The Renaissance artist as plagiarist', *English Literary History* 48 (1981), 476–95.

12 See Ania Loomba, *Gender, Race, Renaissance Drama* (Manchester, 1989), esp. ch. 2; Lynda Boose, 'The getting of a lawful race', in Margo Hendricks and Patricia Parker (eds.), *Women, 'Race' and Writing in the Early Modern Period* (London, 1994), pp. 35–54; Margo Hendricks, 'Managing the barbarian', *Renaissance Drama* ns 23 (1992), 165–88; Ruth Cowhig, 'Blacks in English Renaissance drama', in David Dabydeen (ed.), *The Black Presence in English Literature* (Manchester, 1985), pp. 1–25; Gretchen Gerzina, *Black England* (London, 1995); Peter Fryer, *Staying Power: The History of Black People in Britain* (London, 1984); Kim Hall, *Things of Darkness* (Ithaca, 1995).

13 Cesare Vecellio, *Habiti antichi et moderni di tutto il Mondo*, 1598, repr. as *Vecellio's Renaissance Costume Book* (New York, 1977), p. 133.

14 Quoted by Boose, 'The getting of a lawful race', p. 44.

15 See 'The getting of a lawful race', pp. 42–5.

16 Richard Hakluyt, *The Principal Navigations . . . of the English Nation*, 12 vols. (Glasgow, 1904), VI, pp. 176, 200, 284.

17 J. L. Hughes and J. F. Larkin (eds.), *Tudor Royal Proclamations, 1588–1603* (New Haven, 1969), p. 221.

18 Stephen Orgel, 'Jonson and the Amazons', in Elizabeth Harvey and Katharine Eisaman Maus (eds.), *Soliciting Interpretation* (Chicago, 1990), pp. 119–39.

19 John Donne, *The Satires, Epigrams and Verse Letters*, ed. W. Milgate (Oxford, 1967), p. 212.

20 Herford and Simpson (eds.), *Ben Jonson*, VII, p. 279.

21 Frances Yates, *John Florio* (Cambridge, 1934), p. 248.

22 Graham Parry, *The Golden Age Restor'd: The Culture of the Stuart Court* (Manchester, 1981), p. 42.

CHAPTER 8

Jonson, the antimasque and the 'rules of flattery'
Hugh Craig

As Martin Butler and Tom Bishop have argued in separate essays
in this volume and elsewhere, a doubleness of vision is discernible in
Ben Jonson's *Oberon* (1611) that can best be ascribed to divisions and
ambiguities in the transactions of power at the Jacobean court. These
tensions arise because Prince Henry as Oberon dares to present himself as a significant competitor to his father's (Pan's) royal authority and
pacifist politics. Similar disjunctions are apparent in other Jacobean
masques as well. The contradictions arise not so much from the self-
divided nature of the 'royal mind', as Jonathan Goldberg would have
it,[1] as in the factional differences of a divided court. Leah Marcus too
has recently studied the masque as an expression of factionalism in the
royal family and in aristocratic groupings, conflicts of national policy
regarding traditional holiday pastimes, and competing views on the
national interest in relations with Spain.[2] The authors of this present
book pursue similar aspects of discordant multiplicity in Jacobean courtly
entertainment. The masque emerges today as a polyvocal expression
of Jacobean policy and mythmaking. Its seriousness of purpose is evident in the extent to which it participated in the very historical process
that it undertook to represent. Explored in its full performative and
political context, the masque can lay claim to significant artistic and
cultural value.

Curiously, though, one relic of earlier critical dismissals of the masque
as 'trivial' (see the Introduction, above) remains visible in a key text of
the New Historicism that has otherwise done so much to establish the
contextual significance of genres like the masque. Stephen Greenblatt,
in his *Shakespearean Negotiations*, compares *Henry V* with court entertainments in such a way as to find those entertainments lacking in theatrical magic. Their fault is that they fail to heighten the audience's
involvement through the vital sort of theatrical 'falsification' that Shakespeare so brilliantly deploys by requiring his audience to fill with their

imaginations the gap between the awkward facts and royal ideology, between theatrical performance and historical reality. Because no such gap is exploited in court entertainment, says Greenblatt, celebrations of royal power in that genre are deprived of charisma:

the very doubts that Shakespeare raises [in *Henry V*] serve not to rob the king of his charisma but to heighten it, precisely as they heighten the theatrical interest of the play; the unequivocal, unambiguous celebrations of royal power with which the period abounds have no theatrical force and have long since fallen into oblivion. The charismatic authority of the king, like that of the stage, depends on falsification.[3]

Court entertainment cannot affirm royal absolutism persuasively because it lacks the 'falsification' of presentations on the public stage.

This essay will argue that the Jacobean court masque did have access to the kind of 'falsification' that Greenblatt valorizes, precisely because the masque is not 'unequivocal' or 'unambiguous' in its 'celebration of royal power' as Greenblatt insists. I would like to pursue the idea of multivocality to which this present book is dedicated by looking at the antimasque. That notable feature of court entertainment is anything but unequivocal, and is certainly not devoted to the celebration of royal power; quite the opposite. Especially in Jonson's later years, the antimasque – which he essentially invented – takes on an uninhibited and uncouth violence that unleashes wildness close to the seat of majesty. The figures of Jonson's antimasques are elements of the id allowed provokingly close to the innermost cell of power, restrained only by the masque form's effortful magic.

The central critical question then becomes the now-familiar one of containment versus subversion. If the antimasque is simply contained, in Greenblatt's terms, the taming of its violence might seem to argue that the antimasque too, like the masque itself, merely serves the official – and therefore theatrically inert – purpose of celebrating unambiguously the authority of the monarch. I wish to argue, conversely, that in Jonson's hands the antimasque came to be a vehicle for a kind of uninhibited criticism that the masque itself needed to 'contain' in more discreet forms – though even here, as this present book plentifully suggests, the masque was not the univocal and supine endorsement of royal will too often supposed. The inclusion of the antimasque in court masquing gave opportunity for scenes of barbaric anarchy to be played out in the court with a king as chief spectator. This present essay is concerned with the dialogue that results between antimasque and masque, between unruliness and rule.

The royal masque was certainly created with the intent of supporting and praising the ruling elite. The King or Queen normally commissioned the work, after all, and made sure that the basic plot was
invariably adulatory, climaxing in an apotheosis of sovereign will. As
Strato puts the matter succinctly in *The Maid's Tragedy*, masques are
'tied to rules of flattery'.[4] Jonathan Goldberg, as we have seen, argues
that the masque 'mirrors the royal mind', though he also finds in that
royal mind a thoroughly deconstructed image.[5] Jonson's masques do
indeed tend to celebrate the monarchy, in good part perhaps because
Jonson's own politics accorded with those of James, though even here,
as Peter Holbrook has demonstrated in his essay earlier in this volume,
tensions and ambiguities are everywhere apparent.

Importantly, moreover, Jonson was not the only writer of masques
for the court. His chief predecessor, Samuel Daniel, was anything but
idolatrous, even if he needed to be tactful; his *The Vision of the Twelve
Goddesses* (1604) implies a critical view of James's pacifist foreign policy,
as Holbrook points out. John Pitcher similarly views Daniel's *Tethys'
Festival* (1610) as a masque in which King and court are all reminded of
their final nothingness in the true perspective of Time.[6] The idea is a
philosophical and religious truism, to be sure, but in context it pointedly
deflates any claims to worldly achievement that the court and its colour-
fully costumed masquers might idly entertain about themselves.[7]

Another indirectly critical form of court entertainment is to be found
in what David Norbrook calls the 'reformed' masque, reconstructed by
him from contemporary discussions and plans and from *Comus* (1634).
The reformed masque follows the usual courtly unmasking with a more
searching revelation in which the King and the court are seen as mere
idols when compared with transcendent reality.[8] *Comus* itself, as Barbara
Lewalski argues in this present volume, grew out of an intense dislike of
the Caroline masque by some noble families who were unsympathetic
to the court and its politics.

If, then, the dominant form of the masque was capable of problem-
atizing its own strongly conservative premise, we might well expect to
find some potential subversion lurking in the antimasque, which introduces the unruly and the intemperate into the masquing space. To be
sure, as I have already suggested, one might be tempted to argue that
the disorders of the antimasque are repressed by the masque itself in
a recuperative move of containment. In such a scenario, the unruly
elements of the antimasque make possible a spectacular triumph by
the forces of order, underlining indeed the very need for those forces.

Thus, in a New Historicist economy of subversion and containment, the antimasque creates the anxiety which makes obvious the purpose and importance of containment. Even this interpretation presupposes tension and ambiguity, providing something akin to the 'theatrical force' that Greenblatt professes to find missing in the masque.

An elegant variant of the containment thesis, and indeed a precursor of the New Historical argument, is the notion of seasonal topsy-turvydom, or carnival. In this view, the Saturnalian spirit of the Christmas season and of other festive times of year allows and even encourages boisterousness as a way of ensuring that subversive pressures will not build beyond tolerable limits. Indulgence in indecorous and even potentially treasonous action and dialogue in licensed forms of entertainment presents no real threat to authority. Lampooning of authority ultimately acknowledges the validity of that authority. In Ian Donaldson's view, Jonson's antimasques operate in just this way. The antimasque characters in *Time Vindicated* (1623), for example, like the conspirators in *Catiline*, explore the dark dimensions and ambiguities of 'licence' or 'liberty', until the supervening masque (or play, with its suppression of the conspiracy) reaffirms a 'real and workable social order' by signalling the return of hierarchy.[9] Leah Marcus similarly identifies a 'paradox of state' whereby the 'license and lawlessness' of old pastimes could be 'interpreted as submission to authority'.[10] Graham Parry sees the 'liberties' taken by the Irishmen of *The Irish Masque* (1613–1614) and other Jonson antimasque characters as a reflection of 'the licence of misrule', now 'safely integrated' into the masque, and notes that Misrule appears as a character in *Christmas His Masque* (1616).[11]

Yet a good deal of satirical comment in the antimasques is less easy to reconcile to the idea of a uniformly conservative masque form than these generalizations about containment might suggest. Robin Goodfellow takes advantage of his role in the antimasque of *Love Restored* (1612) to complain about the power of money in the modern world, 'making friendships, contracts, marriages and almost religion' (lines 164–5).[12] These pointed strictures extend well beyond the bounds of the antimasque itself and are, in Roy Strong's view, Jonson's first satirical thrusts in the form.[13] In the full title of his *Mercury Vindicated* (1615) – *Mercury Vindicated from the Alchemists at Court* – Jonson jeeringly suggests that parasites and alchemists are birds of a feather.[14] Court satire is a staple of Jonsonian humour in *News from the New World Discovered in the Moon* (1620), notably in its description of an 'Isle of

Epicoenes'. Most tellingly of all, perhaps, courtiers are pickpockets in *The Gypsies Metamorphosed* (1621).[15]

Jonathan Goldberg ingeniously proposes that James dealt with implied criticisms of his court by simply taking no notice. 'In the *Basilikon Doron*, the king had demanded that he be unaccountable. That meant he must take no account when the masque offered an unflattering mirror of the monarch.'[16] Such a hypothesis does not really explain, however, why the King authorized masquing in the first place, or why satirical commentary on political matters continues to flourish ever more exuberantly in the masques of James's later reign and that of Charles.[17] Indeed, none of the containment theories we have thus far encountered explains the masque's durability and anarchic irreverence. Nor does any of them quite exhaust the energies of rebellion and dissent that we find represented especially in the Jonsonian antimasque.

We must of course be careful not to exaggerate the impact of the libidinous, violent and seditious energies of the antimasque, and cannot afford to ignore the 'formal priorities of the genre as a whole' and 'the hierarchy of discourses' according to which, as Martin Butler insists, 'the plebeian antimasque is subordinated to the aristocratic main masque'.[18] At the same time, we need to explore further the lingering implications of a form of entertainment in which the King was addressed with daring familiarity, and in which unrepentant enemies of decorum and civilization were let loose in the acting area of the Banqueting House. To say that the antimasque was formally subordinated to the masque, as it certainly was, does not distinguish the complexity or degree of subordination in various individual cases.

Marked internal contrast is perhaps more striking in the court masque than in any other Renaissance form of entertainment or literary production. In part, this sense of confrontation arises from the unusual structural pattern of placing the antimasque in the lead position and masque as the sequel. Other Renaissance genres, usually popular in appeal, violate classical decorum by mingling kings and clowns, but do so ordinarily in a way that makes clear the ascendancy of the dominant generic form. Whether in jigs and other comic entertainments written to be performed at the end of a tragedy, or in interspersed scenes of comic buffoonery as in *Doctor Faustus*, multiply plotted works tend to follow a recognizable convention of subordination. The dual strands of the court masque, linked thematically by the nature of a common celebratory occasion and yet radically contrasted in decorum, are well matched in length and emphasis.[19]

The ambiguous standing of the antimasque is evident in uncertainties as to the meaning and origin of the term. Jonson himself constantly redefined its form.[20] Some observers referred to the carnival-like scene he had pioneered as the 'ante-masque', as though calling attention to its place at the start of the entertainment. Others called it an 'antick masque', perhaps attributing to it a classicizing *all'antico* style (though we must not make too much of spelling variations in the early modern period). Jonson himself spoke always of 'anti-masques'. To him, the most significant generic marker may have been the masque's radical polarity.[21]

The contrast of the masque and antimasque is most schematic in Jonson's early masques. Ultimately, the function of the disorderly characters in early antimasques is to be dispelled, as if by magic, in the 'discovery' action of the masque proper. Professional actors originally took the roles of the antimasquers; courtiers undertook roles in the main action. The more decorous roles of the masque proper required no memorizing of lines while conversely maximizing opportunities for dancing and visual display. This confining of speaking parts to the antimasque characters created an art form in which the nominally subordinated element of antimasque became of necessity a substantial and equal part of the whole; it carried the story line and expressed the ideas of the poet, while the masque proper fell more under the purview of Inigo Jones as designer. Poetry and spectacle vied for attention across the generic barrier of antimasque and masque. In later years the distinctions were more blurred: parts of the antimasque were taken up into and modified by the masque, allowing the antimasque element of the entertainment to form a more integral part of the entire production and providing opportunity for courtiers to undertake some of the speaking roles in the antimasque that they evidently were no longer willing to consign entirely to professionals.[22]

The early kind of antimasque accordingly provides Jonson with what he calls a 'foil' to the main masque: a dark ground to make the glitter of the masque jewel all the brighter. He uses the term in the prologue to *The Masque of Queens* (1609), setting forth his version of how the very idea for the antimasque came into being. Queen Anne, he reports, '(best knowing that a principal part of life in these spectacles lay in their variety) had commanded me to think on some dance or show that might precede hers and have the place of a foil or false masque' (lines 9–12). The Queen evidently wanted something more formally contrasting with the masque proper than Jonson had provided in *The*

Masque of Blackness in 1605 and *Hymenaei* in 1606. Responding to royal command, he says, Jonson devised his antimasque of witches, 'not as a masque but a spectacle of strangeness, producing multiplicity of gesture, and not unaptly sorting with the current and whole fall of the device' (lines 17–19). Whether this account describes a genuine act of inspired patronage or is an adroit courtly compliment, the antimasque certainly began under royal protection and was thus shielded from any open criticism.

Jonson's terms for his new device, 'spectacle of strangeness' and 'foil', nicely describe the way in which he originally conceived of the antimasque as something to be used chiefly to enhance the lustre of the main action. As Stephen Orgel observes, the sudden dispersal of the antimasque on the arrival of the masque proper implies that the evil of the antimasque was after all only imaginary.[23] The early masque expresses an unusually pure Manichean view: its evil is as neatly extreme as its forces of good. Its figures tend to be intractably other: witches, satyrs and barbarians, savages who appear innocent in their savagery and yet are greatly distanced from civilization. The action is farcical and 'non-mimetic' in a way that confirms what Northrop Frye says about the antimasque:

> The further comedy moves from irony, the less social power is allowed to the humors. In the masque, where the ideal society is still more in the ascendant, the humors become degraded into the uncouth figures of the Jonsonian antimasque . . . Farce, being a non-mimetic form of comedy, has a natural place in the masque, though in the ideal masque its natural place is that of a rigorously controlled interlude.[24]

The antimasque figures of Jonson's early years generally conform to this pattern. Degraded and deprived of social power, they find their 'natural place' only when they are consigned to a 'rigorously controlled interlude', allowing an 'ideal society' to remain in the 'ascendant'.

What Frye characterizes here as the 'ideal masque' is actually a better description of Jonson's early masque than of his later work, which tends to move more in the direction of comedy and to give the masquing figures an increasing complexity and power. These more mature masques are often Circean in concept, if we can borrow a name from William Browne's masque of *Ulysses and Circe* (1615). In them we characteristically find not strange savages but civilized fellow-humans who are for the moment imprisoned, metamorphosed or disguised in degraded forms as though by enchantment. Several of Jonson's masques are of this type. They are generally from his later years, including *Lovers made Men* in 1617 and *The Gypsies Metamorphosed* in 1621. (*The Masque of Blackness*, 1605, shares some features of the type but was written before Jonson, at Anne's behest, had invented his new form of the antimasque.) The antimasque figures in these later entertainments, though monstrous and deformed, usually prove to be civilized and sometimes noble creatures under a spell.

The later antimasques make increasing use of comic stage routines and out-and-out fooling. Jonson now seems interested in them as independent outlets for comedy. Whereas in *The Masque of Queens* (1609) he is content to describe the antimasque simply as a 'foil' to show the masque proper to best advantage, in *Neptune's Triumph* (1624) he justifies antimasquing on the grounds of pleasing the taste of his audience. The antimasque now exists to satisfy a permanent human need, rather than as a formal complement to the main masque. Jonson's interlocutors on the subject of courtly entertainment are a Cook and Poet, whom this volume of essays has quoted before concerning the role of the artist as a purveyor of delicacies that must offend no stomach. The Cook, who takes pride in knowing 'how to please the palates of the guests' (lines 28–29), patronizingly assures the Poet that he cannot do without an antimasque (lines 155–169). The Poet knows that he is right. As his quotation from Martial puts it, '*Nam lusus ipse triumphus amat*', 'for even a triumph likes fun' (line 223).[25] No matter how much this wry passage may jest at the hapless lot of the writer who must cater to an overly sensitive and easily bored audience, Jonson's acknowledgement of the growing necessity of the antimasque seems clear.

The King himself seems to have given his royal imprimatur to the increasing prominence of antimasquing in courtly entertainments. James called for a repeat performance of two antimasques from Francis Beaumont's *The Masque of the Inner Temple and Gray's Inn* (1613) and one from *The Masque of Flowers* (anonymous, 1614).[26] His enthusiasm for the antimasque of *The Gypsies Metamorphosed* (1621) suggests that he had a taste for the humours of comic low-life. Prompted by such royal encouragement, Jonson's antimasque world had shifted within a decade from one of an imaginary and savage strangeness brought under the rigorous control of an idealized social order to one of irrepressible stage foolery more attuned to the follies of supposedly 'civilized' human behaviour. A shift of this sort was certain to bring with it a marked change in the balance of authority and substance between masque and antimasque.

To begin with, these later antimasques show a marked increase in riot and exuberant subversion. The 'Curious' of *Time Vindicated* (1623)

long not for the solemn spectacle Fame promises but for Saturnalia,
'days of feast and liberty' (line 29). Their unnerving energy betrays a
greediness:

> . . . All the impostures,
> The prodigies, diseases and distempers,
> The knaveries of the time, we shall see all now.
>
> (lines 34–36)

These impulses can take the form of uninhibited violence. In *Pleasure
Reconciled to Virtue* (1618) the Pygmies prepare to revenge themselves
on a sleeping Hercules by '[h]url[ing] him 'gainst the moon, / And
break[ing] him in small portions' (lines 130–1). The complacent security of the masque world seems threatened; Hercules sleeps while danger looms. *For the Honour of Wales* (February 1618), a revision of *Pleasure
Reconciled to Virtue* produced in January, revels in casual violence: '*Jenkin*.
Go to, I will make the hilts conceive a knock upon your pate, and
pershance a bump too if yow talk' (lines 99–100). The violence is
of the Punch-and-Judy sort, curiously carefree, startlingly erratic and
arbitrary. It is all the more disturbing in that it emanates here from
the Welsh, dwelling in that 'uncivilized' territory so near to England.
The allegorical vices of the earlier masques have been replaced by
antimasque figures who are all the more complex and interesting for
being at once human and monstrous. These Welsh are compounded
of little but 'distempers . . . and angers, and passions' (lines 126–7). Their
knockabout antics are, to be sure, a prelude to a reassuring declaration of loyalty: 'though the [Welsh] nation be said to be unconquered,
and most loving liberty, yet it was never mutinous, an't please your
majesty' (lines 372–4). Welshmen are more redeemable than were the
witches and allegorical vices of the earlier masques. Quaint Welsh
pride and broken English may ultimately be turned to good account
by English royal power, whereas the disruptive impulses of the other
can only be caged. Yet the utterances of the Welsh on the serious and
overtly political topic of loyalty raise the spectre of the very sedition
they ultimately eschew; in affirming their present adherence to the
English throne, they state the unthinkable.

The antimasque figures in Jonson's later masques – human or at
least partly human, disfigured, libidinous, potentially violent – necessarily remind us of Caliban in *The Tempest*. The resemblance is no
accident. Shakespeare's play is clearly a response to the Jonsonian
court masque (see David Bevington's essay later in this volume), whereas
Jonson for his part was acutely aware of a Shakespearean dramatic

model with which Jonson found himself in strong disagreement. In his Induction to *Bartholomew Fair* (1614), Jonson proudly insists that there will be no 'servant-monster' in his play – a disclaimer made all the more urgent by the obvious resemblance between Caliban and the 'antiques' who populate the antimasques of courtly entertainments:

If there be never a servant-monster i' the fair, who can help it? he says; nor a nest of antiques? He is loath to make nature afraid in his plays, like those that beget tales, tempests and suchlike drolleries, to mix his head with other men's heels, let the concupiscence of jigs and dances reign as strong as it will amongst you; yet if the puppets will please anybody, they shall be entreated to come in. (Induction, lines 127–34)[27]

The reference to 'tempests' is plainly a hit at Shakespeare's play.

Why does Caliban awaken such scorn in Jonson, given his own penchant for deformed quasi-human figures in his later masques? The answer must have something to do with the way these figures are deployed by their respective authors. Caliban is, for Shakespeare, an 'exotic' character who belongs, as John Gillies observes, to a group of Shakespearean creations – also including Cleopatra, Othello, Titus, and Shylock – who are first mistakenly or weakly tolerated (in the *OED* sense of 'allowing what is not actually approved'), then cause disaster.[28] 'Like the "barbarians" of Athenian tragedy, Shakespeare's exotics are innately transgressive.'[29] Shakespeare, as Gillies shows, is intensely interested in such characters: he 'either goes out of his way to include exotics in plots which don't strictly require them, or he elaborates exotic roles well beyond what they are in the sources'; they are most of all remarkable 'in their ability to monopolise attention'.[30] Shakespeare is fascinated, that is, with the anthropological other, and with the lawless impulse that makes a repressive regime necessary. Caliban legitimates Prospero's rule;[31] the 'foul conspiracy' of which he is a part encapsulates contemporary fears of a revolt of masterless men.[32] Caliban's antimasque, peopled by himself, Stephano and Trinculo, invades, disrupts and threatens the masque world of magical, seamless, unlimited royal absolutism. Drama (conflict) impinges upon masque (Prospero's seemingly effortless dominion over allegorical semi-divinities). If the masque is a dream, Caliban is a rude awakening. Caliban provides the danger, the recalcitrant factor, the dramatic suspense, the missing element of 'time as a series of crises'.[33]

Jonson's antimasque too is an irruption of the outside into the *sanctum sanctorum* of a royal court. Yet his versions of the seditious, violent and pseudo-human grotesque are more allegorical and comic than anthropological. Jonson betrays no sympathy for the anthropological other. His antimasque characters are humorous and satirical. They allegorize an aspect of a universal humanity, or of elements within Jonson's own society, rather than exploring alternative possibilities in human psychology and social organization. He nowhere creates in his antimasques a Caliban with whom we are invited to sympathize, even if momentarily.

Jonson's increasing preference for the conventionally comic in his antimasques rather than for the barbaric and culturally exotic is especially significant because it offered him a way to test the limits and enrich the nuances of deference in speaking with his royal auditor. How was Jonson, as court poet, to flatter the monarch and at the same time offer him counsel in the role of wise humanist he was painstakingly establishing for himself? How did the Jonsonian antimasque adapt to such a pressing need?

As Robert C. Evans has argued, the antimasque was indeed central to Jonson's strategies of self-presentation. The tone of 'licensed familiarity' and the 'teasing' in many of Jonson's masques were calculated to 'enhance his image and appeal'. These features were probably responsible for the popularity of *For the Honour of Wales* and *The Gypsies Metamorphosed*.[34] The 'intimacy' of such moments, argues Evans, represents a sophisticated strategy to please Jonson's patrons:

> It obliquely ratified the authority of those who were its objects by temporarily pushing close to that authority's limits, challenging their power but only in the most playful and non-threatening way. The masques' humorous familiarity could suggest a temporary relaxation of power distinctions, a relaxation as appealing to superiors as to dependents. For superiors the appeal lay in being treated simply as human beings rather than as sources of power to be courted and exploited . . .[35]

The buffoonery of antimasque characters like Jenkins in *For the Honour of Wales* tests the limits of court decorum and distances these comic figures from the poet who created them, emphasizing by contrast Jonson's own 'more dignified' praise of the King.[36]

By developing such a contrast to his own advantage, Jonson seems to have been claiming a special licence as unofficial laureate poet, a privilege to leaven the discourse of deference with reminders of the unruly forces whose existence even the King had to acknowledge. Such a reminder carried with it a tacit compliment that embraces both poet and royal auditor. The freedom to acknowledge the vitality of anarchic forces is an indication of Jonson's intimacy with the King, since no one else would dare; at the same time, it flatters the King by showing the monarch's relaxed and secure hold on power. This strategy reflects in Jonson a self-confidence that rests on the poet's conviction of his own powers and status as artist and humanist. We see Jonson exploring the dimensions of humanistic authority enjoyed by Horace and Virgil in *The Poetaster*, where poets are admitted to the innermost circle of power and deferred to by the emperor himself. At times, Jonson's claims to intimacy even border on the daringly personal. He wrote the lines for Buckingham, after all, who, as gypsy reading the King's palm in *The Gypsies Metamorphosed*, compliments his sovereign on his *mons Veneris* (line 280). Even if he could not exactly be a royal favourite himself, Jonson as poet was able to put himself in Buckingham's place to a significant extent by authoring his speech.[37] Even more risqué is Jonson's glancing at the King's sexuality when, in *Time Vindicated* (1623), Sport warns the widower James that he is in danger from an alliance of Cupid and some of the ladies of the court (lines 311–17). W. Todd Furniss thought this passage 'thoroughly impudent'.[38]

Did Jonson go so far as to ridicule the King? Jonas Barish and William Gifford maintain that he did so in *Bartholomew Fair*, for example, by satirical allusions to James's views on tobacco, Puritans and the moderation necessary in rulers. Ian Donaldson, on the other hand, argues that Jonson reveals the nice judgement of an accomplished court artist; he was sensitive to the question 'of what was or was not dramatically decorous to set before the king'. Cautioning that the issue 'is probably too delicate for us to attempt to decide at this distance in time', Donaldson none the less finds an artistic equilibrium in *Bartholomew Fair* in that play's management of the relationship between monarch and court poet. Some mild liberties might be taken, but the playwright's judgement of how far he could go remained impeccable. The poet's sympathies, both underlying and evident, are with the King and his unquestioned authority.[39]

Donaldson's tactful scenario for *Bartholomew Fair* offers a tempting model for Jonson's comic antimasques as well. Yet the description seems not quite adequate to the persistent pushing of limits that we find in those antimasques. Jonson temperamentally seems to have enjoyed the violent opposites and extremes of deference and flouting of authority. Donaldson himself concedes that the juxtaposition of a world and its 'Antipodes' was Jonson's characteristic way of posing moral questions:

Between a Volpone and a Celia, between a Catiline and a Cicero, between the witches of *The Masque of Queens* – those 'opposites to good Fame', who 'do all things contrary to the custom of men' – and the ladies of that masque who represent true heroical virtue, there can be no real meeting; such figures inhabit opposite sides of the moral globe, antipodeans to each other. The sharp contrasts afforded by Court masque and antimasque evidently suited such a moral temperament as Jonson's.[40]

Jonson's fondness for opposition frequently takes the form, in his plays as in his masques, of an inset performance that is suddenly broken off. In *Volpone*, for instance, both the interlude performed by Volpone's household of zanies and Volpone's sales pitch as Scoto come to abrupt ends. Asinius Lupus interrupts Virgil's reading from the *Aeneid* in *The Poetaster*. The interruption of Prospero's masque in *The Tempest* recalls this incident, as Richard Dutton has suggested; certainly we find in such moments a fruitful 'juxtaposition' of '[h]igh seriousness and satiric farce' in which a royally sponsored masque is disrupted by a threatening presence not easily controlled.[41]

In the same way the antimasque, Jonson's invention, appears as an intrusion on the decorum and orderliness of the masque proper, which is figured as an extension of the court audience and setting. As the leading sylvan of *Oberon* admonishes the satyrs:

> Give place and silence; you were rude too late.
> This is a night of greatness and of state,
> Not to be mixed with light and skipping sport:
> A night of homage to the British court . . . (lines 237–40)

The satyrs do not belong in the royal Banqueting House, the sylvan insists. They are an affront, an embarrassment. At the same time, they are needed as an object on which to exercise and thus demonstrate the power of the forces of order. They infiltrate the masque, and yet their banishment is the climax of the masque; at the moment when a foreign element is expelled, the inviolability of the courtly realm is registered. The antimasquers are interlopers in the masque that are nonetheless required by the very form of the entertainment.

The increasingly delicate boundaries of masque and antimasque in Jonson's court entertainments are evident in *The Gypsies Metamorphosed*. Here the boundaries of masque and antimasque are blurred by the disguise of courtiers as fortune-telling gypsies. Since the disguise of the antimasque is so flimsy – more like a whimsical gambit than a Circean metamorphosis – a second layer of antimasque is required, in the form of the clowns who intrude on the supposed gypsies. These clowns then provide a properly foreign element, outsiders to the court who can be dumbfounded and silenced by the transformation scene, the moment when the gypsies turn into courtiers. As the Patrico, the gypsies' priest, announces triumphantly to the clowns, he can

> Give you all your fill,
> Each Jack with his Jill,
> And show ye the king,
> The prince too, and bring
> The gypsies were here
> Like lords to appear . . .   (lines 1167–72)

These reminiscences of the old antimasque format (closest perhaps to that of *Oberon*) are almost vestigial. The main antimasque, the gypsies, is no longer marked off by any mythical setting or uncanny forces, nor even by any great formal distinction, from the ambient masque world. A courtier speaks to the King – even reads his palm – through only the most transparent of assumed roles. This persona of pickpocket and thief, as the satire of the piece wryly suggests, is in any case no bad approximation for the truth of the real-world behaviour of James's rapacious favourites.

Other parallels between Jonson's stage plays and his masques reveal similar patterns of intrusion and blurring of boundaries between nominally fixed and separate theatrical spaces. The child actors of *Cynthia's Revels*, the stage-keeper of *Bartholomew Fair*, and the onstage audience in *The Magnetic Lady* make their extra-dramatic appearances in order to bracket and re-define the dramatic frame by violating it. This paradox (not of course unique to Jonson) succeeds because such extra-dramatic characters, by seeming to stand outside the dramatic illusion, are able to address the audience with a special directness and thereby establish a sardonic distance from the make-believe of the play's main business. Even if no climactic victory enables the stage world to triumph over its invaders, as in the final triumph of the masque world over its antimasque *doppelgänger*, in both play and masque Jonson violates decorum in order to permit himself a consciously transgressive frankness. And although we cannot safely label these intruders in play or masque as Jonson's mouthpieces, we do sense a distinct *frisson* for the audiences in their iconoclasm, in their sense of betraying an illusion or seeing behind a facade.

The release of anarchic energies that is made possible by these Jonsonian strategies, and that enables him to maintain a fiction of outward disapproval even as he violates the dramatic frame of his masque world, destabilizes the masque in a way that is essential to Jonson's self-defined role as critic and courtly entertainer. Without being directly impudent, Jonson revels in spontaneity and fluidity, implying that the rule of the King is necessary but not quite absolute. The antimasque opens something like the gap that Greenblatt finds in the representation of kingship in *Henry V*, revealing an other which is the reason for kingly rule and its inescapable limitation. The antimasque brings into the masquing world the ruled who make rule active and subjects who make sovereignty transitive. In so doing, Jonson represents himself as a kind of allowed fool bearing witness to the human frailty of the King. This is to argue that a residual element of true Bakhtinian carnival survives the manoeuvres by which antimasques are resolved into the masque proper. The inner logic of the anarchic grotesque, an impulse from popular culture to touch rock bottom of materiality and to challenge official culture,[42] united with Jonson's own drive for recognition and claims to attention, made of the antimasque something which went beyond relief for the pressures created by the self-idealising court, towards a moment when the base-born poet spoke frankly to the King and spilled onto the masquing space the uncouth and unreconciled of the kingdom.

Jonson had to take continually into account, of course, the predilections of his royal master. One explanation for the extravagant contrasts in the masque, the elaborate decorousness and flagrant disruptions, is that they sprang from the ambiguities of James's personality; Leah Marcus holds to that view.[43] Jonathan Goldberg similarly interprets the contrasts within the masque – satire and celebration, demystification and mystification – as reflections of the doubleness of James's regime. Charles I was a very different monarch whose personal style of rule gave less room for daring challenges to decorum, even if, as Kevin Sharpe and others have observed, Caroline antimasques did engage with substantial issues of the day.[44] Certainly Jonson's two masques for Charles, *Love's Triumph through Callipolis* and *Chloridia* (both produced in 1631), have only the most genial and innocuous of subversive gestures in their antimasques.

Yet with all the vagaries of individual monarchical style that required the poet to exercise his tact, and the temptations (evident in early Jonson especially) prompting him to use the masque as a vehicle for making bogeymen of disorderly political opposition that the new regime was anxious to repress, the Jonsonian antimasque modulated into much more than a propaganda weapon or the occasion for conventional compliment. It became a vehicle for the poet's particular brand of iconoclasm. Designedly interruptive and calling attention to its own hyperbole, the antimasque became a form in which Jonson could give expression to uninhibited, libidinous, violent and anarchic impulses as if ventriloquizing them.

As in *Volpone*, where, as David Riggs has persuasively written, Jonson finds a licensed outlet in the antisocial and seditious energies of his comic villains, the later antimasque provides its author with characters who serve precariously as a means of expression for a vigorous if implied outspokenness.[45] In their iconoclasm, these figures do more than indicate the dangers of licence. The antimasque enables Jonson to adopt both the protective colouration and the comic frankness of the court jester, or (to use the phrase of Goneril in *King Lear*) the 'all-licensed fool' (1.4.198). Herford and Simpson indeed argue that the 'zest of the personal allusions' in *The Gypsies Metamorphosed* shows Jonson to have invented a 'literary substitute' for the institution of the Fool.[46] His Welsh or Irish clowns, with their absurd pretensions, remind an audience how artificial the distinctions are between the court and the meanest of the King's subjects. Jonson told Drummond that if he could preach one sermon before the King, he would not care what happened afterwards, 'for he would not flatter though he saw Death'.[47] The antimasque was perhaps as near as he got to that opportunity. Even in the main part of the Jonsonian masque one encounters the voice of one who is taking up an opportunity, if not exactly to preach, then at least to articulate a particular ideology for the court, to cast it in his own ideal form, in the accepted mode of *de laudando praecipere*. Jonson's voice in the antimasque, as has been less well recognised, is also didactic, this time as the allowed Fool.

To interpret Jonson's antimasque as didactic clowning is to open an important perspective on the politics of the Jonsonian masque as a whole. Jonson's comic art does not choose to offer itself as a full-blown apocalyptic vision of the sort David Norbrook reconstructs from contemporary materials under the name of the 'reformed masque'. Jonson's stance is certainly worlds apart from that of Milton's *Comus*. The antimasque of fooling in his later work is more conservative and more personal than this: conservative in its appeal to the traditional privileges of the Fool,[48] and personal in the knowing tone and the self-assertion – not completely discounted by due deference – of the masque-maker who claims for himself the role of poet laureate in all but in name.

We should not be surprised that a poet who promoted hierarchy and ceremony in his masques,[49] and yet who emerges from his writings as a complex and even self-divided artist, should also, in the very heart of the court's self-celebratory form of entertainment, wish to bend the 'rules of flattery' to his own colossal persona. A better way to put the matter might be to say that he partly made up those rules as he went along. While he retained the idealizing main fiction of the early masques in his later productions, Jonson also incorporated a vein of comic frankness and intrusive clowning in such a way that those refreshing qualities were no longer merely subordinated to the affirmations of a deified monarchy as the disruptive forces of the early antimasque had been. Jonson learned how to court an element of risk through his introducing of the antimasque into the masque; from the beginning, a good part of the originality and sustained liveliness of the form as Jonson created it was owing to his wooing of danger in it. The power of the Jonsonian masque came from 'strik[ing] sparks against the crown'[50] as much as from inventive sycophancy.

This power of intrusive clowning is especially apparent when the Jacobean masque is compared with the Caroline masque. Orgel and Strong rightly detect in the Jacobean masques 'a sense of human uncertainty', and note that these masques 'gain much of their richness through their awareness of the realities of passion or politics'.[51] From the beginning, the Jonsonian antimasque explored the controversial boundaries of court decorum. A queen in blackface took some getting used to. Part of Jonson's risk-taking, to be sure, took the form of settling occasional personal scores, attacking George Wither before the court in *Time Vindicated* (1623) and Inigo Jones before the Duke of Newcastle in *Love's Welcome at Bolsover* (1634),[52] but a more daring presumption approaching lese-majesty was also structurally inherent in the antimasque as Jonson conceived it. His appreciation of the risks he ran seems to be echoed in the Shepherd's dismissal of the Fencer in *Pan's Anniversary* (1621):

Faith, your folly may well deserve pardon because it hath delighted; but beware of presuming, or how you offer comparison with persons so near deities. Behold where they are that have now forgiven you, whom should you provoke again with the like, they will justly punish with that anger which they now dismiss with contempt. Away! (lines 131–136)

The King's taste for the antimasque, and reports like Sir John Harington's of occasions on which the execution of the stately parts of a masque reduced them also to farce, suggest that the antimasque resonated as fully and memorably with contemporary courtly audiences as did the solemnly triumphant affirmations of what critics usually mean when they talk about 'the masque'. Perhaps the antimasque was even more vivid and significant to its courtly viewers and participants than the masque proper. In the 1620s the Duke of Buckingham and his friends kept the King entertained with what was termed at the time 'masking and fooling',[53] suggesting once again how masques retained their immediacy and power through their association with dissipation and merriment rather than with the solemn apotheoses of monarchy in the masque itself. If Caliban does not in fact appear in Jonson's antimasques, a Jonsonian Fool does. The poet never realized his fantasy of conversing like Virgil with Augustus, or his dream of preaching a recklessly truthful sermon before a court, but through his antimasque he did achieve a risky but no doubt exceptionally gratifying public familiarity with his King.

NOTES

1 Jonathan Goldberg, *James I and the Politics of Literature: Jonson, Shakespeare, Donne, and Their Contemporaries* (Baltimore, 1983), p. 126.
2 Leah S. Marcus, ' "Present occasions" and the shaping of Ben Jonson's masques', *English Literary History* 45 (1978), 201–25, 'The occasion of Ben Jonson's *Pleasure Reconciled to Virtue*', *Studies in English Literature, 1500–1900* 19 (1979), 271–93, and 'City metal and country mettle: the occasion of Ben Jonson's *Golden Age Restored*', in David M. Bergeron (ed.), *Pageantry in the Shakespearean Theater* (Athens, GA, 1985), pp. 26–47.
3 Stephen Greenblatt, *Shakespearean Negotiations: The Circulation of Social Energy in Renaissance England* (Oxford, 1987), p. 63.
4 [Francis Beaumont], *The Maid's Tragedy* (London, 1619), sig. B1r.
5 Goldberg, *James I*, p. 55. Cf. Stephen Orgel, *The Illusion of Power: Political Theater in the English Renaissance* (Berkeley, 1975), pp. 43, 79.
6 John Pitcher, ' "In those figures which they seeme": Samuel Daniel's *Tethys' Festival*', in David Lindley (ed.), *The Court Masque* (Manchester, 1984), pp. 33–46, esp. pp. 42–3.
7 Pitcher, ' "In those figures" ', p. 39. Daniel seems to be glancing at Jonson in his comments in the dedication to *The Vision of the Twelve Goddesses* on the pretensions of other makers of courtly 'shows'. See D. H. Craig (ed.), *Ben Jonson: The Critical Heritage* (London, 1990), pp. 89–90.
8 David Norbrook, 'The reformation of the masque', in Lindley (ed.), *Court Masque*, pp. 94–110; this comment on p. 99.
9 Ian Donaldson, *The World Upside-down: Comedy from Jonson to Fielding* (Oxford, 1970), pp. 20, 72.

10 Marcus, *The Politics of Mirth: Jonson, Herrick, Milton, Marvell, and the Defense of Old Holiday Pastimes* (Chicago, 1986), p. 3.

11 Graham Parry, *The Golden Age Restor'd: The Culture of the Stuart Court, 1603–42* (Manchester, 1981), pp. 50, 63n.

12 All quotations from Jonson's masques are from Stephen Orgel's *Complete Masques* edition (New Haven, 1969).

13 Roy Strong, *Henry, Prince of Wales, and England's Lost Renaissance* (New York, 1986), p. 175.

14 David Riggs, *Ben Jonson: A Life* (Cambridge, MA, 1989), pp. 219–20.

15 Dale B. J. Randall, *Jonson's Gypsies Unmasked: Background and Theme of 'The Gypsies Metamorphos'd'* (Durham, NC, 1975), p. 10.

16 Goldberg, *James I*, p. 131. Goldberg offers a generous treatment of the satire in Jonson's antimasques in his chapter, but differs from the present account in emphasizing the poet's intimate complicity with James even in this aspect of the masque.

17 Martin Butler, 'Reform or reverence?: the politics of the Caroline masque', in J. R. Mulryne and Margaret Shewring (eds.), *Theatre and Government under the Early Stuarts* (Cambridge, 1993), pp. 118–52.

18 Butler, 'Reform or reverence', p. 124.

19 In *The Gypsies Metamorphosed*, the masque proper is a good deal shorter than the antimasque. See Randall, *Gypsies Unmasked*, pp. 153–61, on the absence of a fully transformed supervening ideal masque world in the conclusion of *Gypsies*.

20 Orgel (ed.), *Complete Masques*, p. 29.

21 See OED, 'antimasque'. Richard Dutton suggests that the use of 'ante-' and 'antick-masque' shows the misunderstanding or alternative preference about the form of masque writers other than Jonson (Dutton, *Ben Jonson: To the First Folio* (Cambridge, 1983), p. 96). Daniel and Middleton use 'antemasque' (for Daniel, see Joan Rees (ed.), *The Vision of the Twelve Goddesses*, by Samuel Daniel, in *A Book of Masques in Honour of Allardyce Nicoll*, ed. T. J. B. Spencer (Cambridge, 1967), p. 21; for Middleton, R. C. Bald (ed.), *The Inner Temple Masque or Masque of Heroes*, by Thomas Middleton, *A Book of Masques*, p. 255). Sir George Herbert uses the term 'ante maskes' in a letter of 1618 (R. A. Foakes (ed.), *Pleasure Reconciled to Virtue*, by Ben Jonson, in *A Book of Masques*, p. 227). For 'antic-masque', see *The Masque of Flowers*, ed. E. A. J. Honigmann, *A Book of Masques*, p. 160.

22 Stanley Wells says this practice was begun by Thomas Campion, in his wedding masque for Lord Hay of 1607: Wells (ed.), *Lovers Made Men, A Book of Masques*, p. 210.

23 Orgel (ed.), *Complete Masques*, p. 9.

24 Northrop Frye, *Anatomy of Criticism: Four Essays* (Princeton, 1957), p. 290.

25 Martial, *Epigrams*, 8.8.10. Translation from Orgel (ed.), *Complete Masques*. The Poet had dismissed antimasques as 'things so heterogene to all device, / Mere by-works, and at best outlandish nothings' (lines 159–60). The Cook's view that antimasques are essential to satisfy the tastes of the

audience recalls the thinking behind James's *Book of Sports* (1618, reissued by Charles in 1633), that public pastimes and diversions satisfy desires that are constants in human nature.

26 Francis Beaumont, *The Masque of the Inner Temple and Gray's Inn*, ed. Philip Edwards, *A Book of Masques*, p. 139; *The Masque of Flowers*, ed. Honigmann, *A Book of Masques*, p. 171.

27 Quotations from Jonson's plays are from the edition by C. H. Herford and P. and E. Simpson, 11 vols. (Oxford, 1925–52).

28 John Gillies, *Shakespeare and the Geography of Difference* (Cambridge, 1994), pp. 99ff.

29 *Ibid.*, p. 99.

30 *Ibid.*, p. 102.

31 Stephen Orgel (ed.), *The Tempest* (Oxford, 1987), p. 24.

32 Curt Breight, '"Treason doth never prosper": *The Tempest* and the discourse of treason', *Shakespeare Quarterly* 41 (1990), 1–28; this comment on 17.

33 Orgel (ed.), *Tempest*, p. 50.

34 Robert C. Evans, *Ben Jonson and the Poetics of Patronage* (Lewisburg, 1989), pp. 226, 241–2.

35 *Ibid.*, p. 242.

36 *Ibid.*, p. 225.

37 Randall comments on the confluence of Buckingham's courtiership and Jonson's satirical purposes at this moment of the masque (*Gypsies Unmasked*, p. 125).

38 W. Todd Furniss, 'Ben Jonson's masques', in Richard B. Young, Furniss, and William G. Madsden, *Three Studies in the Renaissance: Sidney, Jonson, Milton* (New Haven, 1958), p. 118.

39 Donaldson, *World Upside-down*, pp. 72–6, where Barish and Gifford are cited.

40 *Ibid.*, p. 79.

41 Dutton, *To the First Folio*, p. 51; cf. Orgel (ed.), *Tempest*, p. 50.

42 See Mikhail Bakhtin, *Rabelais and his World*, trans. Hélène Iswolsky (Bloomington, IN, 1984), *passim*, and especially pp. 87–96.

43 Marcus, *Politics of Mirth*, introduction, *passim*.

44 Kevin Sharpe, *Criticism and Compliment: The Politics of Literature in the England of Charles I* (Cambridge, 1987), *passim*. See also the contrasting emphasis in Butler, 'Reform or reverence', pp. 120–52.

45 Riggs, *Ben Jonson*, pp. 134–42.

46 Herford and Simpson (eds.), *Ben Jonson*, II, p. 316.

47 Herford and Simpson (eds.), *Ben Jonson*, I, p. 141.

48 Randall draws a parallel between the purposes of *Gypsies Metamorphosed* and those of James's court jester Archy Armstrong (*Gypsies Unmasked*, pp. 167–9, and cf. pp. 175–6).

49 Cf. Norbrook, 'Reformation', p. 97.

50 Furniss, 'Ben Jonson's masques', p. 175.

51 Stephen Orgel and Roy Strong, *Inigo Jones: The Theatre of the Stuart Court*, 2 vols. (London, 1973), I, p. 55.

52 Both brought official disapproval. Butler adds to the list censure for the anti-Spanish sentiment in *Neptune's Triumph* ('Reform or reverence', p. 121).

53 Norbrook, 'Reformation', p. 101.

CHAPTER 9

'Rival traditions': civic and courtly ceremonies in Jacobean London

Nancy E. Wright

The rivalrous political discourses in ceremonial entertainment that provide the subjects of analysis for this book were not limited to the court and its masquing rituals. The court and the City, long-time partners and competitors in the networks of power in medieval and Renaissance England, required ceremonial forms of expression through which to negotiate differences and mutual dependencies. What do we discover when we compare the aesthetic and political economies of civic and courtly ceremonies in Jacobean England as acts of accommodation and realignment?

These two great Jacobean ceremonial traditions, the public shows of the London companies and the private masques of the royal court, have invited a good deal of comparison. The Lord Mayor's Shows, in particular, provoke comparisons to court masques. Paula Johnson, for example, notes that the annual Lord Mayor's Shows are evidence of 'a heightening of civic ritual during the reigns of the early Stuarts, parallel to the increasing costliness and visual elaboration of the court masques'.[1] David M. Bergeron also appreciates similarities in the production of these different kinds of ceremonial entertainments.[2] He directs attention to the great cost of these occasional 'dramas' caused by the number of arts, artists and artificers involved in their preparation. Musicians as well as actors were engaged to perform. Well-known poets published the scripts that they wrote along with descriptions of the performance in commemorative texts. Anthony Munday, Thomas Dekker and Thomas Middleton produced accounts of Lord Mayor's Shows just as Samuel Daniel, Ben Jonson and Thomas Campion devised printed texts of court masques.[3]

Despite the important similarities in the production of Jacobean civic and courtly ceremonials, scholarly consensus designates them 'rival traditions'. 'Indeed it is by no means far-fetched to regard the swelling splendour of the Lord Mayors' Shows in Jacobean and Caroline times as deliberately rivalling the opulent masks of the Court at West-minster', Glynne Wickham contends:

For in the underlying basis of flattery and inflated self-esteem, in the extra-vagance of the expenditure, and in the spectacular quality of both types of entertainment, there is a similarity so remarkable as to be more than coincidence . . . It is possible to sense in the ostentatious Masks of Twelfth Night and Shrovetide on the one hand and the elaborate land and water triumphs of St Simon and Jude's Day a . . . dangerous and aggressive spirit beneath the theatrical cloak of these festivities at Court and in the City.[4]

What Wickham does not explain is why such rivalry should exist between the City and the court. Paula Johnson posits a cause and effect relationship between the changes in the Jacobean court's private enter-tainments and the City of London's public spectacles. She suggests that 'as the enclosed court denies access to its magnificence, the street comes to display a ("rival", one is tempted to say) magnificence of its own'.[5] Magnificence, in Renaissance thought, was a princely virtue associated with royal ceremonies and court masques. Dolora Cunning-ham persuasively argues that the conspicuous consumption evident in the production of masques was the means of manifesting this virtue:

The masque is intended to arouse in the spectators respect for the King and the traditional virtues of kingship, respect for and faith in the established order. Since the aspect of kingship most often honoured is magnificence, the means of honouring royalty must, according to the principle of decorum, be magnificent; they must be proper to their end. The masque, in order to praise this virtue adequately and gain the desired end, must be magnificent in all its parts.[6]

By magnificently fêting its chief magistrate, the Lord Mayor, the City, in Johnson's analysis, usurps an attribute of kingship or courtliness. Indeed, Lawrence Manley sees an ideological significance in these differ-ent displays of magnificence; the City's emulation of the King's cere-monies enacts 'a rivalrous relationship, in which merchants liked to represent themselves as the peers of kings'.[7]

Their rivalry, Theodore Leinwand contends, arises from the efforts of the City's elite symbolically to revise conventional hierarchies of political and social authority. The Lord Mayor's Shows, to Leinwand, are not only 'reassuring images for the City fathers' but also effective displays of 'excessive wealth married to great power'.[8] Leinwand agrees with the argument 'that the City's shows were rivals of the court's masques, the two competing with each other as they sought to impress their respective magnificence upon their constituencies'.[9] Yet this argument, as set forth by Leinwand, defines rather than answers important questions about the function of civic and court ceremonials. For whom were the court masque and Lord Mayor's Show produced? Who belonged to those constituencies? Were they mutually exclusive groups, as the idea of rival traditions and institutions contends? By investigating the relation of these two constituencies, the municipal and business elite of the City of London and the royal court, this essay examines how ceremonies symbolically transform rivalry into reciprocity. The purpose of the ceremonial traditions of the City and the court, I will argue, was not simply to differentiate these constituencies or exacerbate conflict and rivalry. Instead mayoral parades and private civic ceremonies symbolically identified these two groups in order to negotiate long-standing conflicts concerning status and finance. This is well illustrated by the role of Prince Henry in a series of important civic ceremonies produced by the Merchant Tailors' Company from 1607 to 1624.

James as well as Henry participated frequently in events organized by the citizens of London, especially by the twelve great livery companies. In 1609, for example, the King returned from his hunting especially to demonstrate his respect for the Lord Mayor's Show.[10] On such occasions James's conduct was often appropriately ingratiating. The fact that the King was particularly gracious to the London companies sets them apart from other residents of the City on whom, Sir Simonds D'Ewes recorded, the King 'in his sudden distemper would bid a p[ox] or a plague'.[11] The King's dependence upon the financial support of the London companies is the most obvious reason for the special courtesy they received from him and Prince Henry. According to Pauline Croft, the King's councillors understood the economic benefits to be reaped from Henry's popularity with the City and the House of Commons. The installation of Henry as Prince of Wales in 1610 was an elaborate ceremony involving members of Parliament and the municipal government of London who, Sir Thomas Edmondes reported, Robert Cecil hoped would offer 'contributions for the maintaining of his [i.e., the Prince's] estate, which will draw on a charge of £40,000 by the year'.[12] The ceremonial role performed by his son was also intended to benefit King James's exchequer by securing revenues from Parliament to replace those from crown lands handed over to the Prince of Wales. Henry, it must be assumed, willingly participated in the installation ceremony involving both citizens and courtiers in order to promote his own political importance, agenda and revenues.

Henry's parliamentary installation as Prince of Wales and Earl of Chester negotiated an exchange of courtesy and money between the City and the court. Along with the Lords and the Commons, the Lord Mayor and thirty Aldermen attended the ceremony. As Pauline Croft explains, 'the conspicuous honour of an invitation to be present, and seated, at the ceremony was a tacit acknowledgement of London's importance in royal finance and national politics'.[13] The ceremony organized by Robert Cecil and held in Parliament on 4 June 1610 to mark this occasion was financed by a loan of £100,000 from the City Aldermen.[14] Rates levied from London companies paid for two public water entertainments as well. Instructions sent by the court to the Lord Mayor and Aldermen, Croft notes, specified that 'the Prince was to be greeted on the river as he arrived from Richmond, with festivities similar to those for a new lord mayor'.[15] The City employed Anthony Munday to design and write an entertainment in which civic magistrates would participate. The water entertainment, *London's Love To the Royal Prince Henry*, presented speeches by actors figuring Henry's principalities of Cornwall and Wales. What they expressed, however, were 'the endeared affections of London's Lord Mayor, his brethren the Aldermen, and all these worthy citizens, merchants that hold commerce . . . their willing readiness by all means possible to love and honour you'.[16] The first water show enabled the City to participate in Henry's progress from Richmond to Westminster by barge. Following tilting by courtiers, the City presented another water entertainment imitating a sea battle between pirate and merchant ships. The tilting performed by courtiers before the Prince and King was a symbolic demonstration of the court's martial prowess, just as the water battle was a symbolic demonstration of the City's commercial power.[17] The City used these ceremonies as opportunities to symbolize its identity and to negotiate its relationship to the court.

Just as Henry's installation in 1610 had been organized in order to benefit the crown's finances, the court arranged his attendance at the midsummer feast of the Merchant Tailors' Company in 1607 to secure revenue from one of the wealthiest of the twelve great livery companies. Henry, accompanied by King James, attended the private civic ceremony. This feast, at the commencement of Prince Henry's public career,[18] celebrated the annual choice of the master and wardens of this livery company. The *Memorials of the Merchant Tailors* record that members of the Merchant Tailors' Company guided the King to 'a chair of state' at

the upper end of the Hall . . . where his Majesty sat and viewed the Hall, and a very proper child, well spoken, being clothed like an angel of gladness with a paper of frankincense burning in his hand, delivered a short speech containing eighteen verses, devised by Ben Jonson the poet, which pleased his Majesty marvellously well, and upon either side of the Hall in the window were galleries or seats made for music, in either of which were seven singular choice musicians playing on their lutes; and in the ship which did hang aloft in the Hall three rare men and very skilful who sang to his Majesty . . . And his Majesty went up into the king's chamber where he dined alone . . . in which chamber was placed a very rich pair of organs, whereupon Mr. John Bull, Doctor of Music and a brother of this company, did play during the dinner-time . . . And the Prince did dine in the Great Hall . . . And the service to the King and Prince for the first course was carried up by the Knights, Aldermen, Masters, Assistants and Livery which were of the Company . . . And the Master did present his Majesty with a fair purse, wherein was a hundred pounds in gold. And . . . the Clerk did most humbly deliver unto his Majesty a roll in vellum which he had collected out of the ancient books and records of the Company.[19]

The roll recorded the names of nobles and gentlemen who had been members of the Merchant Tailors' Company, including seven kings, one queen, seventeen princes and dukes.[20] At the conclusion of the dinner and presentations, 'his Majesty came down in the Great Hall, and sitting in the Chair of State did hear a melodious song of farewell . . . which song so pleased his Majesty that he caused the same to be sung three times over'.[21]

This private civic ceremony paralleled private court masques in many details. The King's chair of state in the Great Hall placed him as a focus of the civic ceremony just as his seat among the audience of a court masque placed him at a centre of attention. The King was thus a focus of the audience's as well as the performers' gaze.[22] At the upper end of the Merchant Tailors' Hall the King performed an important role himself as the recipient of his subjects' praise and honour expressed in a speech written by Ben Jonson. The Merchant Tailors employed this poet who received so many commissions for the royal court's own private entertainments. Both the production and performance of this private civic ceremonial departed very little from the conventions of early Stuart court masques. The only difference, apparent in this initial description, was the constituency who sponsored the performance, the members of a London livery company. This difference, in fact, only disguised another parallel. From the ranks of the livery company were drawn not only the sponsors but also the performers and audience of the ceremony. Similarly, members of the royal court paid for, and performed in, court masques. In these different ceremonies, members of the Merchant Tailors' Company and the royal court performed analogous functions and dramatic roles.

The Merchant Tailors during the feast invited the King to become a freeman of their company. When James declined because he was free of the Clothworkers' Company, he nominated Prince Henry for the honour offered by the Merchant Tailors. A seventeenth-century account records that the King suggested 'that the Prince his eldest son should be free thereof, and that he would see and be a witness, when the garland should be put on his head'.[23] Having received gifts like those given to his father, a vellum roll and a purse of £50, the Prince prompted his attendants to accept membership in the Merchant Tailors' Company:

> whereupon three ambassadors, eighteen nobles, and some seventy gentlemen signified their willingness to do so. When the Master and Wardens went with garlands on their heads to publish the election, the Prince was graciously pleased to call for the Master's garland and put it on his own head, whereat the King who was watching through the window did very heartily laugh . . . And his Majesty and the Noble Prince and Honourable Lords gave the Company hearty thanks and departed.[24]

The double focus of the Merchant Tailors' ceremonial occurred later in court masques, such as *Oberon, the Fairy Prince*, in which Prince Henry performed before his father. The King performed his customary role as spectator as he watched his son participate in a ceremonial entertainment, as Tom Bishop has shown in an earlier essay in this volume. These roles of the royal guests remained during the dinner, when the King sat separately in an elevated room from which he observed his son through a window. Yet Henry's role changed subtly during the evening when he accepted membership in the livery company; the Prince became a citizen of London, a ceremonially constructed identity that he did not possess previously. He became a freeman of the company – a freedom customarily conferred only for apprenticeship, through patrimony or by redemption (purchase).[25] The Merchant Tailors' Company marked this occasion with not only liberality but magnificence. The expense of the dinner, dramatic monologue and musical entertainments, like the purses of gold given to the King and Prince, demonstrated the magnificence of the institution.

But what did the company accomplish by rivalling the King's own magnificence? The livery company displayed its own magnificence, its wealth and traditions that merited the Prince's respect. The magnificence shared by merchants and the Prince justified a ceremonial union of the constituencies of the royal court and the City. When he asked members of his court to accept the freedom of the company, the Prince extended this union. By symbolizing a network of bonds joining the royal court and the London company, the ceremony negotiated conflicts vitiating their economic relationship.

The citizens of London – that is, the members of the Merchant Tailors and other London companies – comprised the constitutional and economic substructure of the City.[26] Only members of the London companies were able to hold the office of Mayor, Alderman or Common Councillor. It was their business rather than their municipal privileges, however, that constituted their strongest ties to the royal court.[27] Only members of the companies had the freedom of London, which included the rights to keep shop or employ journeymen within the metropolitan square mile east of Temple Bar and the liberties. This restriction protected tradesmen and merchants belonging to existing companies from competitors. The crown's prerogative power to grant charters of incorporation threatened that protected market and as a result frequently caused controversy during the early Stuart period. By supporting the establishment of new companies, James I threatened the profit of existing companies.[28] Another financial bond that caused conflict was the crown's method of rewarding courtiers with, in Robert Ashton's words, 'concessions in kind rather than by payments in cash – by such devices as patents, licences and customs farms'.[29] In order to profit substantially from these 'rewards', courtiers formed syndicates that demanded high prices from merchants whose business and trade depended upon the purchase of licences granting monopolies to make or sell certain products. Profit accruing to London businessmen from such transactions did not eliminate conflict and resentment from their business relationship with Jacobean courtiers.

The role of the City of London as a moneylender to the King must also be taken into account when analyzing their relationship. In April 1610 the Venetian Ambassador remarked, 'as the whole government of this City is in the hands of the merchants, they have acquired great power on account of the need which the King and his Ministers have of them in realizing the revenue and the subsidies'.[30] In the early Jacobean period, the City showed a favourable attitude to the crown's

requests for loans. Before a loan of £60,000 taken out in 1599 was
repaid in 1608, the Corporation of London raised for the King two
other loans.[31] The function of the City in these two loans Robert
Ashton describes as 'that of loan contractor, and was confined to the
assessment of and collection of moneys from the companies, which,
in turn, were secured directly by the Crown'.[32] For the loan in 1604,
the Merchant Tailors' Company was rated the highest amount of the
thirty-five companies required to contribute. It was also one of the two
livery companies to whom the crown repaid this loan last, two years
after its repayment was due. The crown's inability to repay loans to
creditors led the Corporation to provide funding without rating the
companies in later years. For example in 1610, the Aldermen of the
City themselves raised a loan of £100,000 for the crown to pay for
Henry's installation as Prince of Wales. The role of debtor which the
crown played in this relationship seems anything but that of a dominant power.

   As Robert Ashton emphasizes, however, the City was vulnerable to
royal demands because of its dual roles as the commercial and financial
capital and as the municipal government that raised, contracted and
insured loans to the crown.[33] The prosperity of wealthy merchants
who were also Aldermen and Common Councillors, members of the
municipal government, could suffer from the crown's displeasure. Yet
this was not what occurred during the first decade of James's reign
because of the Aldermen's astute economic initiatives. Rather than
providing loans upon request by the crown, the municipal government in 1614 negotiated this request in a manner favourable to the
companies. In 1614 the City offered a gift of £10,000 instead of providing a loan of £100,000 requested by the crown. The records of the
Merchant Tailors indicate that they chose to offer a gift to the crown
whereas other companies were instructed to do so by the Lord Mayor.[34]
The responses of the companies and the City government to the crown's
requests for loans (and presumably to the crown's failure to repay
loans when due) suggest a complex rather than a simple relationship of
a dominant, powerful crown to subordinate clients, the Corporation
and citizens of London. In particular, the City's decision to substitute
a gift for a loan requested by the crown indicates anything but a unilat-
eral exercise of power on the part of the crown. The financial dependence of the crown upon the London companies explains why rather
than provoking royal displeasure, as Ashton notes, 'the Corporation's
substitution of a gift for a loan had the desired effect of diverting the

royal attention from itself to the country at large, and its opportunism was undoubtedly the major factor in the initiation of the general Benevolence of 1614, of which the gift of £10,000 was a part'.[35]

The decision of the City and the Merchant Tailors' Company to distribute a gift to the crown in 1614 provides an important perspective for evaluating the money presented to King James and Prince Henry at the midsummer feast of the Merchant Tailors in 1607.[36] The purses of £100 and £50 given to the King and the Prince during the company's ceremonial were not simply token gifts. The purses symbolized the relation of the royal court to the company who provided a loan free of interest in 1604. This loan, that had fallen due on 24 March 1606, had not been repaid to the Merchant Tailors when the feast occurred in 1607. In these circumstances the company offered to the King and Prince gifts of money that confirmed not only its wealth but also its role as benefactor of the crown. The feast of the Merchant Tailors' Company used gifts of money to symbolize a complex relationship between the crown and its members based on the exchange of money and honours. Treating their 'debtors' with gracious hospitality and liberality, the Merchant Tailors in turn were granted respect and honour when the Prince and other courtiers became members of the company. The feast held by the Merchant Tailors in 1607 was the occasion of a ceremonial exchange of wealth and status that allowed a symbolic identification of merchants, tradesmen, nobles and courtiers. While emphasizing the reciprocity of the court's and City's finances, the private civic ceremony also revealed the desire of citizens to accumulate honour and status. The reciprocal relation of the London companies and the royal court informed the themes of the Lord Mayor's Shows of 1605, 1612 and 1624 to be discussed next.

The Merchant Tailors' efforts to garner status through affiliation with royalty were not first represented in the feast of 1607. The Lord Mayor's Show of 1605, titled *The Triumphs of Reunited Britannia*, catalogued the honours that the Merchant Tailors gathered from many English kings. This civic ceremony paid for by members[37] of the Merchant Tailors' Company celebrated the election of Sir Leonard Holliday as Mayor but throughout praised the King as the 'second Brute'. Indeed a refrain sung by characters figuring Troynovant, or London, the Thames and other rivers presents their greetings 'Unto my second Brute . . . / Welcome King James, welcome great Britain's King'.[38] The legend of Brute in the show effectively represents the relation of the City to the King because, according to legend, as Munday explained,

'Brute thus having the whole land in his own quiet possession, began to build a city, near to the side of the River Thamesis, in the second year of his reign, which he named Troynovant . . . which is, new Troy' (lines 67–70), the fabled origin of London. When discussing the identification of King James with Brute in this ceremonial celebrating the Mayor, David M. Bergeron notes that 'No other Lord Mayor's Show so consciously, explicitly and unrelentingly refers to the sovereign'.[39] The dialogue contains a catalogue of the kings and nobles who honoured the company by accepting membership. The character Pheme (Fame) reported:

> I find recorded in my register,
> Seven kings have honoured this society:
> Fourteen great dukes did willingly prefer,
> Their love and kindness to this Company,
> Threescore eight lords declared like amity,
>   Terming themselves all brethren of this band,
>   The very worthiest lords in all the land.
> Three dukes, three earls, four lords of noble name
> All in one year did join in brotherhood

In the year 1390: Edward, Duke of York, Thomas, Duke of Gloucester, Henry, Duke of Hereford and Earl of Derby, who afterward was King Henry the Fourth, Edward, Earl of Rutland, Thomas, Earl of Warwick, John Holland, Earl of Huntingdon, John, Lord Ros, Rafe, Lord Neville, Thomas, Lord Furnivall, Reginald, Lord Gray of Rithin. (lines 407–20)

Munday might have been fulfilling the company's specifications for his commission by including this information drawn, as the dialogue stated, from the Register of the Merchant Tailors.

The brief history of the Merchant Tailors culminates in an invitation to the new King to follow the precedent of other English kings. The Merchant Tailors ask James to follow the precedent of 'seven Kings [who] have born free brethren's name, / Of this society' (lines 404–5). During the Lord Mayor's Show, an empty chair symbolized the position that James was invited to accept within the company. The symbol of the seat of state, 'Being the most eminent and chiefest place, / With state, with crown and sceptre dignified' (lines 401–2), acknowledged the King's social pre-eminence. While deferring to the King, however, the pageant questioned the nature of social degree signified by a king's crown and a merchant's livery. Henry IV, the dialogue asserted, 'thought it no disgrace to his high state, / To wear the clothing of the Company, / A most majestic royal courtesy' (lines 378–80).

Munday's language levels the difference between members involved in this relationship; the royal benefactor, who gave 'graces' or gifts to the guild, found it no 'disgrace' to be a member of the company. In this manner the pageant advised King James to appreciate and imitate his predecessor's gracious condescension. Henry IV exemplified both royal graciousness and majesty by wearing their livery, a symbolic costume of hood and badge that identified him with the company. The conduct of Henry IV towards the Merchant Tailors, the pageant explained, showed 'Princes lose no part of dignity, / In being affable, it adds to majesty' (lines 386–87). Just as many private court masques sought to educate the King about his conduct, duty and office, the public civic ceremony tutored James so that he could appreciate how citizens understood his relationship to their company. According to the Merchant Tailors, the honour that James could bestow upon the livery company by accepting membership was reciprocated; the status of freeman, in the Merchant Tailors' eyes, augmented his majesty in a measure equal to the honour given them by his gracious condescension.

It was not simply the personnel, both kings and commoners, who were freemen of the Merchant Tailors that related the Stuarts to this company. Instead political and economic ties had been forged by the legal personality, or attributes, bestowed upon the company by various English kings. The history of the 'great grace each Majesty / Gave to the Merchant Tailors Company' (lines 344–45) within the 1605 Lord Mayor's Show specified the particular powers and characteristics conferred upon it by successive kings. Edward III received praise because he confirmed their guild with a charter whereas Richard II allowed them to elect a Master and four 'keepers' and to have a livery.[40] It was Henry IV who received praise for his 'liberality' evident when he made 'Their guild a brotherhood incorporate' (line 377). A royal charter that he granted in 1408 transformed the Tailors' fraternity of St John the Baptist into an immortal corporate body.[41] Henry IV in this manner secured for the crown the gratitude and loyalty of the guild members. As George Unwin has explained, Henry IV used royal charters of incorporation to change the relation of the existing trade fraternity to two other sources of authority, ecclesiastical and civic, who restricted the crown's power. The secular sanction of the crown replaced the previous ecclesiastical sanction that defined such associations as fraternities 'whilst at the same time . . . preserved for the livery companies a basis of voluntary association independent of the civic authority'.[42] The Church or municipal government could not arbitrarily dissolve or reorganize the Merchant Tailors because it was a chartered company. As an artificial person created by royal charter, the Merchant Tailors' Company had authority to exist, and to preserve specified rights, in perpetual succession. The Lord Mayor's Shows of 1612 and 1624 related corporate immortality to fame and virtue in order to assert citizens' claims to honour, status and historical importance customarily assumed to be more properly the attributes of kings and nobles.

The Lord Mayor's Show of 1612 associated virtue with the immortal fame awarded to the name of an individual who was the head of a corporate body. Sir John Swinerton, the mayor elect who was welcomed to 'Fame's high temple' in the civic ceremonial, was the head or highest officer of the municipal government of the Corporation of London. He had been chosen from two names presented to the Court of Aldermen by the liverymen of the chartered London companies.[43] The twelve great livery companies of London in particular received Virtue's praise for their support of 'civil, popular government' (line 221). The Lord Mayor and Aldermen of London depended upon

> Twelve strong pillars . . .
> Upon whose capitals, twelve societies stand,
> (Grave and well-ordered) bearing chief command
> Within this City, and (with love) thus rear
> Thy fame, in free election, for this year.   (lines 224–8)

As James Knowles notes, the image of the building described by Virtue 'concretizes the civilized, ordered and well-founded nature of City- and guild-government, and elaborates a commonplace of Renaissance political thought'.[44] The ceremony praised the twelve great livery companies who provided the economic foundation or edifice of London.

The 1612 show, *Troia-Nova Triumphans*, written by Thomas Dekker, advised Swinerton, the mayor elect, that his virtue could triumph over vices that threaten civic order when he saw Forlorn Castle, defended by a Fury named Envy and her followers, Ignorance, Sloth, Oppression, Riot and Calumny, succumb to Virtue who entered seated on her throne, a pageant car.[45] The settings and characters in this Lord Mayor's Show recalled those in the antimasque of Ben Jonson's *Masque of Queens*. Because of his virtue, the Lord Mayor, like the twelve queens in Jonson's court masque of 1609, was elected to the House of Fame, where his 'name' might

Be as old, and good as Fame.
Ever be remembered here
Whilst a blessing, or a tear
Is in store
With the poor
So shall Swinerton ne'er die,
But his virtues upward fly
And still spring
Whilst we sing
In a chorus ceasing never,
He is living, living ever.[46]

The dialogue associated his fame and immortality not only with the office of Lord Mayor but, more importantly, with the Merchant Tailors, Swinerton's company.

When explaining the immortality of a virtuous name, Dekker referred to the Merchant Tailors, the company rather than the office of the mayor elect. Dekker reserved special praise for the mayor elect's company who, according to custom, paid for, and commissioned, the entire Lord Mayor's Show. In order to confirm 'the high merits / Of thy renowned society', the Merchant Tailors, Fame cited a catalogue of

royal spirits
Of princes holding it a grace to wear
That crimson badge, which these about them bear,
Yea, kings themselves 'mongst you have fellows been,
Styled by the name of a free citizen.   (lines 370–5)

The catalogue, beginning with seven English kings who were free of the Merchant Tailors' Company, concluded with the name of 'Henry Prince of Wales, followed by none, / Who of this brotherhood, last and best steps forth, / Honouring your Hall' (lines 385–87). The affiliation of the English monarchy and the Merchant Tailors seems, in this instance, not simply a singular honour differentiating this great livery company from others. Instead it uses the 'fellowship' shared by kings and merchants to level social degree by equating the status signified by the title 'freeman' held by its members with a royal style, such as 'king' or 'prince'. The honour and status of freemen, shared by both merchants and princes, were to have been represented by those attending the entertainment as well as those participating in the Lord Mayor's Show of 1612. Seats had been prepared for Prince Henry whose attendance, however, was prevented by his fatal illness.

Prince Henry's identity as a freeman remained a theme in the mayoral shows of the Merchant Tailors many years after his death – perhaps, as Tom Bishop and others have noted earlier in this volume, as a token of deep admiration for his chivalrous promise and of dismay at the vacillations and corruptions of James's reign. For example, the 1624 entertainment sponsored by the Merchant Tailors recalled his memory as a freeman of this company and citizen of London. This civic ceremonial, *Monuments of Honour*, written by John Webster, explicitly emphasized the manufacture and trade in which the London companies participated. During a water pageant the Mayor heard Oceanus and Thetis praise 'Drake, Hawkins, Frobisher, Gilbert',[47] English navigators whose voyages secured trade routes for London's 'eminent merchants' (line 52). Then the Mayor proceeded through the City streets to a pageant 'called the Temple of Honour' (line 91). Like the stage car used in Jonson's *Masque of Queens*,[48] characters at the apex of the pageant car sat above actors personating 'famous scholars and poets of this our kingdom, as Sir Geoffrey Chaucer, the learned Gower, the excellent John Lydgate, the sharp-witted Sir Thomas More, and last as worthy both soldier and scholar, Sir Philip Sidney' (lines 99–102). Seated on top of the pageant car were actors representing Troynovant and five centres of trade. Troynovant announces the themes of the show:

> History, Truth and Virtue seek by name
> To celebrate the Merchant Tailors' fame;
> · · · · · ·
>   . . . from low beginnings there oft springs
> Societies claim brotherhoods of kings.
> I Troynovant, placed eminent in the eye
> Of these, admire at my felicity:
> Five cities, Antwerp and the spacious Paris,
> Rome, Venice and the Turks' metropolis:
> Beneath these, five learned poets, worthy men,
> Who do eternize brave acts by their pen;
> Chaucer, Gower, Lydgate, More and for our time
> Sir Philip Sidney, glory of our clime;
> These beyond death a fame to monarchs give,
> And these make cities and societies live.   (lines 116–31)

The theme of social degree or 'eminence' voiced throughout this ceremony eroded deference customarily granted to the King as the individual pre-eminently important in the history of the City. London's 'eminent' place among the five important centres of trade was attributed to merchants and tradesmen. These men deserved their place in the Temple of Honour as much as kings.

Despite the claims to historical importance made for merchants and tradesmen in the Temple of Honour, the ethos of subsequent pageants in the mayoral parade can best be described by Lawrence Manley's adjective 'neo-feudal'.[49] A triumphal chariot, for example, carried not only the heraldic arms of the Merchant Tailors but also 'the honour of the Company (of which records remain in the Hall): eight famous kings of this land, that have been free of this worshipful Company' (lines 166–68). An actor representing Edward III, the first English king to join the fraternity, affirmed that

> the Merchant Tailors' honour springs –
> From this most royal conventicle of kings:
> Eight that successively wore England's crown
> Held it a special honour, and renown
> (The society was so worthy, and so good)
> T'unite themselves into their brotherhood.   (lines 192–7)

Webster described the basis of the relationship of the members of the two constituencies as a reciprocal exchange of honours and virtues, just as Munday had in the 1605 Lord Mayor's Show. Webster's commemorative text of the Lord Mayor's Show, like those of his predecessors Munday and Dekker, detailed the catalogue of royal freemen whose names were recorded in the Register of the Merchant Tailors. It departed from their texts by referring to the 1607 midsummer feast of the Merchant Tailors. In the printed text of *Monuments of Honour*, Webster recorded the honour given the company when it included among its members

with Prince Henry in the year 1607, the Duke of Lennox, the Earls of Nottingham, Suffolk, Arundel, Oxford, Worcester, Pembroke, Essex, Northampton, Salisbury, Montgomery, the Earl of Perth, Viscount Cranborne, Barons, the Lord Evers, Hunsdon, Hay, Burghley, Mr. Howard, Mr. Sheffield, Sir John Harington, Sir Thomas Chaloner, besides States of the Low-Countries, and Sir Noel de Caron their Legier Ambassador. (lines 212–18)

The Company's honour, according to this commentary about the pageant, accrues from the status of members of the pre-eminent social degree, the late Prince and other nobles.

The iconography of the final pageant, the 'Monument of Gratitude', commemorated the honour that the deceased Prince gave to the company. Distinguished by 'four curious pyramids charged with the

Prince's arms, the three feathers', the pageant car set with precious stones

expresses the riches of the kingdom Prince Henry was born heir to, the pyramids, which are monuments for the dead, that he is deceased; on the top of this rests half a celestial globe, in the midst of this hangs the Holy Lamb in the sunbeams, on either side of these, an angel; upon a pedestal of gold stands the figure of Prince Henry with his coronet, George and Garter; in his left hand he holds a circlet of crimson velvet, charged with four Holy Lambs, such as our Company choose Masters with. (lines 308–321)

The monument commemorating Henry joined the heraldic arms of the Prince of Wales and the Merchant Tailors' Company. Pyramids, a symbol of the paradoxical relation of death and immortality also used in the masque car of *The Masque of Queens*, figured the immortal corporate body of the monarchy of which Henry was a part. The iconography also specified efficacious symbols used in courtly and civic ceremonies to confer office. The coronet, St George medal and the Garter, that signified Henry's identity as a member of the Order of the Garter, were compared with the crown of velvet that signified the identity of the freeman elected Master at the annual midsummer feast of the Merchant Tailors. These signs revealed parallels in courtly and civic ceremonies. More important, however, than these practices that the two constituencies had in common was the 'brotherhood' shared by their members. For this reason the *Monuments of Honour* commemorated

> Worthy Prince Henry, fame's best president,
> Called to a higher court of Parliament,
> In his full strength of youth and height of blood,
> And, which crowned all, when he was truly good:
> On virtue, and on worth he still was throwing
> Most bounteous showers, where'er he found them growing.
> . . . . .
> Such was this Prince, such are the noble hearts,
> Who when they die, yet die not in all parts;
> But from the integrity of a brave mind,
> Leave a most clear and eminent fame behind.   (lines 349–62)

The association of Henry's fame with his virtue as well as his participation in the immortal corporate institution of monarchy was conventional in both civic and courtly ceremonials.[50] What seems striking, of course, is the commemoration of Henry as Prince of Wales in the 1624 Lord Mayor's Show, as though expressing a forlorn wish that his policies and leadership were still in practice. At the time the show was performed, Charles was Prince of Wales. This fact is acknowledged at the very conclusion of Webster's *Monuments of Honour* when the speaker advises the mayor elect and his company to set aside their grief for Henry and joyfully remember 'a new phoenix springs up in his stead: / That as he seconds him in every grace, / May second him in brother-hood, and place' (lines 368–70). The Lord Mayor's Show performed on 29 October, 1624 extended an invitation to join the Merchant Tailors to Charles, Prince of Wales, who five months later was King.[51]

The Lord Mayor's Shows of 1605, 1612 and 1624 created occasions for a symbolic reciprocity transferring honours, prestige and identities between the City and the court. Each Lord Mayor's Show prompted the King or Prince of Wales to renew and renegotiate bonds of loyalty and revenue that for much of London's history had circulated between kings, merchants and tradesmen. This was the context within which rivalrous displays of magnificence occurred, as Thomas Dekker perceptively noted. When James I made his procession through London in 1604 marking his coronation, the City, according to Dekker, symbolically transformed its identity. The song 'Troynovant is Now No More a City', Dekker explained, allegorized the effects of the occasion upon which

London (to do honour to this day, wherein springs up all her happiness) being ravished with unutterable joys, makes no account (for the present) of her ancient title, to be called a City (because that during these triumphs, she puts off her formal habit of trade and commerce, treading even thrift itself under foot) but now becomes a reveller and a courtier.[52]

In this explanation of the triumphal entry paid for primarily by the London companies, Dekker stated, the City was not merely personified as in many medieval and Renaissance entertainments. Instead the City participated in the life and ceremonies of the court to the extent that its role and character changed. Its ceremonial role of courtier identified rather than dissociated the two constituencies, during this first civic ceremony acknowledging the Stuart monarchy and its court. The exchange of honours and characteristics in James I's procession of 1604 represented the desire for reciprocity between the crown and citizens. The residence of the royal households in London provided special economic benefits to the City, and encouraged the efforts of the London companies and the Lord Mayor and Aldermen to impress upon James the history of its relation to the kings of England.[53] James and his heir, who depended upon London citizens as moneylenders, acknowledged the companies as benefactors who merited honour and courtesy by attending public and private ceremonials held by the London companies. The benefits arising from the complex relations between royal court and City informed the dynamics of Lord Mayor's Shows and other civic ceremonies of Jacobean London.

NOTES

1 Paula Johnson, 'Jacobean ephemera and the immortal word', *Renaissance Drama* ns 8 (1977), 157.
2 David M. Bergeron (ed.), 'Introduction', *Pageants and Entertainments of Anthony Munday: A Critical Edition* (New York, 1985), p. xi. Cf. David M. Bergeron, *English Civic Pageantry 1558–1642* (Columbia, SC, 1971).
3 Lawrence Manley, *Literature and Culture in Early Modern London* (Cambridge, 1995), p. 268, explains that although the Lord Mayor's Shows had a similar form from 1540 to 1702, only after the mid-1580s was a text of the annual pageant consistently printed.
4 Glynne Wickham, *Early English Stages 1300 to 1660*, 4 vols. (London, 1963), II, Part 1, p. 237.
5 Johnson, 'Jacobean ephemera', p. 156.
6 Dolora Cunningham, 'The Jonsonian masque as a literary form', in Jonas A. Barish (ed.), *Ben Jonson: A Collection of Critical Essays* (Englewood Cliffs, NJ, 1963), p. 167. Cf. Linda Levy Peck, *Court Patronage and Corruption in Early Stuart England* (Boston, 1990), pp. 13–15.
7 Manley, *Literature and Culture*, p. 221. In the *longue durée*, Manley argues, by using ceremony to negotiate the jurisdictions of the King and the municipal government of London, the 'mayoral shows derived . . . new rationales for the City and its bourgeois pursuits' (p. 292).
8 Theodore Leinwand, 'London triumphing: the Jacobean Lord Mayor's Show', *Clio* 11 (1982), 149.
9 *Ibid.*
10 Pauline Croft, 'The parliamentary installation of Henry, Prince of Wales', *Historical Research* 65 (1992), 187 n43. While the mayor elect's pageant only occurred after he had taken his oath of fealty to the crown, the King's presence for such an occasion was not obligatory. The mayor could be sworn in before the monarch's representatives at Westminster. See Manley, *Literature and Culture*, pp. 260, 262–3.
11 Cited in Robert Ashton, *The City and the Court 1603–1643* (Cambridge, 1979), p. 172.
12 *Downshire MSS*, II, p. 199, quoted from Croft, 'Parliamentary installation', p. 185.
13 Croft, 'Parliamentary installation', p. 189.
14 *Ibid.*, p. 186.

15 *Ibid.* Cf. *The Progresses, Processions and Magnificent Festivities of King James the First*, ed. John Nichols, 4 vols. (London, 1828), II, p. 358.

16 Anthony Munday, *London's Love, to the Royal Prince Henry* in *Pageants and Entertainments of Anthony Munday*, lines 156–61.

17 Nichols, *Progresses*, II, p. 361.

18 Roy Strong assumes that this began with his appearance at the Barriers on Twelfth Night 1610, in *Henry, Prince of Wales and England's Lost Renaissance* (London, 1986), p. 141. Cf. Croft, 'Parliamentary installation', pp. 177–8.

19 C. M. Clode, *Memorials of the Guild of Merchant Taylors* (London, 1875), pp. 153–4.

20 *Ibid.*, pp. 155–8.

21 *Ibid.*, p. 160.

22 Recent criticism contests the popular notion that King James was seated at the exact station point of perspective when masques had perspectival scenery. Irrespective of this detail of performance history, the staging of Jacobean court masques, like the 1607 midsummer feast of the Merchant Tailors, verifies Stephen Orgel's argument that 'the entertainment included its audience, both figuratively, by allegorizing its noble spectators and their milieu, and literally' by means of their conspicuous seating in the audience. See Stephen Orgel, ' "To make boards to speak": Inigo Jones's stage and the Jonsonian masque', *Renaissance Drama* ns 1 (1968), 121. During the 1607 midsummer feast, the King's seating reproduced a practice of the court masque that, Orgel explains, affected other spectators whose 'response would have been not simply to the drama, but to the relationship between the drama and its primary audience, the royal spectator'. See Stephen Orgel, *The Illusion of Power: Political Theater in the English Renaissance* (Berkeley, 1975), p. 9.

23 Nichols, *Progresses*, II, p. 141. Cf. Clode, *Memorials*, p. 158.

24 Clode, *Memorials*, p. 160.

25 See Valerie Pearl, *London and the Outbreak of the Puritan Revolution* (Oxford, 1961), p. 35 n98. Cf. Ashton, *The City and the Court*, p. 5.

26 See Pearl, *Puritan Revolution*, pp. 45–68, and Ashton, *The City and the Court*, pp. 5–82.

27 Lionel Cranfield is perhaps the best documented example of the economic relationship between a citizen of London and the royal court. See Menna Prestwich, *Cranfield: Politics and Profits Under the Early Stuarts* (Oxford, 1966); R. H. Tawney, *Business and Politics Under James I: Lionel Cranfield as Merchant and Minister* (Cambridge, 1958); and Linda Levy Peck, *Northampton: Patronage and Policy at the Court of James I* (London, 1982), pp. 37–40.

28 George Unwin, *The Guilds and Companies of London*, fourth edn (London, 1963), p. 170.

29 On syndicates and cartels formed by courtiers in order to increase profits, see Ashton, *The City and the Court*, p. 17.

30 *Calendar of State Papers, Venetian, 1607–1610*, p. 475.

31 Robert Ashton, *The Crown and the Money Market 1603–1640* (Oxford, 1960),
   p. 114.
32 *Ibid.*, pp. 115, 127. In his discussion of the loan of 1617, Ashton analyses the
   Corporation's role as guarantor of the loan to the Crown.
33 *Ibid.*, p. 76.
34 *Merchant Tailors' Hall, Court Minutes*, VII, fo. 128 cited in Ashton, *Crown and
   the Money Market*, p. 122 n22.
35 Ashton, *Crown and the Money Market*, p. 122.
36 Because the purses of money were gifts solely from the Merchant Tailors'
   Company, they differed from the gift customarily presented by the City
   during the entry of a monarch or consort into London. All London companies contributed rates levied by the municipal government for a purse
   of gold or an equivalent 'gift' for a royal entrance. See Manley, *Literature
   and Culture*, pp. 247, 250 on Tudor royal entries. Cf. Carolyn A. Edie, 'For
   "the honour and welfare of the City": London's gift to King Charles II on
   his coming into his kingdom, May 1660', *Huntington Library Quarterly* 50
   (1987), 119–31.
37 Manley, *Literature and Culture*, p. 261, explains that a Lord Mayor's Show
   was produced by 'the individual guild from whose membership the mayor
   had been elected in a given year. Commissioned and paid for by the
   "bachelors" of the company, scores of whom were raised to this livery
   from the lower yeomanry whenever a company's candidate was elected
   mayor, the show was the company's gift to one of its illustrious members'.
   Cf. Steven Rappaport, *Worlds within Worlds: Structures of Life in Sixteenth-
   Century London* (Cambridge, 1989), p. 229.
38 *The Triumphs of Reunited Britannia* in *Pageants and Entertainments of Anthony
   Munday*, lines 314–36.
39 *Pageants and Entertainments of Anthony Munday*, p. xiii.
40 *Triumphs*, lines 388–91, specifies that it was Edward IV who changed the
   title of 'keepers' to Wardens.
41 Unwin, *Guilds and Companies*, pp. 158–59, explains that the charter granted
   to the Merchant Tailors in 1390 merely confirmed previously held rights,
   such as the right to hold their guild of St John Baptist, to make a livery, to
   hold their assemblies and their annual feast at midsummer, and to make
   ordinances. It only added a provision for the election of a master and four
   wardens. The later charter of 1408 'constitutes them "a sound perpetual
   and corporate fraternity", which is to have a common seal, may plead
   and be impleaded, may have and hold lands, etc.'.
42 *Ibid.*, p. 170.
43 Ashton describes the selection of the mayor as an annual 'process which
   is a characteristic blend of the elective and the oligarchic principles'. See
   The City and the Court, p. 10.
44 James Knowles, 'The spectacle of the realm: civic consciousness, rhetoric
   and ritual in early modern London', in J. R. Mulryne and Margaret

Shewring (eds.), *Theatre and Government Under the Early Stuarts* (Cambridge, 1993), p. 174.

45 On the theme of civic order and virtue, see Sergei Lobanov-Rostovsky, '*The Triumphs of Gold*: economic authority in the Jacobean Lord Mayor's Show', *English Literary History* 60 (1993), 879–98. Cf. Gordon Kipling, 'Triumphal drama: form in English civic pageantry', *Renaissance Drama* ns 8 (1977), 37–56, and A. A. Bromham, 'Thomas Middleton's *The Triumphs of Truth*: City politics in 1613', *The Seventeenth Century* 10 (1995), 1–25.

46 *Troia-Nova Triumphans*, in *The Dramatic Works of Thomas Dekker*, ed. Fredson Bowers, 4 vols. (Cambridge, 1958), III, lines 496–506.

47 *Monuments of Honour* in *The Complete Works of John Webster*, ed. F. L. Lucas, 4 vols. (London, 1927), III, line 70.

48 'Men-making Poets' supported heroes within the House of Fame. See Ben Jonson, *The Masque of Queens*, in C. H. Herford, P. and E. Simpson (eds.), *Ben Jonson*, 11 vols. (Oxford, 1925–52), VII, line 86. Cf. Jonson's *Golden Age Restored*, line 117, that names a similar catalogue of English poets.

49 Manley, *Literature and Culture*, p. 221.

50 The monarchy, like the Merchant Tailors' Company, was an immortal corporate entity. See Ernst Kantorowicz, *The King's Two Bodies: A Study in Mediaeval Political Theology* (Princeton, 1981), pp. 314–450, and Nancy E. Wright, 'Legal fictions and interpretation in *Attorney General v Pickeringe* (1605) and Ben Jonson's *Masque of Queens* (1609)', *Newcastle Law Review* 1 (1995), 55–72.

51 Charles became a freeman of the Merchant Tailors' Company. See Nichols, *Progresses*, II, p. 138.

52 Dekker, *The Magnificent Entertainment Given to King James . . . Through his Honourable City (and Chamber) of London (1604)*, in *Works*, II, lines 915–24.

53 Robert Ashton, 'Popular entertainment and social control in later Elizabethan and early Stuart London', *London Journal* 9 (1983), 3–19.

CHAPTER 10

The Tempest *and the Jacobean court masque*

David Bevington

A book-length study on the Jacobean court masque is necessarily deprived of the full presence of William Shakespeare, since he differs from most of his major contemporaries in the theatre in never having been commissioned to write a court masque. John Webster, Ben Jonson, Francis Beaumont, George Chapman, Thomas Dekker, Samuel Daniel, Thomas Campion – the list of playwrights and other authors with whom this book has dealt is all the more striking in view of Shakespeare's absence from it. Yet Shakespeare did portray a masque in *The Tempest*, as Stephen Orgel has noted in his discussion of Prospero as Renaissance theatre magician and as Hugh Craig has noted in comparing Caliban with Jonson's antimasque figures. This essay will argue that *The Tempest* offers important implications about the politics of masquing, and that it does so from the point of view of a leading popular playwright and independent artist. Shakespeare re-presents the masque for heterogenerous public audiences who would not be invited to court, making clear as he does so that his artistic and professional allegiances are to the many spectator-patrons who have in effect commissioned him to write.

Was *The Tempest* written to celebrate the betrothal and wedding of King James I's only daughter, Princess Elizabeth, to Frederick V, the Elector Palatine? Many have argued that it was ultimately aimed at that event, even though it had been written and performed in anticipation of the marriage itself. The masque in *The Tempest*, in this view, was especially designed for a court occasion.[1] We do know that the first recorded performance of the play was at court on 11 November 1611, when on 'Hallowmas night was presented at Whitehall before the King's Majesty a play called *The Tempest*'. The actors were 'the King's players' (Revels Account).[2] Presumably this performance occurred shortly after the play was written, since Simon Forman, who testified to having seen *Cymbeline* and *The Winter's Tale* in 1611, made no mention of *The Tempest*; Forman died in September of that year. When next heard from, *The Tempest* was again presented at court during the winter of 1612–13, this time 'before the Princess Highness the Lady Elizabeth and the Prince Palatine Elector'. The elaborate and costly festivities for this politically and dynastically important season of entertainment included at least thirteen other plays performed by the King's Men and three masques.[3]

Early production history of *The Tempest*, then, links it closely to a royal court that was noted for its extravagant and ideologically meaningful masquing entertainments. The critical inclination on the part of some critics to see *The Tempest* as a part of the Jacobean courtly scene is also part of a larger scheme of tying a number of Shakespeare's plays to the Tudor and Stuart court: *A Midsummer Night's Dream* and some important wedding, *The Merry Wives* and the installation ceremony for Knights of the Garter, *Macbeth* and James's royal lineage, and the like.[4]

The evidence seems to me slim or nonexistent, however, that any of Shakespeare's plays was ever commissioned in the first instance for royal performance. The fetching story of Queen Elizabeth I's wanting to see Falstaff in love, and of her commanding that *The Merry Wives* be finished in fourteen days, is the nearest we have to direct testimonial on the subject, and it is an eighteenth-century tradition from the fertile pen of John Dennis (1702).[5] Even if taken at face value, the story describes a wish with no promise of money attached; we cannot assume that such a royal command amounted to a commissioning in the important sense of guaranteeing financial backing. On the other hand, royal interest in the plays of Shakespeare was always in itself a valuable cachet, as attested by the various quarto title pages of his plays (the 'Pied Bull' *King Lear*, for example) proclaiming 'as it was played before the King's Majesty at Whitehall upon St Stephen's Night in Christmas holidays' and the like. Even a title page like that adds, for its advertising purposes, 'By his Majesty's servants playing usually at the Globe on the Bankside'. Shakespeare's company was first and foremost a professional acting company that needed steady revenues at the gate. The ultimate patronage for a capitalist free enterprise company was the public. Being known as 'the King's Players', being entitled to wear his livery, being invited to perform before the royal presence – these things were valuable because they brought public attention and acclaim. They also brought a nice fee for command performances, but in overall financial terms this was a relatively minor consideration.

I wish to argue, under these circumstances, that *The Tempest* does indeed celebrate in part the betrothal and wedding of the Princess Elizabeth and Frederick, but not in the sense of its having been royally commissioned for the occasion. Shakespeare's play capitalizes on public sentiment about the wedding. It offers a wedding masque for those many persons who were not invited to the three costly, one-time masques staged at court for its own exclusive membership. It gives the nation as a whole, or at least that central part of the English nation located in London and involved in attending plays, a chance to do what the royal family and the courtly entourage did to honour the occasion of this state marriage: to be present at a ceremonially splendid mythologizing of a wedding, and to ponder the dynastic and metaphysical implications of such a union. The event resonates with suggestions of the Jacobean pacifist foreign policy that Peter Holbrook has analysed earlier in this volume. At the same time, the producers of the show are independent of the court; their tribute is freely offered in the name of the people of England and London, rather than being dictated at royal command to those on the official payroll. Shakespeare's company capitalizes on the occasion in a multiple sense: they seize a fruitful opportunity, and they capitalize it out of their own venture capital. In this sense, *The Tempest* may represent with a special clarity the kinds of political, economic and social tensions and cooperative urges that linked Whitehall to city and nation (as discussed in the previous essay by Nancy Wright) while also marking its separation.

In political terms, then, the masque in *The Tempest* engages with a number of burning issues of the day. The royal marriage of 1613 was integral to James's strategy of mediating peace between Protestant and Catholic Europe. Frederick was a Protestant prince, whose acceptance of the Bohemian throne in 1619 would undo James's careful work, as Peter Holbrook has argued, by embroiling England in German politics and in the growing conflagration that would become the Thirty Years' War, but in 1613 the prospects were bright for a peaceful balancing of power that would play off Spain and France as traditional enemies. James's Queen Anne gave James access to the Habsburg Catholic powers of Europe; Frederick represented the Protestant connection, over which the commercial might of the Dutch bid fair to exercise an authority that might threaten England's role in continental affairs. The masque in *The Tempest* chooses an event that any public audience would be encouraged to see in these topical terms, for here too the wedding is a means of preserving a balance of power and a reconciliation of warring principalities. The play's stance is not one of special pleading on a geopolitical level; it was written well before the marriage, for a popular audience rather than an exclusively courtly one, and takes a broadly national view of things. Perhaps because no queen is present to represent Anne's pro-Catholic position, the masque is genially chauvinistic and Protestant in its promotion of the marriage; insofar as the audience is invited to think of the Elector Palatine Frederick when it beholds Ferdinand, the image of the royal son-in-law is romantically positive. The major emphasis is on harmony, and on Prospero's role as stage-manager and conciliator.

At the same time, insofar as the play invites the Jacobean spectator to ponder James's role as monarch through the image of Prospero, the portrait is not uniformly flattering. Recent critical views of Prospero as indulgent and yet irritatingly managerial, learned and yet foolishly inattentive to public responsibility, visionary about peace and yet impolitic as a ruler, all find inviting parallels in current historical debates about James.[6] Like the 'wisest fool in Christendom', Prospero is capable of both arrogance and inattentiveness to duty; we learn that in his earlier days, as neglectful ruler of Milan, he delegated too much power to his ambitious younger brother. Antonio, for his part, demonstrates all too vividly the abuses of cultivating favourites for which James was angrily denounced. Perhaps public audiences would see some resemblance to their Scottish king in both Prospero and Antonio, even though personal likenesses (especially to James's notoriously slovenly habits) are entirely lacking.

Prospero's learning, like James's, is impressive but it is also oppressive, and leads him to accept a surcease from the burdens of authority as he comes to acknowledge his own flawed humanity. Political power itself is seen as a paradoxical thing of enormous potential for good and evil. These are commonplaces about power, to be sure, and royal weddings designed to improve international relations are a constant occurrence in Renaissance Europe; we must not press the connection any further than it will allow. The play's implied observations on marriage and power remain at a sufficiently general level to insulate Shakespeare and his royally sponsored company from anything remotely seditious. On balance, moreover, Prospero is a force for good and his political balancing act through masquing and marriage an admirable performance. These suggestive resemblances between fiction and political reality do nonetheless focus our attention on the masque of *The Tempest* in the context of the court masques that were presumably written under more explicitly political circumstances.

A comparison of the masque in *The Tempest* with one of the three masques actually sponsored by and produced by the court in 1613 – Thomas Campion's *The Lords' Masque* – gives us an opportunity to explore the stagecraft of a commercial play designed to provide its paying customers the vicarious experience of attending a masque. The other two masques designed for the wedding festivities, George Chapman's *Masque of the Middle Temple and Lincoln's Inn* and Francis Beaumont's *Masque of the Inner Temple and Gray's Inn*, offer similarly revealing contexts for *The Tempest* which this essay will not explore in detail. Important differences immediately become apparent in Shakespeare's sharing with his audience a theatrical self-awareness of the fact that the experience in his theatre is for a heterogeneous commercial audience rather than for a single and costly court occasion. From that perception of difference can arise further understandings: about the role of the artist fashioning a commercial play versus that of the writer devising a commissioned masque, about Shakespeare's sense of his own achievement and limitations, and about closure – how we return from the experience of a masque or a commercial play to the world we ordinarily inhabit.

The Lord's Masque features lyrics and dialogue by Thomas Campion, the famous musician and lyric poet, whose professional status made him dependent to a degree on court patronage. (He also practised medicine.) He had been commissioned to write a masque in celebration of the weddings of Lord Hay in 1607 (as we will see in David Lindley's essay about the politics of music in the court masque), and was to write another in 1613 for the wedding of the Earl of Somerset, King James's favourite; he also wrote two 'Entertainments' devised to welcome royalty on 'progress'. *The Lords' Masque* was commissioned by the King himself for the event of the wedding night, 14 February, 1613, and was financed by the royal Exchequer.[7] Campion thus undertook an obligation to create with Inigo Jones and with Mr Confesse (the dancing master) an artifact exclusively for court performance on a single momentous occasion, paid for by royal patronage.[8] *The Tempest* was written two years or so before the royal marriage, and, however much it may have been inspired by the betrothal of Elizabeth and Frederick, had to find a more general audience. Shakespeare lacked both the opportunity and the constraint of working with a demanding genius like Inigo Jones. Thus the conditions of conception and execution were strikingly different.

Shakespeare's masque in *The Tempest* and Campion's *The Lords' Masque* do resemble each other in significant ways. Both are masques; both are suddenly interrupted. They both celebrate a royal wedding: that of Elizabeth and Frederick explicitly in Campion's case, and perhaps implicitly the same in *The Tempest*, but in any event the wedding of Miranda and Ferdinand. Dynastic consequences of the marriages are central. For that reason, both poets invoke the gods to bring down their blessings from the heavens. The gods are Olympian; they are also manifestly theatrical, in that both masques call attention to the devices of artifice by which the gods are presented. Movements of ascent and descent dominate the action onstage, which otherwise inclines to be static. The stage picture makes much of contrasts between the heavens and the lower world of human affairs. In both plays, human love and marriage are enriched and ennobled by the gods' blessing. Both masques are in that sense epiphanies, incarnations of the divine in human life. The royal couple and the bride's royal or ducal father are present as witnesses to the masque and are integral to the semiotic signs used to convey political, social, religious and ethical meaning.

All that being said, *The Lords' Masque* takes a very different approach from Shakespeare's to the sense of occasion in a masque. Campion is continually interested in the creative process and its dependent relation on a hierarchical structure of authority. He chooses as his fable the freeing of Entheus, or Poetic Fury, from the bondage of Mania, goddess of madness, in order that Entheus may be allowed to sing in praise of the royal marriage. The arts are implicitly under attack; too long has Entheus suffered the 'affliction' of his monstrous 'wrong', that of being pent up with madmen. His imprisonment has been in Mania's 'earthy den', a place presumably under the earth (and implicitly under the stage) where fury 'confounds' the senses (lines 1–76). Mania and her mad entourage, the antimasque characters, present madness as a malady: Madness lives in 'darkness, which my humour fits', in the company of the 'frantic'st wits'. She is 'Brainsick', and appears '*wildly out of her cave*' in a '*confused and strange, but yet graceful*' attire. Though she acknowledges the ultimate authority of Jove's hand, she is herself a creature of darkness. Her twelve 'Fantastics' dancing in the antimasque present themselves in 'sundry habits and humours' of the Self-Lover, the Melancholic Man 'full of fear', the Schoolman or pedant 'overcome with fantasy', the 'overwatched Usurer', and the like, all in 'an absolute medley of madness' (lines 56–60). Their music sounds in a 'mad measure'. Campion is at pains, then, to mark a distinction between true madness, represented by Mania, and poetic fury, represented by Entheus.

Lamentably, madness and *furor poeticus* are too often confused by the undiscerning. The poet's task is to free Poetic Fury from an unjust imprisonment, and to insist that this exalted kind of rage is 'divine, / Full of celestial rapture', deservedly 'exempt / From vulgar censure' (lines 35–8). Repeatedly, the text accentuates the impassable gulf between a 'mad age' that is 'senseless' of true poetic beauty and a 'celestial rage' that abounds in qualities of 'excelling rapture', 'light', and of course 'musics, shows, and revels'. Poetic Fury thus comes under the purview of 'Divinest Orpheus', to whom Entheus owes his deliverance from 'vulgar censure'. A cluster of images associates Poetic Fury with the 'sacred wings' and 'Phoebean brain' of Orpheus, the legendary Thracian poet and follower of Dionysus whose perform-ances on the lyre were capable of spellbinding wild beasts and of persuading Persephone to allow Eurydice to return from Hades to the land of the living (lines 82–4). Poetic Fury, similarly brought back by Orpheus from a Hades-like cave of madness to the world of the Jacobean court, is to be the genius of the evening: he is to 'create / Inventions rare' in celebration of the night's nuptials. His imprisoned spirit is to enjoy once again her 'liberty and fiery scope' (lines 88–92).

Several aspects of this defence of poetic freedom are notable in relation to *The Tempest*. Here, in Campion's world of the court, poetic genius is sharply divided from the world of the populace at large. The age as a whole is guilty of censorious disapproval and misunderstand-ing of what Poetic Fury has to offer. The 'reinless fury' (line 45) char-acteristic of Mania and her entourage is also the characteristic of public taste and opinion. Only in the court can Entheus find the sanction to be free. Not surprisingly, Entheus's courtly world is one in which a number of authority figures provide the guidance, protection and pat-ronage necessary to guarantee poetic freedom. Orpheus is the first such figure of authority, speaking on behalf of Jove. The language is that of royal will: as Orpheus says to Entheus, 'Jove . . . by me com-mands thee to create / Inventions rare' (lines 89–90). It is through Jove's power that Entheus has been freed. Orpheus is an intermediary, a courtier, influential with the divine ruler of all. Entheus readily and gratefully acknowledges his dependency: 'Jove I honour still / And must obey' (lines 93–4). Jove is not only patron but muse: 'I feel the fires / Are ready in my brain, which Jove inspires'. The implications for the Jacobean masque as creative event are significant. The poet is protected from 'vulgar censure' by a royal godlike patron who not only frees Poetic Fury to do his work in a courtly environment but directly inspires his creativity.

Along with Orpheus and Jove, the chief sponsoring authority in *The Lords' Masque* is Prometheus. Entheus addresses him as 'Patron of mankind, powerful and bounteous' (line 130). Prometheus is to aid in solemnizing the marriage rituals; he is to 'fill the lookers' eyes / With admiration of thy fire and light'. He is accompanied by 'fiery sprites' who 'Break forth the earth like sparks' attired in flames, *'with fiery wings and bases, bearing in either hand a torch of virgin wax'* (lines 194–7). Being as he is 'one of the ancient heroes' (lines 128–9) who created mankind out of clay and then stole fire from heaven on their behalf, Prometheus is potentially in conflict with Jove or Jupiter; according to ancient legend, the chief of the gods punished the theft by creating Pandora and sending her to undo the human race with her seductive guile. Indeed, these well-known stories about Prometheus are emblematically represented in *The Lords' Masque* by four *'noble women-statues of silver'*, each in a separate niche in the lower part of the *'scene'* representing the human world:

In the first was Prometheus, embossing in clay the figure of a woman; in the second he was represented stealing fire from the chariot-wheel of the sun; in the third he is expressed putting lye with this fire into his figure of clay: and in the fourth square Jupiter, enraged, turns these new-made women into statues. (lines 220–5)

Yet the Prometheus of this masque is ultimately not at war with the king of the gods. Resident in his astrological heavenly 'house' amid *'an element of artificial fires, with several circles of light, in continual motion'* (lines 190–1), Prometheus is instead one more figure of semi-divine authority who offers intercession and patronage to Poetic Fury. As patron and as ally of Jove, Prometheus's role is not unlike that of the powerful male courtiers of James's court who danced this masque. Prometheus descends to earth in a figure of epiphany, to the accompaniment of *'the music of a full song'* (line 207), leading the eight Masquers who are transformed into human shape and who are to dance with the ladies. The women too are transformed; no longer statues representing Pandora as a means of Jove's vengeance toward Prometheus and mankind, they are made 'new-born women' so that Prometheus's 'new-born men' may 'entertain' them 'with love'. Jove's wrath, that has transformed into statues these dames whom Prometheus 'long since out of thy

purchased flames / Didst forge with heav'nly fire', now 'relents', and
has signalled his willingness to let Entheus and the new-born men
implore Jove's aid for 'the life' of the four statue-women 'and then for
more' (lines 238–57). When four more ladies are '*new-transformed*' from
statues into living human dancers, the numbers are 'complete' and
symmetrical: each man and woman has a partner; Jove's reconciliation is manifested in this cessation of 'strife'. 'See, Jove intends / To
fill your number up, and make all friends.' Orpheus and Entheus are
to 'join your skills once more, / And with a hymn the Deity implore'
(lines 277–91). Music and poetry thus join in perfect harmony of dance
and song.

Campion has rewritten the story of Prometheus and Pandora in
a hyperbolic revamping of mythology characteristic of much courtly
art. The tributes to Jove as 'powerful' and able to reconcile conflict
through his own beneficence clearly idealize James I's presiding role in
the Jacobean court; Campion's implied politics are thus close to Ben
Jonson's, as described by several essays earlier in this volume. James
is implicitly like the Jove of this production, who does not appear directly in the action but who is invoked as the all-powerful champion
of artists and patron of their work. The Jacobean Jove of this masque
issues his commands through Orpheus and Prometheus, who, like courtiers, also exercise a powerful role in the system of patronage as inter-
mediaries and sponsors in their own right. Some of those who took
part as masquers, including the Earls of Montgomery and Salisbury,
Lord Hay and Anne Dudley, may have seen themselves in positions of
power not unlike that of Orpheus and Prometheus. Their names suggest Campion's allegiance in this masque to the peace faction at court
supporting James's foreign policy of accommodation: the Earl of Salisbury was William Cecil, son of Sir Robert Cecil, first Earl of Salisbury
and Viscount Cranborne, who had died in 1612; the Earl of Montgomery, Philip Herbert, was a favourite of the King's who danced in a
number of Ben Jonson's masques; and Lord Hay was another favourite, having come with James from Scotland.[9]

The place of Campion, Inigo Jones, and their performers and actors
in this world of adoring praise of the monarchy is implicit in the role of
Entheus and, to some degree, Orpheus: poet and scene designer are to
'join' their 'skills', assisted by their performers, offering their hymns of
praise to a deity-like monarch and to others of the court who provide
sponsorship and patronage. Campion does not claim the humanist's
role of educating the court in a mirror for magistrates, as Jonson was

wont to do with asperity and even arrogance, even if Campion's political stance is close to that of Jonson; Campion's tone is one of gratitude and complicity as he implicitly compliments the monarchy and its court for fostering true art and freeing it from the constraints of 'vulgar' taste. Any remembrance of conflict between a monarch and the creative artist invoked by the Prometheus legend is refashioned into a new world in which the inherent tension between politics and art is wholly resolved by the graciousness of the monarch and the intelligent creativity of the artists who adoringly serve him.

By the same token, any mythological recollection of women as seducers and troublemakers is similarly dispelled by the artful rewriting of mythology. Pandora is only an unhappy memory. Though the lordly men and women of this masque enact through their dance a representation of 'passion', of seductive 'persuasion', and of 'Bold assaults' that 'are fit for men, / That on strange beauties venture' (lines 270–7), music and its harmonies (as David Lindley will show) transform potential conflict into the productive tensions and reconciliations of sexual difference and mating. In this way, Campion's mythological fiction and the accompanying dance are made appropriate to the marriage being celebrated by these festivities. 'Beauty and youth' are united 'both in one':

> Live with thy bridegroom happy, sacred bride;
> How blest is he that is for love envied.   (lines 307–9)

Sybilla's prophecies of fame to the couple's posterity, a song in praise of Cupid's 'Hymenaean right', and a last dance of the Masquers bring to a close *The Lords' Masque* by acknowledging explicitly the presence of the royal couple who have been the implicit focus of the entire evening. A harmony of art and of celebratory occasion leads to a promise of sexual fulfilment, of political alliance, and of the long-continuing European peace that James so earnestly (but at last unsuccessfully) pursued. At the same time we should remember that this masque is called *The Lords' Masque*, giving to the men (prominently including James's favourites) a dominant role in the resolution of sexual and political conflict. Here we can see an anticipation of the new ascendency of James's male entourage in the masquing at court that Leeds Barroll has described in his essay. *The Lords' Masque* celebrates the marriage of the young people, and assigns a presiding role to James as Jove, but it does not seem to provide equal honour for Queen Anne. James is implicitly in charge of his royal family once more; the threat of feminine and irrational passion associated with Pandora is controlled.

Inigo Jones's staging design for *The Lords' Masque* provides a rich visual dimension to the dominant motif of hierarchical harmony between magnanimous royal patron and happily dependent artist. Throughout, the set or '*scene*' is divided '*from the roof to the floor*' into upper and lower parts. The lower world, 'discovered' first to view, shows a wood in perspective with a cave on one side to represent the dwelling of Mania and a thicket on the other from which Orpheus emerges. The cave, on the left, brings with it associations of the lower world, of frantic strife and of darkness. Renaissance audiences familiar with church architecture and with religious plays would readily associate the left with the north, as in a cathedral with its north stair leading down into the crypt. The right, conversely, is associated with ascent. The struggle for control of Entheus with Mania and her twelve 'Frantics' on the left and Orpheus on the right thus visualizes a familiar spiritual psychomachia that accords aptly with the theme of incarceration and deliverance from 'affliction'. Costuming visually reinforces contrastive verbal images of brainsick fury and of sweetly divine rapture: Mania appears in '*habit confused and strange*', while Orpheus is '*attired after the old Greek manner, his hair curled and long, a laurel wreath on his head, and in his hand . . . a silver bird*'. Entheus, the figure over whom these polarized contestants quarrel, is decorously attired with a wreath of laurel and wings, and holds in his hands a book and a pen, all of which identify him with the laurel-crowned Orpheus and with true creativity rather than with the wildly costumed entourage of Mania (lines 1–81).[10] Horizontal antithetical symmetry is thus paired with vertical separation as a major element of Jones's playful but politically Jacobean cosmology.

Action in '*the upper part of the scene*' emphasizes the splendour of a heavenly firmament that beneficently protects those earthlings whom heaven loves – that is to say, the court of King James and especially the newly married couple. The dominant motif is one of epiphany, of incarnation. Hyperbole and paradox transform a religious idea of the gods made manifest in human affairs into an extravagant flattery of the Jacobean court. The spirits who come down to earth in this masque will find a better world among mortals. As Prometheus puts it:

> Wait, spirits, wait, while through the clouds we pace,
> And by descending gain a higher place.   (lines 201–2)

The vertical and hierarchical relationship between heaven and earth is thus paradoxical and interconnected. Just as Jove is reconciled with Prometheus, just as the legend of Pandora yields to a new order in

which the women of the Jacobean court are desirably amorous and yet
nobly virtuous, so too the court of King James subsumes the heavenly
qualities of the starry world above. Jones's and Campion's visual ideology here is unnervingly close to the Neoplatonic and cavalier representations of Caroline royal absolutism that Barbara Lewalski will discuss
below.

Accordingly, Inigo Jones's visual effects execute ingenious variations
on a single idea: a metamorphosis in which the heavens in the '*upper
part of the scene*' yield their divine qualities to the human dancers and to
the royal couple present at the masque. Prometheus first appears in
the front of the upper scene amid clouds of fiery and silver colours and
eight stars '*of extraordinary bigness*', placed so that they seem '*to be fixed
between the firmament and the earth*' (lines 123–9). By Prometheus's stealth,
these 'heav'n born stars' are to become 'sublunars' and to show their
'native beauties' in 'this place' (lines 139–40). The elaborate conceit is
that Prometheus's stealing of fire from heaven is to be re-enacted this
night, culminating in the masque itself. Small wonder, then, that Jove
is reconciled to this theft, for its very product is the Jacobean court and
the marriage being celebrated. The court subsumes the qualities of
heaven itself, not in a revolutionary overthrow but in an epiphany and
through the medium of art.

Campion's description insists on the '*exceeding strange and delightful
manner*' and the '*neat artifice*' through which the stars suddenly vanish,
only to be incarnated in eight dancers. No less wondrous are the
sixteen Pages attired like fiery spirits, who dance a '*lively measure*' below
and attend on the eight Masquers as they descend from heaven on '*a
bright and transparent cloud*' which reaches '*from the top of the heavens to the
earth*' (lines 173–209). Below, in the part of the scene representing earth,
the chief visual effects are of transformation, as eight statues of ladies
are changed into living women. The huge expense needed to bring
about these theatrical effects is itself part of the point: in the studied
artifice of the Jacobean court masque, mythology and artistic convention are all brought to bear on the central purpose of celebrating the
court and its dynastic function. The medium becomes the message.[11]

The last stage vision of *The Lords' Masque* is again paradoxical, con-
trived, and self-conscious: having transformed Jove's statues into living
women, the masque finally presents us with '*statues of the Bridegroom and
Bride, all of gold, in gracious postures*' (lines 342–3). The Princess Elizabeth
and the Elector Palatine have not taken roles in this masque, though
they have been taken out to dance '*in these solemn revels, which continued*

a long space' (lines 323–6). Their dance is '*broken off*' with a song of welcome to the Sybilla and to her prophetic utterance of long life and numerous progeny for the wedded couple. We end with statues and with dance and song, all emblematic of the kind of art that has enabled this masque to undertake its social and political role of celebrating the monarchy. The artists – Jones, Campion, the musicians, the professional dancers – serve the court by engendering contrivances of art. Their hyperbolical overstatement and rewriting of mythological history join to produce a closure that is self-consciously statuesque and artificial. The idealized image of the married couple, frozen into lifelessness in golden splendour, bespeaks the role of courtly art as the giver of eternal fame. *The Lords' Masque* is thus a defence of an art that unites poetry, music and theatre in a rhetoric of praise. It honours a royal patronage without which such art would lose its essential function.

Presumably *The Lords' Masque* does not end with applause. As in other masques, the final indications are of a dance: '*The last new dance of the Masquers, which concludes all with a lively strain at their going out*'. The King and his court, and especially the newly married couple, who have been so much a part of the spectacle, are still present in the hall. Royal husband and wife are the final reality of this show, and their living presence is an explicit reminder that courtly life goes beyond mere artistic representation. As Prometheus insists, gesturing in their direction:

> Turn, turn, and honour now the life these figures bear;
> Lo, how heav'nly natures far above all art appear!
>
> (lines 389–90)

In the real presence of this royal couple, the artifice ceases. The event returns to what is the central entity of any court masque: the court itself, ongoing and intensely political. The hall used to stage the masque resumes its familiar courtly dimensions. The lords and ladies who have masqued set aside their disguises and resume their roles as courtiers, while the musicians and the professional actors who undertook the antimasque of Mania and her 'Frantics' pack up their gear and go home. The expensive set, erected for this single occasion, is struck. As with the statues of the final scene, the semiotics of closure underscores the nature of priorities and relationships in a court masque. Art and artifice are ornaments used to adorn court magnificence and to fashion its image of greatness. The court is the great patron and the artist is its celebrant.

An analysis of Chapman's *Masque of the Middle Temple and Lincoln's Inn* and Beaumont's *Masque of the Inner Temple and Gray's Inn* would reveal similar patterns of patrician sponsorship of the arts, especially as undertaken by the Inns of Court in an attempt to define their power and influence in the Jacobean court.[12]

The masque in Shakespeare's *The Tempest* also celebrates an aristocratic couple whose union is of great dynastic consequence, and does so by invoking the gods to descend with their blessings. Self-aware contrivance dominates the action; the spectacle is an artifact produced by Ariel and his spirits at Prospero's behest to entertain and honour the young couple, who are as aware as we of how the mimesis is created. Juno's descent in a chariot from the 'heavens' above the stage (the Folio stage direction reads, '*Juno descends*', 4.1.72) calls further attention to overt theatrical effects. Yet in matters of authority and control, this masque is presented under strikingly different auspices. Prospero is in charge from first to last. His servant Ariel creates the illusions; spirits obedient to Prospero personify the gods. And, whereas this structural relationship sounds at first like a courtly one in which a duke or king sponsors and authorizes a royal entertainment for his own pleasure and that of his marrying children, the crucial difference is that Prospero is the fictive creation of Shakespeare and his company. Prospero's masque does not end with a return to the reality of courtly power and magnificence. It closes with a return to Shakespeare's play, in which Prospero will ultimately bid farewell by asking his commercial audience to applaud.

As a consequence, the masque in *The Tempest* presents itself as a version of a courtly masque at one remove: not for the court in the first instance (though the play was taken to court), and not for the actual wedding of Elizabeth and Frederick, but for a paying audience interested in what a court wedding masque would be like. Prospero plays at being the royal master who has ordered the occasion; Ariel is his producer, his Inigo Jones and Thomas Campion all rolled into one; his goddesses and spirits are the professional musicians and dancers performing the antimasque of the reapers and nymphs '*in a graceful dance*'; and Ferdinand and Miranda stand in for the royal couple whose marriage is being celebrated.[13] Their marriage is 'real' enough, of course in the fiction of the play, but it is not a mere allegory for the royal wedding of 1613.

The differences between Shakespeare's dramatic version and the commissioned wedding masques written by Campion, Chapman and

Beaumont are signalled not so much in the masque of *The Tempest* itself
as in its surrounding theatrical context. The masque as it stands is a
plausible replica, and must have been intended as such. '*Soft music*'
attends the entrance of Iris (4.1.59). Her language, like that of Ceres
and Juno, is heightened and formal, in a pastoral mode; Iris speaks of
'rich leas / Of wheat, rye, barley, vetches, oats, and peas', 'turfy moun-
tains', 'nibbling sheep', meadows, swollen streams, vineyards, and still
more. These invocations of a bountiful nature betoken the foison that
will attend the marriage of Ferdinand and Miranda. Iris's words suggest a natural world put to the service of humankind, providing harvest
and plenty. The goddesses of this masque are, appropriately, vegetation
goddesses and presiders over marriage. Iris, the rainbow, promises a
hopeful message from the gods and a pathway between heaven and
earth; Ceres represents the generative power of nature, and is an earth
deity; Juno is the goddess of women and of child-bearing, sometimes
associated with the moon.

Staging of this masque is manifestly simpler than that of *The Lords'*
Masque, and yet it capitalizes on resemblances to the more elaborate
courtly entertainments that would be produced for the royal wedding.
The costumes in *The Tempest* are evidently splendid and meaningful in
their symbolism. Iris is a 'many-colored messenger' with 'saffron wings'
(lines 76–8); Ceres is addressed as 'rich Ceres' in such a way as to
suggest that her dress conjures up images of harvest; and Juno is of
course habited as befits the 'Highest Queen of state, / Great Juno'
(lines 101–2). The antimasque figures are visually contrasted with the
goddesses: the 'sunburned sicklemen' are '*suitably habited*' in 'rye-straw
hats', and they dance with the 'temperate nymphs' or 'naiads' in 'sedged
crowns' of reeds suggesting the 'windring brooks' and 'crisp channels'
from which they have been summoned by Iris (lines 128–37). Shakespeare's company, like other professional troupes, expended considerable resources on costuming; it was their chief opportunity for ornate
visual display, in the absence of movable scenery. The actors of the
three goddesses add to the spectacle with their skill in impersonating
greatness and divinity: as Ceres says of Juno, in reference to the regal
bearing as queen of the gods, 'I know her by her gait' (line 102). Ceres
must mean 'bearing or carriage while moving' (*OED* sb.¹) when she
talks of 'gait', as well as 'manner of walking'; Juno '*descends*' in the Folio
stage direction at line 72 and appears to reach the stage shortly before
Ceres announces her arrival. The actor or actress then has time enough
to display what divine or royal 'gait' can be.

Most of all, the poetic images of the goddesses' speeches invoke spectacle through language. The absence of Jones's devices is a paradoxical blessing, for Shakespeare is required to invent a masque largely through verbal magic. Iris call up images of meadows, sheep on turfy mountainsides, swollen springs and vineyards. She herself is a 'watery arch and messenger' who diffuses refreshing showers in honeydrops upon flowers and, with each end of her 'blue bow', crowns the 'bosky acres and unshrubbed down' of Ceres like a 'rich scarf' to the 'proud earth' (lines 78–82). The Queen of the gods is drawn through the air by her 'peacocks'. Perhaps they are figured on the chariot by which Juno presumably descends from 'the heavens' to the main stage, but evidently not with the elaboration of scenic design and trompe l'oeil effects employed by Jones at court; no elaborate stage direction, so typical of the court masque, attests to visual magic in this recollection of Juno's peacocks.

Other gods are present, too, through poetic imagination rather than through stage contrivance. Venus is recalled, 'Cutting the clouds towards Paphos, and her son / Dove-drawn with her'. Being as she is 'Mars's hot minion', Venus is out of favour, and her 'waspish-headed son' Cupid has 'broke his arrows' in a pet at being unable to tempt the marriage couple into sexual pleasure before 'Hymen's torch be lighted' (lines 93–101). The naiads summoned to dance a 'country footing' with the 'sunburned sicklemen' in the antimasque conjure up for us pastoral worlds of cold brooks and harvested fields. These figures represent a harmonious resolution of sexual conflict, one in which males and females are visibly very different and yet complementary, united in the graceful antithesis of a dance.[14] Thus an entire psychomachia of love and desire, pitting Venus and Cupid against Juno, is acted out in imaginative verse without the questionable benefit of overt representation that a masque would be more equipped to provide. The royal couple witnessing this masque are at the fictive centre of the celebratory event, as in *The Lords' Masque*, but much of the conflict surrounding them is not visible in the masquing space.

To be sure, Juno does descend from the 'heavens' of the theatre in an elaboration of staging not seen in early Shakespearean drama (it appears also in the late *Cymbeline*). If she is provided with a chariot it is no doubt a handsome one, perhaps festooned with peacocks. Shakespeare's company must have provided as artful a descent as possible. The very fact that Juno descends so slowly, beginning her descent (according to the Folio stage direction) at line 72 as Iris announces

Juno's intent to 'come and sport' 'in this very place' and continuing
through Ceres's entrance and conversation with Iris down to line 101,
when her presence is finally proclaimed, makes for impressive spectacle; Juno is aloft for twenty-nine lines of a masque that is only seventy-
eight lines long in all, some ten lines of which (lines 118–27) constitute
an interruption by Prospero and Ferdinand. Juno is in the air for
nearly half of the masque's spoken lines.

The place at which Juno arrives is repeatedly referred to as 'Here
on this grass plot, in this very place', 'this short-grassed green', and
'this green land' (lines 73, 83, 130), using much the same sort of language used to greet Queen Elizabeth, for example, when she visited
Elvetham in 1591.[15] The insistent reference to 'here' is metatheatrical,
as in *The Lords' Masque*, and has a similar effect of confounding the
fictional setting of the masque's text with the theatrical space occupied
by the actors and their royal audience. The 'green' is presumably
imaginary in Shakespeare's theatre, but 'here' has its own reality. It is
a place, as in the masque, 'To come and sport', to 'be merry' and
'Make holiday' (lines 74, 135–6). It is essentially a theatrical space that
includes the marrying couple. As in *The Lords' Masque*, they are specifically referred to: Juno bids Ceres 'Go with me / To bless this twain,
that they may prosperous be, / And honored in their issue' (lines 103–
4). In the song by Juno and Ceres that follows, the young couple are
directly addressed: 'Hourly joys be still upon you! / Juno sings her
blessings on you', sings the Queen of the gods, to which Ceres echoes,

> Spring come to you at the farthest
> In the very end of harvest!
> Scarcity and want shall shun you;
> Ceres' blessing so is on you.   (lines 106–17)

Ferdinand and Prospero can converse with each other without responding to the goddesses. The actors in the masque occupy their own theatrical and fictional space, to which Prospero, Ferdinand and Miranda
are witnesses, and yet these three are fictional characters in the larger
context of *The Tempest*. We as audience watch them watching the
masque, much as courtly attendants at *The Lords' Masque* watched
the King and the marrying couple witnessing the work of Campion
and Jones.

At the same time, Ferdinand, Miranda and her father do not participate in the dance. Dancing is assigned strictly to the antimasque
figures of sunburned sicklemen and fresh nymphs, so that the entertainment more resembles the 'burgomask dance' of *A Midsummer Night's*

Dream in the marriage festivities for Duke Theseus than it does the masquing of *The Lords' Masque*, where the essential purpose of the evening is to allow the ladies and gentlemen, with the marrying couple at their head, to dance at considerable length. Moroever, the audience is in a different position. In *The Lords' Masque*, the audience is 'here' where the entertainment takes place; the dance serves to erase barriers between the mythological fiction and the present reality of courtly celebration. The stars in the heavens become courtiers; the statues become their ladies. Their fictional identity spills out onto the dance floor. Prospero and his family, by contrast, are sealed off from the masque by a fictional barrier that is like a one-way mirror, allowing the masquing goddesses to speak to the human audience but not the reverse.

Nowhere is this difference more apparent than in the manner in which the two masques are interrupted. In the climactic dance of *The Lords' Masque*, the Masquers of both sexes '*take out others to dance with them, men women, and women men, and first of all the princely Bridegroom and Bride were drawn into these solemn revels, which continued a long time, but in the end were broken off with this short song*' (lines 323–6). The interruption is simply a means of ending this dance so that the masque can continue to its end; the singer bids the dancers 'Cease, cease, your revels, rest a space', so that they can behold 'New pleasures press into this place'. The interruption does not challenge the spatial fiction of the entertainment, for dancers and actors alike occupy 'this place' and have nowhere else to go. Prospero, conversely, has concocted a show for his own purposes that must yield to other necessities, especially the 'foul conspiracy' of Caliban and his confederates (lines 139–40). This masque comes abruptly to an end when Prospero calls to mind what he must do about Caliban. The masque is seemingly unfinished, if only in the sense that a masque does not traditionally end with the antimasque and without the participation on the dance floor of the marrying couple. The actors in the masque – namely, Ariel and his spirits – have been given no warning of this abrupt ending. The implication is that they have prepared something still to come.

How do the actors of the masque exit, given the suddenness of Prospero's interruption? The Folio text gives only the sparse indication that '*Prospero starts suddenly, and speaks; after which, to a strange, hollow, and confused noise, they heavily vanish*'. How do they vanish? The theatrical requirements of the moment are compelling. The dancers, Iris, and Ceres have presumably entered on foot and can leave in a similar way,

even if they must do so unexpectedly and with no motivation for going
away. The stage direction indicates confusion and hubbub. Most of
all, Juno's exit provides a problem. Is she to be cranked back up in her
chariot, presumably more swiftly than she descended? Her presence
for long would distract from the immediately following dialogue about
Prospero's anger at Caliban. Or does she exit on foot while the chariot
is pulled up into the heavens and stored away? The difficulties suggest a deliberate move on Shakespeare's part to call attention to the
contrivance of Prospero's fiction, and indeed to all theatrical fiction.
Prospero's famous lines describing how 'Our revels now are ended'
(lines 148ff.), usually quoted in the context of Shakespeare's presumed
farewell to his art, take on in the present circumstance a direct comment on the fictional nature of Prospero's masque. 'These our actors,
/ As I foretold you, were all spirits and / Are melted into air, into thin
air', he informs Miranda and Ferdinand. The remark about 'thin air'
takes on a comic dimension when we visualize a chariot disappearing
into the 'heavens', perhaps with a disarranged Juno still aboard. Does
Prospero gesture in Juno's direction as he alludes to 'These our actors'
and 'thin air'? If so, the comedy is in keeping with Shakespeare's wry
comments elsewhere (as in the end of *A Midsummer Night's Dream*) about
the illusory nature of his art and indeed of all art.

Prospero's actors are indeed 'all spirits'. Prospero makes no secret of
the fact that his illusions are manufactured by Ariel and his attendants,
just as Ariel has earlier impersonated a harpy. 'Now come, my Ariel!'
commands Prospero, exultingly: 'Bring a corollary, / Rather than want
a spirit' (lines 57–8). Ariel is thus bidden to have fresh reserves on
hand; no expense is to be spared (as in a court masque) in making this
a show to be long remembered. And, whereas the masque deals too
in self-conscious impersonation, the fiction in *The Tempest* points to a
different kind of theatrical experience. In a masque, the impersonation
is frankly allegorical; the purported gods are devices of flattery for the
courtly audience and claim little substance in their own right. They
are created by the poet and scene-maker according to the conventions
of the genre. The gods of *The Tempest* are Prospero's creations. They
are also Shakespeare's, of course. In both senses, they express the power
of art to inform, to move, to persuade. The masque of *The Tempest* is
created to honour Miranda and Ferdinand, but it is also there to
demonstrate Prospero's authority as artist and his authority over the
couple. Not by coincidence does this masque serve as the text for

Prospero's famous sermon on the cloud-capped towers and gorgeous palaces that will dissolve like 'the great globe itself' and 'Leave not a rack behind' (lines 151–6).

The masque in *The Tempest* is a demonstration of, and a tribute to, dramatic art and poetry of the imagination.[16] The ultimate authority is not a royal spectator surrounded by his courtiers and bridal couple but the dramatist in his own theatre, speaking to the patrons who signal their approval by their paid admission and their applause. Juno, Ceres and Iris are not figures like Prometheus, Orpheus and Entheus in *The Lords' Masque* whose ultimate function is to defer to the royal authority of King James. The gods of *The Tempest* are Prospero's creatures. The incessant reflexivity of the play makes clear that Prospero is supreme in his artistic kingdom. If gods appear, it is because he causes them to appear; they are Ariel's fabrications at the behest of Prospero. Although *The Tempest* is not quite agnostic in its fabricating of divine beings, since Prospero does acknowledge an overall 'Providence divine' that has brought Miranda and himself to this island (1.2.160), on the island he arrogates to himself all the powers that gods exercise and invents other gods as fictions to serve his artistic ends. The final figure of authority is Prospero himself, and his authority is that of the poet.

Such a poet, in the professional theatre of the English Renaissance, maintains his artistic independence with the aid of his clientele. Shakespeare had apparently tried the path of aristocratic patronage early in his career, writing poems for the Earl of Southampton's family. He found his lasting success in the theatre, where in a market economy of culture he had to continue to 'sell' his product to paying audiences or else face unemployment and oblivion. The motif of competitive excellence in a capitalist economy of the public theatre thus underlies Prospero's request for applause. This is how Shakespeare chooses to end a play that manifestly assesses the final achievement of his own dramatic art: Prospero asks his paying audience to signify that they have gotten their money's worth. The same kind of near-blasphemy that prompts Prospero to invent fictional gods as the extensions of his own power as dramatist now suggests to Prospero a secularized version of prayer. His art will have failed unless he is applauded; his ending will otherwise be 'despair'. The only 'prayer' that can relieve him is applause.[17] This kind of prayer, in Prospero's conceit, is exactly like intercession; it 'pierces so that it assaults / Mercy itself, and frees all faults' (Epilogue, lines 13–18). In *The Lords' Masque*, the intercessors are Prometheus and Orpheus, and the deities whom they implore are the royal couple, the King and the court. *The Tempest* addresses its final plea instead to its paying audience. Here is Prospero's church and his salvation. 'As you from crimes would pardoned be, / Let your indulgence set me free' (lines 19–20). The wit of the conceit pardons the lighthearted tone in the use of ecclesiastical concepts. 'Indulgence', in the Catholic theology that many Protestant spectators might find suspiciously applicable to Queen Anne and the Jacobean court, is at once a remission of punishment for sin and a kind of lenient humouring. In Prospero's church, he and his paying audiences are the only authorities that can claim lasting sanction.

Applause is thus a choice for Shakespeare. It seems to us an inevitable and appropriate way to conclude any performance, but this has not always been so. We do not know that Greek tragedies ended to applause, though Aristophanes's comedies (in a markedly more topical and contemporary kind of genre) ask unashamedly for applause and for first prize. Medieval religious drama could not have been applauded when performed in church as part of the order of worship or even when played as individual pageants under the auspices of craft guilds. Religious drama is not a 'performance' in our sense of the term. Applause becomes appropriate when actors put on mimetic entertainments for audiences whose approval they must secure if they are to find new audiences, like the itinerant players of *Mankind* in the late fifteenth century who take up a collection before the play will be allowed to continue. Shakespeare's requests for applause sound conventional to our ears, but they are not. His epilogues – to *A Midsummer Night's Dream*, to *As You Like It*, to *2 Henry IV*, to *Henry V*, to *The Tempest*, to *Henry VIII*, even to *Troilus and Cressida* – are exercises in genteel begging. They urge the audience to come back; they hold out promise of new material; they flatter the audience for its sagacity and good judgement; they lay the fortunes of the acting company at the feet of the only patron that really matters. Much then can be seen in the apparent fact that *The Lords' Masque* ended without applause on its single evening of performance whereas *The Tempest* chooses the topic of applause as its means of closure. Shakespeare's politics of masquing, in this play that is insistent upon public performance and that also suggests some implicit criticism of James as a 'wise fool' even while it appears to mirror patriotic approval of the Protestant marriage of James's daughter, is a politics of independent artistry.

NOTES

1 Frank Kermode, in the Introduction to his edition of *The Tempest* (London, 1954), pp. xx–xxiii, reviews and argues against the formidable roster of historical scholars who have seen the masque in *The Tempest* as especially created to celebrate the wedding in 1613. One of the more elaborate theories is that of Henry David Gray, 'Some indications that *The Tempest* was revised', *Studies in Philology* 18 (1921), 129–40. For the view that Prospero's masque-like pageant recalls the coronation festivities of James I, see Enid Welsford, *The Court Masque* (New York, 1962), p. 342, and Kermode (ed.), *Tempest*, p. lxxiii. An account of the celebratory devices for 'The King's Entertainment through the City of London' in 1603–4 is to be found in John Nichols, *The Progresses, Processions and Magnificent Festivities of King James the First*, 4 vols. (London, 1828), I, pp. 339ff. Allardyce Nicoll, *Stuart Masques and the Renaissance Stage* (New York, 1938), pp. 119–21, sees the masque in *The Tempest* as thoroughly indebted to various court masques, proposing for example that the towers, palaces and temples invoked by Prospero in *The Tempest* (4.1.152–3) are from Jonson's *Oberon* (1611), that 'the great globe itself' (line 153) alludes to the stage globe of Jonson's *Hymenaei* (1606), and that the dissolving 'rack' (lines 154–6) refers to stage clouds in Jacobean court masques such as *Hymenaei*. See also Graham Parry, 'The wedding of Princess Elizabeth', in his *The Golden Age Restor'd: The Culture of the Stuart Court, 1603–42* (Manchester, 1981), pp. 95–107, and Clifford Geertz, 'Centers, kings, and charisma: reflections on the symbolics of power', in his *Local Knowledge: Further Essays in Interpretive Anthropology* (New York, 1983), pp. 121–46, esp. pp. 125–9, for a comparable analysis of the way in which Queen Elizabeth's charisma grew out of the allegories of royal virtue and power for which her reign was well noted. The theory of topical relevance to a royal wedding in *The Tempest* is still very much alive, as Parry makes plain. See Leah Marcus, *Puzzling Shakespeare: Local Reading and Its Discontents* (Berkeley, 1988), pp. 49–50 and *passim*.

2 Printed in E. K. Chambers, *William Shakespeare: A Study of Facts and Problems*, 2 vols. (Oxford, 1930), II, p. 342.

3 John Heminge received payment in May 1613 for 'fourteen several plays' acted by the King's Men at court 'before the Princess's Highness the Lady Elizabeth and the Prince Palatine Elector', including *Much Ado about Nothing*, 'Sir John Falstaff,' *Othello*, *The Winter's Tale*, and *The Tempest*, along with Beaumont and Fletcher's *Philaster*, *A King and No King*, and *The Maid's Tragedy*. See the Chamber Accounts in E. K. Chambers, *The Elizabethan Stage*, 4 vols. (Oxford, 1923), IV, p. 180; also printed in Chambers, *Shakespeare*, II, p. 343. See also W. R. Streitberger (ed.), *Jacobean and Caroline Revels Accounts, 1603–1642* (Oxford, 1986), pp. 55–6; Inga-Stina Ewbank, ' "These Pretty Devices": a study of masques in plays', in T. J. B. Spencer and Stanley Wells (eds.), *A Book of Masques in Honour of Allardyce Nicoll* (Cambridge, 1969), pp. 407–48; Robert C. Fulton, *Shakespeare and the Masques*

(New York, 1988); Suzanne Gossett, *The Influence of the Jacobean Masque on the Plays of Beaumont and Fletcher* (New York, 1988), and Jean Wilson, *Entertainments for Elizabeth I* (Woodbridge, 1980).

4 See, for example, Paul A. Olson, '*A Midsummer Night's Dream* and the meaning of court marriage', *English Literary History* 24 (1957), 95–119; H. J. Oliver (ed.), *The Merry Wives of Windsor* (London, 1971), pp. lxiv–lii, reviewing theories of the play's occasion and purported satire; and Henry N. Paul, *The Royal Play of 'Macbeth'* (New York, 1950).

5 John Dennis, *Epistle* to *The Comical Gallant* (1702), a play based on *The Merry Wives*. Two years later, in *The Person of Quality's Answer to Mr. Collier's Letter* (1704), Dennis sharpened the sense of drama in this questionable recollection by specifying that the Queen had commanded Shakespeare to write the comedy 'in ten days' time, so eager was she for the wicked diversion'. Reprinted in Chambers, *Shakespeare*, II, p. 263.

6 Recent revisionist criticism of Prospero often sees him as a colonialist and slave-owner obsessed with 'producing legitimacy'; see, for example, Paul Brown, ' "This thing of darkness I acknowledge mine": *The Tempest* and the discourse of colonialism', in Jonathan Dollimore and Alan Sinfield (eds.), *Political Shakespeare: New Essays in Cultural Materialism* (Manchester, 1985), pp. 48–71, who argues that the colonialist discourse in *The Tempest* 'voices a demand both for order and disorder, producing a disruptive other in order to assert the superiority of the coloniser' (p. 58); and Francis Barker and Peter Hulme, ' "Nymphs and reapers heavily vanish": the discursive con-texts of *The Tempest*', in John Drakakis (ed.), *Alternative Shakespeares* (London, 1985), pp. 191–205, who argue cogently that Prospero's masque is 'deeply concerned with producing legitimacy' (p. 201). For a sceptical critique from a psychoanalytical perspective, see Meredith Skura, 'Discourse and the individual: the case of colonialism in *The Tempest*', *Shakespeare Quarterly* 40 (1989), 42–69. A measured and complex assessment is to be found in John Gillies, *Shakespeare and the Geography of Difference* (Cambridge, 1994), esp. pp. 140–55.

On differing historical evaluations of King James, see William Lloyd McElwee, *The Wisest Fool in Christendom: The Reign of King James I and VI* (New York, 1958); D. H. Willson, *King James VI and I* (London, 1956); Robert Ashton (ed.), *James I by his Contemporaries* (London, 1969); Linda Levy Peck (ed.), *The Mental World of the Jacobean Court* (Cambridge, 1991), especially the essays by Wormald, Sommerville and Christianson; Maurice Lee, Jr., *Great Britain's Solomon: James VI and I in his Three Kingdoms* (Urbana, IL, 1990); Kenneth Fincham and Peter Lake, 'The ecclesiastical policy of James I', *Journal of British Studies* 24 (1985), 169–207; Derek Hirst, *Authority and Conflict: England, 1603–1658* (London, 1986); and A. G. R. Smith (ed.), *The Reign of James VI and I* (London, 1973).

7 Thomas Campion, *The Lords' Masque*, ed. I. A. Shapiro, in *A Book of Masques*, pp. 95–123. The warrant showing the King's commission of this masque is printed in John Payne Collier, *Annals of the Stage*, 3 vols. (London,

1831), I, p. 378. The masques written for the weddings of Lord Hay and the Earl of Somerset are to be found in Walter R. Davis (ed.), *The Works of Thomas Campion* (Garden City, NY, 1967).

8 On the dancer Confess, see Chambers, *Elizabethan Stage*, I, p. 202 and III, pp. 244, 386–7. He also had a professional role in Jonson's *Oberon* (1611) and *Love Freed* (1611). In this last masque he was paid £50 for teaching the dances; for the others, his fee ranged from £20 to £40. A payment to him of £30 is recorded on 16 June 1613 for employment 'in His Majesty's late masque'; see *Issues of the Exchequer . . . during the Reign of King James I*, ed. Frederick Devon (London, 1836), p. 165.

9 William Cecil married Lady Catherine Howard in 1608 and succeeded to his father's title as Earl of Salisbury in 1612. Philip Herbert, younger brother of William, third Earl of Pembroke of the second creation, was created Earl of Montgomery in 1605, and succeeded his brother as fourth Earl of Pembroke in 1630. He danced in a number of Ben Jonson's masques, and was, with his brother, a patron of the Shakespeare First Folio of 1623. James Hay came from Scotland to England with James I, was knighted, and became a Gentleman of the Bedchamber. He was later named Baron Hay, first Viscount Doncaster, and first Earl of Carlisle. Anne Dudley was Elizabeth's lady of honour. See Davis (ed.), *Works of Campion*, pp. 204 and 232–3, and the *Dictionary of National Biography*.

10 Several of Inigo Jones's sketches for the costumes in *The Lords' Masque* are extant in the collection of the Duke of Devonshire, including that for Entheus. See Stephen Orgel and Roy Strong, *Inigo Jones: The Theatre of the Stuart Court*, 2 vols. (London, 1973), I, pp. 240–52; and *Designs by Inigo Jones for Masques and Plays at Court*, with Introduction and Notes by Percy Simpson and C. F. Bell (Oxford, 1924), pp. 48–9, frontispiece, and plate VIa. The latter work observes that the accessories for Entheus's costume are taken from Cesare Ripa's *Iconologia*.

11 Nicoll, *Stuart Masques*, pp. 72–5, characterizes the transformational effects in *The Lords' Masque* as 'something much more elaborate than any masque had previously offered', and suggests mechanical solutions that may have been used to make such effects possible, including cloud-machines and a system of *periaktoi* of the sort recorded in Nicolà Sabbatini, *Practica di fabricar scene e machine* (1638). *The Lords' Masque* also makes use of a falling curtain.

12 *The Masque of the Middle Temple and Lincoln's Inn*, written by Chapman and designed by Inigo Jones, was performed on 15 February 1613, before the King, the bride and bridegroom, the Privy Council, and 'our chief nobility'. Chapman speaks like a humanist on the defensive, touchily responding to 'certain insolent objections made against the length of my speeches and narrations'. Like Campion's masque, this work distinguishes between the *Insania* that prompts vainglorious writing and true *Divinus Furor*. The text indulges in jokes about the poverty of poets. Conversely, Plutus, god of riches, and Capriccio, a man of wit, celebrate the huge expenditure of

wealth on the present wedding occasion. Capriccio is the kind of crabbed railer one finds in the satire of the period. The masque thus gives prominent attention to the role of the satirist poet as a kind of moral arbiter of court life, as in Jonson's *Cynthia's Revels*; although the poet fawns at times on the royal graciousness that has commanded his services as author, he also stakes out a claim for himself as a sort of Diogenes.

Beaumont's *The Masque of the Inner Temple and Gray's Inn* was presented only a few days later, on 20 February. The readers at Gray's Inn were assessed £4 apiece to help cover expenses. The role of the Inns of Court was underscored by its members setting forth from Winchester House to Whitehall in the King's own royal barge, 'with the rich furniture of state, and adorned with a great number of [wax] lights placed in such order as might make best show'. They were attended by the Prince's barge and 'a multitude of barges and gallies', etc. The masque itself features many details that remind us of *The Tempest*: Jupiter and Juno dispatch their messengers, Mercury and Iris to do honour to the marriage of the two famous rivers, Thames and Rhine (i.e. Elizabeth and Frederick). Iris's role, as in *The Tempest*, is to represent Juno as 'the Queen of Marriage'. Like Jupiter and Juno, Mercury and Iris contend with each other for primacy, until all is amicably resolved. The staging requires various 'descents' and 'traverses'. King James seems to have preferred at least the comic parts of this masque to Chapman's, for 'It pleased His Majesty to call for it [the second antimasque dance] again at the end, as he did likewise for the first antimasque'. This masque is edited by Philip Edwards in Spencer and Wells (ed.), *A Book of Masques*, pp. 125–48.

13 On Prospero as an illusionist, presenting in the betrothal masque 'his own version of Gonzalo's utopia, a vision of orderly nature and bountiful fruition', see Stephen Orgel, 'Shakespeare and the cannibals', in Marjorie Garber (ed.), *Cannibals, Witches, and Divorce: Estranging the Renaissance* (Baltimore, 1987), pp. 40–66, esp. pp. 64–5. Howard Felperin makes a similar point in *Shakespearean Romance* (Princeton, 1972), pp. 266–8. On Prospero as a masque-presenter throughout *The Tempest*, see Barbara A. Mowat, *The Dramaturgy of Shakespeare's Romances* (Athens, GA, 1976), pp. 62–3 and elsewhere; Kermode (ed.), *Tempest*, pp. xxxxiv–lxxxviii; and Welsford, *Court Masque*, pp. 339ff. Donna B. Hamilton writes on the language of spectacle in this play as that of the Jacobean court masque in *Virgil and 'The Tempest'*: *The Politics of Imitation* (Columbus, 1990), pp. 67–104.

14 For an analysis of how Prospero inverts the usual order of antimasque and main masque, see Ernest B. Gilman, '"All eyes": Prospero's inverted masque', *Renaissance Quarterly* 33 (1980), 214–30. Leah Sinanoglou Marcus, 'Masquing occasions and masque structure', *Research Opportunities in Renaissance Drama* 24 (1981), 7–16, takes exception to what she sees as an oversimplification in Gilman's argument. See also Clifford Leech, 'Masking and unmasking in the last plays', in Carol McGinnis Kay and Henry E. Jacobs (eds.), *Shakespeare's Romances Reconsidered* (Lincoln, NE, 1978), pp. 40–59.

15 *The Honourable Entertainment given to the Queen's Majesty in Progress, at Elvetham in Hampshire, by the Right Honourable Earl of Hertford*, 1591, in *The Complete Works of John Lyly*, ed. R. Warwick Bond, 3 vols. (Oxford, 1902), I, pp. 431–52; see, for example, the song on p. 439.

16 On Prospero as a magus whose art is magic depending upon 'the crucial role of the imagination' and achieving its effects chiefly by means of quasi-theatrical spectacles, see Karol Berger, 'Prospero's art', *Shakespeare Studies* 10 (1977), 211–39, esp. 217 and 234ff. Neil H. Wright discusses Prospero as an artist 'whose medium is the imaginary and the preternatural, a poet who reveals truth through illusion', in 'Reality and illusion as a philosophical pattern in *The Tempest*', *Shakespeare Studies* 19 (1977), 241–70, esp. 244. See also Stephen Orgel, *The Illusion of Power: Political Theater in the English Renaissance* (Berkeley, 1975), pp. 45–8.

17 On the way in which Prospero's final soliloquy 'hovers uncertainly between the options of applause and prayer', see Harry Berger, Jr., 'Miraculous harp: a reading of Shakespeare's *Tempest*', *Shakespeare Studies* 5 (1969), 253–83, esp. 278–9.

'Virgin wax' and 'hairy men-monsters': Unstable movement codes in the Stuart masque

Barbara Ravelhofer

Once the mechanics had cleared the scene at the close of a masque, the literati controlled the afterlife of the performance. Spectacle gave way to literature, as writers undertook the difficult task of verbalizing what was not intrinsically a matter of language. Present-day critics, reporting on action, try to make sense of what has already been mediated through masque libretti,[1] letters and other early modern sources. How do we cope with texts that only refract the stage effects, the lyrics, the sounds and movements of a courtly entertainment? Elusive masque dances not only challenged seventeenth-century writers, they continue to perplex modern exegetes in pursuit of the ephemeral. We possess the verbal choreographies of Ben Jonson, William Davenant, and others. Deciphering these literary versions of dance, however, does not resurrect the pure movement itself. Gestures, like the accounts which attempted to preserve them, do not have a fixed and unalterable quality, but depend on their context. It matters who executed the dance steps and it matters who watched and evaluated them. To introduce the ambiguity of described dance movements I shall discuss a celebrated Jonsonian libretto passage. In order to examine the ambiguities of casting and audience response, I shall focus on the French style of courtly dancing fashionable in the circle of the Duke of Buckingham, and the allegations of effeminacy that it attracted both on stage and off, before turning to the question of child performers and their aesthetic function in a context where 'manliness', given their tender age, could scarcely have been expected of the boys, but in which they had a unique role to fulfil.

I

In what has become an almost canonical definition of the ephemeral character of these entertainments, Ben Jonson remarks of *Hymenaei* (1606) that the spectacle wanted nothing either in riches, or strangeness of the habits, delicacy of dances, magnificence of the scene, or divine rapture of music. Only the envy was that it lasted not still, or . . . cannot by imagination, much less description, be recovered to a part of that spirit it had in the gliding by.[2]

To characterize the masque, Jonson uses an expression which evokes dancing, pre-eminently an action 'gliding by'. How can such movements be captured in words? Choreographies form perhaps the most elusive part of masques. Yet authors and eyewitnesses treat them as textual and attempt to pin down in words what has been performed on stage, no matter how hard dances are to explain. Some retrospective masque libretti include architectural details and musical scores in their accounts. Others minutely report on entries and exits of the performers (with most of the description devoted to costumes). More generous masque narratives disclose the names of the dance styles or comment that the Caroline revellers enjoyed *sarabandes*. Typically, that is all. These vestigial impressions of a rich spectacle leave us with a superficial understanding of the dance scores themselves.

How exactly did masquers practise *sarabandes* – dances of supposedly Spanish origin? What precisely do the ubiquitous 'measures' represent? In some sources they appear to denote the activity of dancing in its most general sense, but elsewhere a specially invented device.[3] In pursuit of the lost choreography, the researcher must try to decipher masque texts. What are we to make, for instance, of Jonson's lines introducing the noble masquers in *Pleasure Reconciled to Virtue* (1618)?

> Come on, come on; and where you go,
> So interweave the curious knot,
> As ev'n th' observer scarce may know
> Which lines are Pleasure's and which not.
> First, figure out the doubtful way
> At which awhile all youth should stay,
> . . . . . .
> Then, as all actions of mankind
> Are but a labyrinth or maze,
> So let your dances be entwined,
> Yet not perplex men unto gaze;
> But measured, and so numerous too,
> As men may read each act you do,
> And when they see the graces meet,
> Admire the wisdom of your feet.[4]

The passage is as labyrinthine as the choreography it evokes; to the reader who wishes to elicit some information on steps and figures, it seems a strangely evasive account of the physical trouble taken by the masquers. But is it Jonson's intention to provide a faithful choreographic description? He is expounding the effects of the art of dancing. Dance should be simple, so that everybody can understand what is happening on stage. It should be complicated, since it reflects life. How can masquers ever realise both ambitions? The lyrics reveal Jonson's ambivalence towards both the performance (in its enacted and textual manifestation) and its impact on the audience. On the one hand, he is convinced that masque dances had a self-explanatory potential which allowed the viewer to read the performers' inherent virtue from their moving bodies. Words are redundant and inadequate to express the 'dignity and reverence' to be found in such 'true motions'.[5] On the other hand, these lines seriously question the didactic capacity of masque dances themselves. Here is a maze in which modal verbs – 'may', 'should' – are the unreliable signposts to the doubtful ways of the written dance. Such rhetorical strategies weaken the claim that the audience may rise to the moral implications of the choreographies. The speaker has to appeal to the dancers not to perplex their audience by their numerous variations, and yet the observer may 'scarce know' how to interpret the spectacle on stage.

Seventeenth-century critical responses to dance were as varied as the measures danced at these entertainments and their literary treatment in written sources. Choreographies both enthralled and incensed the public. The gestures included within choreographies were not confined only to masques but represented, beyond the event, one manifestation of the movement code current at the Stuart court. The way courtiers moved on stage overlapped with manners and deportment they adopted off stage. In order to understand something about the conventions of dancing in this period, we need to answer questions about the meaning of particular gestures or movements. If we want to know how to analyse the bodily dynamics of choreographies, we need to know how fashionable nobility displayed proper bowing or ways of walking in daily life.

The skills of those who participated in masques were not unanimously admired. Detractors regarded masques not as visions of delight but schools for scandal where, as the extreme Puritan William Prynne charged in 1633, 'effeminate cinque-pace coranto-frisking gallants' and 'rustic hobbling satyrs' wasted their time.[6] They charged courtiers with indecency and affectation in their movements off as well as on stage in ways that linked the two:

Now as no other reason appeared in favour of their choice but handsomeness, so the love the King showed was as amorously conveyed as if he had mistaken their sex, and thought them ladies. Which I have seen Somerset and Buckingham labour to resemble in the effeminateness of their dressings. Though in w– looks and wanton gestures they exceeded any part of womankind my conversation did ever cope withal.

Nor was his love . . . carried on with a discretion sufficient to cover a less scandalous behaviour; for the King's kissing them after so lascivious mode in public, and upon the theater as it were of the world, prompted many to imagine some things done in the tiring-house that exceed my expressions no less than they do my experience.[7]

What were these 'w[horish] looks and wanton gestures' which troubled Francis Osborne in his retrospective account of Jacobean court life? Unfortunately, the comments of those who condemned behaviour and morals at the Jacobean court are less explicit than the allegedly improper movements they observed. These seemingly offensive gestures might be elucidated by studying the personalities of the presumed malefactors and their private lives.

Osborne's *exemplum* of the perverted courtier was, somewhat conventionally, George Villiers, Duke of Buckingham, the favourite of the King as well as of contemporary satirical writers, who thereby unwittingly magnified what they sought to diminish.[8] A monopoliser of patronage, the Duke had truly been born 'under the star of a galliard' (*Twelfth Night*, 1.3.130). The attractive dancer exploited his charms to the full in dazzling masque performances such as Ben Jonson's *Vision of Delight* (1617) and *Pleasure Reconciled to Virtue* (1618), where he saved the performance with his nimble capers.[9] He also commissioned masques himself, competing with the spendthrift James Hay, Viscount Doncaster, in setting up costly private entertainments such as *The Gypsies Metamorphosed* (1621) and the masques given in honour of the Spanish and French ambassadors at York House.[10]

Buckingham promoted French customs at the Stuart court. He was educated in France and travelled there on several diplomatic missions. A veritable ambassador of Stuart court culture, he conveyed the masque spirit abroad as well. In 1625, the Duke left a lasting impression at the Louvre, being the only guest at a ball to wear a costume:

en habit à la Persienne, avec un chapeau de velours tout couvert de plumes et de pierreries, et des chausses si troussées, qu'elles laissoient voir non seulement toute la forme de ses jambes qu'il avoit belles, mais aussi beaucoup audessus des genoux. Cette invention estoit bien hardie et bien douteuse, et mesme dans une Cour étrangère, où tant de . . . grands Seigneurs, qui luy portaient envie, ne cherchoient qu'à le tourner en ridicule . . . le Duc . . . dança de si bon air, que les Dames qui rioient d'abord pour s'en moquer, ne rioient sur la fin de bal, que pour luy plaire, et qu'avec sa parure bizarre et surprenante, il effaça la mode Françoise, et les plus galans de la Cour.[11]

The eyewitness dwells on Buckingham's bizarre appearance, which highlighted his shapely legs. He does not inform us which gestures formed the *cantus firmus* of Buckingham's fascinating self-display, but it must have been a style cultivated in France. French-style deportment not only fed general popular associations with effeminacy but also became specifically related to the Duke of Buckingham. In 1627/1628 these anonymous verses were composed after the return of the Duke from the Isle de Rhé expedition:

> Stay, stay at Court then, and at tennis play;
> Measure French galliards out on Killewgray.
> Venus' pavilions doth befit thee best;
> Periwigs with helmets are not to be pressed.
> T'o'errun Spain, win Calais, or conquer France
> Requires a soldier's march, no courtier's dance.[12]

A pacifist camp longhair? It is difficult to define a catalogue of 'male' and 'female' gestures, since every society shapes its own categories of gender. There is more to sixteenth- and seventeenth-century courtly repertoire than a binary opposition between thrusting phallocrats 'relentlessly' penetrating 'the air' and victimised female performers involuntarily flashing their 'orgiastic feet', as some dance criticism would have it.[13] A martial body does not necessarily signify priapic virility; in our age of Tarzan, narcissistic bodybuilders might also be regarded as examples of gay body consciousness.

Male and female characteristics in dance have interested writers since antiquity. A classic definition by Lucian relating to the theatrical dancers of his time distinguishes extremes of masculinity and femininity:

When they exceed the due limit of mimicry and put forth greater effort than they should, if something large requires to be shown, they represent it as enormous, if something dainty, they make it extravagantly effeminate, and they carry masculinity to the point of savagery and bestiality.[14]

The standard Renaissance reference provided by Castiglione states that a man should display 'a certain manliness, full and steady' and 'a certain dignity, tempered notwithstanding with a handsome and sightly sweetness of gestures' in his dancing style.[15] Castiglione considered excessive ornamentation in movements and garments as effeminate affectation.[16]

In the same way, Sir Thomas Elyot associated vehemence and fierceness with the male dancer as opposed to the delicate, less 'advancing' comportment of women.[17] Following what Renaissance commonplaces on dancing and his particular critics mentioned about 'female' body language, Buckingham's bodily rhetoric tended, it seems, to the gliding, suave, ornate side available in the spectrum of dance vocabulary. In his appearance and deportment, he functioned as an arbiter of fashion who shaped the tastes of the Jacobean and Caroline aristocracy both within and outside masques. Yet his dancing body constituted simultaneously a veritable anatomy of abuse. What Prynne deplores about the English gentry reads like a belated and unsympathetic obituary of the Duke five years after his assassination:

> . . . they are now so fantastic in their apparel, so womanish in their frizzled periwigs, love-locks, and long effeminate . . . pounced hair; so mimical in their gestures . . . so player-like in their deportment; so amorous in their speeches; so lascivious in their embracements; so unmanly, degenerous and unEnglish (if I may so speak) in their whole conversation; is it not principally from their resort to plays, to masques, and such like antic, apish pastimes, the very schools to train them up in all effeminacy and fantastic folly?[18]

Prynne was an ideologue, but even those who themselves produced these 'immoral' spectacles occasionally vented their spleen on what they saw as the excesses of the genre. In addition to the familiar catalogue of mannerisms to be deplored, tight corsets frequently worn by gallants as well as dancers[19] came in for criticism. Ben Jonson remarked on effeminate gentlemen of his age, as he must have encountered them in the streets of London and in the more exclusive circles of Whitehall:

> All must be as affected and preposterous as our gallants' clothes, sweet bags, and night-dressings, in which you would think our men lay in, like ladies . . . There is nothing valiant or solid to be hoped for from such as are always kempt and perfumed and every day smell of the tailor; the exceedingly curious, that are wholly in mending such an imperfection in the face, in taking away the morphew [*sic*] in the neck; or bleaching their hands at midnight, gumming and bridling their beards; or making the waist small, binding it with hoops, while the mind runs at waste. Too much pickedness is not manly.[20]

Reviewing the reviews, we find that the association of effeminacy with affectation is often tinged with xenophobia: bad habits are unEnglish and tend to be imported from southern countries. Here we find the gestural counterpart to the courtier who is too exuberant in speech ('For rhetoric, he could not ope / His mouth but out there flew a trope').[21]

Dance experts of the period do not, of course, censure the verbal infelicities of their students; instead, they provide whole catalogues of vices based on exaggerated gesture and carriage. In the bestselling dance book *Nobiltà di dame* (1600), for instance, the prominent choreographer Fabritio Caroso harbours deep suspicions of knees spread too far apart as if 'to urinate'.[22] Did a Jacobean audience also associate this movement with urination? Was this the body language of gipsy-courtiers who had their faces greased with yellow ointment and delivered lines such as 'Claw a churl by the arse, and he'll shite in your fist'? Fascinating as a detour into scatological conjecture would be, I would like to confine my study to two French dance treatises of the period that definitely shadow English practice and discuss how they reflect popular fears of gestural exaggeration. It is worth considering in greater detail how dance and conduct books treated the histrionics of male and female deportment.

Two French sources, both dating from the early 1620s, are intimately connected with Buckingham and the English court. Hoping to gain the patronage of the aristocratic couple, the dance theorist François de Lauze addressed his book *Apologie de la danse* (1623) to Buckingham and his wife Katherine. Bartholomew de Montagut was a professional choreographer who worked for Buckingham and participated as dancer in masques such as Davenant's *Luminalia* (1638). Montagut seems to have known de Lauze personally; his work *Louange de la danse* represents in parts a pirated copy of de Lauze's dance manual.[23] Both manuals, together with another treatise from about 1610 found in Germany, provide valuable French accounts of dancing in the early seventeenth century. Montagut's and de Lauze's books are also the last before the introduction of French dance repertoire in Feuillet notation at the end of the seventeenth century.

The *Louange* and the *Apologie* offer a repertoire of dance types as commonly practised in courtly circles, and they describe it in almost the same terms. However, they differ greatly in style from those in other dance sources of the period. A *galliard* (*cinquepace*) as described in the *Apologie de la danse* has little in common with, say, the *gagliardas* integrated in the dance suite-like creations of Fabritio Caroso in the late sixteenth century. Equally, de Lauze and Montagut share only a few common elements with another French dance instruction manual, Thoinot Arbeau's *Orchésographie* (1588). Hence, de Lauze's and Montagut's contributions supplement the range of treatises usually consulted in research on masque dances.[24] If it is legitimate to predicate a

'French school' based on de Lauze and Montagut which influenced English courtly dancing of the period, then their works represent the first expositions of a new fashion. For the purpose of this discussion, we need only note some of its predominant features: the turn-out of the feet, a kind of *plié*, highly accomplished leaping, circular movements of the feet and regular rising on tiptoe. This new style was smooth and gliding in character and markedly different from that in English dance sources.[25]

'French' elements, as has been shown, were sufficiently well known and practised to allow for literary puns by the time Jacobean masquers were adorning the stage. In 1598, John Marston had already objected to the affectations of a love-sick gallant, fittingly called 'Lucian': 'Having kissed his hand', he 'stroke up his hair' and then bowed in a tearful 'French conge' to the bedpost in his chamber which he took for his lady, thereby making a private scene unnecessarily theatrical.[26] Masque texts poke fun at gesture codes which must have been applied in the dances of aristocratic performers, not in the derogatory context of the antimasque only. In a typical example of two aesthetic-kinetic principles being at odds with each other within the same genre, Momus in Thomas Carew's *Coelum Britannicum* (1634) derides the 'fellow who to add to his stature thinks it a greater grace to dance on his tiptoes like a dog in a doublet than to walk like other men on the soles of his feet.'[27]

If the fashion of dancing on tiptoes was unfavourably received, the turn-out of the feet did not fare much better. When Jacobean courtiers occupied the masque stage, the turn-out was still not a common convention. Only gradually did dancers shift from a closed, parallel foot position to one where feet closed at the heels only and toes pointed emphatically outwards, as we see in the most extreme form in today's first position in classical ballet. The influential Milanese dancing master Cesare Negri, choreographer for Philip III of Spain, whose students became important performers at the European courts of the time, had advocated in his later works a slight turn-out of the feet.[28] But it was later choreographers such as de Lauze and Montagut who insisted even more in their dance manuals on a visible turn-out with toes pointing strongly to the sides. This style verged on what later developed into a Baroque ballet standard for both men and women.

Other features predominantly to be found in de Lauze's and Montagut's treatises as well as in later Baroque repertoire were the *temps en rond* and the *plié*. In the *temps en rond*, dancers described a small circle to the side with one leg, beginning from a basic position with feet closed at the heels and toes pointed strongly outwards.[29] Melusine Wood has noted that this choreographical element developed into a specific 'circular' walking style which became fashionable in French courtly circles from the early seventeenth century onwards.[30]

The *plié* involved bending the knees and was one way in which dancers might bow in greeting their partners. Bowing and bending, however, together with pointing the toes outwards, were movements to be carried out with great delicacy. Thoinot Arbeau, a late sixteenth-century writer who lived on the Continent, comments in his dance book *Orchésographie* on the pitfalls of the *révérence*, a movement used to greet partners or to introduce a dance:

As for feet close together, or toes too positively turned out, these have a feminine appearance. And in the same way that it ill becomes a damsel to assume a masculine bearing so we should avoid feminine poses. This is demonstrated in the révérence, because in making it the men cross one foot smartly to the rear of the other and the damsels bend both knees gently and arise in like manner.[31]

Arbeau has the woman bend both knees, anticipating the way Montagut and de Lauze would later describe their *plié*. The man, however, tries bowing by bending one leg only, which he crosses behind the other which is kept straight. This seems to be a specific French way of curt-seying, one of the few practices shared between Arbeau and his insular colleagues. This is the type which Marston seems to caricature. The moralist Brathwaite satirizes it, too, in his conduct books of the 1630s: the 'compliment' of a 'fantastic gallant' performing his 'formal congies' resembles that of an 'ape'.[32]

The rigid leg, however sufficient it may have been for Arbeau as a mark of gender difference, did not gratify Richard Brathwaite in his critical assessment of Stuart fashions. When, in his popular books on etiquette, *The English Gentleman* and *The English Gentlewoman*, he sets out to portray what he calls the 'effeminate' man marked by 'delicacy in fare, sumptuousness in attire', the movement catalogue of bending and subtle turns is always implicit.[33] It seems no coincidence that Brathwaite chooses the adjectives 'supple' and '*plia*ble in their joints' to characterise the ubiquitous 'Jackanapes in gay clothes',[34] whose mere sight he detests, whether they are dancing or merely socialising in other ways. Lamenting the bygone days in which 'legs were held for useful supporters, but no complimental postures', he sets out to draft the portrait of a degenerate aristocratic society in which men and women alike embark on the excesses of the 'outlandish salute', the 'congies, cringes, . . . of which error, I would this age wherein we live, did not too much labour'.[35]

It is only natural that Brathwaite should address both men and women in *The English Gentlewoman*, since he sees so much reason to inveigh against men's effeminate affectation both on the street and in courtly dancing. On the one hand, he finds that women resemble in habit and conceit 'neither women nor men'.[36] It appears that they must have followed the same dance fashions as men, practising the *temps en rond* and affecting it in their way of walking: 'What a circular gesture we shall observe some use in their pace, as if they were troubled with the vertigo!'[37] On the other hand he notices how introduction at court initially embarrasses the ignorant swain: 'should a rustic or boorish behaviour accompany one who betakes himself to the court, he might be sure to find a controller in every corner to reprove him.' The swain is soon transformed, however, and adapts himself to the ruling tastes. The result, Brathwaite notices frowningly, is 'a fantastic dressing, or some antic compliment, which the corruption of an effeminate state hath brought in'.[38] Clearly such gender confusion is in part the consequence of overdiligent dancing practice. Teachers such as Montagut and de Lauze must be blamed for this development. After all, it is de Lauze, who, as Melusine Wood put it, arrogantly asserted that courtiers would not even be able to walk, let alone dance properly, without his instruction.[39] Stuart aristocracy no longer relies on legs as supporters, as Brathwaite would have it, but 'learns to pace'. Such learning ends in the loss of male/female distinction, and the English Gentleman turns into the English Gentlewoman. In a manner which almost anticipates an academic who faces a postmodern crisis of representation, Brathwaite reflects that 'these unstaid dimensions argue unsettled dispositions'.[40]

We have seen that the style described in the French treatises was practised in English masque productions. It reverberated in contemporary writing and fashionable manners, leaving traces in conduct books, choreographical instruction and such everyday behaviour as salutation and walking. However, reading the movements depended on the onlooker who decided what he wanted to see. The interweaving knots of labyrinthine masque dances, as Jonson described them, left enough space for interpretation. 'Effeminate hairy men-monsters'[41] using a gesture code associated with the other sex may well have turned into a 'circle of celestial bodies'[42] from the appropriate perspective. Performer and critic decide how to understand a choreography. A certain dancing style might conjure up differing audience responses, if realised by different sets of dancers.

II

Masque casts and audiences consisted of different factions grappling for power at a polycentric court, as this present volume attests.[43] It is the great achievement of the masque genre that, despite the diversity of interests, alliances and attitudes towards an aestheticised display of monarchical power, such spectacles could take place at all. Everybody played his or her social role – if with various degrees of enthusiasm – and even those most averse to 'illusions of power' on stage attended such spectacles. They were also likely to try to initiate their children into the world of a masque event with an eye on their future careers. These young performers' skills were exploited for two purposes: to integrate them into an aristocratic ensemble both on stage and off, and to secure their later advancement. Many observers of the period regarded masques as dubious in their political and aesthetic qualities, but at the same time as indicators of distinction and guarantees of an exclusive social position in the establishment of the Stuart court. Masques, with all their ambiguities, were connective events by which a group, though internally diversified, manifested its stability, identity and sociopolitical influence. Ambiguity was essential to a genre that needed to satisfy heterogeneous participants and onlookers. In this, masques were similar to modern-day social functions. People will attend the most tedious party if 'everybody else' will be present too; and by introducing their offspring at such occasions, they hope to enable them to make important contacts and secure for them status and prestige. How did Stuart society involve their young sons and daughters in masques?

The instabilities between 'male' and 'female' movement codes as previously outlined become even more complex if we consider that 'male' and 'female' masquers were not timeless. Age has been a less popular object of masque studies than gender. For modern criticism, the agile performer, somewhat indefinitely hovering between the teens and forties, dominates the scene, the youngest leading an invisible backstage existence. Children, however, took an active part in masque productions, and it was their dancing skills that pushed them into the limelight.

Illustrating performing skills of aristocrats in greater detail, critics have focused predominantly on the memorable examples of full-grown, 'mature' dancers, emphasising the role of Sir Christopher Hatton under

Elizabeth I, or Buckingham in the Stuart period. Castiglione's *Il Cortegiano* and the literary sequels it provoked made it clear that dance training held an important place in the armoury of the would-be courtier. John Holles recorded in his 1614 correspondence that 'an assured, free and civil conversation, running at the ring, dancing' as practised in France were 'qualities in these times most respected in our Court'. Holles was to spend some time in France with the English ambassador. His father urged him to acquire some accomplishments at the Academy and advised:

> Practise your riding, weapon and dancing seriously and diligently that you may be a proficient and master in each occupation, all which qualities adorn not only, but are so necessary to a young gentleman, as who can not express himself in them as he ought shall be disesteemed . . . for as these governed with discretion and fellowed with other powers of the mind, create a perfect courtier, so to intend to be one of them only brings rather obloquy, as to dance only belongs to a ballarin, to fence only to a fencer, and to ride only to a cavallerizzo. All must therefore go together . . . These things at your return will grace you with the Prince, and by your ability to serve him and the King therein, will give you place and precedence in their affections. You have examples before you, for those that run at the ring, tilt, dance, viz. do at those times only their master, the Court and the Kingdom service and honour, all others are held for burden in the best sense, number, and the filling up of the chamber.[44]

In such contexts it seems only logical that aspirants should begin at an early age to meet the manifold requirements of courtly deportment. Young noble dancers in masques demonstrate their claim to belong to a courtly society because they are up to its standards. Excellence in dancing may launch a distinguished future career.

Within the genre of the masque, however, courtly dances also fulfil a two-fold didactic purpose: they can make not only the beholder but the young performer wise. Elaborate choreographies aimed at integrating audience and participants into Stuart culture, both for the duration of a masque production and within the greater framework of the society that arranged such events and endeavoured to maintain its stability through festive occasions. This latter aspect appears to be particularly important for young masquers, who might still be as impressionable as the 'virgin wax'[45] flambeaux they brandished. The sixteenth century is certainly not the age of developmental psychology, but didactic notions of forming the young mind circulated in handbooks such as those of Erasmus or Roger Ascham.[46] Virtuous behaviour and specific social rules were best acquired while the individual was still young and

malleable. Already Elyot had advocated dancing as a proper educational means of inculcating virtuous behaviour – for instance the 'moral
virtue called prudence':

> This virtue being so commodious to man . . . that as soon as opportunity may
> be found, a child or young man be thereto induced. And by cause that the
> study of virtue is tedious for the more part to them that do flourish in young
> years, I have devised how in the form of dancing now late used in this realm
> among gentlemen, the whole description of this virtue prudence may be found
> out and well perceived, as well by the dancers as by them which standing by
> will be diligent beholders and markers.[47]

The Jesuit colleges, which had changed the face of upper-class education on the Continent, did not instruct their pupils in courtly dance
simply to have them shine in public theatrical presentations, elaborate
and fully choreographed shows; these skills were also directed towards
a greater social adaptability: 'Give me the child, and I will give you the
man'. To discuss the didactics of spectacle and strategies of career
planning, I shall now turn to dancing children in masques and the
aristocratic tradition which prompted their appearance on stage.

Did masques have age requirements? In a period when, for a time,
audiences crowded to plays staged by the childrens' companies, the
fashion for young performers permeated courtly spectacles as well, and
with success, if the favourable accounts of such events may be trusted.
It was presumably John Finnett, Master of Ceremonies, who wrote of
Daniel's *Tethys' Festival* (1610) that the 'little Duke of York', attended
upon by 'twelve little ladies, all of them the daughters of earls or
barons', performed

> their dance to the amazement of all the beholders, considering the tenderness
> of their years and the many intricate changes of the dance which was so
> disposed that, which way soever the changes went, the little Duke was still
> found to be in the midst of these little dancers.[48]

The 'influences of the stars' in *Tempe Restored* (1632) had an average
age between nine and thirteen years.[49] Jonson's entertainment for
Henry's first masque as Prince of Wales featured a ballet of ten small
page boys.[50] In masque texts we often read of nymphs or pages and
'young lords' carrying flambeaux. This suggests that the performers
may well have been children. In her survey of courtly masque dances,
Jean Knowlton suggests that children were frequently among the torch-
bearers.[51] 'Young lords and noblemen's sons' had preceded the main

masquers, lighting the scene in Carew's *Coelum Britannicum*. These performers were between nine and fourteen, among them 'Lord Brackley', aged eleven. This was John Egerton (1623–86) who played the 'Elder Brother' in Milton's *Comus* the same year, and he had already taken part two years before in Townshend's *Tempe Restored*.[52]

The daughter of the Duke of Buckingham invited admiration for her prowess as an immature performer no less than do the pyrotechnical improvisations of her prominent father. Mary Villiers could hardly walk when she took her first dancing lessons. Her mother Katherine Villiers wrote in a letter to her husband, who had accompanied Prince Charles to Spain on the latter's abortive bride-finding mission:

> . . . when she is set to her feet and held by her sleeves she will not go subtly but stamp and set one foot afore another very fast that I think she will run before she can go. She loves dancing extremely and when the saraband is played she will set her thumb and her finger together offering to snap and then, when Tom Duff is sung, then she will shake her apron and when she hears the tune of the clapping dance my Lady Frances Huberd taught the prince she will clap both her hands together and on her breast and she can tell the tunes as well as any of us can and as they change the tunes she will change her dancing . . . She is so full of pretty play and tricks and she has got a trick that when they dance her she will cry hah hah and Nicolae will dance with his legs and she will imitate him as well as she can. She will be excellent at a hat for if one lay her down she will kick her legs over her head but when she is elder I hope she will be more modest . . .[53]

'Pretty Mall', then about two years old, grew into the entertainment culture of the Caroline court and was able to participate in large productions such as *Tempe Restored*, when she was not much older than eleven, representing one of the stellar influences. Later, she was one of the lady masquers in *Salmacida Spolia* (1640). She married in succession Charles, Lord Herbert (son and heir of Philip, Earl of Pembroke and Montgomery), then James Stuart (fourth Duke of Lennox and first Duke of Richmond), and finally Thomas Howard (brother to Charles, Earl of Carlisle), all of them at some point participants in masque productions. 'Mall', then, proved an influential figure in aristocratic circles. She owed her career to family ties and the social talents she displayed at various occasions, and in particular, masques. In her case, success stories appearing in courtly literature of the period came true. 'Mall' mirrors Deletia, the heroine of Margaret Cavendish's story 'The Contract'. Cavendish, later Duchess of Newcastle (1623–1673), was Maid of Honour to Queen Henrietta Maria. When Cavendish described the

Figure 11.1 Children torchbearers in a masque of Diana and Mercury. A detail
from the Memorial Portrait of Sir Henry Unton, 1596.

education of Deletia, she may have been inspired by real examples at court:

from the time of four years old, she was taught all that her age was capable of, as to sing, and to dance; for he [Deletia's well-meaning uncle and sponsor] would have this artificial become as natural, and to grow in perfection, as she grew in years. When she was seven years of age, he chose her such books to read in as might make her wise, not amorous, for he never suffered her to read in romancies, nor such light books; but moral philosophy was the first of her studies, to lay a ground and foundation of virtue, and to teach her to moderate her passions, and to rule her affections. The next, her study was in history . . .[54]

Pretty rigorous training for young Deletia! Yet the tuition in courtly repertoire does not seem to have made her monstrous or affected but accomplished. When finally unveiled at a court masque, aged sixteen and 'a meteor of the time',[55] she eclipsed both her female rivals and the scenic effects of the stage machinery. She was also quite stunning as a dancer.

That the early dance education of aristocratic ladies and fictional heroines started at a time when their speaking skills were developing as well is not surprising and must be placed within a courtly tradition reaching beyond the 'Fortunate Isles' and the reign of Charles I. Already in the fifteenth century, Italian princesses had had their personal dancing teachers from a tender age; at the age of seven, Isabella d'Este invented her own *balli* to French tunes which she sang while she was dancing. The dancing master Cornazano dedicated his treatise to his nine-year-old pupil Hippolita Sforza.[56] Pastorals and masques *en miniature* with young performers were also popular at German courts. A particularly intriguing example is a Nuremberg childrens' ballet with barriers of the later seventeenth century, featuring knights from all five continents and French dialogues, presented by more than sixty boys and girls between six and twelve.[57] In England, a throng of dancing masters kept up the standards in courtly repertoire; best known among them were Sir William Erwin, teacher to Henry Prince of Wales, Thomas Giles, Hierome Herne, Bochan and Confesse, all of them significantly involved in Jacobean masque productions, and Simon Hopper, tutor to the family of Charles I in the 1630s. Thanks to the efforts of his teachers, Prince Henry could astonish the Spanish Ambassador at the age of ten with a daring galliard.[58]

Early choreographic training of the nobility answers to the need to express oneself with the necessary decorum not only in speech but in

Figure 11.2 Children practising a dance. From Hans and Paul Vredeman de Vries, *Palace Architecture, c.* 1596.

gesture. Accordingly, de Lauze and Montagut emphasize that the beginner should not have reached an age 'which is too advanced'.[59] Clearly, such statements reflect the pressures towards an impeccable presentation on the public stage. The great court masques in particular attracted a sophisticated, cosmopolitan audience which had seen similar feats at other European courts and was quick to note flaws. Observers like Orazio Busino carefully scrutinized the noble masquers:

> The Prince [Charles], however, excelled them all in bowing, being very formal in making his obeisance both to the King and to the lady with whom he danced, nor was he once seen to do a step out of time when dancing, whereas one cannot perhaps say so much for the others. Owing to his youth he gets winded easily; nevertheless, he cut a few capers very gracefully.[60]

Apart from the assertion that beginners should not be too old before they embarked on courtly dancing, almost nothing is known about choreography for children. Dancing masters distinguished sometimes between rules for men and women, but devised no instructions for boys and girls. They were predominantly concerned with levels of proficiency, hence between beginners and advanced practitioners, often grading their instructions according to level of difficulty. De Lauze is not Piaget. A 'Young Person's Guide to Courtly Dancing' does not exist in the literature on the subject. Step repertoire particularly tailored to childrens' needs has not been traced in any dance treatise up to the Stuart period. However, it is the dance that integrates young performers into the masque spectacles, offering them an active participation, and placing at their disposal the same step vocabulary as their adult counterparts.[61]

Significantly, dancing children were often used as messengers announcing the elder generation. In *Coelum Britannicum*, the young torch dancers, representing celestial influences, preceded adult main masquers dressed as stars who followed them on the illuminated stage. The sung lyrics accompanying the entry of the young performers in *Tempe Restored* evoke a promising future:

Harmony:	And these the beams and influences are
	Of constellations, whose planetic sway,
	Though some foresee, all must alike obey
Chorus:	Such a conjunction, of auspicious lights,
	Meet but in honour of some regal rights.
Harmony and	. . . there are stars to rise,
her choir:	That far above our song
	Are music to all eyes.[62]

Young masquers made a time perspective visible on stage in addition to the three-dimensional statements of architecture and the space mapped out by the movements of the performers. Although not a grand courtly masque, the smaller-scale *Entertainment at Richmond* (1636) illustrates the four-dimensionality of the genre in an exemplary way. Here the children did not precede the elder generation but rather presented, as messengers from the past, a choreographic epilogue. Eight years after George Villiers had been assassinated, his sons appeared on stage to demonstrate the mutual attachment of the Villiers family and the Royal House of the Stuarts beyond the generations of King James, King Charles and the first Duke of Buckingham. George, born in 1628, and his brother Francis, born posthumously in 1629,[63] danced together with the Prince and future King Charles II, then six. They entered dressed in ancient Roman fashion. After they had delivered their measures in the presence of a priestly chorus, six dwarfish squires leapt in, carrying shields each bearing an *impresa*, and laying them at the feet of the Prince's mother, Henrietta Maria.

The *imprese* do not represent virtues, muses or deities attributed *ad libitum* to the individual dancer. Rather, they seem to target specifically each young performer, the family history, the allegiance to the crown, or the future inherent for the child by its family connections. The princely emblem represented 'the sun scarce risen', 'peeping behind a mountain, and shedding light upon the world'. The explanation read '*Nondum conspectus illuminat orbem* [the sight does not yet illuminate the world]'.[64] The *subscriptio* of Buckingham's sons is most revealing:

My L. DUKE of Buckingham's: A fair well-spread tree, and tall, blown down to the ground by a tempest, out of it a straight young tree springing, over which a black cloud dropping, and through that cloud the sun breaking with his beams and shining upon that young tree. The word: *Sub his radiis sic iterum resurgam.*

My L. FRANCIS VILLARS: A square altar of green turf, upon which is placed a heart crowned, over against this Cupid with a bow in his hand broken with a shot. At the bottom of the altar a shaft fastened as shot from the bow, and a second shaft in the middle way between Cupid and the altar, yet flying towards it. The word: *Etiam fracto arcu huc destinatur.*[65]

In the present collection, Tom Bishop points out how much the spectacle of the Stuart period needs the presence of the living body and how much representative art uses the image of the body even in its absence. The presence of a dead dancer is felt throughout *The*

Figure 11.3 Francis, George and Mary Villiers, from the tomb of the
Duke of Buckingham, Westminster Abbey.

Entertainment at Richmond. The exertions of the sons seem like a repetition of the father's successes. In a quasi-ritualistic scenario, the movements of Francis and young George recall the figures of their father, living bodies reconfiguring an absent one. The depictions on the shields enhance the dynamics on stage. In a significant movement between past, present and future, the anonymous narrator verbalises the image on the young Duke's shield as a 'blown down' tree, using a past passive participle. The tense changes to the present: 'a straight young tree springing', the 'sun breaking' through the skies; both processes leading into the future. The participles connect the present and a very close future, describe something which will happen and is already happening.

The Latin motto ends with an optimistic outlook, some certainty assumed. The future will be fulfilled when the sun of Charles II has fully risen.

Child performers carried all the authority they inherited from their cultural and social background. George Villiers, second Duke of Buckingham, presented as spotless youth, has apparently only inherited the virtues of his father. The historical references in the masque text often sound rather unArcadian,[66] as the characters raise unpalatable contemporary issues. A dialogue between a Captain and a Druid, for instance, alludes to undisciplined soldiers ravaging the countryside ('He that kills men for money, does no better / Than common hangmen, perhaps he does worse'[67]). The childrens' performance, by contrast, comes through as an untainted, innocent activity, the young prince being a messianic icon of chivalry:

> Why stay you there brave knights? Descend!
> And let these ladies see
> The action that your looks portend,
> Which is love's chivalry.
> Why should you fear their eyes to meet?
> You have a sure defence,
> That might a greater danger greet:
> Your age and innocence.[68]

The qualities of 'age' and 'innocence' bestowed on child performers an authority in conveying political messages which might range even beyond that of adult masquers. Were George and Francis really innocent boys, noble naive creatures who would have outstripped Rousseau's painfully docile Emile? It does not matter. What counts is their use as a rhetorical vehicle within an entertainment promoting Caroline courtly ideology. By employing young performers in the aesthetics of innocence, masque authors and designers played with images of childhood and clichés of an unspoilt existence. Diminutive knights in white, dressed *à l'antique*, truly worthy heirs of the heroic British past, carry virgin wax candles into an uncontaminated future.[69] How bizarre that the step repertoire of Prynne's 'hairy men-monsters' might be turned to the auspicious 'planetic sway' of the new-born stars.

The author of *The Entertainment at Richmond* did not trust his own work. Ironically, it is the libretto which has come down to us, and not the choreographic devices, which apparently formed the most impressive part of the event:

Then was the curtain let fall, and this folly (as all others do) had consumed itself, and left no impression in the spectators, or hearers, had it not been that much admiration was conceived at the great quickness, and aptness of the Prince, who varying figures so often, was so far from being out, that he was able to lead the rest.[70]

It is dance that singles out festive occasions and transforms them into unforgettable events. Such success derives from the workings of the very same art which Prynne considered ruinous for the character of young people. Notwithstanding hostile criticism, it is precisely the dance of child performers which is felt to have a strong artistic and moral impact on the audience. Although elsewhere signifying vice incarnate, ambiguous French style seems here a component of the aesthetics of innocence and good fortune, aiming to impress the viewer through virtue made visible.

Spectacles such as *Coelum Britannicum* or *The Entertainment at Richmond* show how moving bodies may reconfigure the past in their dance formations or give a preview of the future. In this, child performers play a central role. However, they do not refer merely in linear time to the heroic origins of Stuart court culture or prophesy its impending apotheosis. Immature dancers share with the masque as genre a kind of self-perpetuating property which requires further analysis.

From her perspective as a dance historian, Jane Gingell has characterized the masque as 'incestuous art, which existed to define, express and reinforce the court which produced it'.[71] Tom Bishop elaborates on this complicated interplay between feedback and impulse in terms of the 'future perfect'; the masque is generated by the past and, as political statement, gives impulses for a future definition of the court.[72] Giving body to this abstraction, it could be argued that the child performer, then, represents the incestuous principle *in nuce*. If, following Bishop, the masque seeks to be its own precedent, then the child performers are their own precedents. Originating from and shaped by the courtly society which surrounds them, young dancers express the culture in which they have been raised. The presence of boy and girl torchbearers in historicising costumes links back to the past and invokes the glorious mythical background of the events happening on stage. At the same time, they invite a glance into the future. After introductory measures, they must give way to the adult generation performing the grand masque dances, merely illuminating their entries. All the same, young courtiers, though not yet physically grown to maturity, carry within themselves the full potential of the future. They draw from the same step vocabulary as the main masquers, and they participate in the spectacle with the same authority. Except for their age or size, the nymphs, fairies and torchbearers have at least as much aesthetic and didactic force ascribed to their performance as the main masquers do. They could even, as at Richmond, sustain a full-scale performance. Why? They are the prelude and the main act. They are already what they are going to be, perfect utopian embodiments of the ideal courtier *en miniature*: Do as we do, do better than we do. Referring to what is to come, they add a perspective of time, a fourth dimension to the three-dimensional topology of the stage. The display of future events and the future encapsulated in the young performers authorises and reinforces present action.

At least as long as the spectacle lasts, children masquers impersonate the values of the Stuart court. Masques may attempt a prognosis of the perfect future, but only for the duration of the performance. The actions of the young dancers can only be predicted for the timespan of an entertainment. Once outside this frame of reference, the future perfect turns into an open-ended forecast.

Children grow, although they may be fixed in masque texts and pictures by way of their momentary activities. As the court painter de Vries portrays the children practising their dancing in his panorama of courtly life (fig. 11.2), they blend perfectly into the social and geometrical architecture of his landscape. The ape in the foreground illustrates the imitative aspects of the art of dancing, and indeed the children imitate the grown-up world in their endeavour at courtly accomplishment. The ape also signifies 'apishness' and artful dissimulation. They cannot for ever retain the 'virgin wax' quality which society ascribes to them:

Youth, being indeed the philosopher's *tabula rasa*, is apt to receive any good impressure [*sic*], but spotted with the pitch of vice, it hardly ever regains her former purity.[73]

'Learning to pace', the children may acquire arts of which they would better have remained ignorant. The 'tabula rasa' of 'virgin wax' could turn into a chronicle of scandal. Young dancers might later be judged according to their 'manliness' in masque choreographies and they are likely to face allegations of effeminacy in the theatre of the world as well. Becoming mature, performers may not only deviate aesthetically in the view of onlookers but politically from orthodoxies expounded by masques, defying the didactics of the spectacles in which they danced. Looking back to *Tempe Restored* (1632), we find among the cast Mr Charles Cavendish, aged twelve, and Lord Thomas Grey of Stamford, aged ten, among the heavenly 'Influences' announcing the 'regal rites' to come.[74] Years later, Charles Cavendish would become a royalist. Thomas Grey metamorphosed from 'auspicious light'[75] to regicide. Some of the hands that carried the torches would sign the death warrant for the King.

NOTES

1 In his study *Music in the English Courtly Masque, 1604–1640* (Oxford, 1996), Peter Walls objects to the term 'libretto', since it implies a single composer setting the libretto text. In masques, various kinds of music by several composers relate to the poetical device (p. 42). In my essay, however, I am not discussing the origins of opera, to which Walls refers shortly, nor am I dealing with various composers of music. I understand as 'libretto' merely a written device which (retrospectively) accompanies and explains an action happening on the masque stage.

2 C. H. Herford and P. and E. Simpson (eds.), *Ben Jonson*, 11 vols. (Oxford, 1925–1952), VII, p. 229, lines 572–9.

3 John Ward, 'Newly devis'd measures for Jacobean masques', *Acta Musicologica* 60 (1988), 111–42.

4 Herford and Simpson (eds.), *Ben Jonson*, VII, pp. 488–9, lines 253–68.

5 *Ibid.*, p. 489, lines 292–3.

6 William Prynne, *Histriomastix*, facs. edn (New York, 1974), p. 232.

7 Francis Osborne, *Historical Memoirs on the Reigns of Queen Elizabeth and King James* (London, 1658), part II, pp. 127–8.

8 On Buckingham's biography, see Roger Lockyer, *The Life and Political Career of George Villiers, First Duke of Buckingham, 1592–1628* (London, 1981); on the literary images of favourites, see Ruth Little, 'Perpetual Metaphors: The Configuration of the Courtier as Favourite in Jacobean and Caroline Literature' (unpub. PhD, University of Cambridge, 1993).

9 For a more specific comment on Buckingham's prowess, see the famous account by Orazio Busino of *Pleasure Reconciled to Virtue* (London, 24 January 1618): *Calendar of State Papers, Venetian*, XV, pp. 111–14, also Herford and Simpson (eds.), *Ben Jonson*, X, pp. 580–4, and Andrew Sabol (ed.), *Four Hundred Songs and Dances from the Stuart Masque* (Hanover, NH, 1982), Appendix B, p. 545.

10 For French influence, see Marie-Claude Canova-Green, *La Politique-spectacle au grand siècle: les rapports franco-anglais.* (Paris, 1993); on Buckingham as patron, see John Orrell, 'Buckingham's patronage of the dramatic arts: the Crowe accounts', *Records of Early English Drama* 2 (1980), 8–17, and James Knowles, 'Change partners and dance: a newly discovered Jacobean masque', *TLS* 9 August (1991), 19. For influence of French *ballet de cour* and the role of Buckingham and Lord Hay, see Timothy Raylor,

'Who danced in *The Essex House Masque* (1621)?', *Notes & Queries* 242 (1997), 530–3.

11 The Duke of Buckingham appeared in a Persian costume, with a velvet hat all covered in feathers and jewels, and with breeches so slashed [tucked] that they revealed not only the shape of his legs, which were very fine, but a good deal above the knee as well. This idea was extremely audacious and risky, particularly in a foreign court, where a host of handsome people and great lords, who were envious of him, were only too willing to treat him as a laughing-stock. However, the Duke succeeded in carrying off his entry so well, and danced so gracefully, that the ladies who at first had laughed to mock him, were by the end of the ball laughing only to please him, and that with his strange and surprising appearance he eclipsed the fashion of France and the most stylish people of the Court.

Chevalier de Méré, *De la conversation* (Paris, 1677), in Méré, *Oeuvres complètes*, ed. Ch.-H. Boudliors, 3 vols. (Paris, 1930), II, pp. 131–2. Quoted from Ruth Little, *Perpetual Metaphors*, p. 224, translation slightly modified.

12 GB-Cu MS Gg.IV.13 (D). For another version of this poem, 'Listen jolly gentlemen', and further studies on Buckingham and effeminacy, see J. Knowles, 'Dirty dancing', paper given at the conference *Dance, Gesture and Representation: The Performance of the Renaissance Body*, University of Warwick, 14 June 1996, and 'Change partners and dance', p. 19.

13 Quoted from Skiles Howard, 'The Politics of Courtly Dancing' (unpub. PhD, University of Columbia, 1993), p. 26 ('the air was relentlessly penetrated') and p. 71. See also Skiles Howard, 'Rival discourses of dancing in early modern England', *Studies in English Literature* 36 (1996), 31–56. The essay invokes a standard constellation of male dancers dominating their female partners (p. 33); an exception is only granted to outstanding figures as 'patriarchal' queens, or characters of Greek mythology. For other works on female subjection in a courtly context, see Rudolf zur Lippe, *Naturbeherrschung am Menschen* (Frankfurt am Main, 1974, rev. edn 1981), II. Mark Franko offers a more sophisticated analysis in *Dance as Text: Ideologies of the Baroque Body* (Cambridge, 1993). Generally, such studies tend to read a Foucauldian scenario into contemporary dance sources at the expense of performance practice and historical fact.

14 Lucian, *Peri Orcheseos / The Dance*, ed. A. M. Harmon, 8 vols. (London, 1936), V, pp. 284–5.

15 Baldassare Castiglione, *The Book of the Courtier*, trans. Sir Thomas Hoby, ed. W. H. D. Rouse (London, 1928), p. 99, and on the exercises of the body, p. 189.

16 Castiglione, *The Book of the Courtier*, pp. 98–9. For an interpretation of Castiglione and gendered courtly dancing, see Jane Gingell's excellent paper 'Man and woman in dance: social and sexual functions of dances for men and women in 16th-century Italy, 17th-century Spain and 18th-century England', given at the conference *Europese Vereniging van Danshistorici: Man en Vrouw in de dans*, 2–4 November 1990, Leuven, Belgium.

17 Thomas Elyot, *The Book Named the Governor*, facs. edn (Menston, Yorks., 1970), fol. 83.
18 Prynne, *Histriomastix*, fol. 546v.
19 The early seventeenth-century dance treatises by François de Lauze and Bartholomew de Montagut mention the *busque du pourpoint*, a close-fitting sleeveless doublet with stays. In later usage, the term denotes primarily a woman's corset. I shall discuss these treatises later in this essay.
20 *Discoveries*, Herford and Simpson (eds.), *Ben Jonson*, VIII, p. 581; 'De mollibus & effeminatis', p. 607. I am grateful to Ian Donaldson for drawing my attention to this passage.
21 Samuel Butler, *Hudibras*, 'The Presbyterian Knight', lines 81–2. From Alastair Fowler (ed.), *The New Oxford Book of Seventeenth Century Verse* (Oxford, 1991), p. 497.
22 See Caroso's updated version of *Il Ballarino* (Venice, 1581), *Nobiltà di dame* (Venice, 1600); the latter edited by Julia Sutton (New York, 1995), p. 98, rule II.
23 De Lauze, *Apologie de la danse*, facs. edn (Geneva, 1977); Montagut's version represents in parts a pirated early draft of de Lauze's book, which was published in 1623; see Montagut, *Louange de la danse*, ed. Barbara Ravelhofer, in *Renaissance Texts from Manuscripts*, gen. ed. Jeremy Maule (Cambridge, forthcoming).
24 The most frequently quoted sources in research on masque dances are Caroso's *Il Ballarino* and *Nobiltà di dame*; Cesare Negri, *Le gratie d'amore* (Milan, 1602); Arbeau, *Orchésographie* (Lengres 1588, repr. 1589), all of them available in modern editions. For the connection between masque choreographies and Italian dance texts, see, among others, John C. Meagher, *Method and Meaning in Jonson's Masques* (Bloomington, IN, 1966), ch. 4; Judy Smith and Ian Gatiss, 'What did Prince Henry do with his feet on Sunday 19 August 1604?', *Early Music* 14.2 (May 1986), 199–207; Anne Daye, 'Skill and invention in the Renaissance ballroom', *Historical Dance* 2.6 (1988/91), 12–15. For English repertoire at the Inns of Court, see Ward, 'Newly devis'd measures'; an excellent general survey is provided in Peter Holman, *Four and Twenty Fiddlers: The Violin at the English Court, 1540–1690* (Oxford, 1993), and Walls, *Music in The English Courtly Masque*. On Renaissance gesture in general, see Anna Bryson, 'The rhetoric of status: gesture, demeanour and the image of the gentleman in sixteenth- and seventeenth-century England', in Lucy Gent and Nigel Llewellyn (eds.), *Renaissance Bodies: The Human Figure in English Culture, c. 1540–1660* (London, 1990), pp. 136–53.
25 For a fuller discussion, see Joan Wildeblood's introduction in her edition of the *Apologie de la danse* (London, 1952); David Buch (ed.), *Dance Music from the Ballets de Cour, 1575–1651: Historical Commentary, Source Study and Transcriptions from the Philidor Manuscripts* (Stuyvesant, 1993), pp. 9–11; Mône Dufour, 'Contribution à l'étude de *l'Apologie de la danse et la parfaite méthode de l'enseigner tant aux cavaliers qu'aux dames* (de Francis de Lauze, 1623)', *La Recherche en*

danse 4 (1986/87), 13–17; Magnus Blomkvist, 'François de Lauze und seine *Apologie de la danse* (1623)', in Sybille Dahms and Stephanie Schroedter (eds.), *Tanz und Bewegung in der barocken Oper*. Kongreßbericht Salzburg 1994 (Innsbruck, 1996), pp. 31–44; Montagut, *Louange de la danse*, Introduction.

26 *Certain Satires* (1598), III, 'Quedam et sunt, et videntur', in Arnold Davenport (ed.), *The Poems of John Marston* (Liverpool, 1961), p. 79, lines 69–71. It is not clear where the idiosyncracy of kissing one's hand before giving it to the partner originated. See my Introduction to Montagut, *Louange de la danse*.

27 Thomas Carew, *Coelum Britannicum*, in David Lindley (ed.), *Court Masques: Jacobean and Caroline Entertainments, 1605–1640* (Oxford, 1995), p. 170, lines 155–7.

28 Negri, *Le gratie d'amore*, p. 37: 'con le punte de' piedi in fuora', 'la punta delli piedi vn poco infuora, accioche le gambe, & le ginocchia stiano ben dritte'.

29 De Lauze and Montagut employ the *temps en rond*, for instance, in the chapter on the *courante reglée*. In the interpretation of the *temps en rond* I follow Lieven Baert and Dorothee Wortelboer, who kindly discussed with me the style in these two manuals.

30 Melusine Wood, *More Historical Dances* (London, 1956), p. 81. Wood suggests that this circular way of walking may have facilitated accommodating boots with their large brims as they were worn in this period. I think she was right in her assumption about the circular walking style. Her enthusiastic book is still worth reading for interesting details and sources; what she states about the masque, however, is entirely misconceived.

31 Arbeau in the edition by Julia Sutton and Mary Stewart Evans, *Orchésographie* (New York, 1967), p. 83.

32 Richard Brathwaite, *The English Gentlewoman* (London, 1631), has an illustration of this *congé* type performed by a courtier on the title page. The explanation follows on a folio attached.

33 Richard Brathwaite, *The English Gentleman* (London, 1630), p. 18.

34 *Ibid.*, p. 204.

35 *Ibid.*, pp. 63–70; p. 63 seems to be directed to the excesses of women, p. 70 reflects on men, p. 61 is addressed to both.

36 *Ibid.*, p. 75.

37 *Ibid.*, p. 82. Melusine Wood notes this passage in *More Historical Dances*, p. 81.

38 Brathwaite, *The English Gentlewoman*, p. 71.

39 Wood, *More Historical Dances*, p. 81. De Lauze says about the 'façon de cheminer toute grave & noble' that is is impossible to learn graceful walking without 'l'instruction que i'en donne' (*Apologie de la danse*, p. 27).

40 Brathwaite, *The English Gentlewoman*, p. 83. The original quotation is 'learned to pace'; the alteration in the main text does not change the meaning.

41 Prynne, *Histriomastix*, p. 202.

42 *The Masque of Blackness*, Herford and Simpson (eds.), *Ben Jonson*, VII, p. 173, line 121.

43 See also the standard works of Malcolm Smuts, *Court Culture and the Origin of a Royalist Tradition in Early Stuart England* (Philadelphia, 1987); Martin Butler, *Theatre and Crisis, 1632–1642* (Cambridge, 1984), and Kevin Sharpe, *Criticism and Compliment: The Politics of Literature in the England of Charles I* (Cambridge, 1987).

44 P. R. Seddon (ed.), *Letters of John Holles, 1587–1637*, 3 vols. (Nottingham, 1975), I, pp. 53–5, no. 136. 'Instructions for travel that my father gave me the 22 of July 1614, being to go over into France with Sir Thomas Edmunds Liedger ambassador there for his Majesty.' I am grateful to David Lindley for drawing my attention to this passage.

45 Carew, *Coelum Britannicum*, in Lindley (ed.), *Court Masques*, p. 188, lines 897–8.

46 Roger Ascham, *The Schoolmaster*, ed. John E. Mayor (New York, 1967), pp. 58–9. The 'first book teaching the bringing up of youth' recommends 'learning joined with pastimes', among these dancing, since 'learning should always be mingled with honest mirth and comely exercises'. Apparently, Ascham proposes an integrative model *avant la lettre* aimed at advancing morals as well as brains and health by an increased fun-factor.

47 Elyot, *The Book Named the Governor*, fol. 84v.

48 Winwood, *Memorials*, III, pp. 180–1; in Steven Orgel and Roy Strong (eds.), *Inigo Jones: The Theatre of the Stuart Court*, 2 vols. (London, 1973), I, p. 192.

49 The identification of the masquers is partly derived from the index of masquers in Lindley, *Court Masques*, pp. 272–281, partly from the *Dictonary of National Biography*. One of the 'influences', Lord Rich of Holland, is identified by Lindley as Henry Rich, the Earl of Holland (p. 276). A more likely candidate seems to be his son, twelve at the time, while the father would have been a forty-two-year-old dancer among children.

50 Anonymous translation from a Spanish eyewitness account of *Oberon*. See Sabol (ed.), *Four Hundred Songs*, Appendix A, and Historical Manuscripts Commission report on the manuscripts of the Marquess of Downshire (London, 1938), III: *The Papers of William Trumbull the Elder*, 1611–12, pp. 1–2.

51 Jean Knowlton, 'Some Dances of the Stuart Masques Identified and Analyzed', 2 vols. (unpub. PhD, University of Indiana, 1966), I, p. 65.

52 Lindley, index of masquers, *Court Masques*, pp. 272–81.

53 Letter from York House, 16 July 1623, GB-Lbl, MS Harl. 6987, no. 58(64), fols 119v–120 (142 crossed out). Joan Wildeblood cites the letter in her Introduction to the *Apologie de la danse* but does not provide a precise reference.

54 'The Contract', in Margaret Cavendish, *The Blazing World and Other Writings*, ed. Kate Lilley (Harmondsworth, 1994), p. 5. I am grateful to Anne Barton for this reference.

55 Cavendish, 'The Contract', p. 7.

56 Antonio Cornazano, *The Book on the Art of Dancing*, ed. M. Inglehearn and P. Forsyth (London, 1981), introduction.

57 J. M. L. [Jacob Lang?], *Kurtzer Entwurff/Eines anmuthigen/Kinder-Ballets* (Nürnberg, 1668). The ballet was presented at the occasion of the birth of a prince.

58 Smith and Gatiss, 'What did Prince Henry do with his feet on Sunday 19 August 1604?', pp. 199–207. See note 24.

59 De Lauze, *Apologie de la danse*, p. 26, and Montagut, *Louange de la danse*, fol. 12v.

60 Busino referred to a performance of Ben Jonson's *Pleasure Reconciled to Virtue* (1618): *Calendar of State Papers, Venetian*, xv, pp. 111–14; Herford and Simpson (eds.), *Ben Jonson*, x, pp. 580–4; Sabol (ed.), *Four Hundred Songs*, Appendix B, p. 545.

61 There would be an emphasis on spectacular male solo performances going along with certain restrictions on female dancers concerning more vigorous improvisations and jumps. A differentiated evaluation of such exclusion strategies exceeds, however, the scope of this discussion and will be attempted elsewhere.

62 *Tempe Restored*, p. 98, in Cedric C. Brown (ed.), *The Poems and Masques of Aurelian Townshend with Music by Henry Lawes and William Webb* (Reading, 1983).

63 *Dictionary of National Biography*.

64 *The Entertainment at Richmond* (Oxford, 1636), p. 27.

65 *Ibid.*, pp. 27–8.

66 On the political implications of *The Entertainment at Richmond*, see Martin Butler's analysis in 'Entertaining the Palatine Prince: plays on foreign affairs, 1635–1637', *English Literary Renaissance* 13 (1983), 319–44, in particular 338–41.

67 *The Entertainment at Richmond*, p. 20.

68 *Ibid.*, pp. 26–7.

69 As in Carew, *Coelum Britannicum*, p. 188.

70 *The Entertainment at Richmond*, p. 31.

71 Gingell, 'Man and woman in dance'. See note 16.

72 See his essay 'The gingerbread host' in this volume.

73 Richard Brathwaite, *The English Gentleman*, p. 4.

74 Townshend, *Tempe Restored*, p. 98.

75 *Ibid.*, p. 98.

CHAPTER 12

The politics of music in the masque

David Lindley

Scholarly attention devoted to music in the masque has tended either to concentrate on its role in the evolution of musical styles (especially as an antecedent of opera), or else to focus on its symbolic function as image of cosmic harmony.[1] The reason is not far to seek. Because music, as 'pure contraption', in Auden's phrase,[2] seems impossible to pin down to referential meaning, it is tempting either to focus upon the internal logic of musical language and the history of forms and styles, or else to retreat to general statements about the symbolic potential music carries, and fall with relief upon Renaissance notions of the music of the spheres reflected in *musica mundana*. In recent years, however, cultural historians have increasingly complicated our understanding of the ways in which music functions within society, and musicologists have begun to deploy strategies derived from literary and historical theorists to locate political significance in the workings of musical texts themselves. The possibility this offers for a more nuanced view of music's cultural function, and at the same time for close attention to political resonances in the musical vocabularies deployed in the masque, means that analysis of this, the least obviously political element in masque's performance, can appropriately be brought within the purview of a volume which sets out to explore the multiplicity of voices which contributed to the circulations of power enacted in and through the celebratory rituals of the Stuart court.

Music's referential indeterminacy was, of course, recognized in the early modern period. As Richard Hooker wrote, music 'is in truth most admirable, and doth much edify if not the understanding because it teacheth not, yet surely th'affection because it therein worketh much'.[3] Working upon the individual at the level of feeling, music has the power both to salve and to inflame. Robert Burton, for example, asserted on the one side that 'it is so powerful a thing that it ravisheth the soul, *regina sensuum*, the queen of the senses, by sweet pleasure (which is a happy cure), and corporal tunes pacify our incorporeal soul', but also argued on the other that it can be 'most pernicious . . . for music enchants, as Menander holds, it will make such melancholy persons mad'.[4] Or, as Hooker put it:

In harmony the very image and character even of virtue and vice is per- ceived, the mind delighted with their resemblances and brought by having them often iterated into a love of the things themselves. For which cause there is nothing more contagious and pestilent than some kinds of harmony; than some nothing more strong and potent unto good.[5]

Here Hooker is gesturing towards the consequences that the double potential of music has in the public as well as the private realm. Music incites and unites the crowd, whether in worship or revolt; it may celeb- rate the triumphs of state as well as the processional rituals of charivari. At the same time, he is reaching for a means of discrimination between different musics. For, as Jacques Attali observes: 'Music, the quintes- sential mass activity, like the crowd, is simultaneously a threat and a necessary source of legitimacy; trying to channel it is a risk that every system of power must run'.[6] Richard Leppert, in similar vein, writes that 'In hierarchical societies there cannot be one undifferentiated body of music. The musics that exist must be classified, and their differences must be articulated *in words*. Unclassified sound, sound- scape without the registration of difference, is the sonoric allowance of either democracy or anarchy'.[7] It is precisely the attempt to classify sound and to differentiate its positive and negative potentials that, in the early modern period, characterized arguments over the place of music in church, its function in popular culture, its perilous association with women and effeminacy – and also conditioned its deployment in the masque. In earlier treatments of the politics of the masque, as Martin Butler and others have stressed in previous essays in this vol- ume, it tended to be axiomatic that masques simply represented and enacted the ideology of the court. A major aim of this present book is to explore ways in which these courtly displays were engaged in more complex – and more anxious – processes of legitimation, and I will be arguing that music plays an interesting and ambiguous part in these processes precisely because of its inherent instability of signification and the complex ways in which it therefore functioned in the larger cultural scene.

There is, however, a difficulty which must first be confronted. One reason, perhaps, why music has commanded relatively little attention in treatment of the masque is simply that not much of it, comparatively, survives; there is no extant masque for which a complete musical score could be provided.[8] Even where they exist, the musical traces are difficult to interpret. Dance tunes simply called 'The Prince's Masque', for example, might be attached to any number of different masques. Furthermore, the music, both for dance and song, is often preserved only as a melody with bass line, or else arranged in three or four parts, and this gives very little sense of how it might have sounded when orchestrated for the full resources of the King's Music. Yet that sound was itself very much part of the statement the music was making. Up to 100 musicians, it would seem from Bulstrode Whitelocke's account of James Shirley's *The Triumph of Peace* (1634),[9] might have been employed, an ensemble only possible at court, and making therefore a significant contribution to the assertion of royal magnificence which, according to Jonson, 'rightly becomes' the personages for and by whom the masques were presented.[10] If one listens to a modern reconstruction such as that by Jakob Lindberg and fellow-lutenists on the recording *Three, Four and Twenty Lutes*,[11] where Robert Johnson's 'Three Masque Dances' are scored for the full band, then to our amplifier-deafened ears the sound might be nothing special – just Caliban's 'twangling instruments'[12] – but to the Jacobean audience its opulence, together with the visual spectacle it offered, must have been remarkable.

Problematic though it is to reconstruct the actual sound-world of the masque, enough survives in musical score and in cues and descriptions within the masque texts for it to be clear that there was frequent effort to discriminate and distinguish between different musical kinds. The discordant, libidinous voices of the antimasque, discussed in Hugh Craig's essay earlier in this volume, might be characterized in part by the instruments associated with them. In *Pan's Anniversary* (1621), for example, the disruptive Boetians are accompanied by a tinker who 'beats the march to the tune of "ticklefoot, pam, pam, pam" ' (p. 310), upon a tinging kettle which immediately invokes the 'rough music' of the charivari, and in *Britannia Triumphans* (1638), the First Entry 'of a mock music of five persons' is played by a viol, a tabor and pipe, knackers and bells, tongs and key, gridiron and shoeing horn.[13] In Whitelocke's account of the procession through the streets which acted as a prelude to *The Triumph of Peace*, instrumentation (which is not specified in the printed text) includes 'music of keys and tongues and the like' associated with the antimasque of beggars and 'bagpipes, hornpipes and such kind of Northern music, speaking the following antimasque of Projectors to be of the Scotch and Northern quarters'. (This last, indeed, gives

a political pointedness and specificity to the satire that the published
text of the masque suppresses.) The clear demarcation of musical ter-
rain is evident in Whitelocke's contrasting of these antimasquers with
the Gentlemen who 'had their music, about a dozen of the best trumpeters proper for them'.[14]

That sense of 'proper' music is continued at the moment of transition from antimasque to masque, which was frequently signalled by
'the loud music'. In *The Masque of Queens* (1609), for example, 'In the
heat of their [the Witches'] dance on the sudden was heard a sound of
loud music, as if many instruments had made one blast; with which
not only the hags themselves but the hell into which they ran quite
vanished, and the whole face of the scene altered' (p. 134). At one level,
it is the simple physical shock of the sound which drives away the
witches. Iconologically, however, the 'loud music', perhaps performed
by trumpets and drums, or else by sackbuts (trombones), hautboys
(oboes) and cornets,[15] conventionally signifies martial masculinity, here
opposed to the female transgression of the witches. But, as Whitelocke's
comment indicates, it was also associated with the upper classes, and
particularly with the ceremonies of royalty.[16] The loud music at this
moment of transition is therefore appropriate in several different ways
to the introduction of the masquers, who, though women, led by the
Queen, are defined by heroic, martial virtues. The demarcation of
worlds by such 'loud music' persists throughout the masque's history;
even in the more complex arrangement of *The Triumph of Peace*, for
example, 'Here with loud music the masquers descend'.[17] But the association of the loudest sound with royalty is evident even before the
antimasque became fixed, as when in Thomas Campion's *Lord Hay's
Masque* (1607), three consorts of instruments and sundry singers, hitherto playing as separate and distinct groups, unite for the first time to
set words of praise to King James.[18]

If differentiation was achieved in part through instrumentation, the
courtliness of the masque proper was also marked by songs which were
increasingly influenced by a declamatory musical vocabulary, stylistic-
ally 'new' and sophisticated.[19] Such songs characteristically avoid simple
tunefulness, are rhythmically irregular and often of extended vocal
range, thus marking themselves off clearly from antimasque songs, sometimes characterized as 'ballads', associated with the rude and popular,
and presumably rhythmically emphatic and melodically limited in range.
Very few antimasque songs survive (and many antimasques contain no
songs), but the difference is clear from comparison of examples 1 and 2:

Example 1 Alfonso Ferrabosco, *Oberon*

Example 2 Robert Johnson, *Gypsies Metamorphosed*

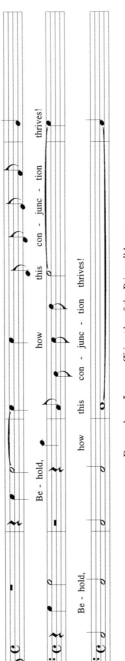

Example 3 Lawes, *Triumphs of the Prince d'Amour*

In setting the lyrics it was certainly possible for a composer to accommodate musical detail to illustrate and thereby reinforce the political message of a particular entertainment. Davenant's *The Triumphs of the Prince D'Amour* was offered early in 1635 by the Inns of Court to Princes Charles and Rupert, the two sons of the Elector Palatine, who had arrived late the year before to solicit Charles's restoration to the Palatinate. Davenant apologised to readers of the printed text that the work had been hastily prepared, but none the less the masque seems designed to control and deflate the incitement to warlike action in Europe which their visit might threaten to arouse. The work introduces first the Priests of Mars, who celebrate warlike behaviour; they are followed by Priests of Venus, urging a surrender of bellicose instincts to the charms of love, and then by the Priests of Apollo, who reconcile the opposed forces under the ægis of wisdom. In the song which ends the masque proper William Lawes neatly marries musical language to political address. The reconcilement of Venus and Mars is celebrated by the Priests of Apollo in the song 'Behold how this conjunction thrives', and each section of the song begins with a canonic passage enacting the conjunction of which they speak (example 3). After the banquet which followed the presentation of gifts to the princes, a Valediction recapitulated the movement of the masque as a whole. Here a solo priest of Mars gives place to a duet of Venus's priests, and finally to an Apollonian trio. Each section, as is usual, concludes with a chorus, and the final words pray: 'May our three gods so long conjoin / To raise your soul and rarify your sense'.[20] The variation of style between the three sections illustrates the nature of the three gods, as is evident in the incipits given in example 4, while the gradual build-up of the number of singers embodies the moral and political statement that the work is aiming to inculcate.

Thus far it might seem that it is a comparatively unproblematic task to see the masque as a dialectical form in which the virtues of courtly civility surmount or contain the subversive energies of the disruptive antimasques, and to claim that this dialectic is enacted through differentiation of musical codes. But such a reading, however tempting, is scarcely adequate. In a number of different ways the music of the masque served rather to complicate than to clarify such distinctions.

In the first place, musical codes themselves are always inherently slippery, and particularly so in the early modern period, when composers might construct elaborate sets of keyboard variations on popular song tunes,[21] or write airs which imitated popular styles,[22] or when

Example 4 Lawes, *Triumphs of the Prince d'Amour*

ballads might be set to versions of courtly airs, or, conversely, when John Dowland's *Lacrimae* was well-enough known to be referred to in passing in a number of dramas for the popular stage.[23] Ballads might be symptomatic of the 'popular', as they are in *Neptune's Triumph* (1624) where the Poet dismisses 'th'abortive and extemporal din / Of balladry' (p. 414); but in *Christmas His Masque* (1616) they stand for the warm-hearted affection of the populace as against stiff-necked Puritan attempts to banish such festivity. Furthermore, when one looks at the collections of surviving dance tunes for the masque, it is frequently difficult to be sure that one could distinguish a tune labelled 'antimasque' from a 'masque' dance on musical grounds alone. Indeed, as John M. Ward has demonstrated, the music for the specially choreographed masquers' dances were probably put together from the dancing-master's repertory of conventional motifs.[24] Even the 'loud music' could be transformed into an image of dangerous violence, as it is in *The Golden Age Restored*, where the antimasque of the Iron Age is accompanied by 'two drums, trumpets and a confusion of martial music' (p. 226). The difficulty is precisely that the polemic direction is given by words and surrounding actions, rather than necessitated by musical language itself.

Milton's *Comus* struggles effortfully with the problem of maintaining musical distinctions, especially with the difficulty of 'placing' rural music. Early in the masque the Attendant Spirit disguises himself as a conventional swain 'Who with his soft pipe, and smooth-dittied song, / Well knows to still the wild winds when they roar'.[25] Yet the Lady subsequently hears Comus's revelry as

> the sound
> Of riot, and ill-managed merriment,
> Such as the jocund flute, or gamesome pipe
> Stirs up among the loose unlettered hinds
> When for their teeming flocks, and granges full
> In wanton dance they praise the bounteous Pan.
>
> (lines 170–5)

The pipe is the same, but the effect is quite opposite; only Milton's adjectival urging forces a distinction. Later in the masque, celebrating shepherds acquire a positive colouration when the Attendant Spirit includes in his description of Sabrina's benign power an invocation of 'the shepherds at their festivals' who 'Carol her goodness loud in rustic lays' (lines 846–7). But then, in a further twist, a troupe of 'Country

Dancers' are permitted to do homage at Bridgewater's festival, but, their dance over, they are condescendingly dismissed:

> Back, shepherds, back, enough your play
> Till next sunshine holiday,
> Here be without duck or nod
> Other trippings to be trod
> Of lighter toes, and such court guise
> As Mercury did first devise.   (lines 957–62)

Thus do the musical markers of social class and moral probity slip and slide in this masque. The problem is embodied in the person of Henry Lawes himself, the actor of the role of Attendant Spirit and at the same time the composer of the music of the masque. He is disguised as a shepherd, but employs a musical language in the masque's surviving songs which is emphatically removed from the taint of the popular.

The second complication of an easy compartmentalization of musics follows from the aestheticisation of the figures of the vices in the antimasques, and their enactment by accomplished performers. This opens up the possibility of a response to the spectacle in which an audience's pleasure in their performance clouds the clarity of moral distinction. In *Salmacida Spolia* (1640), for example, an elaborate series of twenty entries concludes with the comment: 'All which antimasques were well set out and excellently danced, and the tunes fitted to the persons'.[26] But even in *The Masque of Queens*, where demarcation would seem to be absolute, there is an overlap between the description of the dances of Witches and Queens. The Witches 'fell into a magical dance, full of preposterous change and gesticulation . . . excellently imitated by the maker of the dance, Master Hierome Herne' (p. 134), whereas the Queens' two dances are described as 'right curious, and full of subtle and excellent changes, and seemed performed with no less spirits than of those they personated' (pp. 139–40). The aesthetic desideratum of 'variety' is common to both performances, and the pleasure to be taken in them by the audience is therefore curiously similar. The closeness of masque and antimasque in this respect is signalled in *The Triumph of Peace*, where the first antimasque figures presented are of Madame Novelty and Signior Fancy, who themselves debate the appeal of antimasques. Though they are presented satirically, mocking those for whom masques are merely superficial display, the qualities they represent are not far removed from those of invention and imagination upon which the masque prided itself. Indeed, as we have seen, it is precisely the novelty of musical style in the songs of the masques that

is the ground upon which they are distinguished from the 'rough'
or 'popular'. In general terms, then, the complicity of an audience's
delight in the spectacles of strangeness of the antimasques carries an
inherently subversive potential.

This becomes clear later in *The Triumph of Peace*, when, after the
entry of the masquers, the action is interrupted by a band of figures representing those who had been instrumental in putting on the
night's performance, including, for example, a Carpenter, a Painter and
a Tailor. This disruption of conventional form carries direct political
implication,[27] but for present purposes what is significant is that, embar-
rassed, the Tailor suggests that

> 'tis our best course to dance a figary ourselves, and then they'll think it a piece
> of the plot, and we may go off again with the more credit (we may else kiss
> the porter's lodge for't). Let's put a trick upon 'em in revenge, 'twill seem a
> new device too.

In order for this device to work, the Tailor must hope 'the musicians
knew but our minds now'. Fortunately the musicians comply, and
'the violins play', allowing the antimasque to 'go off cleanly'.[28] It is a
moment rich in implication. By converting themselves into an aesthetic
spectacle, diverting thereby the laughter and scorn of the audience,
these characters defuse the threat they offer to courtly exclusivity. The
music, which the royal musicians already know, becomes a means,
therefore, not of dramatizing their natures as disruptive figures, but
of controlling them and of conditioning the response to them. From
a New Historicist perspective this might seem only too obviously to
enact the ways in which the court masque operates to contain the
subversion it itself calls into being. But at the same time, I would
suggest, the episode registers something of the masque's omnipresent
anxiety about its own legitimacy.

A striking example of this anxiety, and its registration in and through
music, is offered by *Lovers Made Men* (1617). In the fiction of this work
(presented at the house of Lord Hay to the French Ambassador) there
are no separate antimasque characters; instead the masquers are first
characterized as misled and drowned by love, and play out an 'antimasque in several gestures, as they lived in love' (p. 259). They are
healed by Mercury's order that they 'bow unto the reverend lake' of
forgetful Lethe and thus become 'themselves again', and 'dance forth
their entry'. Cupid then appears, claiming that 'these are the motions
I would see' (p. 260), but Mercury sternly enjoins them:

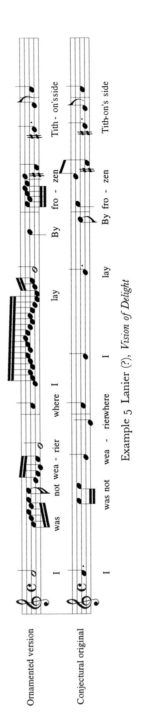

Example 5 Lanier (?), *Vision of Delight*

Look, look unto this snaky rod,
And stop your ears against the charming god;
His every word falls from him is a snare:
Who have so lately known him should beware.

(pp. 260–1)

But after their 'main dance' Cupid points out that to follow Mercury's prescription would disqualify them from completing the necessary ritual of the masque by taking out the ladies in the communal dances:

Come, do not call it Cupid's crime
    You were thought dead before your time.
If thus you move to Hermes' will
    Alone, you will be thought so still.
Go, take the ladies forth, and talk,
    And touch, and taste too: ghosts can walk.
'Twixt eyes, tongues, hands, the mutual strife
    Is bred that tries the truth of life.
They do indeed like dead men move
    That think they live, and not in love! (p. 261)

Mercury must finally be content to let the masquers remain as virtuous lovers.

Lovers Made Men, in thus celebrating the redirecting of Love to virtuous ends, was engaged in an attempt to ward off the criticism of masques as wanton, lascivious and intemperate so frequently made by the court's opponents.[29] In this work it is essential to the argument that masque and antimasque should not be opposed in dialectical fashion, but seen as a process of redefinition. (In this respect its structure is very like Campion's earlier *Lord Hay's Masque*, where the narrative is one of reformation.) The music may have contributed significantly to this blurring of boundaries. In the 1640 folio (though not the 1617 Quarto) the *whole* of the work, including the antimasque, is reported as having been 'sung (after the Italian manner) *stylo recitativo* by Master Nicholas Lanier'.[30] The uniformity of musical surface this must have produced in performance leads Mary Chan to observe that the music was 'simply decorative' and 'could have had no mythic or symbolic function'.[31] But the very absence of overt musical contrast at this level paradoxically highlights the problematic nature of such elaborate and novel musical style in the relationship it generates between the audience and the masque as a whole.

For the declamatory style anticipated a manner of performance in which the singer improvised elaborate embellishment upon the spare vocal line, as may be seen in example 5. There are two major

implications of this musical practice. First, such elaborate ornamentation must have drawn attention to the virtuoso, individual nature of
the singer's performance. The masque is a genre which is usually
assumed to have asserted and celebrated a collective courtly identity,
but it was also a site of individual competition. Buckingham's exploits
as a dancer, for example (as in his well-known rescue of the performance of *Pleasure Reconciled to Virtue*) did him no harm in his pursuit of
courtly favour. (Tom Bishop, in his essay earlier in this volume, has
made a similar argument for the performative importance of the dancer
as a way of indicating whose political agenda was on display, especially
when Prince Henry danced in *Oberon* in 1611.) Though the musicians
who sang, like the actors who most often spoke the lines, were unambiguously servants, yet the conspicuous individuality of their virtuoso
performance might threaten to disturb the collectivity of the masque's
statement. It is significant, therefore, that very frequently songs in
masques are structured as solos with chorus. This structure is characteristic, for example, of the great majority of William Lawes's surviving
songs, where a dance-like sinfonia gives way to a declamatory solo,
which in turn is gathered in by choruses of generally straightforward
texture. It is also the pattern of Dowland's lovely songs composed for a
now lost entertainment, and included in *A Pilgrim's Solace* (1612).[32] The
way so many songs subsume the individuality of the solo singer into
the corporate identity of the chorus may be seen as a taming of music's
individualizing danger.

Secondly, recitative style and an elaborate singerly performance were
unambiguous markers of sophistication. In Campion's *Caversham Entertainment* (1613), as Queen Anne proceeded through the park she was
greeted by a series of scenes and songs, each more musically sophisticated than the last, until finally, when she arrived 'near the house, this
song was sung by an excellent countertenor voice, with rare variety of
division [embellishment] unto two unusual instruments'.[33] Yet to Puritan
opponents it was precisely such a style, ornamented by divisions and
trills, which seemed most to embody the dangerous potential of music.
William Prynne, for example, argued that

Modest and chaste harmonies are to be admitted by removing as far as may
be all soft effeminate music from our strong and valiant cogitation, which
using a dishonest art of warbling the voice, do lead to a delicate and slothful
kind of life. Therefore, chromatical harmonies are to be left to impudent
malapertness, to whorish music crowned with flowers.[34]

In such a context, the novelty of musical style which Lanier employed to characterize and to dignify the purification of desire dramatized by *Lovers Made Men* might serve only to confirm, even to intensify, the very qualities of the court masque which most incensed its critics.

The particular association Prynne makes here between music and effeminacy was, of course, a staple ingredient of Puritan censure both of certain kinds of music and of the masque itself. The appeal of music to the senses, its capacity either to elevate or to corrupt, was readily mapped onto conventional perceptions of womankind.[35] The distinction which Prynne offers between 'masculine' and 'feminine' harmonies ultimately looks back to Greek attempts to attribute distinct qualities to the different modes – theories that continued to circulate even after the modal basis of Greek music had long passed into oblivion. But the whole issue of music and effeminacy was confronted daringly and directly in Aurelian Townshend's *Tempe Restored* (1632). The masque begins with a song of Circe in a rage for the loss of her lover, which is answered by the female figure of Harmony as a prelude to the introduction of the Queen as Divine Beauty. There is some distinction made between the character of the first two women in the nature of the lyrics they sing. Circe begins:

> Dissembling traitor, now I see the cause
> Of all thy fawning was but to be free.
> 'Twas not for nothing thou hadst teeth and claws,
> For thou hast made a cruel prey of me.[36]

It is a song of individual feeling (though contained by choral comments of a moralizing kind by 'Her four Nymphs'). Harmony, by contrast, begins:

> Not as myself, but as the brightest star
> That shines in heaven, come to reign this day;
> And these the beams and influences are
> Of constellations . . .[37]

The difference between music as expressive of individual appetite in the first, but of an abstract celestial harmony in the second, is plain enough. What makes this masque particularly interesting, however, is that these two roles were taken by women: Madame Coniack and Mistress Shepherd, the first female singer/actresses to take part in public performance.[38] It would seem highly unlikely that the musical language of the two songs would have been very different; both are structured as an air and chorus, and, in the allegory appended to the

masque, we read of the 'sweetness of her [Circe's] voice'. The dangerous allure of effeminising music is thus powerfully and physically present
in the masque, and, we must imagine, working too upon the spectators,
especially because of the novelty of women singing.[39]

The fiction of the masque goes some way to containing the danger.
The brutish love that Circe inspires is contrasted with the admiration
inspired by Divine Beauty (represented by the Queen) which in turn is
placed under the direction of the rational Heroic Virtue represented
by the King. Indeed, masculine control is implied throughout, from
the figures painted on the scene – a female Invention, but a masculine
Knowledge – through the appearance of a male singer (Lanier once
more) as 'The Highest Sphere' to the introduction of Jupiter as the
final agent of harmony. But in theatrical terms the biggest surprise was
the female singers, and the central spectacle on which Jones lavished
all his art surrounded and celebrated the Queen. It was in the year of
this masque that Prynne published *Histriomastix* with its attack upon
the Queen's theatricals and upon the effeminacy of music and dancing.
It is surely the case that the insinuating song of Circe not only enacts
a subversive gesture that the work as a whole fails quite to subdue, but
also that it embodies a wider cultural uncertainty and anxiety about
the power of music, which could function as an expression of larger
political and moral anxieties.

It is not surprising, then, that as the Queen descended, an attempt is
made to confine and define the limits of musical power. The Chorus
tells the audience:

> The music that ye hear is dull,
> But that ye see is sweet indeed,
> In every part exact and full,
> From whence there doth an air proceed,
> On which th'Intelligences feed,
> Where fair and good, inseperably conjoined
> Create a Cupid, that is never blind.[40]

Just as the chaste and rational married love of the Queen and King
redirects and thereby ratifies sensual appetite, so the contemplation of
the beauty of the Queen herself translates and thereby subdues music's
subversive potential. Townshend's strategy in this song raises one of
the most fundamental questions about the deployment of music in the
masque – its co-option in the symbolism of the monarchical state.

It has, of course, been a commonplace of Renaissance musical criticism for many years to observe that music's authority was sanctioned

through an assertion of the correspondence between earthly music and the heavenly music of the spheres. Just as God had created the world through number, weight and measure, so the earthly musician, in shadowing that consonance, both brought down the heavenly power to earth and lifted up the earthly listener to divine contemplation. So long as this belief had a quasi-scientific status it invested the power to move specifically in the music itself.[41] The job of the masque musician in this context can be seen as harnessing the educative and curative properties that music derives from its heavenly affinity, and bringing them down to earth in the ceremonious masque.

Campion's *The Lord Hay's Masque* embodies precisely this doctrine. At the beginning of the masque, music initiates the disclosure of the scene; it later enables the trees in which the Knights of Apollo have been imprisoned to dance by its solemn enchantment, and then draws on specifically religious associations in the 'solemn motet' which accompanies the tribute paid by the masquers to the tree of Diana. So too, the disposition of the musical ensembles suits with the masque's number symbolism, in which everything is organized in threes. Music's power to work upon its audience in this masque derives from a heavenly authority which lies outside the political system which the masque is celebrating. The musical climax, when the musicians unite in praise of James, is made as an offering to him in a masque of which he remains the privileged spectator (and in which he is offered advice). Just as the imprisoned nobles are freed by talismanic magic which calls down the power of the moon, so this celebratory music works to educate its hearers, including the monarch, through its reflection of a celestial order.

As the masque evolves, however, the power of music is increasingly subordinated to, and seen as a reflection of, royal power. In part this is enabled by the terms in which royal authority itself is explicated. James's address to his 1610 Parliament, one of the most familiar articulations of his theory of kingship, contains the following assertion:

Kings are justly called gods, for that they exercise a manner or resemblance of divine power upon earth: for if you will consider the attributes to God, you shall see how they agree in the person of a king. God hath power to create, or destroy, make or unmake . . . and to God are both soul and body due. And the like power have kings: they make and unmake their subjects . . . And to the king is due both the affection of the soul, and the service of the body of his subjects.[42]

Both James's speech and the traditional terminology used to describe music's efficacy are sustained by a correspondence between divine and human worlds. The crucial ideological elision that the King performs in suggesting that power is maintained by the due return of the 'affection of the soul',[43] echoes the conventional view of music's capacity to solicit the affections of its hearers and move the body to respond by the 'heavenly' power implanted in it. But if this overlap enabled music's co-option, developments in musical theory threatened at the same time to unpick the seamless correspondence.

For, as Gretchen Finney and John Hollander amongst others demonstrate,[44] the undermining of the scientific status of Greek cosmology turned the 'music of the spheres' into an increasingly empty image, and relocated the source of music's persuasive power in a rhetorical model of affective persuasion. The consequences of this shift are far-reaching, raising troubling questions about the validating source of music's effect. It is in the uncertain area between an increasingly absolutist theory of monarchical power and a growing sense of the rhetorical sources of musical effect that masques increasingly operate.

Something of the nature of this change can be seen in the way in which Campion's 1613 entertainment, *The Lords' Masque* (discussed in David Bevington's essay above, as a reflection of royal will) differs from his earlier work. At its opening, when Orpheus, that most potent figure of music's symbolic power, calls for music to charm Mania from 'her earthy den', she responds:

> What powerful noise is this importunes me
> T'abandon darkness which my humour fits?
> Jove's hand in it I feel, and ever he
> Must be obeyed, ev'n of the frantic'st wits.[45]

Jove here stands for James, and so, right at the beginning of the masque, the power of music is identified with the political power of the King. The identification continues as Orpheus speaks of the way in which

> ... Jove into our music will inspire
> The power of passion, that their thoughts shall bend
> To any form or motion we intend.

Throughout this masque the source of the rhetorical power of music is identified as Jove/James. Jove controls every detail of the masque, and the means of his control are, in major part, musical. For the audience, then, the power of the King to command the affections of his subjects is represented in the 'naturally given' power of music to direct the affections both of the participants in and the audience of the masque.

In Jonson's *Irish Masque at Court*, performed in December 1613, and again in January 1614, the monarch's dictation is even more obvious. The central device of this work is the arrival of Irish Lords to do honour to the marriage of Frances Howard and Robert Carr. Their first dance is performed dressed in Irish mantles to the Irish music of harps. After this dance a gentleman summons the Irish bard:

> Advance, immortal bard, come up and view
> The gladding face of that great king in whom
> So many prophecies of thine are knit.
> This is that James of which long since thou sung'st
> Should end our country's most unnatural broils;
> And if her ear, then deafened with the drum,
> Would stoop but to the music of his peace,
> She need not with the spheres change harmony.
> . . . . . .
>
> Sing then some charm, made from his present looks,
> That may assure thy former prophecies.   (p. 211)

Transformation is here made possible, not through the power of music in itself, but through the power of the King, for which the music stands merely as metaphor. Indeed, the music of James's peace renders the music of the spheres irrelevant, so dethroned is the old 'science' of music's power. Very much the same image is employed in *Pan's Anniversary*, where the audience is informed that the figure of James/ Pan 'From his loud music all your manners wrought, / And made your commonwealth a harmony' (p. 313). The monarch is not simply offered a musical tribute; he (or she) is represented as in effect writing the tunes. The political implication of this shift is powerfully registered in *The Tempest*, where Prospero angrily remembers that his brother 'set all hearts i'th' state / To what tune pleased his ear' (1.2.84–5). Here, as pervasively throughout the play, the power of music is asserted, but our attention is drawn at the same time to its manipulable and shaky authority.[46]

It is perhaps not surprising that Milton, musician as he was, should have meditated on the question of the source of music's authority in his masque. When Comus responds to the Lady's singing of 'Sweet Echo' he says:

> Can any mortal mixture of earth's mould
> Breathe such divine enchanting ravishment?
> Sure something holy lodges in that breast,
> And with these raptures moves the vocal air
> To testify his hidden residence;   (lines 243–7)

The Lady's singing is compared to that of his mother Circe and the sirens, which itself had Orphic power to charm Scylla and Charybdis to quietness. As Gretchen Finney observes: 'The difference in effect does not derive from the relations of earthly music to divine, or even from differences in musical modes – Phrygian, Dorian or Lydian – but from the character and emotion of the singer'.[47] This moment typifies the drift of the masque as a whole, which is to sidestep the conventional agency of the monarch or noble masquers in generating moral transformation.[48]

In the masque at court the old Neoplatonic resonances of music were still being employed albeit with increasing strain. *Salmacida Spolia*, that last attempt to bring together jarring faction,[49] ends with a by now familiar coercive version of musical symbolism:

> So musical as to all ears
> Doth seem the music of the spheres,
> Are you unto each other still,
> Tuning your thoughts to either's will.
>
> All that are harsh, all that are rude,
> Are by your harmony subdued;
> Yet so into obedience wrought,
> As if not forced to it, but taught.[50]

The masque sought, by its foundation in antiquity and solid learning, to validate the symbolic authority of the monarch; but even as the musical medium through which it so significantly worked came to be seen as fundamentally rhetorical in its effect, so the kingly power it celebrated was shortly to be exposed for the rhetoric it was. There is a poignancy in the 'As if' of this, the final song of the final masque performed at court.

Whilst the music of the masques, throughout the life of the genre, participated in their effort of courtly self-validation, its inherent instability of signification also embodied and enacted many of the ambiguities and ideological tensions that always threatened to disrupt that project. As Edward Said observes, 'the transgressive element in music is its nomadic ability to attach itself to, and become a part of, social formations, to vary its articulations and rhetoric depending on the occasion as well as the audience'.[51] It is precisely because of music's immediate solicitation of feeling and eliciting of response, its resistance to single referential meaning, that its political workings could never, quite, be fixed.

NOTES

1 A significant exception is Peter Walls, *Music in the English Courtly Masque, 1604–1640* (Oxford, 1996), which appeared after this essay was largely completed, and adds enormously to the discussion of masque music, its performers, composers and practices. Its focus, however, is very different from that offered in this essay.

2 *W. H. Auden: Collected Poems*, ed. Edward Mendelson (London, 1976), 'The Composer', p. 148, line 7.

3 *Laws*, 5.38, in *The Folger Library Edition of the Works of Richard Hooker*, ed. W. Speed Hill, 6 vols. (Cambridge, MA, 1977–93), II, p. 153.

4 Robert Burton, *The Anatomy of Melancholy*, ed. Nicholar K. Keisling, Thomas C. Faulkner and Rhoda L. Blair, 3 vols. (Oxford, 1994), II, pp. 113–14.

5 Hooker, *Laws*, 38.1, in *Works*, II, p. 151.

6 Jacques Attali, *Noise: The Political Economy of Music*, trans. Brian Massumi (Manchester, 1985), p. 19.

7 Richard Leppert, *The Sight of Sound: Music, Representation, and the History of the Body* (Berkeley, 1993), p. 28.

8 The most comprehensive published source for the music of the masque is Andrew J. Sabol (ed.), *Four Hundred Songs and Dances from the Stuart Masque* (Providence, RI, 1978), but it is not complete, and many of its ascriptions of pieces to particular masques are open to question. See also Murray Lefkowitz (ed.), *Trois Masques à la Cour de Charles I* (Paris, 1970), and Sabol's attempted recreation of a full score for Campion's *The Lords' Masque* (Hanover, NH, 1993).

9 Murray Lefkowitz, *William Lawes* (London, 1960), p. 209. This number was probably exceptional, though Campion speaks in *The Lord Hay's Masque* of forty-two musicians.

10 *Hymenaei*, in Stephen Orgel (ed.), *Ben Jonson: The Complete Masques* (New Haven, 1969), p. 75. All subsequent references to Jonson's masques are to this edition, and given in the body of the text.

11 BIS CD341 1985/6.

12 *The Tempest*, 3.2.139 (it is possible that Caliban may be recalling precisely this courtly sound).

13 Stephen Orgel and Roy Strong, *Inigo Jones: The Theatre of the Stuart Court*, 2 vols. (London, 1973), II, p. 664.

14 *Ibid.*, p. 541.

15 Walls comments that 'it is not easy to say exactly how the "loud music" would have been constituted on a particular occasion' though suggests it could have been drawn from the sackbuts, oboes and cornetts (*Music in the Courtly Masque*, p. 152).

16 There were more trumpeters in the King's Music than any other kind of musician, and it would seem that they travelled everywhere with the monarch.

17 Orgel and Strong, *Inigo Jones*, II, p. 552.

18 David Lindley (ed.), *Court Masques* (Oxford, 1995), p. 30.

19 For discussion of the declamatory style, see Ian Spink, *English Song: Dowland to Purcell* (London, 1974), pp. 38–71; John Duffy, *The Songs and Motets of Alfonso Ferrabosco the Younger* (Ann Arbor, 1980); Elise Bickford Jorgens, *The Well-Tun'd Word: Musical Interpretations of English Poetry, 1507–1651* (Minneapolis, 1982), pp. 173–89; and Walls, *English Courtly Masque*, ch. 2. The term 'declamatory air' is something of an imprecise catch-all covering a range of musical styles, but it is convenient shorthand in the context of this essay.

20 Sabol (ed.), *Songs and Dances*, pp. 139–46.

21 See, for example, many sets of variations on popular tunes in *The Fitzwilliam Virginal Book*, ed. J. A. Fuller Maitland and W. Barclay Squire (repr. New York, 1963).

22 See David Lindley, *Thomas Campion* (Leiden, 1986), pp. 74–6.

23 See Diana Poulton, *John Dowland*, second edn (London, 1982), pp. 131–3, 143.

24 John M. Ward, 'Newly devis'd measure for Jacobean masques', *Acta Musicologica* 60 (1988), pp. 111–42.

25 *A Masque Presented at Ludlow Castle*, in John Carey and Alastair Fowler (eds.), *The Poems of John Milton* (London, 1968), lines 86–7.

26 Orgel and Strong, *Inigo Jones*, II, p. 732.

27 See Martin Butler, 'Politics and the masque: *The Triumph of Peace*', *The Seventeenth Century* 2 (1987), p. 133.

28 Orgel and Strong, *Inigo Jones*, II, pp. 552–3.

29 Its effort was reduplicated in the much more complex *Pleasure Reconciled to Virtue*, performed at court the following year.

30 McDonald Emslie, in 'Nicholas Lanier's innovations in English song', *Music and Letters* 41 (1960), 13–27, suggested that the fact that the description only appeared in the later printing casts serious doubt upon whether recitative was in fact used. Walls, however, has persuasively argued that at the very least the settings must have 'resembled extended declamatory dialogues' (*Music in the Courtly Masque*, pp. 89–95).

31 Mary Chan, *Music in the Theatre of Ben Jonson* (Oxford, 1980), p. 274.

32 The songs are 'Up Merry Mates', 'Welcome, Black Night' and 'Cease These False Sports'. They may have been performed at a wedding masque for Lord Howard de Walden in 1611. See Edward Doughtie (ed.), *Lyrics from English Airs, 1596–1622* (Cambridge, MA, 1970), pp. 411–12, 617–18, and Diana Poulton, *John Dowland*, pp. 311–14.

33 Lindley (ed.), *Court Masques*, p. 97. See also Lindley, *Campion*, pp. 211–16. Unfortunately, as so often, no music survives.

34 William Prynne, *Histriomastix* (London, 1633), p. 275.

35 For detailed consideration of this process see two articles by Linda Phyllis Austern, ' "Sing again syren": the female musician and sexual enchantment in Elizabethan life and literature', *Renaissance Quarterly* 42 (1989), 420–48, and ' "Alluring the auditorie to effeminacie": music and the idea of the feminine in early modern England', *Music and Letters* 74 (1993), 343–54.

36 Lindley (ed.), *Court Masques*, p. 157.

37 *Ibid.*, p. 159.

38 For a discussion of this event from a rather different feminist perspective, see Suzanne Gossett, '"Man-maid be gone": women in masques', *English Literary Renaissance* 18 (1988), 96–113. Little is known of either of these performers; Roy Booth persuasively suggests that Madam Coniack is the subject of Thomas Randolph's poem 'Upon a very deformed gentlewoman, but of a voice incomparable sweet' ('The first female professional singers: Madam Coniack', *Notes and Queries* 242 (1997), 533.

39 That women performed and sang in private entertainments is well-known. Aurelian Townshend, indeed, wrote a poem (set by Henry Lawes) 'On Hearing Her Majesty Sing'.

40 Lindley (ed.), *Court Masques*, p. 161.

41 See Frances Yates, *The French Academies of the Sixteenth Century* (London, 1947), ch. 11, for the application of these ideas to French court entertainments.

42 Johann P. Sommerville (ed.), *King James VI and I: Political Writings* (Cambridge, 1994), p. 181.

43 Precisely that elision is enacted in *Love Restored*, where it is argued that the King's triumph is 'secured by love', rather than by coercion.

44 Gretchen Ludke Finney, *Musical Backgrounds for English Literature: 1580–1650* (New Brunswick, 1962); John Hollander, *The Untuning of the Sky* (Princeton, 1970).

45 I. A. Shapiro (ed.), *The Lords' Masque*, in T. J. B. Spencer and Stanley Wells (eds.), *A Book of Masques* (Cambridge, 1967), p. 106.

46 For an extended discussion of musical rhetoric in the play, see my 'Music, masque and meaning in *The Tempest*', in David Lindley (ed.), *The Court Masque* (Manchester, 1984), pp. 47–59.

47 Finney, *Musical Backgrounds*, p. 169.

48 David Norbrook suggests that the stress on music as agent of transformation 'can be seen as a formal equivalent of Milton's suspicion of idolatry'. ('The reformation of the masque', in Lindley (ed.), *The Court Masque*, p. 105). He underplays, however, the degree to which its difference from the court masque's characteristic troping of music can be seen as part of the work's political statement.

49 See Martin Butler, 'Politics and the masque: *Salmacida Spolia*', in Thomas Healy and Jonathan Sawday (eds.), *Literature and the English Civil War* (Cambridge, 1990), pp. 59–74.

50 Orgel and Strong, *Inigo Jones*, 11, p. 734.

51 Edward Said, *Musical Elaborations* (London, 1991), p. 70.

CHAPTER 13

Milton's Comus *and the politics of masquing*

Barbara K. Lewalski

When Milton accepted commissions to write two aristocratic entertainments, *Arcades* (1632?) and *Comus* (1634), he had to determine how
to situate himself in the culture wars that intensified in the early 1630s.
Charles I and his French Roman Catholic queen were promoting a
fashionable cult of Platonic Love as a benign representation and vindication of royal absolutism and the personal rule (1629–1640), when
Charles ruled without Parliament. In the court masques of the early
1630s the royal pair displayed themselves under various mythological
and pastoral guises as enacting the union of Heroic Virtue (Charles)
and Divine Beauty or Love (Henrietta Maria).[1] Their marriage was
idealized in Neoplatonic and pastoral terms as the stimulus for reforming Jacobean debauchery and current Cavalier licentiousness. The King
and Queen themselves danced in several masques, symbolizing their
personal and active control of all the discordant elements represented
in the antimasques – unruly passions, disorderly or mutinous elements
in the populace and threats from abroad.

Caroline masques were even more exotic and prodigiously expensive than Jacobean masques, sets and machinery were more elaborate,
antimasques were much more numerous, and dramatic speech was
more prominent. They ended in the usual way, with the royal and
noble masquers unmasking and participating with other members of
the court in the revels dances, figuring the continual intermixing of the
ideal world and the Stuart court. At times, Caroline masques alluded
to contemporary problems and insinuated some covert critique of the
personal rule, but their primary effect was to mystify and reinforce it.

During the 1630s Charles sought to extend the cultural control of
the court and the Laudian church throughout the country. He reissued
Jacobean proclamations commanding the gentry and nobility back
to their country estates to keep hospitality in the traditional fashion,
especially at the Christmas and Easter seasons. He also reissued King

James's *Book of Sports*, prescribing the continuance of traditional holiday festivities and Sunday sports in every parish. Puritans denounced both court festivities and country sports on religious grounds: they regarded masques, maypoles and morrises as palpable occasions of sin and the Sunday sports as profanations of the Sabbath. Also, many saw connections between Queen Henrietta's court entertainments, with their sophisticated pastoralism and Neoplatonism, and her Roman Catholicism. Some specific points of connection were: the elaborately staged masses and masque-like processions in her private chapel; the representations of religious rituals in many masques; the many conversions to Rome among the noblewomen who performed in her masques and pastorals; the emphasis both in masques and in Tridentine aesthetics on magnificence and splendour, seeking the spiritual by stimulating the senses; and the idealization of both the Queen and the Virgin in terms of Platonic beauty and love.[2] The contemporary Puritan historian Lucy Hutchinson underscored the politics of the court-sponsored entertainments, identifying both masques and country sports as vehicles for spreading the court's immorality and idolatry throughout the kingdom and thereby distracting the people from true religion and the political crisis:

The generality of the gentry of the land soon learnt the court fashion, and every great house in the country became a sty of uncleanness. To keep the people in their deplorable security until vengeance overtook them, they were entertained with masques, stage plays, and other sorts of ruder sports. Then began fornication and all sorts of ribaldry to be no concealed but countenanced vices, favoured wherever they were privately practised because they held such conformity with the court example.[3]

Arcades and *Comus* develop a stance toward art and recreation that repudiates both court aesthetics and the Puritan wholesale prohibitions. Associating this better aesthetics with the values of a virtuous Protestant aristocracy, Milton's entertainments seek both to confirm and to educate these noble families in these good values. Both works undertake to reform the court genres and the values associated with them; both have at their centre a journey to a virtuous aristocratic household; and both emphasize the curative powers of local pastoral figures and of good art – poetry, song and dance.

Soon after he left Cambridge for Hammersmith, or possibly even before, Milton was invited to contribute to festivities in honor of Alice Spencer, Dowager Countess of Derby, taking his place in a long line of reformist Protestant writers she patronized, including Spenser.[4] He may have obtained the invitation through Henry Lawes, music master to the Countess's Egerton grandchildren.[5] There is some dispute as to when these festivities took place, but as Cedric Brown argues, August-October 1632 seems most likely.[6] The text in Milton's Trinity Manuscript is not a first draft but Milton continued to work on it, entering several pre- and post-performance changes.[7]

The Dowager Countess of Derby was the widow of Lord Strange, Earl of Derby, as well as of Lord Keeper Egerton; her estate, Harefield in Middlesex, was only a few miles from Milton's then residence at Hammersmith. In 1632 she was seventy-three years old and the matriarch of a large family, supporting and educating several grandchildren at Harefield.[8] In a separate household she helped support her daughter Anne and Anne's eldest daughter Elizabeth after Anne's second husband Castlehaven was executed in May 1631 for outrageous sexual abuse of them both.[9] The Dowager Countess's second daughter Frances, wife of Sir John Egerton, Earl of Bridgewater, lived at Ashridge, sixteen miles away. Milton's entertainment makes tactful use of the Dowager Countess's role as a bulwark of strength and model of virtue for her family without referring directly to the notorious Castlehaven scandal.

With *Arcades* [the Arcadians], performed in the great hall of Harefield by some of the Dowager Countess's resident and visiting grandchildren, Milton begins a critique of contemporary court entertainments and masques as well as the politics and aesthetics they embody. The heading Milton supplied to this work in the Trinity Manuscript, 'Part of an Entertainment',[10] relates it to the genre usually employed to welcome visiting royalty or their deputies to a noble house; the topics of an entertainment typically praise the visitor who is seen to bring the benefits and virtues of the court ethos to the hosts. Milton would likely have known Jonson's entertainments at Althorp (1603), Highgate (1604), and Theobalds (1607), all published in the 1616 Folio; also, Sidney's entertainment for Elizabeth, 'The Lady of May', was often published with the *Arcadia* in the 1620s and 1630s. *Arcades*, however, is structured more like a masque, in that the visitors pay homage to, and locate the fountain of virtue in, the Countess, who occupies the State. This device gains significance from the family's considerable experience with court masques: the Dowager Countess had danced in Queen Anne's masques and her Egerton granddaughters had by this time danced in several Caroline masques: Penelope in *Chloridia* (1631), Alice (the Lady of *Comus*) and her elder sisters Katherine and Elizabeth in *Tempe Restored* (1632).[11] In *Arcades* the visitors are imagined to have come from Arcadia (the court), where they have previously danced, to Harefield where (the final song suggests) they will now do so.[12]

Arcades is positioned against the Christmastide court masques of 1631 and 1632, which reconceived that genre in Caroline terms. Milton may have heard of them from Lawes or others, or read the quartos published at the time of performance.[13] In these masques the King, as Heroic Virtue or Heroic Love, is irresistibly drawn to and joined with the Queen as Divine Beauty, conceived in Neoplatonic terms as the manifestation of her chaste virtue and the stimulus for transforming the court into a *locus amoenus*. The King is complimented by masque structures associating him with classical antiquity, architecture and art, while the Queen is associated with pastoral ideality – not rural nature but elegant gardens where art enhances every natural delight.

The 1631 masques were the last cooperative productions of Ben Jonson and Inigo Jones. *Love's Triumph Through Callipolis*, danced by King Charles and his gentlemen on Twelfth Night, praises the Queen, sitting in state, as the ideal beauty that dispels the antimasques of depraved lovers (termed 'certain Sectaries', line 23), and attracts several varieties of true lovers, including the King as Heroical Love. The Chorus then purges the city with incense and swinging censers in a ceremony reminiscent of Catholic and Laudian Anglican ritual.[14] After the revels the court scene changes to a beautiful garden in which Venus and other gods celebrate the union of Heroical Love and Divine Beauty, Charles and Henrietta, as the source of all good to the kingdom. The Shrovetide masque, *Chloridia*, danced by the Queen and her ladies, presents the Queen as Chloris/Flora, the nymph who transforms the earth in Springtime, as in the Neoplatonic programme of Botticelli's *Primavera*. The antimasques threatening earth's beauty and harmony are unruly passions released from hell by rebellious Cupid, and also fierce tempests and storms. Juno dispels them and establishes Chloris in a delicious bower – pastoral nature enhanced by art – as mistress and guardian of the Spring. Chloris and her nymphs (fountains and rivers) imprint the earth with springtime beauty through their dances, after which they are celebrated by Fame and blessed by 'airy spirits' above.

The 1632 masques are by Jones and Aurelian Townsend. The Twelfth Night masque, *Albion's Triumph*, presents the King as a Roman emperor celebrating a triumph – a figure of his autocratic rule. It is moralized by the presenter Platonicus to his literal-minded interlocutor Publius (the public) as representing the King's conquests over the wild beasts

of passion, since he himself has been conquered by the beauty of
Queen Alba, which has 'a great affinity with all purity and white-
ness'.[15] The antimasques – various spectacles that would appeal to a
crude public – readily give way to the masquers, who are subdued by
Alba's beauty. They dance in a 'pleasant grove' before the Temple of
Jove where a chorus of high priests and sacrificers also celebrate Alba.[16]
As Charles takes the seat of state beside Queen Henrietta, the heavens
open to reveal the companions of Peace that spring from their union –
Innocence, Justice, Religion, Affection to the Country and Concord –
and also the celestial gods who protect them. The Shrove Tuesday
masque, *Tempe Restored*, danced by the Queen and her ladies, begins
with a Circe figure (natural beauty and desire) who inhabits a delicious
bower and sumptuous palace in the Vale of Tempe, which is the valley
of the Muses. The antimasques are persons naturally bestial (Indians
and Barbarians) and others half-transformed into beasts by passion.
The Queen, as Divine Beauty, leads the spheres and stars in the masque
dances; and songs celebrating her affirm, in Neoplatonic terms, the
supremacy of the arts of vision which make manifest the conjunction
of beauty and virtue:

> The music that ye hear is dull,
> But that ye see is sweet indeed,
> In every part exact and full,
> From whence there doth an air proceed,
> On which th'Intelligences feed,
> Where fair and good, inseparably conjoined,
> Create a Cupid, that is never blind.[17]

Finally Circe, prompted by Jupiter, Cupid and Pallas, resigns the Vale
of Tempe to the King and Queen, indicating that this union of Heroic
Virtue with Divine Beauty has purged all licentiousness from the arts
at court.

Milton's entertainment, *Arcades*, proposes to reclaim pastoral, intimating the superiority of the Harefield festivities and the virtues of the
noble Protestant Countess and her household over the Queen and her
courtly Arcadia. For reformist Protestants, the Queen as promoter of
Roman Catholic idolatry (often figured in her entertainments) was anything but the fountain of virtue and reform. By making the seventy-
three-year-old Countess of Derby's virtue the sole source of her worth
and that of her estate, Milton challenges the Neoplatonic assumption
that beauty is the clear manifestation of inner virtue. Milton's entertainment presents visitors (the dowager Countess's grandchildren and

others) who come in pastoral guise from the 'Arcadian' court to pay homage to a far superior rural queen of a better Arcadia, directed by Genius, its guardian spirit. The Countess in the chair of state replaces the King and Queen, exhibiting royal and even divine accoutrements. A 'sudden blaze of majesty' flames from her 'radiant state' and 'shining throne', which is also a 'princely shrine' for a 'deity . . . unparalleled': 'Such a rural Queen / All Arcadia hath not seen'.[18] The critique of the court is sharpened by a pair of lines added to the final song by Genius: 'Though Syrinx your Pan's mistress were, / Yet Syrinx well might wait on her'.[19] Since the Arcadia/Pan myth had long been adopted by the Stuarts,[20] these lines exalt the Countess above Henrietta Maria and the pastoral ethos of the Caroline court.

In another revisionary gesture, Milton locates the source of Harewood's virtues not only in the ruling Lady but also in the power of good art – here, poetry and music, not the Neoplatonic arts of vision given priority in *Tempe Restored*. Genius – probably acted by a servant-musician attached to the Countess's household – is the gardener and guardian of the place, embodying the curative and harmony-producing powers of music and poetry. By his 'puissant words' (line 60) Genius nourishes all nature and cures conditions that symbolize the evils of the fallen world – noisome winds, blasting vapors, evil dew, worms with cankered venom. Also, he hears the music of the spheres (inaudible to mortals) and praises music's capacity 'To lull the daughters of Necessity, / And keep unsteady Nature to her law' (lines 69–70). His own songs participate in that function as they both celebrate and nurture the Countess's virtue.

With the publication in November 1632 of William Prynne's *Histriomastix* the culture wars intensified. Prynne staked out the most extreme Puritan position in his passionate tirade of over one thousand pages against stage-plays, masques, masque dancing, maypoles and rural festivals, country sports on the Sabbath, Laudian ritual, stained-glass windows and much more. Several passages strike directly at the King and Queen, among them cautionary tales of monarchs and magistrates who met untimely ends after encouraging or participating in theatrical productions. Both monarchs were implicated in Prynne's attacks on Christmastide masques as promoting 'amorous, mixed, voluptuous, unchristian, that I say not, Pagan dancing, to God's, to Christ's dishonour, Religion's scandal, Chastity's shipwrack, Sin's advantage, and the eternal ruin of many precious souls'. But he especially targetted Henrietta Maria: 'Queens . . . are commonly most devoted to it'.[21]

Also, his index entry to 'Women actors, notorious whores', and his reference to 'scurrilous amorous pastorals' were taken to refer to the Queen, who was then rehearsing her ladies for a presentation of *The Shepherd's Paradise* by Walter Montagu, a Laudian Anglican who converted to Rome in 1635.[22] Prynne explicitly associated the court arts – 'effeminate mixed dancing, lascivious pictures, wanton fashions, face painting . . . amorous pastorals, lascivious effeminate music' – not only with effeminacy and licentiousness but also with seduction to popery. Many actors, he claims, are 'professed papists'; masque dancing is like a Devil's Mass where 'he that danceth, maintaineth his pomp, and singeth his Mass' while the 'parishioners' look on; and pastorals present amorous songs and 'lust-provoking' poems such as were formerly heard in churches.[23] In February 1633 Prynne was tried and imprisoned by the Star Chamber; a year later he was stripped of his academic degrees, ejected from the legal profession, pilloried at Westminster and Cheapside, had his books burned and his ears cropped and was remanded to life imprisonment. The severity of the sentence indicates the perceived danger of his cultural critique, epitomized in the remark by one judge, 'This book is to effect disobedience to the state, and a general dislike unto all governments'.[24]

Partly in response to Prynne, on 18 October 1633 King Charles reissued James I's highly controversial *Book of Sports* (1618), to mandate the continuance of traditional rural sports and festivities in every parish under the careful supervision of the clergy:

For our good people's lawful recreation, our pleasure likewise is, that after the end of divine service our good people be not disturbed, letted or discouraged from any lawful recreation, such as dancing, either men or women; archery for men, leaping, vaulting, or any other such harmless recreation, nor from having of May-games, Whitsunales, and morris dances; and the setting up of maypoles and other sports therewith used.[25]

The ordinance also instructed bishops to constrain 'all the Puritans and precisians' either to conform or leave the country, thereby striking down 'the contemners of our authority and adversaries of our Church'. This proclamation links Laudian Church ritual with rural festivities, making them (like the court masques) instruments of royal authority and control.

At court Queen Henrietta continued to present and define herself in terms of Neoplatonic ideology and the pastoral mode. On 10 January 1633 she and her ladies presented and played roles in Montagu's very long pastoral romance, *The Shepherd's Paradise*, which required about eight hours to perform. Modelled on French romances as well as Sidney's *Arcadia*, the work alludes to the adventures of Buckingham (Agenor) and Prince Charles (Basilino) in France and Spain, during which Charles relinquished his intended Spanish bride to wed a French princess (Bellesa/Saphira), played by Henrietta.[26] The scene is a new Arcadia to which a company of royal and noble women and men resort to escape assorted love troubles. They take a vow of chastity, not to be broken upon pain of death except 'upon design of marriage'; the women annually elect the most beautiful – and thereby the most virtuous – among them as Queen; and their society has a quasi-Catholic or Laudian flavor with its vows, rituals, ceremonies, priests, altars and prayers. The characters spend their time in lengthy dialogues about the perfection of courtship and love, articulating several versions of Neoplatonism. But the work revises the usual Neoplatonic ideal of love rising above the senses to the worship of ideal Beauty, to honour the Caroline version exhibited in Charles and Henrietta: love that refines but does not bypass the senses, finding its highest realization in chaste marriage.

On Twelfth Night 1634 the Queen presented a revival of Fletcher's pastoral tragicomedy, *The Faithful Shepherdess*, which had been a dismal failure at its first presentation at Blackfriars during James's reign (*c.* 1610) but which accorded well with the Caroline ideology of a court purified by Henrietta Maria's Neoplatonism.[27] In Fletcher's play, Arcadia is overrun with unruly passions, magic potions producing mistaken identities, wanton shepherdesses, dangers of rape, a heroine twice wounded by her jealous lover's sword and a vicious Sullen Shepherd who embodies lustful desire and cruelty. Pan, now united with his Syrinx, is transformed into a Neoplatonic deity, and his priests attempt to purge the unruly passions of young lovers. But the restoration of Arcadia is accomplished by the shepherdess Clorin, whose magical powers are linked to a vow of perpetual virginity. Unleashing the 'secret virtue' that resides in 'herbs applied by a virgin's hand' (lines 39–40) she cures both physical wounds and unchaste desires for all the erring lovers, joining the right mates together in virtuous love and expelling the incorrigible Sullen Shepherd from the land. Her virginity itself has magical powers, shielding her from all harm and threat.

The court masques of 1634 respond to the heightened anxiety over court and country recreations. They are lavishly hyperbolic in their praises of the monarchs, but introduce ambiguities that define some space for political critique and at least implicit advice and admonition.[28]

A Shrovetide masque, *The Triumph of Peace* by James Shirley and Inigo Jones, was presented to the King on 3 February by the Inns of Court, in response to a hint that some such gesture of loyalty would be in order since the notorious Prynne had been a member of Lincoln's Inn.[29] It cost some £20,000, was preceded by an elaborate procession through the streets of London, and was repeated ten days later at the King's request in the Merchant Tailors' hall, with the Lord Mayor as host. The setting is the Piazza of Peace, and the governing device presents the return to earth of Irene (Peace), Eunomia (Law) and Dike (Justice), who identify Charles and Henrietta as their parents, Jove and Themis. The masquers are the sons of Peace, Law and Justice who, with the Hours, sing and dance the praises of the King and Queen. However, the lawyers offer their own oblique comment on the King's arbitrary rule when Irene (Peace) and Eunomia (Law) agree that 'The world shall give prerogative to neither / We cannot flourish but together' (lines 539–540). Other ambiguities are introduced by a long sequence of antimasques that seem to represent various unworthy effects of the King's Peace, or follies and vices not really reformed – frequenters of taverns, foolish projectors, monopolists, a Don Quixote tilting at windmills.[30] That critique is partly, but only partly, deflected by the nature of the presenters – Folly, Opinion, Confidence, Novelty and Jollity – some of whom are cast as social climbing gentry visiting London. The masque dances and songs are interrupted by a late antimasque of common people who helped produce the scenery, props and costumes for the masque and now demand to see it – registering class discontents that the court may not always be able (as here) to construct as another antimasque and so contain. After the revels the scene changes to a pastoral countryside as the light of dawn concludes the night splendours.

Coelum Britannicum, by Thomas Carew and Inigo Jones (with music, perhaps, by Henry Lawes), was the King's return offering on Shrove Tuesday (18 February) for the Queen's presentation of the Fletcher pastoral.[31] It was the most spectacular, elaborate and hyperbolic of the Caroline masques, with lengthy speeches and magnificent sets: classical ruins of ancient Britain; Atlas upholding a mountain with England, Scotland and Ireland displayed on it; a rock opening up to decant Picts and English heroes; a delicious garden with walks, parterres, fountains, grottos and a stately palace (Windsor). Among the dancers were the young Egerton sons who would soon perform in *Comus*, John, Lord Brackley and Thomas Egerton. The device strains hyperbole to its limit, as the Caroline court and especially the example of marital chastity in Charles and Henrietta are seen to provide a model for reforming the heavens themselves. Viewing the earthly monarchs' virtue, Jove has repented his lustful ways and Juno her jealous furies, and they have expelled from the heavens the constellations and astronomical signs derived from licentious Ovidian myths. Those figures of natural deformity and vice are antimasques, as are the new pretenders to the vacated heavenly places: Plutus or wealth (rustics), Poenia or poverty (gypsies), Fortune (battles) and Hedone or pleasure (the five senses). Assertions of power by these pretenders carries a note of critique and challenge to the Caroline reforms – especially forceful in Hedone's appeal to the decadent pleasures of court life. The strongest admonitory note sounds in the comic dialogue of the presenters, Mercury (Platonic idealist and also god of thieves) and Momus (satirist and god of ridicule, who was banished the heavens for finding fault with the gods). Momus is termed Theomastix, in allusion to Prynne. Their discussions allude to contemporary political disputes, with Momus turning praise into parody as he questions the motives, the value and the effectiveness of Jove's (Charles's) ordinances: the demand that judges uphold the King's prerogative; regulations on monopolies and patents; edicts dispatching the gentry and nobility to their estates to hold hospitality; promotion of American emigration as a means to purge 'virulent humours' from the politic body; censorship of arts and manners. The persistence of Cavalier licentiousness under the Neoplatonic facade is indicated in Momus's comment that, though virtue alone now wins a place in the purged heavens, yet a handsome lady will find that Jupiter, 'notwithstanding his age and present austerity, will never refuse to stamp beauty, and make it current with his own impression' (lines 290–4). But Momus departs as the antimasques end, and the displaced constellations and false claimants are replaced with new stars (the masquers) who represent virtuous garter knights and heroes of the Stuart court. Then the scene changes to a delicious garden of love where the Queen (as Beauty) joins in the revels with her ladies, after which Religion, Truth, Wisdom, Concord, Government and Reputation bless the monarchs from the heavens.

Milton's *Mask* for the Earl of Bridgewater, performed on Michaelmas night (29 September 1634) in the great hall at Ludlow Castle, has a very different, and quite radical, political agenda. Its critique is directed not to specific abuses but to the fundamental values of the court genre, as they were insinuated through the version of Neoplatonism and pastoralism associated with the Queen and (often) with her Catholicism. Sometime in 1634 Milton received a commission for a masque to honour the Earl upon his first visit to the regions he would administer as Lord President of the Council of Wales and Lord Lieutenant of the Welsh and Border counties.[32] The invitation may have come directly from the family, who knew Milton from *Arcades*, but it was more likely tendered by Henry Lawes who, as servant to Bridgewater and music master to his children, probably had charge of planning the entertainment. Lawes contributed some and perhaps all of the music for *Comus*.[33] Bridgewater's character and Ludlow's distance from the court allowed Milton to create a reformed masque: though a royalist and a friend of the King and Buckingham, Bridgewater seems to have been a Calvinist, a political moderate who resisted Laud's efforts to impose rigid religious conformity in his region and a conscientious judge.[34] Milton's device builds brilliantly upon the specific occasion, presenting the Earl's three unmarried children (Lady Alice, age fifteen, the young heir John, Lord Brackley, age eleven and Thomas, age nine) on a journey to their father's house for a celebratory occasion, attended by their music master, Lawes. But their journey also has overtones of the journey of life to a divine Father's house, undertaken in the contemporary milieu. The children are lost in a dark forest where the Lady must confront the temptations of Comus, who with his bestial rout figures Cavalier licentiousness, Laudian ritual, the unruly pastimes promoted by the *Book of Sports* and the depravities of court masques and feasts – as well as the seductive power of false rhetoric, perverse art and the threat of rape.

Milton titled his work simply *A Mask*, and the text, dated 1634 in the Trinity Manuscript, shows several kinds and stages of revision, all in Milton's hand.[35] Pre-performance changes involve shifting or adding to some passages and altering stage directions as Milton gained, probably from Lawes, a better sense of the resources available – singers, dancers, machinery. He probably began writing in the Spring of 1634 and gave a fair copy (now lost) to Lawes before Lawes left London in early July to accompany the Egertons on their 'Progress' in the region.[36] Subsequently, performance requirements and social decorum led someone, probably Lawes, to make extensive revisions which do some violence to Milton's conception; the Bridgewater Manuscript is in essence a record of that acting version.[37] Part of the Epilogue is transferred to the beginning to make a catchy opening song for the Attendant Spirit. Lady Alice's long part is shortened, in part perhaps to make fewer performance demands on the young girl but chiefly to blunt the sexual threat to her: her expressions of fear and vulnerability are cut, as are Comus's explicit sexual advances and his arguments against virginity. Not surprisingly, the parts of the brothers are expanded: in the acting version though not in Milton's text the Elder Brother helps to summon Sabrina and direct the return home. Clearly, the young heir had to be given a more active and more successful role than Milton had allowed for.

Late in 1637 or early in 1638 Lawes published the text of *Comus* without Milton's name, dedicating it to Lord Brackley who had played the Elder Brother. He has published the work, he explains, because, 'Although not openly acknowledged by the author . . . [it is] so lovely, and so much desired, that the often copying of it hath tired my pen to give my several friends satisfaction'.[38] This suggests that Lawes had already presented fair copies of the acting version to Bridgewater and others.[39] But Milton evidently did not want to publish the acting version, with its cuts, its changed opening and its redistribution of parts. Before publication he also made other additions and changes to the version in the Trinity Manuscript and added two substantial passages: a long speech by the Lady extolling the 'Sun-clad power of Chastity' and the 'sage / And serious doctrine of Virginity', followed by Comus's awestruck testimony to that power manifested in her (lines 779–806); and a much expanded epilogue that reworks the Venus/Adonis and Cupid/Psyche myths as a commentary on the masque action.[40] Milton's decision to remain anonymous may testify to some uneasiness about the reception of a work that defies expectations, generic and cultural.[41]

In all its stages, Milton's *Mask Presented at Ludlow Castle* is a reformed masque. It enacts the poet's educative role as it locates virtue in, and teaches virtue to, a worthy noble family, and then to a wider reading audience. It puts on display the sound education and virtue of the young Egertons, implying that the moral health of the nation depends upon the formation of such young aristocrats, not upon the suspect court reformation promoted by the Queen. Moreover, it censures the fundamental assumptions of Caroline court masques and entertainments by restoring the elided perspective of the fallen human condition. Milton's masque explores the nature of temptation, the problem of deception and illusion in a fallen world where external form does not (in Neoplatonic fashion) reflect internal worth, and the fallacy of expecting the easy conquest or expulsion of evil usual in court masques. The sensualist magician Comus, son of Circe and leader of a beast-headed rout, recalls and reworks the Circe figures in the *Odyssey*, in

Ovid and in *Tempe Restored*, as well as Comus in Jonson's masque *Pleasure Reconciled to Virtue* and Hedone in *The Triumph of Peace*. The Lady's temptation recalls but contrasts with Spenser's Amoret enslaved by Busirane (*Faerie Queene* 3.12); Comus paralyzes the Lady by magic and tries to seduce her by powerful rhetoric but unlike Amoret she produces a powerful verbal defence. The chaste nymph Sabrina who releases the Lady recalls the curative role of the virgin healer Clorin in Fletcher's *Faithful Shepherdess*, and the Elder Brother's glorification of chastity also owes much to Fletcher. But Milton's masque design forces a radical revision of the views on chastity voiced by Clorin and the Elder Brother.

Milton's *Mask* outdoes even Shirley and Carew in its extensive use of dialogue, and it supplies some real dramatic tension in the Lady's encounter with Comus. Yet the work is not a drama *manqué* but a masque with the essential masque elements, as its title indicates. Dances are central, though we cannot now recover their visual impact: the antic dances of Comus's rout, the rustic dances of the shepherds, the masque dances of the children at Ludlow Castle, probably followed by revels.[42] Also, song has special prominence: the Lady's haunting song invoking Echo, the Attendant Spirit's song invoking Sabrina, Sabrina's lovely lyrics, the Attendant Spirit's song presenting the children to their parents at Ludlow. The dialogues are chiefly debates (as with Mercury and Momus, or Publius and Platonicus): formal presentations of opposed positions, first by the two brothers, then by the Lady and Comus. The resolution comes through Sabrina's songs and ministrations and the children's masque dance at Ludlow, in which, the Spirit declares, they 'triumph in victorious dance / O'er sensual folly and intemperance' (lines 974–75).

In form, theme and ethos, however, this *Mask* reflects Puritan religious and political sensibilities.[43] It requires no expensive and elaborate machinery – no cloud machines for the Attendant Spirit, no elaborate sets. The principal characters (the three children) are not, as is usual, allegorical or mythic figures in masks; only Comus, Sabrina and the Attendant Spirit (Lawes, disguised as the Shepherd Thyrsis) are true masquers. And while the lost Lady sees 'visibly' the forms of those virtues especially necessary to her in her plight – faith, hope and chastity – they are not masque personifications (as they would be in a court production), but the inhabitants of her own mind. More important, the Platonism in this masque is a far cry from that of the Caroline court, and evil is conceived in Protestant, not Platonic terms. The ideal masque world is Ludlow Castle, not the court, and it is attained through pilgrimage; it does not, as is usual, simply appear and dispel all dangers. At the end of this masque evil remains: the dark wood is still dangerous to pass through and Comus (unlike other antimasque figures) is neither conquered, nor transformed, nor contained, nor reconciled. And neither the monarchs nor their deputies are agents of cure and renewal: that role belongs to the nymph Sabrina as an instrument of divine grace from the region, the Welsh countryside, and as an embodiment of the transformative power of song and poetry.

Comus is the court masquer: he wields 'dazzling spells' and marvellous spectacles but they only 'cheat the eye with blear illusion' (lines 155). He deceptively claims the world of pastoral by his shepherd disguise and his offer to guide the Lady to a 'low / But loyal cottage' (lines 319–20) – in allusion to the court's deceptive pastoralism. But instead he leads her to a decadent court with an elaborate banquet and a beast-headed entourage – a none-too-subtle allusion to the licentious Cavaliers. In formal terms, this scene would surprise a masque audience, who would expect the court scene to be the main masque after the antimasque in the dark wood with its antic dances of Comus's rout. Instead, Milton presents the court as another antimasque: it is not the locus of virtue and grace but is Comus's own residence. The reversal of the usual politics of masquing could not be more complete.

Milton's masque also sets in opposition alternative styles of life and art. Comus's perversion of natural sensuality is contrasted to the 'Sunclad power of Chastity' in the Lady – with both concepts receiving nuanced and complex definition over the course of the work. Milton's Comus is not the traditional belly God of drunkenness and gluttony but (like Hedone or Townshend's Circe) he has the power and attractiveness of a natural force and a contemporary cultural ideal. As Cedric Brown notes, he is the right tempter for the occasion, presenting these young aristocrats with the refined, dissolute, licentious, effeminate Cavalier model they must learn to resist.[44] His beast-headed rout images the deformation of human nature when passions supplant reason, and the antimasque dances display the art associated with this manner of life: 'Midnight shout and revelry, / Tipsy dance and Jollity', producing the sound 'Of Riot and ill-managed Merriment' (lines 103–4, 172). Poised against the Comus-ideal are the Lady's chastity and the better art embodied in the songs of the Lady, the Attendant Spirit and Sabrina, and the masque dances at Ludlow castle.

Milton also sets the Lady's chaste virginity over against the Queen's Neoplatonic mystifications of chaste marital love. Milton's masque exalts chastity as the virtue that orders sensuality, pleasure and love, holding nature, human nature and art to their right uses, but he detaches that virtue from the 'idolatrous' Catholic queen and vests it in a learned Protestant virgin. The Miltonic concept of chastity is clarified by later autobiographical comments in the *Apology* (1642), employing images from *Comus* – the Circean sorceress's cup and the twin birth produced by spiritual love.[45] The expanded passages on virginity in the 1637 *Comus* do not glorify that state as an ideal permanent condition or as inherently superior to marital chastity – a point Milton insists on in the *Apology*. Rather, they emphasize the virgin's honour and power as a subset of 'the Sun-clad power of Chastity', the subset appropriate to the Lady in her present condition of life:

> to him that dares
> Arm his profane tongue with contemptuous words
> Against the Sun-clad power of Chastity
> Fain would I something say, yet to what end?
> Thou hast nor ear nor soul to apprehend
> The sublime notion and high mystery
> That must be uttered to unfold the sage
> And serious doctrine of Virginity.   (lines 780–7)

It may be, however, that Milton's new emphasis on the Lady's virginity in 1637 is in part a response to the Queen's Shrovetide masque of 1635, *The Temple of Love*, by William Davenant and Inigo Jones. That masque makes the largest claims yet for the power of the Queen's Neo-platonism to reform both poetry and the court ethos.[46] In the device, Indamora (the Queen is to restore the Temple of Love 'by the influence of her beauty' (sig. A 2), thereby bringing chaste love and the rule of Truth to Britain. The Temple was hidden by Divine Poesy because certain Magicians misused it, seducing many noble knights and ladies and scoffing at the 'frozen Winter' of chastity and the 'new sects' of Platonic Love inspired by Indamora, 'Which must not woo or court the person, but / The mind; and practise generation not / Of bodies but of souls' (sig. B 2). They call up antimasques to counter her power, including 'fine precise fiends [Puritans] . . . sworn enemy of poesy, music, and all ingenious arts, but a great friend to murmuring, libelling, and all seeds of discord' (sigs. B 4-C). Masque dances by noble Persian youths display their transformation by Indamora from licentious to

Platonic lovers; and the songs of Orpheus and his priests display poetry's service to the courtly Neoplatonism. Then the masque dances of the Queen and her ladies uncover the Temple of Love, occupied by Sunesis (Reason) and Thelema (Will); and after the revels Amanteros (Chaste Love) flies down from Heaven to celebrate his pattern in Charles and Henrietta Maria. At another level, the presentation of this masque in the presence of the first accredited representative of the Pope to England, Gregorio Panzani, invites association of the Temple of Love with the Queen's nearly completed Catholic chapel in Somerset House, as an augury of her desire to restore Catholicism to the land.[47] Milton may have added the passages on virginity in 1637 to sharpen the distinction between the Lady's chastity and the Queen's, which had been so extravagantly celebrated and mystified in this 1635 masque.

Significantly, while Milton's masque exalts virginity and chastity it undermines claims for their magical powers, as developed in the court masques and in Fletcher. The haunting music and poetry of the Lady's Echo Song leave Comus awestruck, but he is not deflected from his licentious purposes, as Fletcher's Satyr is by viewing the virgin Clorin. In the debate between the Lady's brothers, the younger, a pessimistic realist, expects his sister to suffer rape and worse, given her exposed condition in an evil world, while the elder, a Platonic idealist, believes that chastity alone will protect her from savages, bandits or any other evil – as if she were 'clad in complete steel' (line 421) like a Diana, or a Clorin, or a Bellesa, or a militant Britomart:

> 'Tis chastity, my brother, chastity:
> She that hath that, is clad in complete steel,
> And like a quivered Nymph with arrows keen
> May trace huge forests and unharboured heaths,
> · · · · ·
> No savage fierce, bandit or mountaineer
> Will dare to soil her virgin purity:
> Yea there, where very desolation dwells,
> By grots and caverns shagged with horrid shades,
> She may pass on with unblenched majesty,
> Be it not done in pride or in presumption.
> Some say no evil thing that walks by night
> In fog or fire, by lake or moorish fen,
> · · · · ·
> No goblin or swart faëry of the mine
> Hath hurtful power o'er true virginity.   (lines 420–37)

His speech closely echoes the claims of Fletcher's virgin shepherdess, Clorin, demonstrated by the behaviour of the rough Satyr to her:

> Yet I have heard (my mother told it me)
> And now I do believe it, if I keep
> My virgin flower uncropped, pure, chaste, and fair,
> No goblin, wood-god, fairy, elf, or fiend,
> Satyr or other power that haunts these groves,
> Shall hurt my body, or by vain illusion
> Draw me to wander after idle fires,
> Or voices calling me in dead of night,
> To make me follow.
> ·   ·   ·   ·   ·
>   . . . sure there is a power
> In that great name of virgin that binds fast
> All rude uncivil bloods, all appetites
> That break their confines; then strong chastity
> Be thou my strongest guard, for here I'll dwell
> In opposition against Fate and Hell.
>   (*Faithful Shepherdess*, lines 111–29)

But in the Lady's sounder view, chastity is a principle of spiritual integrity, not a physical state or a magic charm. In the dark wood and when paralyzed in Comus's chair she confronts the reality of deception, physical danger and sexual violence, insisting only upon her power of spiritual resistance:

> Thou canst not touch the freedom of my mind
> With all thy charms, although this corporal rind
> Thou hast immanacled, while Heav'n sees good.
>   (*Comus*, lines 663–5)

At Comus's castle, Comus and the Lady display their opposed values and rhetorical styles in a formal debate about what kind of pleasure accords with Nature, and the nature of Nature. In an initial exchange Comus offers the Lady his Circean cup of sensual pleasure, ease, refreshment, balm and joy as the true principle of Nature, while she, pointing to his earlier lies and to the beast-headed creatures, retorts that 'none / But such as are good men can give good things' (lines 702–3). In richly sensuous language, mesmerizing in its very sounds and rhythms, Comus then proposes a vision of Nature so prolific in its abundance and vitality that its bounty bids fair to strangle the world unless humans consume, consume, consume with riotous abandon. His language also evokes the opulence of masque spectacle and festivity:

Wherefore did Nature pour her bounties forth
With such a full and unwithdrawing hand,
Covering the earth with odors, fruits, and flocks,
Thronging the seas with spawn innumerable,
But all to please and sate the curious taste?
·   ·   ·   ·   ·

       . . . If all the world
Should in a pet of temperance feed on pulse,
·   ·   ·   ·   ·

[Nature] would be quite surcharged with her own weight,
And strangled with her waste fertility;
Th'earth cumbered, and the wing'd air darked with plumes.
                              (lines 710–30)

Drawing the issue to the folly of virginity in such a Nature, Comus echoes countless Cavalier seduction poems on the themes of *carpe diem* and *carpe floream*:

> List, Lady, be not coy, and be not cozened
> With that same vaunted name Virginity;
> Beauty is nature's coin, must not be hoarded,
> But must be current, and the good thereof
> Consists in mutual and partaken bliss,
> Unsavory in th'enjoyment of itself.
> If you let slip time, like a neglected rose
> It withers on the stalk with languished head.
> Beauty is nature's brag, and must be shown
> In courts, at feasts, and high solemnities
> Where most may wonder at the workmanship;
> It is for homely features to keep home.   (lines 737–48)

The Lady's incisive rejoinder is couched in trenchant language with a satiric edge, challenging Comus's vision of a madly prolific nature and the rhetorical excess he uses to describe it – the 'dazzling fence' of his 'dear Wit and gay Rhetoric' (lines 790–1). Her description of nature squares with the fallen world of common experience. Directly challenging the social vision of *The Triumph of Peace* and *Coelum Britannicum* that locate the evils of social disorder in the lower classes, Milton's Lady censures the wasteful court and the wealthy elites, offering (for the time) a remarkable egalitarian argument for the right of the poor to an equitable distribution of nature's resources:

> If every just man that now pines with want
> Had but a moderate and beseeming share
> Of that which lewdly-pampered Luxury

Now heaps upon some few with vast excess,
Nature's full blessings would be well dispensed
In unsuperfluous even proportion,
And she no whit encumbered with her store.

(lines 768–74)

Though the Lady scornfully refuses to answer Comus's challenge to chastity and virginity, insisting that he is utterly unable to understand those concepts, her few words opening that topic leave Comus awestruck, as her song did earlier. But only temporarily. When Comus finds his rhetorical art countered by her 'sacred vehemence', he turns to force.

The rescue scenes demystify the divine interventions and the male heroics common in masques. Set against Comus's role as magician and masquing illusionist is the Attendant Spirit's role as teacher, dispensing heaven's aid through human means, not miracles. He advises the brothers on the way to rescue their sister, and provides them with haemony (sound education in temperance, perhaps, or in Scripture) which protects them from Comus as the moly protected Ulysses from Circe. But the brothers' swordplay, surprisingly, achieves only a partial rescue: their brave but impetuous attack chases Comus away but cannot release the Lady – perhaps because as males they cannot reverse the phallic power of Comus's wand. Instead, the Lady is rescued by the power of a female deity evoked through poetry. The Spirit recalls from his teacher Meliboeus (Spenser, in *Faerie Queene* 2.10.19) the tale of an innocent virgin murdered because she was the product of an adulterous union, and then transformed into the nymph of the Severn river which flows near Ludlow into Wales. The chaste Sabrina's tainted origin points to original sin as the source of the Lady's plight: she is paralyzed in a chair 'smeared with gums of glutinous heat' – subject, despite her virtue, to unruly sensuality and unable to attain salvation by her own merits. Sabrina is an appropriate agent for the divine grace necessary to counter these effects because she is now a being from another order, the world of poetry and myth, not (like Fletcher's Clorin or like the Queen) a woman whose virginity or chaste love supposedly give her magical powers.

When the Attendant Spirit invokes Sabrina in song, the masque transformations begin, and songs and dances resolve issues only partly worked out in debate. As female deity and as poet Sabrina provides the Lady with an appropriate model. As daughter of Locrine, Sabrina calls up the heroic myths of Trojan Britain as an impetus for national reformation. As nymph of the local river, she brings the Lady into the region her father governs, and to a virtuous household that can partly control fallen nature and nurture good pleasures. And as a personage in Spenser's poem and a poet herself, she figures the power of true poetry to counter unruly sensuality and debased rhetoric. She is the good poet whose elegant songs and rituals free the Lady from the spells of the bad rhetorician, Comus, and confirm her in the arts of song. Significantly, the final masque scene at Ludlow Castle is prefaced by the rustic dances of shepherds, a gesture that recuperates pastoral from Comus and the court. Then comes the presentation song by the Attendant Spirit, and the children's masque dances that figure and display their triumph. The scene presents the virtuous pleasure, beauty, dance and song that accord with the life of chastity, intimating that they can be best nurtured in the households of the country aristocracy.

The Spirit's epilogue provides another perspective on virtue and pleasure. In lines added to the Epilogue in the 1637 *Mask*, the Attendant Spirit flies to his own region, the Garden of the Hesperides, which is filled with sensuous delights but which is still, like Ludlow, a place where fallen nature is only mending, not wholly cured. In explicit contrast to the joyous and free lovemaking of Venus and Adonis in Spenser's Garden of Adonis, and especially to the fusion of the Caroline court with the court of heaven in *Coelum Britannicum*, Milton underscores the distance between earthly virtue and heavenly perfection. Adonis here is only 'Waxing well of his deep wound' inflicted by the boar (commonly allegorized as sensuality), and Venus sits 'sadly' beside him (lines 999–1002). But the Spirit points to a higher realm where the cures and pleasures are perfect, where the celestial Cupid will at length welcome Psyche (a figure for the Soul, the Lady and the Bride of Revelation) after her long journeys and trials, and where she will give birth to the twins, 'Youth and Joy' (line 1011).

Milton's *Comus* is in every respect a reformed masque, a generic tour de force that conjoins and explores, as one subtle and complex ideal, chastity, true pleasure and good art, setting them against what he saw as their debased counterparts, nurtured by the pastoralism and Neoplatonism of the Caroline court masques.

NOTES

1 See Graham Parry, *The Golden Age Restor'd: The Culture of the Stuart Court, 1603–42* (Manchester, 1981), pp. 184–259, and Stephen Orgel, *The Illusion of Power: Political Theater in the English Renaissance* (Berkeley, 1975).

2 For an exploration of these and other connections, see Erica Veevers, *Images of Love and Religion: Queen Henrietta Maria and Court Entertainments* (Cambridge, 1989), *passim*. She sees the fusion of piety and pleasure as the core of the Queen's version of *preciosité*, Salesian devout humanism and Neoplatonic love. The cornerstone for the Queen's elaborate Catholic chapel in Somerset House, designed by Inigo Jones, was laid in 1632, and the work was completed in 1636.

3 Lucy Hutchinson, *Memoirs of the Life of Colonel Hutchinson*, ed. Julius Hutchinson (London, 1968), p. 62. Written at some periods during the 1650s and 1660s, it was first published in 1806.

4 Milton may have hoped to attract some settled patronage in a noble Protestant household like that of the Dowager Countess or her son-in-law, the Earl of Bridgewater. He was at this juncture very doubtful about taking orders in the church, as he had earlier planned.

5 It seems likely (though there is no evidence) that Milton's father, a well-known amateur musician, knew and by this time had introduced his son to Henry Lawes, member of the royal music, who taught singing to Alice Egerton (the Lady of *Comus*) and her older sister Mary. Milton senior also had various business connections with relatives of Bridgewater and the Countess of Derby, but the commission seems less likely to have come by that route. See Cedric Brown, *John Milton's Aristocratic Entertainments* (Cambridge, 1985), p. 181, n1.

6 See Brown, *Aristocratic Entertainments*, pp. 7–26, 47, and Brown, 'Milton's *Arcades*: context, form, and function', *Renaissance Drama* 8 (1977), 245–74. The 1632 date is supported by the fact that *Arcades* is the first item in the Trinity Manuscript; the third item is a heavily corrected autograph letter composed directly in that notebook early in 1633. The title *Arcades* was probably added for publication in 1645, in Milton's *Poems*.

7 See Brown, '*Arcades* in the Trinity Manuscript', *Review of English Studies* ns 37 (1986), 542–49. The subtitle, 'Part of a Masque', is corrected to 'Part of an Entertainment', suggesting that Milton was uncertain as to the scope of the festivities and the place of dancing in them. The opening lines are crossed out and verses more suited to song are substituted. Several other changes in stage directions and text indicate that his conception evolved as he learned more about what was wanted and needed for the occasion. John Shawcross argues, I think implausibly, that the changes are all post-performance ('Speculations on the dating of the Trinity MS of Milton's Poems', *Modern Language Notes* 75 (1960), 11–17).

8 The group included two daughters of her youngest daughter Elizabeth, Countess of Hastings, whose family was in dire financial straits; and three children of her eldest daughter Anne, Countess of Castlehaven, from her first marriage to Baron Chandos. See Brown, *Aristocratic Entertainments*, pp. 16–26.

9 On numerous occasions Mervin Touchet, Earl of Castlehaven, had his servants rape his wife and stepdaughter (who was married to his own son);

he was also accused of sodomy with his servants and of popery. See Barbara Breasted, '*Comus* and the Castlehaven scandal', *Milton Studies* 3 (1971), 201–24.

10 The heading in the 1645 *Poems* is 'Arcades. Part of an entertainment presented to the Countess Dowager of Derby at Harefield by some noble persons of her family, who appear on the scene in pastoral habit, moving toward the seat of state.' The title suggests that this brief work served as prologue to an evening's festivities.

11 The Dowager Countess danced in Samuel Daniel's *The Vision of the Twelve Goddesses* and Jonson's *Masque of Beauty*. Some Egerton grandchildren also danced in later Caroline masques: John, Lord Brackley and Thomas Egerton in *Coelum Britannicum* (along with their cousin, George, Lord Chandos); Mary in *The Temple of Love* (1635); and Elizabeth in *Luminalia* (1638).

12 There is no formal call for revels or dancing in the text, suggesting that Milton did not know whether there would be revels. Yet the song – 'Nymphs and Shepherds dance no more / By sandy Lodon's lillied banks. / On old Lycaeus or Cyllene hoar, / Tip no more in twilight ranks, / . . . Here ye shall have greater grace, / To serve the Lady of this place' (lines 96–105) – opens the way to dances as a manifestation of this new service. I cite *Arcades* and *Comus* from *John Milton: Complete Poems and Major Prose*, ed. Merritt Y. Hughes (Indianapolis, 1957).

13 Ben Jonson and Inigo Jones, *Love's Triumph through Callipolis. Performed in a Masque at Court, 1630* [1631] *by his Majesty with the Lords and Gentlemen Assisting* (London, 1631). Ben Jonson and Inigo Jones, *Chloridia. Rites to Chloris and her Nymphs Personated in a Masque at Court by the Queen's Majesty and her Ladies at Shrovetide, 1630* [1631] (London, 1631); Aurelian Townshend and Inigo Jones, *Albion's Triumph. Presented in a Mask at Court* (London, 1631 [1632]); Aurelian Townshend and Inigo Jones, *Tempe Restored. A Masque Presented by the Queen and Fourteen Ladies to the King's Majesty at Whitehall on Shrove Tuesday, 1632* (London, 1631 [1632]).

14 See Stephen Orgel and Roy Strong, *Inigo Jones: The Theatre of the Stuart Court*, 2 vols. (London, 1973), I, p. 53.

15 Cited from *The Poems and Masques of Aurelian Townshend*, ed. Cedric Brown (Reading, 1983), p. 75.

16 *Ibid.*, p. 83.

17 Lines 218–24. Quoted from the edition in David Lindley (ed.), *Court Masques: Jacobean and Caroline Entertainments, 1605–1640* (Oxford, 1995), p. 161.

18 Lines 2, 14–25, 36, 108–9. As a maternal deity she is said to surpass in her own merit and in her noble progeny wise Latona (mother of Apollo and Diana), Cebele (mother of a hundred gods), and even Juno.

19 Lines 106–7. In the Trinity Manuscript the lines are added twice – to the second song and the third – suggesting that Milton considered carefully how to place them for best effect. I suspect these lines were spoken at the performance, though we cannot be certain of this; they could have been added when the text was prepared for publication in 1645.

20 In Jonson's *Entertainment at Althorpe* (1603), published in 1604 and in the 1616 Folio, Queen Anne is Syrinx and James is Pan. In *Pan's Anniversary, or The Shepherds' Holiday* (1621), laid in Arcadia, Pan is a figure for King James and the Arcadians are his subjects.

21 William Prynne, *Histriomastix: The Players' Scourge, or Actors' Tragedy* (London, 1633), pp. 225, 236.

22 Walter Montagu, *The Shepherd's Paradise. A Comedy* (London, 1659 [1629]).

23 *Histriomastix*, Introduction and pp. 142, 230, 261. See Veevers, *Images of Love and Religion*, pp. 89–90.

24 *Documents relating to the Proceedings against William Prynne*, ed. S. R. Gardiner (Westminster, 1877), p. 16.

25 Charles I, *The King's Majesty's Declaration to His Subjects Concerning Lawful Sports to be Used* (London, 1633).

26 For a detailed discussion of the analogues, more clearly pointed by the use of a stiff Spanish costume for Fidamira and a flowing modern one for Bellesa, see Veevers, *Images of Love and Romance*, pp. 41–43. The chief French romance model is A. Remy's *La Galatée* (Paris, 1625), which makes its historical allegory explicit: *Histoire de Nostre Temps où sous Noms Feints sont Représentez les Amours du Roy et de la Reyne d'Angleterre*.

27 Quarto editions were published in 1610 and 1629. A third edition was published in 1634, prompted by the revival of the play at court and at Blackfriars. Citations are from the edition by Cyrus Hoy in *The Dramatic Works in the Beaumont and Fletcher Canon*, gen. ed. Fredson Bowers, 10 vols. (Cambridge, 1966–1996), III.

28 For various positions on this issue see, e.g., Jennifer Chibnall, '"To that secure fix'd state": the function of the Caroline masque form', in Lindley (ed.), *The Court Masque* (Manchester, 1984), pp. 78–91; Joanne Altieri, *The Theatre of Praise: The Panegyric Tradition in Seventeenth-Century English Drama* (Newark, 1986), pp. 74–87; Lawrence Venuti, *Our Halcyon Dayes: English Pre-Revolutionary Texts and Postmodern Criticism* (Madison, 1989), pp. 165–211; Martin Butler, 'Reform or reverence?: the politics of the Caroline masque', in J. R. Mulryne and Margaret Shewring (eds.), *Theatre and Government under the Early Stuarts* (Cambridge, 1993), pp. 118–42.

29 *The Triumph of Peace. A Masque Presented by the Four Honourable Houses or Inns of Court before the King and Queen's Majesties in the Banqueting House at Whitehall, February the Third, 1633* [1634] (London: 1633 [1634]). Citations are from the edition by Clifford Leech in T. J. B. Spencer and Stanley Wells (eds.), *A Book of Masques in Honour of Allardyce Nicoll* (Cambridge, 1970).

30 The presenters at first scoff at the rumoured intention to have no anti-masques, reinforcing the theory of the *Book of Sports* that such impulses cannot be expelled.

31 *Coelum Britannicum. A Masque at Whitehall in the Banqueting House on Shrove Tuesday Night, the 18 of February, 1633* [1634] (London: 1633 (1634)). Citations are from the edition in Lindley (ed.), *Court Masques*. The masque, published anonymously, is a reworking of Giordano Bruno's *Spaccio de la Bestia Trionfonte* (1584).

32 Though he was appointed in 1631, his first visit was delayed until the summer of 1634.

33 A manuscript of Lawes's music (BL Add. 53723) contains in Lawes's autograph the music and lyrics for five songs: 'From Ye Heav'ns Now I Fly', 'Sweet Echo', 'Sabrina Fair', 'Back Shepherds Back' and 'Now My Task is Smoothly Done'. Other music, including Sabrina's song and the dance music, may have been written by Lawes but not included in this manuscript, or else supplied by some other musician attached to the household.

34 William Riley Parker supplies evidence of Bridgewater's moderation in the controversies relating to royal absolutism and especially Laudianism in *Milton: A Biography*, 2 vols. (Oxford, 1968), II, p. 792, n42. Cf. Maryann Cale McGuire, *Milton's Puritan Masque* (Athens, GA, 1983), pp. 171–2. Leah Marcus, in *The Politics of Mirth: Jonson, Herrick, Milton, Marvell and the Defense of Old Holiday Pastimes* (Chicago, 1986), pp. 172–9, offers a careful resumé of the conflicting interpretation of his politics in the 1630s and after. In 'The milieu of Milton's *Comus*: judicial reform at Ludlow and the problem of sexual assault', *Criticism* 25 (1983), 293–327, Marcus discusses Bridgewater's judicial probity, especially in relation to a rape case involving an aristocrat and a country girl.

35 The best account of these revisions is S. E. Sprott's Introduction to *A Maske: The Earlier Versions* (Toronto, 1973), pp. 3–33. This edition presents the Trinity manuscript, the acting version represented in the Bridgewater manuscript and the 1637 published version side by side, to highlight changes.

36 Brown, *Aristocratic Entertainments*, pp. 26–40, discusses Bridgewater's two visits to Ludlow in July and September, and the route of his 'Progress'. Several entertainments were presented to him *en route*, including one at Chirk Castle which highlights his viceregent status, as one speaker briefly mistakes the Earl and his wife for 'Mars and the Queen of Love'. Cf. Brown, 'The Chirk Castle entertainment of 1632', *Milton Quarterly* 11 (1977), 77–86. The family, including Lawes, also made a three-week visit to Lyme Park in Cheshire.

37 This fair copy is not in Milton's hand or Lawes's. I agree with Cedric Brown that Milton could have had little or nothing to do with this version.

38 *A Mask Presented at Ludlow Castle, 1634 on Michaelmas night before the Right Honorable John, Earle of Bridgewater, Vicount Brackly, Lord President of Wales, and One of His Majesty's Most Honorable Privy Council* (London, 1637), sig A 2^{r-v}. The work was not entered into the Stationer's Register. Henry Wotton, erstwhile Provost of Eton and ambassador to various foreign nations, claimed on 6 April 1638 to have seen it 'some good while before, with singular delight' along with a copy of Thomas Randolph's *Poems*, dated 1638. He thanks Milton 'for intimating unto me (how modestly soever) the true artificer', *Complete Prose Works of John Milton*, ed. Don M. Wolfe *et al.*, 8 vols. (New Haven, 1953–82), I, p. 341.

39 The Bridgewater Manuscript, which remained at Bridgewater House until this century, has the names of the three children and their parts inscribed on the title page.

40 The exchange between the Lady and Comus about chastity and virginity is not in the Trinity Manuscript; the first epilogue in that manuscript is crossed out, and the expanded version added there.

41 He hints at some other reasons in the title page epigraph from Virgil's Second Eclogue: 'Eheu quid volui misero mihi! floribus austrum Perditus –' (Alas what wish, poor wretch, has been mine? I have let in the south wind to my flowers). This might suggest the fastidiousness of a gentleman wishing to avoiding public display, but also the anxiety of a young artist about his first foray into the public arena with a work that might be misunderstood. Henry Wotton's praises might have reassured him, but Wotton addressed only the 'Doric delicacy in your Songs and Odes, whereunto I must confess to have seen yet nothing parallel in our language' (Milton, *Prose Works*, I, p. 341).

42 Neither the Trinity Manuscript nor the printed text have stage directions for revels dances. Milton could hardly take it upon himself to dictate on this matter, but his text invites and makes place for them between the masque dances and the Spirit's epilogue.

43 See McGuire, *Milton's Puritan Masque, passim.*

44 Brown, *Milton's Aristocratic Entertainments*, pp. 57–77.

45 Thus from the laureate fraternity of poets, riper years and the ceaseless round of study and reading led me to the shady spaces of philosophy, but chiefly to the divine volumes of Plato and his equal Xenophon. Where if I should tell ye what I learnt, of chastity and love, I mean that which is truly so, whose charming cup is only virtue which she bears in her hand to those who are worthy. The rest are cheated with a thick intoxicating potion which a certain sorceress the abuser of love's name carries about; and how the first and chiefest office of love begins and ends in the soul, producing those happy twins of her divine generation knowledge and virtue . . . But having had the doctrine of holy Scripture unfolding those chaste and high mysteries with timeliest care infused, that *the body is for the Lord and the Lord for the body*, thus also I argued to my self, that if unchastity in a woman, whom Saint Paul terms the glory of a man, be such a scandal and dishonour, then certainly in a man who is both the image and glory of God, it must, though commonly not so thought, be much more deflowering and dishonourable . . . Nor did I slumber over that place expressing such high rewards of ever accompanying the Lamb, with those celestial songs to others inapprehensible, but not to those who were not defiled with women, which doubtless means fornication: For marriage must not be called a defilement. (Milton, *Prose Works*, I, pp. 891–3)

46 Inigo Jones and William Davenant, *The Temple of Love. A Masque Presented by the Queen's Majesty and her Ladies at Whitehall on Shrove Tuesday, 1634* [1635] (London, 1634 [1635]). It was presented three times, on 10, 11, 12 February.

47 Panzani arrived in December 1634. See Veevers, *Images of Love and Religion*, pp. 136–43.

CHAPTER 14

Valediction
In which,
the scene closed up and the revels ended,
the masquers take their leave

Leah S. Marcus

Here, at the end of our revels, in this instance a multidisciplinary and international collection of essays devoted to revelry itself, it is appropriate to look back in reflection upon our recent fascination with the Tudor and Stuart masque. Why has the form become so interesting of late? Because, as someone once said of climbing a mountain, it is there? Because, having run ourselves dry in more traditional literary studies, we yearn for a subject that still feels fresh and untrammelled? Because, with the new fluidity of traditional disciplinary boundaries, we are finally free to move outside the limits by which canonical drama has been set apart from less clearly 'literary' forms of entertainment? Because we have become secretly or not so secretly fascinated with Tudor–Stuart displays of power?

As the present volume's editors have suggested and the foregoing essays amply demonstrate, there has been a revamping during the past decade and a half of the implicit political paradigm adopted by scholars studying the masque. The paradigm has changed in response to the recent work of revisionist historians – who have complicated the idea of early modern 'royal absolutism' sufficiently that the phrase has for the most part been replaced by the less monolithic 'royal prerogative powers' – but also in response to the end of the Cold War, which the work of revisionist historians may be said to have anticipated. For scholars of the postwar era, the masque was made visible by the path-breaking work of Stephen Orgel. He gave the masques of Ben Jonson accessibility and definition through his important critical study and edition. Along with Roy Strong, he posited the arch-Artificer Inigo Jones as co-author of the masques whose surviving vestiges are reproduced in two sumptuous volumes entitled *Inigo Jones*. Perhaps most important of all as a bellwether of the times, Orgel insisted in *The Illusion of Power* (1975) on the centrality of absolutist ideology to the structure and meaning of these seemingly frivolous entertainments. In the United States at least, during the mid to late 1970s, amidst the many post-Vietnam upheavals that restructured many elements of university life and thought, those of us who wrote on the masque felt obliged to defend ourselves against the implicit charge of irrelevance. The early modern court masque seemed important to us in part because its spectacles of state displayed government power in ways that eerily resonated with the public posturing and polarization of the Cold War era. Appropriately for the decade, the Stuart masque seemed profoundly polarizing and bivocal, offering through its miniature worlds a clean divide between the disruptive nay-saying subversion of the antimasques and the orderly containment of royal vision in the main masque. Very much in the manner of the centrifugal and centripetal models of cultural community promulgated during the same decade by Clifford Geertz and Michel Foucault, the masque was a ritualized performance by which the monarch at the centre of the community expelled negative elements and remade the nation at least symbolically in the image of his own ideals. Stephen Orgel's work (which I have oversimplified here and which has by no means remained within the straitjacket parameters I have sketched out for it) made the court masque a subject of fascination for a whole generation of scholars. Given the Cold War environment of the nation at large, there was an uneasy but compelling congruence in perspective between the absolutist model proposed for the masque and dominant Anglo-American attitudes towards the threat of post-Stalinist communism. To what extent, some of us secretly wondered, might our interest in and at least implicit vindication of Stuart rituals of state relocate a fascination with less artful and more contemporary displays of power?

The absolutist model of the 1970s gave us access to detailed correspondences between the seemingly trivial pleasures of a night of revelry and major policy initiatives of James I and Charles I. Indeed, the masque as a form may be said to have aided in the *creation* of a myth of Stuart absolutism – both for its contemporaries and for us looking back upon the age – through its display of instant, vast transformations wrought through the exercise of the royal will. This bipolar model works well for some of the entertainments designed specifically for James or Charles, but less well for masques designed for other members of the royal family or for a politically divided family, as in Jonson's masques during the 1620s. I vividly remember the frustration

I myself felt as I tried unsuccessfully to extend the style of topical political-allegorical interpretation I had used to elucidate and unify Jonson's *Pleasure Reconciled to Virtue* and *The Vision of Delight* to later masques, which the same interpretive techniques seemed to fragment rather than unify.

What was needed, of course, was a new, less centripetal model, being provided even then by revisionist historians, quickly adapted to literary study by innovative scholars like Martin Butler, and reflected throughout the present volume. As befits the modesty topos, Butler's contribution in this book underplays the importance of his own work to more recent developments in the field. What Orgel was to the seventies and early eighties, Butler has been to the nineties. He has insisted on the absence during the early Stuart era of the totalitarian imagination as we have observed it in various regimes during the mid to late twentieth century; he has redefined the masque away from the bipolar model that seemed so attractive in the 1970s and toward a less constricting, multiple and multiply-centred vision of its political rhetoric; he has remodelled the form as a site for the intersection and interplay of numerous personal and political agendas. That is not to suggest that there is no room left for interpretations of the masque based on the idea of a single historical individual as instigator or imaginative centre of any given entertainment. More could still be made of Kevin Sharpe's provocative suggestion that Charles I used the masque as a confessional. More work of the kind Leeds Barroll and Stephen Orgel have done here on Queen Anne as patroness and central figure of *The Masque of Queens* and *The Masque of Blackness* still needs to be done for Charles I's consort, Queen Henrietta Maria, who, like Anne, had her own political and cultural interests separate from those of the King. Of course, Butler's decentring of absolutist ideology works better for some masques than for others. It is perhaps noteworthy that most of the essays in the present volume concentrate on the same handful of entertainments. Nevertheless, the revitalizing shift in political paradigms goes along with a massive alteration in our perceptions of the West in relation to the rest of the world, not to mention a concomitant alteration in our view of the place and importance of women as subjects and political instigators in their own right. Although many scholars of my generation appear not to have noticed its passing, the myth of Stuart absolutism has been successfully dismantled by recent historians along with the confrontational subversion/containment mentality that helped to nurture it. Masque study has survived, indeed renewed itself, amidst the dispersal of what was perhaps the strongest single impetus behind its fascination for its mid to late twentieth-century practitioners: its seductive, lethal display of absolute power.

As the essays gathered here and in David Lindley's *The Court Masque* (1984) bear witness, it is no longer taboo for historically minded scholars to be interested in aesthetic effects. Moreover, it is now possible for scholars studying the masque to imagine the form as aesthetically successful and nevertheless eclectic and even fragmented in terms of its range of political meanings. Although the introduction to the present volume makes a gesture towards the by now traditional defence of the seriousness of the masque, one of the liberating agendas of this book is that for many of its contributors, the loveliness, rarity and delicious refinement of the masque can be acknowledged without apology alongside its (perhaps multiple and conflicting) political purposes. The category of the aesthetic has, at least to some degree, been disentangled from its disreputable imbrication within a myth of early modern royal power. We have in some ways gone back full circle to Enid Welsford's pioneering *The Court Masque* (1927), in which English entertainments were interpreted (with little need for apologia) as spectacles of wonder with many debts to French or Venetian or Florentine shows and revels. Were English masques understood by their contemporaries as part of a vaster, pan-European interplay of visually encoded political rituals? Surely there must be compelling reasons why the English, as reflected in newsletters and pamphlets of the period, seem to have hungered for even minute details about foreign entertainments. Little of Welsford's interest in the masque's transnational eclecticism is reflected in the present volume, but the groundwork is laid here for new work on continental sources and echoes of the Tudor-Stuart masque. English 'quotation' of foreign originals may have signalled continuities and alterations in foreign policy in the same way that, as Nancy E. Wright's essay here demonstrates, the Jacobean court masque and London civic entertainments not only borrowed each other's imagery for purposes of rivalry, but also engaged in a free and fruitful interplay of mutual gratulation.

There are other ways, less clearly visible in the present volume, in which the breakup of the absolutist paradigm that underlay earlier masque criticism has opened up the field to new interpretation. What about masques apart from court? The sole examples offered here, in Barbara Lewalski's essay, are *Arcades* and the often-discussed *Comus*, but what of other, similar productions that may have been launched elsewhere? What of the possibility (unearthed among the many local records made newly available to us through the Records of Early English Drama project) that another masque featuring Comus (or perhaps the same *Comus* as Milton's) may have been performed during the 1630s before the Earl of Bridgewater's fellow in office, Thomas Wentworth, Earl of Strafford, Lord President of the Council of the North? With the discovery of previously unknown masques and entertainments, even if the records are sometimes disappointingly fragmentary, we are primed to expand the vision offered in this volume of the political and geographic multivalence of the masque as a form beyond the milieu of the court. And what of the new, revisionist work on Elizabethan progresses (in London and elsewhere) in which the Queen appears less as an instant quick-fix for the economic and social ills of a region and more as a player among others in a vaster pattern of meanings that she did not control? Paul Hammer's essay here on the Earl of Essex's upstaging of Elizabeth in the Accession Day celebrations of 1595 provides a splendid paradigm for revisionist work on the 'local' meanings carried by other entertainments, tilts, May-games and civic shows diverse and sundry. During the 1970s, it seems to me in retrospect, masque studies operated under a Puritan (or Jonsonian) interdiction of pleasure: they were acceptable only insofar as they unmasked unrecognized forms of royal hegemony. Now, the power to be unmasked, or rather acknowledged, in all such cultural forms is the more fundamental human power to lift life out of the everyday and bring it into resonance with mysterious and portentous significance beyond itself.

Two decades ago, if someone had suggested to me that fundamentally the masque was about beauty and harmonious interaction among diverse political and social entities, I would have secretly written off the approach as hopelessly retrograde and morally troubling in its evasion of the disturbing realities of Stuart power. But now, with the dispersal of some of the highly charged binaries that gave containment culture such moral hegemony even over those of us who thought we were resisting it, an interpretive agenda that postulates at least limited autonomy for the aesthetic as a shaper of culture in its own right seems new again, and newly promising. As Ben Jonson recognized, even though he profoundly mistrusted the visual spectacle of the masques, these entertainments, whatever else they may have accomplished, brought their audiences into contact with 'more removed mysteries' – infused the often sordid life of the court with harmonic reverberations that seemed to partake of the uncanny and to promise healing and rejuvenation. For all our overt resistance to it and despite the local political meanings that we have revelled in here, I suspect that most of us who have taken the trouble to write about the Tudor–Stuart masque are more susceptible to its aesthetic power than we let on. In the masque, an ordinary grove can become a temple peopled by satyrs or priests or goddesses; looming rocks can dissolve into light and motion; seeming chaos can crystallize in an instant into exquisite form. Whatever the masque and its kindred entertainments may accomplish in terms of rhetorical persuasion and whomever it may celebrate, it also offers the promise, as seductive now as ever, that the future can be made to conform to our hopes for it, and that the past can be reimagined to fit our desired image of it. It offers the seductive and not-so-hidden promise that life – for fleeting moments at least – can be lived as art.

Index